Readings in World Civilizations

Volume 2: The Development
of the Modern World

Readings in World Civilizations

Volume 2: The Development of the Modern World

KEVIN REILLY

St. Martin's Press • New York

Library of Congress Catalog Card Number: 87-060524
Copyright © 1988 by St. Martin's Press, Inc.
210
f

For information, write St. Martin's Press, Inc.
175 Fifth Avenue, New York, NY 10010

cover design: Darby Downey
cover photo: From Michael Kidron and Ronald Segal,
The New State of the World Atlas.
By permission of Simon and Schuster © 1988
and Pluto Projects (a division of
Visionslide, Ltd.)

ISBN: 0-312-00430-3

For my friends in the World History Association

CONTENTS

PREFACE

When I began my teaching career at Rutgers University in the 1960s, there was no course in world history. We taught a course called "Western Civilization" that had developed in American universities between World War I and World War II. It was a course that identified America's fate with that of Europe; the idea of "Europe" or "the West" made more sense to Americans swept up in European wars than it did to many Europeans (who taught their national histories). A course in western civilization also seemed the appropriate way for an American population largely descended from Europeans to find their roots.

There were problems with this idea from the beginning. One was that it ignored the heritage of Americans whose ancestors came from Africa and other parts of the world. Another was that the world was becoming a much smaller place. Transoceanic journeys that formerly took a week or more had been reduced by jet planes to a few hours. Since the 1960s, the importance of the non-European world for Americans has increased even more. Trade with Japan has become larger than that with European countries. More new American immigrants have come from Asia and Latin America than from Europe. The daily newspaper carries more stories concerning the Middle East, Asia, Africa, and Latin America than Europe. The interests of the United States are more global than ever. For these good reasons, increasingly colleges and universities (including Rutgers) are now offering world history or "World Civilizations."

Compiling an anthology for use in such introductory world history classes is a task that requires many decisions and that benefits from many friends. The instructor who considers using the result should be apprised of both.

First the decisions. These two volumes are intended for introductory courses. For me, that consideration prescribes a survey format that encompasses all of world history. (The two volumes of this work divide roughly at the year 1500.) It also mandates that the readings be understandable, at least in their essentials, by typical first-year college students.

In nearly every chapter I have included both primary and secondary sources. Primary sources were selected partly to represent "great works" and cultural legacies and partly to provide students with an authentic glimpse of a particular historical time and place. Some readings do both. The Epic of Gilgamesh in volume 1, for example, is a "great work" that also opens a window on Sumer. From it students can learn about Sumerian religion, gender roles, and ideas of kingship and also acquire a basis for making important historical comparisons—the Biblical account of the flood is often compared with the flood in Gilgamesh. The selection in volume 2 from *Aké*, the autobiography of Nobel Prize winner Wole Soyinka, illuminates the process of westernization in a Nigerian village in the 1940s.

Secondary sources were chosen for their capacity to challenge students with information and points of view probably not found in their survey texts, as well, of course, for their interest and accessibility. Some readings will introduce students to the work of leading modern historians—such as William H. McNeill, Philip Curtin, Natalie Davis, Fernand Braudel, and L. S. Stavrianos—and perhaps even induce them to read further in the writings of these great scholars. In some cases the selections may lead students to look at additional primary sources beyond what I have been able to include here. In volume 1, for example, S. G. Brandon's "Paul and His Opponents" should encourage students to examine the New Testament letters of Paul with a keener eye. In volume 2, the secondary readings on "Dependence and Independence" in Africa and Latin America (chapters 15 and 16) will enable students to get more out of their daily newspapers.

I wanted each reading to be able to stand on its own. (I do expect, however, that most students will also be assigned a survey text.) I know how frustrating it can be to find that a favorite selection or passage has been so condensed as to become almost worthless. Although space considerations have dictated that some abridging be done, I have tried very hard to be as sensitive as possible to this concern.

I also wanted students *to read the readings*. Therefore the readings are not preceded by lengthy introductions that, in students' minds, may make the readings seem superfluous. For each reading I have provided an introduction that establishes a context but that principally directs students with a series of questions. These questions ask: What is said? What is the evidence? What conclusion or judgment can be drawn? They are intended to aid students in developing critical thinking skills—recall, analysis and evaluation, and self-expression.

The historical understanding that, I am hopeful, will develop from the study of these volumes is qualitative. Different students will remember different specifics. All, however, should gain an increased understanding of past civilizations and ways of life and a greater awareness of the connections and contrasts between past and present. My ultimate goal for these two volumes is that they help students to live in a broader world, both temporally and spatially.

Now for the friends. A work like this would not have been possible without many historian friends and colleagues. As president of the World History Association, I am fortunate in having many people who are both. Many members of the association—too many to name—offered suggestions, read drafts, sent me favorite selections, and in general helped me improve this work. But I am especially indebted to Lynda Shaffer of Tufts University, Steve Gosch of the University of Wisconsin–Eau Claire, Marc Gilbert of North Georgia College, Marty Yanuck and

Margery Ganz of Spelman College, Robert Roeder of the University of Denver, and Jerry Bentley of the University of Hawaii. Their criticisms and also, of course, the work of an earlier generation of world historians, especially William H. McNeill, Philip Curtin, and Leftan Stavrianos, have been invaluable. Additionally, many thanks go to Joe C. Dixon of the Air Force Academy, Joe Gowaskie of Rider College, Charles F. Gruber of Marshall University, D. Brendan Nagle of the University of Southern California, Richard A. Overfield of the University of Nebraska at Omaha, and Ken Wolf of Murray State University for their constructive comments.

My own institution, Raritan Valley Community College (with the assistance of New Jersey Department of Higher Education grants), gave me the opportunity to discuss with colleagues from different disciplines the selection and classroom use of readings for the introductory humanities course.

I have also been extremely fortunate in that a preliminary draft of these volumes was class-tested at Iona College. In 1986, when Iona decided to institute world civilization as a core course for all first-year students, the history faculty chose to use this work as "the core of the core." Thus, thanks to the support of Iona's president and administration and the active participation of the members of the history department, particularly Ernst Menze, Mary Evelyn Tucker, Zehra Arat, and the late Michael Zaremski, I was able to revise this book for publication with the benefit of extensive classroom use and student response.

I also want to thank Michael Weber, whose idea this work was, Andrea Guidoboni, and Emily Berleth of St. Martin's Press. Without their suggestions, encouragement, and hard work, and the superb copyediting of Denise Quirk, this would be a far lesser work.

And I thank Pearl for her presence and her love.

A NOTE ABOUT THE COVER

St. Martin's Press and I have chosen for the covers of these volumes maps that are both historically valuable and, we hope, attractive. On volume 1, courtesy of the Rare Book Room, New York Public Library, we have reproduced a rare map of the world, the *Ptolemaeus Cosmographia*, printed in the German city of Ulm in 1482. The Ulm map is a copy of one originally drawn by the Greco-Egyptian mathematician, astronomer, and geographer Ptolemy, who worked in the second century A.D. For volume 2 we have adapted from *The New State of the World Atlas* by Michael Kidron and Ronald Segal (New York: Simon & Schuster, 1988) a "cartogram" in which each country's size is drawn so as to indicate its share of the world's trade in the 1980s. Thus Brazil and the Soviet Union, for example, despite their large actual size, appear quite small on the map, while Japan appears relatively large.

KEVIN REILLY

Readings in World Civilizations

Volume 2: The Development of the Modern World

INTRODUCTION

This is a collection of readings from and about the human past. Those that are from the past are usually called *primary sources*. They can be anything from an old parking ticket to a famous ancient poem. Those that are about the past are what we call *secondary sources*, interpretations, or just plain "histories." They can be written immediately after the events they describe or centuries later, by professional historians or by average people.

We read primary sources and histories for the same reason: to find out what happened in the past. Different people have different motivations for finding out about the past. Some people are curious about everything. Some people are interested in knowing what it was like to live in a particular time or be a particular kind of person. Some people are interested in how things change, or how the world got to where it is. Some people wonder about human variety, trying to figure out how different or similar people have been throughout history. My hope is that this book will answer all of these questions.

The reading selections are what is important in this book. Each reading is preceded by an introduction that poses some questions. These questions are designed to guide your reading and to suggest approaches to the reading. There are no particular ideas or pieces of information that everyone should get from a particular reading. What you learn from a reading depends very much on who you are, what you already know, and how much attention you give it. My hope is that you get as much from each reading as you can. Each reading should affect you in some way. Some you will like more than others, but each should open a world previously closed.

Treat these readings, especially the primary sources, as openings to a lost world. Keep your eyes and ears open. Notice everything you can. But don't worry if you miss a sign, a name, or even the meaning people attach to some things. This is your discovery. In some cases, I have added explanatory notes, but I have tried to keep these to a bare minimum. Ultimately there are never enough explanations. But more importantly, I do not want my explanations to become the information that is read, remembered, and studied for an exam. The readings should bring you your own insights, discoveries, and questions. Like a good travel guide they should help you see, not tell you what you saw.

I. THE EARLY MODERN WORLD: 1500 TO 1750

Mogul Emperor Akbar (1542–1605) hunting. (The Metropolitan Museum of Art, the Theodore M. Davis Collection. Bequest of Theodore M. Davis, 1915.)

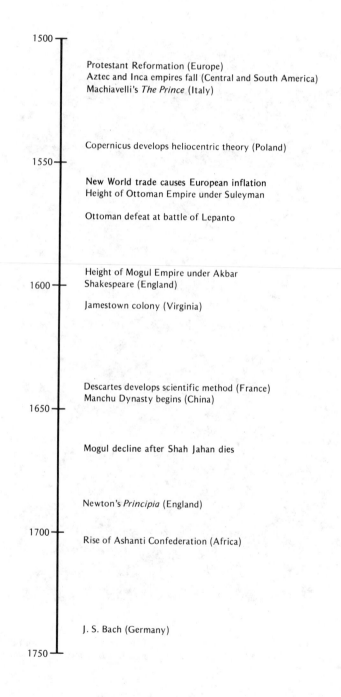

1500 — Protestant Reformation (Europe)
Aztec and Inca empires fall (Central and South America)
Machiavelli's *The Prince* (Italy)

Copernicus develops heliocentric theory (Poland)

1550 — New World trade causes European inflation
Height of Ottoman Empire under Suleyman

Ottoman defeat at battle of Lepanto

Height of Mogul Empire under Akbar
1600 — Shakespeare (England)

Jamestown colony (Virginia)

Descartes develops scientific method (France)
Manchu Dynasty begins (China)
1650 —

Mogul decline after Shah Jahan dies

Newton's *Principia* (England)

1700 — Rise of Ashanti Confederation (Africa)

J. S. Bach (Germany)

1750 —

1. Renaissance and Reformation in Europe

THE PRINCE

NICCOLÒ MACHIAVELLI

Machiavelli's The Prince, *written in 1512 for Prince Lorenzo de Medici, who had just regained control over the city of Florence after a period of relative democracy, is a very modern book. Paying only lip service to traditional religious and ethical concerns, it advises rulers to ask only what works.*

This little book has been called the work of the devil, the first essay in political science, the burial of political morality, the beginning of the modern "religion" of the state, and the first breath of nationalism. Which, if any, of these characterizations seems most accurate? What is "modern" about the book? Do we, or do politicians, think this way today?

NICCOLÒ MACHIAVELLI TO LORENZO THE MAGNIFICENT SON OF PIERO DI MEDICI

It is customary for those who wish to gain the favour of a prince to endeavour to do so by offering him gifts of those things which they hold most precious, or in which they know him to take especial delight. In this way princes are often presented with horses, arms, cloth of gold, gems, and suchlike ornaments worthy of their grandeur. In my desire, however, to offer to Your Highness some humble testimony of my devotion, I have been unable to find among my possessions anything which I hold so dear or esteem so highly as that knowledge of the deeds of great men which I acquired through a long experience of modern events and a constant study of the past.

With the utmost diligence I have long pondered and scrutinised the actions of the great, and now I offer the results to Your Highness within the compass of a small volume: and although I deem this work unworthy of Your Highness's acceptance, yet my confidence in your humanity assures me that you will receive it with favour, knowing that it is not in my power to offer you a greater gift than that of enabling you to understand in a very short time all those things which I have learnt at the cost of privation and danger in the course of many years. I have not sought to adorn my work with long phrases or high-sounding words or any of those superficial attractions and ornaments with which many writers seek to embellish their material, as I desire no honour for my work but such as the novelty and gravity of its subject may justly deserve. Nor will it, I trust, be deemed presumptuous on the part of a man of humble and obscure condition to attempt to discuss and direct the government of princes; for in the same way that landscape painters station themselves in the valleys in order to draw mountains or high ground, and ascend an eminence in order to get a good view of the plains, so it is necessary to be a prince to know thoroughly the nature of the people, and one of the populace to know the nature of princes.

May I trust, therefore, that Your Highness will accept this little gift in the spirit in which it is offered; and if Your Highness will deign to peruse it, you will recognize in it my ardent desire that you may attain to that grandeur which fortune and your own merits presage for you.

And should Your Highness gaze down from the summit of your lofty position towards this humble spot, you will recognize the great and unmerited sufferings inflicted on me by a cruel fate.

1: The Various Kinds of Government and the Ways by Which They Are Established

All states and dominions which hold or have held sway over mankind are either republics or monarchies. Monarchies are either hereditary in which the rulers have been for many years of the same family, or else they are of recent foundation. The newly founded ones are either entirely new, as was Milan to Francesco Sforza, or else they are, as it were, new members grafted on to the hereditary possessions of the prince that annexes them, as is the kingdom of Naples to the King of Spain. The dominions thus acquired have either been previously accustomed to the rule of another prince, or else have been free states, and they are annexed either by force of arms of the prince himself, or of others, or else fall to him by good fortune or special ability. . . .

5: The Way to Govern Cities or Dominions That, Previous to Being Occupied, Lived Under Their Own Laws

When those states which have been acquired are accustomed to live at liberty under their own laws, there are three ways of holding them. The first is to despoil them; the second is to go and live there in person; the third is to allow them to live under their own laws, taking tribute of them, and creating within the country a government composed of a few who will keep it friendly to you. Because this government, being created by the prince, knows that it cannot exist without his friendship and protection, and will do all it can to keep them. What is more, a city used to liberty can be more easily held by means of its citizens than in any other way, if you wish to preserve it.

There is the example of the Spartans and the Romans. The Spartans held Athens and Thebes by creating within them a government of a few; nevertheless they lost them. The Romans, in order to hold Capua, Carthage, and Numantia, ravaged them, but did not lose them. They wanted to hold Greece in almost the same way as the Spartans held it, leaving it free and under its own laws, but they did not succeed; so that they were compelled to lay waste many cities in that province in order to keep it, because in truth there is no sure method of holding them except by despoiling them. And whoever becomes the ruler of a free city and does not destroy it, can expect to be destroyed by it, for it can always find a motive for rebellion in the name of liberty and of its ancient usages, which are forgotten neither by lapse of time nor by benefits received; and whatever one does or provides, so long as the inhabitants are not separated or dispersed, they do not forget that name and those usages, but appeal to them at once in every emergency, as did Pisa after so many years held in servitude by the Florentines. But when cities or provinces have been accustomed to live under a prince, and the family of that prince is extinguished, being on the one hand used to obey, and on the other not having their old prince, they cannot unite in choosing one from among themselves, and they do not know how to live in freedom, so that they are slower to take arms, and a prince can win them over with greater facility and establish himself securely. But in republics there is greater life, greater hatred, and more desire for vengeance; they do not and cannot cast aside the memory of their ancient liberty, so that the surest way is either to lay them waste or reside in them. . . .

8: Of Those Who Have Attained
the Position of Prince by Villainy

But as there are still two ways of becoming prince which cannot be attributed entirely either to fortune or to ability, they must not be passed over, although one of them could be more fully discussed if we were treating of republics. These are when one becomes prince by some nefarious or villainous means, or when a private citizen becomes the prince of his country through the favour of his fellow-citizens. And in speaking of the former means, I will give two examples, one ancient, the other modern, without entering further into the merits of this method, and I judge them to be sufficient for any one obliged to imitate them.

Agathocles the Sicilian rose not only from private life but from the lowest and most abject position to be King of Syracuse. The son of a potter, he led a life of the utmost wickedness through all the stages of his fortune. Nevertheless, his wickedness was accompanied by such vigour of mind and body that, having joined the militia, he rose through its ranks to be praetor of Syracuse. Having been appointed to this position, and having decided to become prince, and to hold with violence and without the support of others that which had been constitutionally granted him; and having imparted his design to Hamilcar the Carthaginian, who was fighting with his armies in Sicily, he called together one morning the people and senate of Syracuse, as if he had to deliberate on matters of importance to the republic, and at a given signal had all the senators and the richest men of the people killed by his soldiers. After their death he occupied and held rule over the city without any civil strife. And although he was twice beaten by the Carthaginians and ultimately besieged, he was able not only to defend the city, but leaving a portion of his forces for its defence, with the remainder he invaded Africa, and in a short time liberated Syracuse from the siege and brought the Carthaginians to great extremities, so that they were obliged to come to terms with him, and remain contented with the possession of Africa, leaving Sicily to Agathocles. Whoever considers, therefore, the actions and qualities of this man, will see few if any things which can be attributed to fortune; for, as above stated, it was not by the favour of any person, but through the grades of the militia, in which he had advanced with a thousand hardships and perils, that he arrived at the position of prince, which he afterwards maintained by so many courageous and perilous expedients. It cannot be called virtue to kill one's fellow-citizens, betray one's friends, be without faith, without pity, and without religion; by these methods one may indeed gain power, but not glory. For if the virtues of Agathocles in braving and overcoming perils, and his greatness of soul in supporting and sur-mounting obstacles be considered, one sees no reason for holding him inferior to any of the most renowned captains. Nevertheless his barba-rous cruelty and inhumanity, together with his countless atrocities, do not permit of his being named among the most famous men. We cannot attribute to fortune or virtue that which he achieved without either.

• • •

Some may wonder how it came about that Agathocles, and others like him, could, after infinite treachery and cruelty, live secure for many years in their country and defend themselves from external enemies without being conspired against by their subjects; although many others have, owing to their cruelty, been unable to maintain their position in times of peace, not to speak of the uncertain times of war. I believe this arises from the cruelties being exploited well or badly. Well committed may be called those (if it is permissible to use the word well of evil) which are perpetrated once for the need of securing one's self, and which afterwards are not persisted in, but are exchanged for measures as useful to the subjects as possible. Cruelties ill committed are those which, although at first few, increase rather than diminish with time. Those who follow the former method may remedy in some measure their condition, both with God and man; as did Agathocles. As to the others, it is impossible for them to maintain themselves.

Whence it is to be noted, that in taking a state the conqueror must arrange to commit all his cruelties at once, so as not to have to recur to them every day, and so as to be able, by not making fresh changes, to reassure people and win them over by benefiting them. Whoever acts otherwise, either through timidity or bad counsel, is always obliged to stand with knife in hand, and can never depend on his subjects, because they, owing to continually fresh injuries, are unable to depend upon him. For injuries should be done all together, so that being less tasted, they will give less offence. Benefits should be granted little by little, so that they may be better enjoyed. And above all, a prince must live with his subjects in such a way that no accident of good or evil fortune can deflect him from his course; for necessity arising in adverse times, you are not in time with severity, and the good that you do does not profit, as it is judged to be forced upon you, and you will derive no benefit whatever from it.

· · ·

17: Of Cruelty and Clemency, and Whether It Is Better to Be Loved or Feared

Proceeding to the other qualities before named, I say that every prince must desire to be considered merciful and not cruel. He must, however, take care not to misuse this mercifulness. Cesare Borgia was considered cruel, but his cruelty had brought order to the Romagna, united it, and reduced it to peace and fealty. If this is considered well, it will be seen that he was really much more merciful than the Florentine people, who, to avoid the name of cruelty, allowed Pistoia to be destroyed. A prince, therefore, must not mind incurring the charge of cruelty for the purpose of keeping his subjects united and faithful; for, with a very few examples, he will be more merciful than those who, from excess of tenderness, allow disorders to arise, from whence spring bloodshed and rapine; for these as a rule injure the whole community, while the executions carried out by the prince injure only individuals. And of all princes, it is impossible for a new prince to escape the reputation of cruelty, new states being always full of dangers.

Nevertheless, he must be cautious in believing and acting, and must not be afraid of his own shadow, and must proceed in a temperate manner with prudence and humanity, so that too much confidence does not render him incautious, and too much diffidence does not render him intolerant.

From this arises the question whether it is better to be loved more than feared, or feared more than loved. The reply is, that one ought to be both feared and loved, but as it is difficult for the two to go together, it is much safer to be feared than loved, if one of the two has to be wanting. For it may be said of men in general that they are ungrateful, voluble, dissemblers, anxious to avoid danger, and covetous of gain; as long as you benefit them, they are entirely yours; they offer you their blood, their goods, their life, and their children, as I have before said, when the necessity is remote; but when it approaches, they revolt. And the prince who has relied solely on their words, without making other preparations, is ruined; for the friendship which is gained by purchase and not through grandeur and nobility of spirit is bought but not secured, and at a pinch is not to be expended in your service. And men have less scruple in offending one who makes himself loved than one who makes himself feared; for love is held by a chain of obligation which, men being selfish, is broken whenever it serves their purpose; but fear is maintained by a dread of punishment which never fails.

Still, a prince should make himself feared in such a way that if he does not gain love, he at any rate avoids hatred; for fear and the absence of hatred may well go together, and will be always attained by one who abstains from interfering with the property of his citizens and subjects or with their women. And when he is obliged to take the life of any one, let him do so when there is a proper justification and manifest reason for it; but above all he must abstain from taking the property of others, for men forget more easily the death of their father than the loss of their patrimony. Then also pretexts for seizing property are never wanting, and one who begins to live by rapine will always find some reason for taking the goods of others, whereas causes for taking life are rarer and more fleeting.

26: Exhortation to Liberate Italy from the Barbarians

Having now considered all the things we have spoken of, and thought within myself whether at present the time was not propitious in Italy for a new prince, and if there was not a state of things which offered an opportunity to a prudent and capable man to introduce a new system that would do honour to himself and good to the mass of the people, it seems to me that so many things concur to favour a new ruler that I do not know of any time more fitting for such an enterprise.

. . .

May your illustrious house therefore assume this task with that courage and those hopes which are inspired by a just cause, so that under its banner our fatherland may be raised up, and under its auspices be verified that saying of Petrarch:

> Valour against fell wrath
> Will take up arms; and be the combat quickly sped!
> For, sure, the ancient worth,
> That in Italians stirs the heart, is not yet dead.

FREE WILL AND PREDESTINATION

ERASMUS AND LUTHER

One of the major issues that separated Catholics and Protestants in the early years of the Protestant Reformation was whether God's creatures have free will. This was not an abstract philosophical debate. A recognition of human free will was politically advantageous to Catholics because it allowed them to hold Protestant radicals responsible for their actions. It also was part of a general sense among Catholics that human action, law, and institutions (including the church, papacy, and sacraments) are beneficial. Protestants, on the other hand, found the concept of predestination more in keeping with their pessimism about worldly institutions like the church. Their position of revolt against the dominant political forces was fueled by their conviction that they acted helplessly in doing God's will.

The following selection consists of a sermon by the Catholic theologian, Erasmus of Rotterdam, in which he challenges the Protestant Martin Luther's doctrine of predestination, and Luther's response. Notice how Erasumus and Luther approach each other. What kind of people do they appear to be? Are there personality differences between a believer in free will and a believer in predestination? Who is more convincing?

A DIATRIBE OR SERMON CONCERNING FREE WILL
by Desiderius Erasmus of Rotterdam

Among the many difficulties encountered in Holy Scripture—and there are many of them—none presents a more perplexed labyrinth than the

Erasmus and Luther: *Discourse on Free Will*, translated and edited by Ernst F. Winter. © 1961 by The Ungar Publishing Company. Reprinted by permission of the publisher.

problem of the freedom of the will. In ancient and more recent times philosophers and theologians have been vexed by it to an astonishing degree, but, as it seems to me, with more exertion than success on their part. Recently, Carlstadt and Eck restored interest in the problem, debating it, however, with moderation. Soon thereafter, Martin Luther took up the whole controversy once more—and in a rather heated fashion—with his formal *Assertion* concerning the freedom of the will. And although more than one has answered his *Assertion*, I, too, encouraged by my friends, am going to try to see whether, by the following brief discussion, the truth might not become more visible.

Luther's Supposed Infallibility

Here some will surely close their ears and exclaim, "Oh prodigy! Erasmus dares to contend with Luther, a fly with an elephant?" In order to assuage such people, I only want to state at this point, if they give me the time for it, that I have actually never sworn allegiance to the words of Luther. Nobody should therefore consider it unseemly if I should openly disagree with him, if nothing else, as one man from another. It is therefore by no means an outrage to dispute over one of his dogmas, especially not, if one, in order to discover truth, confronts Luther with calm and scholarly arguments. I certainly believe that Luther will not feel hurt if somebody differs in some instances from his opinion, because he permits himself not only to argue against the decisions of all the doctors of the church, but also appeals against all schools, church councils and Popes. Since he asserts this freely and openly, his friends must not hold it against me if I do likewise. . . .

In my opinion the implications of the freedom of the will in Holy Scripture are as follows: if we are on the road to piety, we should continue to improve eagerly and forget what lies behind us; if we have become involved in sin, we should make every effort to extricate ourselves, to accept the remedy of penance, and to solicit the mercy of the Lord, without which neither the human will nor its striving is effective; for all evil let us consider ourselves responsible, but let us ascribe all good to Divine Benevolence alone, for to It we owe even what we are; and in all things must we believe that whatever delightful or sad happens to us during life, God has caused it for our salvation, and that no injustice can come from Him who is by nature just, even if something should befall us which we deem undeserved; nobody should despair of forgiveness by a God who is by nature most merciful. In my opinion, it used to be sufficient for Christian piety to cling to these truths. . . .

Let us assume the truth of what Wycliffe[1] has taught and Luther has asserted, namely, that everything we do happens not on account of our free will, but out of sheer necessity. What could be more useless than to publish this paradox to the world? Secondly, let us assume that it is true, as Augustine has written somewhere, that God causes both good and evil in us,[2] and that he rewards us for his good works wrought in us and punishes us for the evil deeds done in us. What a loophole the publication of this opinion would open to godlessness among innumerable people? In particular: mankind is lazy, indolent, malicious, and, in addition, incorrigibly prone to every impious outrage. How many weak ones would continue in their perpetual and laborious battle against their own flesh? What wicked fellow would henceforth try to better his conduct? Who could love with all his heart a God who fires a hell with eternal pain, in order to punish there poor mankind for his own evil deeds, as if God enjoyed human distress? Most people would react as they are sketched above. People are universally ignorant and carnalminded. They tend towards unbelief, wickedness and blasphemy. There is no sense in pouring oil upon the fire.

Thus Paul, the prudent disburser of the divine word, frequently consults charity and prefers to pursue what serves the neighbor, rather than what is permissible. Among the mature he speaks with the wisdom he possesses. But before the weak he displays no other knowledge but that of Jesus Christ, the crucified.[3] Holy Scripture knows how to adjust its language to our human condition. In it are passages where God is angry, grieved, indignant, furious; where he threatens and hates. Again in other places he has mercy, he regrets, he changes his intentions. This does not mean that such changes really take place in the nature of God. These are rather modes of expression, benefitting our weakmindedness and dullness. The same prudence should, I believe, adorn all who have taken up preaching the divine word. Some things can be noxious, because like wine for the feverish, they are not fitting. Hence such matters might be treated in discourses among the educated or also in theological schools, although it is not expedient even there I think unless done with caution. Definitely, it seems to me, it is not only unsuitable, but truly pernicious to carry on such disputations when everybody can listen.

In short, one should be persuaded to waste neither time nor ingenuity in such labyrinths; neither to refute nor to endorse Luther's teachings. Perhaps I deserve the reproach of having been too verbose in this preface. But all of it appears more important than the disputation proper.

---

1. John Wycliffe (1330–1384), one of the early influential English reformers tried, as a philosophical realist, to explain predestination and free will.
2. Erasmus was admittedly not well versed in Augustinian theology and philosophy.
3. Corinthians 2: 1–6.

REPLY OF MARTIN LUTHER

To the Venerable master Erasmus of Rotterdam, Martin Luther wishes Grace and Peace in Christ.

That I have been so long in answering your Diatribe on the free will, venerable Erasmus, has happened against the expectation of all and against my usual wont, because thus far I have not only gladly embraced such opportunities for writing, but have also freely searched for them. . . . I concede to you openly, a thing I have never done before, that you not only surpass me by far in literary prowess and intellectuality (which we all grant to you as your due, and the more so, since I am a barbarian occupied with the barbarous), but that you have in two ways also dampened my spirits and impetuousness, and slackened my strength before the battle began. First, because artfully you debate this matter with wonderful and continuous restraint, preventing thereby my becoming angry with you. Second, because by chance or fortune or fate you say nothing on so great a subject which has not already been stated before, and you say even less, and attribute more to free will than the Sophists[1] hitherto did (I shall speak more of this later), so that it seemed quite superfluous to answer your invalid arguments.

I have already often refuted them myself. And Philip Melanchthon has trampled them underfoot in his unsurpassed book *Concerning Theological Questions.*[2] His is a book which, in my judgment, deserves not only being immortalized, but also being included in the Church's canon, in comparison with which your book is, in my opinion, so contemptible and worthless that I feel great pity for you for having defiled your beautiful and skilled manner of speaking with such vile dirt. . . . To those who have drunk of the teaching of the Spirit in my books, we have given in abundance and more than enough, and they easily despise your arguments. But it is not surprising that those reading without the Spirit are tossed like a reed with every wind. . . . Hence, you see, I lost all desire to answer you, not because I was busy, or because it would have been a difficult task, nor on account of your great eloquence, nor for fear of you, but simply because of disgust, indignation and contempt, which, if I say so, expresses my judgment of your Diatribe. . . . If I do answer, it is because faithful brethren in Christ press me to it. . . . And who knows but that God may even condescend to visit you, dearest Erasmus, through me, His poor weak vessel, and that I may (which from my heart I desire of the Father of mercies through Jesus Christ our Lord) come to you in this book in a happy hour and gain a dearest brother. For although you write wrongly concerning free will, I owe you no small thanks, because you have confirmed my own view. Seeing the

---

1. Luther calls the Scholastics such, because he condemns their theology as sophistry.
2. *Loci Theologici*, 1521.

case for free will argued with such great talents, yet leaving it worse than it was before, is an evident proof that free will is a downright lie. It is like the woman of the gospel: the more the physicians treat her case, the worse it gets.[3]

Therefore I shall be even more grateful if you gain greater certainty through me, just as I have gained in assurance through you. But both are the gift of the Spirit, and not the work of our own endeavors. So we should pray to God that He will open my mouth, and your and all men's hearts: that He may be the teacher in the midst of us, who may in us speak and hear.

My friend Erasmus, may I ask you to suffer my lack of eloquence, as I in return will bear with your ignorance in these matters. God does not give everything to each and we cannot all do everything. As Paul says, "Now there are varieties of gifts, but the same Spirit" (1 Corinthians 12:4). It remains, therefore, that these gifts render a mutual service. One with his gift bear the burden of the other's lack. Thus we shall fulfill the law of Christ.[4]

. . . It is not irreligious, curious or superfluous, but extremely whole-some and necessary for a Christian to know whether or not his will has anything to do in matters pertaining to salvation. This, let me tell you, is the very hinge upon which our disputation turns. It is the crucial issue between you and me. It is our aim to inquire what free will can do, in what it is passive, and how it is related to the grace of God. If we know nothing of these things, we shall know nothing whatsoever of Christi-anity, and shall be worse off than all the heathens. Whoever does not understand this, let him confess that he is not a Christian. But he who derides and ridicules it, should know that he is the greatest foe of Christians. . . . It is necessary to distinguish most clearly between the power of God and our own, between God's works and ours, if we are to live a godly life.

Foreknowledge of God

. . . In this book, therefore, I shall harry you and all the Sophists until you shall define for me the power of free will. And I hope so to harry you (Christ helping me) as to make you heartily repent ever having published your Diatribe. It is then essentially necessary and wholesome for Christians to know that God foreknows nothing contingently, but that he foresees, purposes and does all things according to His immu-table, eternal and infallible will. This thunderbolt throws free will flat and utterly dashes it to pieces. Those who want to assert it must either deny this thunderbolt or pretend not to see it. . . .

3. Cf. Luke 8: 43 and Mark 5: 26.
4. Cf. Galatians 6: 2.

CITY WOMEN AND RELIGIOUS CHANGE

NATALIE ZEMON DAVIS

In this essay a modern historian examines the role of women in the cities of sixteenth century France because it was there that the appeal of the Protestant Reformation was strongest. Did Protestantism improve the lives of women? In what ways did the Huguenot movement, Calvinism, or the Reformed Church (all expressions of the Protestant Reformation in France) change women's lives or appeal to them?

Looking back on the birth and progress of the Calvinist heresy in the course of his own lifetime, the Bordeaux jurist Florimond de Raemond remarked on how much easier it was to entrap women into heresies than men. The Church Fathers had warned us of this long before. Women were weak and imbecile. They could be as precious as pearls or as dangerous as venomous asps. Very often in our religious quarrels, de Raemond went on, their distaffs spun more evils than could ever be wrought by the partisan slash of seditious swords. He knew this from his own experience, for during a few misguided years in the 1560's he had been part of the Huguenot movement himself.

De Raemond was not the only Catholic male to try to discredit the Protestant cause by associating it with the weak will and feeble intellect of the female. Protestant polemicists returned the compliment by characterizing Catholic women as at best ignorant and superstitious and at worst whorish and frenzied. Most modern historians of the Reformation go them one better: they scarcely mention women at all.

Oh yes, there have been and are exceptions. In a tradition of women's history that goes back to Plutarch and Boccaccio, portraits of individual women have been collected—of the wives of Luther and Calvin, for instance, and of Protestant duchesses and queens—which show that, after all, women had something to do with the Reformation. More than a century ago the Scottish pastor James Anderson published his *Ladies of the Reformation, Memoirs of the Distinguished Female Characters Belonging to the Sixteenth Century;* and even today are appearing the charming and useful vignettes by Roland Bainton called *Women of the Reformation.* Furthermore, the great political and literary leaders have been given their due: Marguerite de Navarre, sister of King Francois I of France, whose poetry and patronage were so important in the early days of the French Reformation, and her militant daughter, the Huguenot Jeanne d'Albret, queen of Navarre.

Few social studies exist, however, that try to look systematically at the role of women in religious change in the sixteenth century. Did the Reformation have a distinctive appeal to women? If so, what was it and to what kinds of women? What did Protestant women do to bring about religious change? And what innovations did the Reformation effect in the lives of women of different social classes?

Some hypotheses have been offered. First, there are those that pick out features of a religious movement most likely to attract women. Max Weber has suggested in his *Sociology of Religion* that women are always especially receptive to nonmilitary and nonpolitical prophecy and to religious movements with orgiastic, emotional, or hysterical aspects to them. Weber's assumptions remind us uncomfortably of the Church Fathers and Florimond de Raemond, but in any case we will want to ask whether such criteria could apply to a religion as disciplined as Calvinism. A broader approach is found in Keith Thomas' study of women in the civil war sects of seventeenth-century England. He suggests that the spiritual status and scope of activity—emotional or non-emotional activity—offered to women are what drew them to new religions. The more spiritual equality of the sexes, the more women in the movement.

A second set of hypotheses concerns the state of life of women before religious conversion. Some historians stress a prior sense of uselessness, of imprisonment, from which fresh religious commitment served as an escape. Speaking of the attraction of Protestantism for the women of the English aristocracy, Lawrence Stone comments, "Given the idle and frustrated lives these women lived in the man's world of a great country house, it is hardly surprising that they should have turned in desperation to the comforts of religion." Robert Mandrou attributes the same kind of motivation to the wives of traders, artisans, and unskilled workers in sixteenth-century France: "Stuck in their houses, wholly occupied by their little courtyards and inner world of family and children, these women no doubt found in religious movements a kind of liberation." Other historians, however, talk about this liberation as if it had begun to occur even before women were caught up in religious reform. Nancy Roelker sees the Huguenot noblewomen as strong-minded and already quite independent wives and widows who found in the Reformed cause a way to enhance their activities (by converting their relatives, protecting pastors, giving money and strategic advice to male leaders, and so on) while at the same time preserving their feminine identities. Similarly, Patrick Collinson thinks that it was the education and relative freedom of social life that prepared English gentlewomen and merchants' wives to respond positively to Puritanism in the sixteenth century. "The example of modern Islamic societies," Collinson writes, "leads one to expect the enthusiastic, even violent adoption of political causes by a partially emancipated womanhood. Translated into sixteenth-century categories, we are perhaps witnessing something of the same sort in the vigorous religious partisanship of the women of that time."

Which of these hypotheses best fits the case of the Protestant women in French cities? We will answer this question in the course of this essay. We may note in passing, however, that both of them invoke psychological solutions but do not address themselves to the actual content and organization of the new religious movements. Indeed, Robert Mandrou says that his little housewives might be liberated either by Protestantism or by the transformed Catholicism of the Counter-Reformation; it did not matter which.

A third group of hypotheses has to do with the consequences of the Reformation for women. It is usually argued that it was life within the family that changed most for Protestant women, and for the better. Not only the elimination of clerical celibacy but also the definition of marriage as the school of character is supposed to have led to greater friendship and more equal partnership between Protestant spouses than was possible between Catholic spouses of the same period. Less attention has been paid, however, to the changed roles of women within the life, liturgy, symbolism, and organization of the Reformed Church. Some speculation has been made about the social and psychological origins of Protestant opposition to Mariolatry, but how did banning the cult of Mary affect attitudes toward women and sexual identity?

Let us ask some of these large questions about an important category of women in France—not the great noblewomen already examined by Nancy Roelker, but the women of the cities. Hopefully, some of the conclusions drawn about France may, with appropriate adjustments, be relevant to other parts of Europe.

The growing cities of sixteenth-century France, ranging from ten thousand inhabitants in smaller places to sixty thousand in Lyon and a hundred thousand in Paris, were the centers of organization and dissemination of Protestantism. The decades in question here are especially those up to the Saint Bartholomew's Day Massacre of 1572—the years when it still seemed hopeful, in the words of a female refugee in Geneva, that the new Christians might deliver their cities from the tyranny and cruelty of the papist Pharaohs. For a while they were successful, with the growth of a large Protestant movement and the establishment in 1559 of an official Reformed Church in France. After 1572, the Huguenot party continued to battle for survival, but it was now doomed to remain a zealous but small minority.

Apart from the (nuns), almost all adult urban women in the first half of the sixteenth century were married or had once been so. The daughter of a rich merchant, lawyer, or financial officer might find herself betrothed in her late teens. Most women waited until their early twenties, when a dowry could be pieced together from the family or one's wages or extracted from a generous master or mistress.

And then the babies began and kept appearing every two or three years. The wealthy woman, with her full pantry and her country refuge in times of plague, might well raise six or seven children to adulthood. The artisan's wife might bury nearly as many as she bore, while the poor woman was lucky to have even one live through the perils of a sixteenth-century childhood. Then, if she herself had managed to survive the first rounds of child-bearing and live into her thirties, she might well find that her husband had not. Remarriage was common, of course, and until certain restrictive edicts of the French king in the 1560's a widow could contract it quite freely. If she then survived her husband into her forties, chances are she would remain a widow. At this stage of life, women outnumbered and outlived men, and even the widow sought after for her wealth might prefer independence to the relative tutelage of marriage.

With the death rate so high, the cities of sixteenth-century France depended heavily on immigration for their increasing populations. Here, however, we find an interesting difference between the sexes: men made up a much larger percentage of the young immigrants to the cities. The male immigrants contributed to every level of the vocational hierarchy—from notaries, judges, and merchants to craftsmen and unskilled day laborers. And although most of the men came from nearby provinces, some were also drawn from faraway cities and from regions outside the kingdom of France. The female immigrants, on the other hand, clustered near the bottom of the social ladder and came mostly from villages and hamlets in surrounding provinces to seek domestic service in the city.

Almost all the women took part in one way or another in the economic life of the city. The picture drawn in Renaissance courtesy books and suggested by the quotation from Robert Mandrou—that of women remaining privily in their homes—is rather far from the facts revealed by judicial records and private contracts. The wife of the wealthy lawyer, royal officer, or prosperous merchant supervised the productive activities of a large household but might also rent out and sell rural and urban properties in her own name, in her husband's name, or as a widow. The wives of tradesmen and master craftsmen had some part in running the shops, not just when they were widowed but also while their husbands were alive: a wife might discipline apprentices (who sometimes resented being beaten by a woman's hand), might help the journeymen at the large looms, might retail meats while her husband and his workers slaughtered cattle, might borrow money with her husband for printing ventures, and so on.

In addition, a significant proportion of women in artisanal families had employ on their own. They worked especially in the textile, clothing, leather, and provisioning trades, although we can also find girls apprenticed to pinmakers and gilders. They sold fish and tripe; they ran inns and taverns. They were painters and, of course, midwives. In Paris they made linen; in Lyon they prepared silk. They made shoes and gloves, belts and collars. In Paris, one Perette Aubertin sold fruit at a stall near the Eglise des Mathurins while her husband worked as a printer. In Lyon, one Pernette Morilier made and sold wimples while her husband worked as a goldsmith. And in an extraordinary document from Lyon, a successful merchant-shoemaker confesses that his prosperity was due not so much to his own profits as to those made by his wife over the preceding 25 years in her separate trade as a linen merchant.

Finally, there were the various semiskilled or unskilled jobs done by women. Domestic service involved a surprisingly high number of girls and women. Even a modest artisanal family was likely to have a wretchedly paid serving girl, perhaps acquired from within the walls of one of the orphan-hospitals recently set up in many urban centers. There was service in the bath-houses, which sometimes slid into prostitution. Every city had its *filles de joie*, whom the town council tried to restrict to certain streets and to stop from brazenly soliciting clients right in front of the parish church. And there was heavy work, such as ferrying people across the Saône and other rivers, the boatwomen trying to argue up their fares as they rowed. If all else failed, a woman could dig ditches and carry things at the municipal construction sites. For this last, she worked shoulder to shoulder with unskilled male day workers, being paid about one-half or two-thirds as much as they for her pains.

The public life of urban women did not, however, extend to the civic assembly or council chamber. Women who were heads of households do appear on tax lists and even on militia rolls and were expected to supply money or men as the city government required. But that was the extent of political participation for them. Male artisans and traders also had little say in these oligarchical city governments, but at least the more prosperous among them might have hoped to influence town councillors through their positions as guild representatives. The guild life of women, however, was limited and already weaker than it had been in the later Middle Ages. In short, the political activity of women on all levels of urban society was indirect or informal only. The wives of royal officers or town councillors might have hoped to influence powerful men at their dining tables. The wives of poor and powerless journeymen and day laborers, when their tables were bare because the city fathers had failed to provide the town with grain, might have tried to change things by joining with their husbands and children in a well-timed grain riot.

What of the literacy of urban women in the century after the introduction of printing to Europe? In the families of the urban elite the women had at least a vernacular education—usually at the hands of private tutors—in French, perhaps in Italian, in music, and in arithmetic. A Latin education among nonnoble city women was rare enough that it was remarked—"learned beyond her sex," the saying went—and a girl like Louise Sarrasin of Lyon, whose physician-father had started her in Hebrew, Greek, and Latin by the time she was eight, was considered a wondrous prodigy. It was women from these wealthy families of bankers and jurists who organized the important literary salons in Paris, Lyon, Poitiers, and elsewhere.

Once outside these restricted social circles, however, there was a dramatic drop in the level of education and of mere literacy among city women. An examination of contracts involving some 1,200 people in Lyon in the 1560's and 1570's to see whether those people could simply sign their names reveals that, of the women, only 28 percent could sign their names. These were almost all from the elite families of well-off merchants and publishers, plus a few wives of surgeons and goldsmiths. All the other women in the group—the wives of mercers, or artisans in skilled trades, and even of a few notaries—could not sign. This is in contrast to their husbands and to male artisans generally, whose ability to sign ranged from high among groups like printers, surgeons, and goldsmiths, to moderate among men in the leather and textile trades, to low—although still well above zero—among men in the food and construction trades. Thus, in the populous middle rank of urban society, although both male and female literacy may have risen from the mid-fifteenth century under the impact of economic growth and the invention of printing, the literacy of the men increased much more than that of the women. Tradesmen might have done business with written accounts; tradeswomen more often had to use finger reckoning, the abacus, or counting stones. Only at the bottom of the social hierarchy, among the unskilled workers and urban gardeners, were men and women alike. As with peasants, there were few of either sex who were literate.

And where would women of artisanal families learn to read and write if their fathers and husbands did not teach them? Nunnery schools received only a small number of lay girls, and these only from fine families. The municipal colleges set up in the first half of the sixteenth century in Toulouse, Nîmes, and Lyon were for boys only; so were most of the little vernacular schools that mushroomed in even quite modest city neighborhoods during these years. To be sure, a few schoolmistresses were licensed in Paris, and there were always some Parisian schoolmasters being chided for illegally receiving girls along with their boy pupils. But in Lyon, where I have found only five female teachers from the 1490's to the 1560's, I have come upon 87 schoolmasters for the same decades.

Thus, in the first half of the sixteenth century, the wealthy and well-born woman was being encouraged to read and study by the availability to her of printed books; by the strengthening of the image of the learned lady, as the writings of Christine de Pisan and Marguerite de Navarre appeared in print; and by the attitude of some fathers, who took seriously the modest educational programs for women being urged by Christian humanists like Erasmus and Juan Luis Vives. Reading and writing for women of the common people was more likely to be ridiculous, a subject for farce.

Into this picture of city women separated from their parish clergy and from male religious organizations, one new element was to enter, even before the Reformation. Women who could read or who were part of circles where reading was done aloud were being prompted by vernacular devotional literature and the Bible to speculate on theology. "Why, they're half theologians," said the Franciscan preachers contemptuously. They own Bibles the way they own love stories and romances. They get carried away by questions on transubstantiation, and they go "running around from . . . one (female) religious house to another, seeking advice and making much ado about nothing." What the good brothers expected from city women was not silly reasoning but the tears and repentance that would properly follow a Lenten sermon replete with all the rhetorical devices and dramatic gestures of which the Franciscans were masters.

Even a man who was more sympathetic than the Franciscans to lettered females had his reservations about how far their learning should take them. A male poet praised the noble dame Gabrielle de Bourbon in the 1520's for reading vernacular books on moral and doctrinal questions and for composing little treatises to the honor of God and the Virgin Mary. But she knew her limits, for "women must not apply their minds to curious questions of theology and the secret matters of divinity, the knowledge of which belongs to prelates, rectors and doctors."

The Christian humanist Erasmus was one of the few men of his time who sensed the depths of resentment accumulating in women whose efforts to think about doctrine were not taken seriously by the clergy. In one of his *Colloquies*, a lady learned in Latin and Greek is being twitted by an asinine abbot (the phrase is Erasmus'). She finally bursts out, "If you keep on as you've begun, geese may do the preaching sooner than put up with you tongue-tied pastors. The world's a stage that's topsy-turvy now, as you see. Every man must play his part—or exit."

The world was indeed topsy-turvy. The Catholic Church, which Erasmus had tried to reform from within, was being split by Protestants who believed that man was saved by faith in Christ alone and that human work had nothing to do with it, who were changing the sacramental system all around and overthrowing the order of the priesthood.

After 1562 the Reformed Church of France started to settle into its new institutional structures and the promise of Protestantism began to be realized for city women. Special catechism classes in French were set up for women, and in towns under Huguenot control efforts were made to encourage literacy, even among all the poor girls in the orphanages, not just the gifted few. In certain Reformed families the literate husbands finally began teaching their wives to read.

Some Protestant females, however, had more ambitious goals. The image of the new Christian woman with her Bible had beckoned them to more than catechism classes or reading the Scriptures with their husbands. Consider Marie Dentière. One-time abbess in Tournai, but expelled from her convent in the 1520's because of heresy, Dentière married a pastor and found her way to Geneva during its years of religious revolution. There, according to the report of a nun of the Poor Clare order, Marie got "mixed up with preaching," coming, for instance, to the convent to persuade the poor creatures to leave their miserable life. She also published two religious works, one of them an epistle on religious matters addressed to Queen Marguerite de Navarre. Here Dentière inserted a "Defense for Women" against calumnies, not only by Catholic adversaries but also by some of the Protestant faithful. The latter were saying that it was rash for women to publish works to each other on Scriptural matters. Dentière disagreed: "If God has done the grace to some poor women to reveal to them by His Holy Scriptures some good and holy thing, dare they not write about it, speak about it, and declare it, one to the other? . . . Is it not foolishly done to hide the talent that God has given us?"

Dentière maintained the modest fiction that she was addressing herself only to other females. Later women did not. Some of the women prisoners in the French jails preached to "the great consolation" of both male and female listeners. Our ex-Calvinist jurist Florimond de Raemond gave several examples, both from the Protestant conventicles and from the regular Reformed services as late as 1572, of women who while waiting for a preacher to arrive had gone up to pulpits and read from the Bible. One *théologienne* even took public issue with her pastor. Finally, in some of the Reformed churches southwest of Paris—in areas where weavers and women had been early converts—a movement started to permit lay persons to prophesy. This would have allowed both women and unlearned men to get up in church and speak on holy things.

An examination of a few other areas of Protestant reform reveals the same pattern as in reading Scripture and preaching: city women revolted against priests and entered new religious relations that brought them together with men or likened them to men but left them unequal.

The new Calvinist liturgy, with its stress on the concerted fellowship of the congregation, used the vernacular—the language of women and the unlearned—and included Psalms sung jointly by men and women. Nothing shocked Catholic observers more than this. When they heard the music of male and female voices filtering from a house where a conventicle was assembled, all they could imagine were lewd activities with the candles extinguished. It was no better when the Protestant movement came into the open. After the rich ceremony of the mass, performed by the clergy with due sanctity and grandeur, the Reformed service seemed, in the words of a Catholic in Paris in the 1560's, "without law, without order, without harmony." "The minister begins. Everybody follows—men, women, children, servants, chambermaids. . . . No one is on the same verse. . . . The fine-voiced maidens let loose their hums and trills. . . so the young men will be sure to listen. How wrong of Calvin to let women sing in Church."

To Protestant ears, it was very different. For laymen and lay-women in the service the common voice in praise of the Lord expressed the lack of distance between pastor and congregation. The Catholic priests had stolen the Psalms; now they had been returned. As for the participants in the conventicles, the songs gave them courage and affirmed their sense of purity over the hypocritical papists, who no sooner left the mass than they were singing love songs. The Protestant faithful were firmly in control of their sexual impulses, they believed, their dark and sober clothes a testimonial to their sincerity. And when the women and men sang together in the great armed street marches of the 1560's, the songs were a militant challenge to the hardened Catholics and an invitation to the wavering listeners to join the elect.

2. American Civilizations and the Columbian Exchange

THE AZTEC CIVILIZATION OF MEXICO

BERNAL DIAZ

Aztec civilization was the last of a long line of native American civilizations that had sprung up in the central highlands of Mexico. In this selection it is described by Bernal Diaz, a conquistador who accompanied Cortes to Mexico in 1519. In what ways was the Aztec civilization like that of Spain? In what ways was it different?

When it was announced to Cortes that Motecusuma [Montezuma] himself was approaching, he alighted from his horse and advanced to meet him. Many compliments were now passed on both sides. Motecusuma bid Cortes welcome, who, through Marina, said, in return, he hoped his majesty was in good health. If I still remember rightly, Cortes, who had Marina next to him, wished to concede the place of honor to the monarch, who, however, would not accept of it, but conceded it to Cortes, who now brought forth a necklace of precious stones, of the most beautiful colours and shapes, strung upon gold wire, and perfumed with musk, which he hung about the neck of Motecusuma. Our commander was then going to embrace him, but the grandees by whom he was surrounded held back his arms, as they considered it improper. Our general then desired Marina to tell the monarch how exceedingly he congratulated himself upon his good fortune of having seen such a powerful monarch face to face, and of the honour he had done us by coming out to meet us himself. To all this Motecusuma answered in very appropriate terms, and ordered his two nephews, the princes of Tetzuco and Cohohuacan, to conduct us to our quarters. He himself returned to the city, accompanied by his two other relatives, the princes of Cuitlahuac and Tlacupa, with the other grandees of his numerous suite. As they passed by, we perceived how all those who composed his majesty's retinue held their heads bent forward,

From *The Memoirs of the Conquistador Bernal Diaz de Castillo*, translated by I. I. Lockhart. London: J. Hatchard, 1844.

no one daring to lift up his eyes in his presence; and altogether what deep veneration was paid him.

The road before us now became less crowded, and yet who would have been able to count the vast numbers of men, women, and children who filled the streets, crowded the balconies, and the canoes in the canals, merely to gaze upon us? . . .

We were quartered in a large building where there was room enough for us all, and which had been occupied by Axayacatl, father of Motecusuma, during his life-time. Here the latter had likewise a secret room full of treasures, and where the gold he had inherited from his father was hid, which he had never touched up to this moment. The apartments and halls were very spacious, and those set apart for our general were furnished with carpets. There were separate beds for each of us, which could not have been better fitted up for a gentleman of the first rank! Every place was swept clean, and the walls had been newly plastered and decorated.

When we had arrived in the great court-yard adjoining this palace, Motecusuma came up to Cortes, and, taking him by the hand, conducted him himself into the apartments where he was to lodge, which had been beautifully decorated after the fashion of the country. He then hung about his neck a chaste necklace of gold, most curiously worked with figures all representing crabs. The Mexican grandees were greatly astonished at all these uncommon favours which their monarch bestowed upon our general.

Cortes returned the monarch many thanks for so much kindness, and the latter took leave of him with these words: "Malinche, you and your brothers must now do as if you were at home, and take some rest after the fatigues of the journey," then returned to his own palace, which was close at hand.

We allotted the apartments according to the several companies, placed our cannon in an advantageous position, and made such arrangements that our cavalry, as well as the infantry, might be ready at a moment's notice. We then sat down to a plentiful repast, which had been previously spread out for us, and made a sumptuous meal.

This our bold and memorable entry into the large city of Temixtitlan, Mexico took place on the 8th of November, 1519. Praise be to the Lord Jesus Christ for all this. . . .

The mighty Motecusuma may have been about this time in the fortieth year of his age. He was tall of stature, of slender make, and rather thin, but the symmetry of his body was beautiful. His complexion was not very brown, merely approaching to that of the inhabitants in general. The hair of his head was not very long, excepting where it hung thickly down over his ears, which were quite hidden by it. His black beard, though thin, looked handsome. His countenance was rather of an elongated form, but cheerful; and his fine eyes had the expression of love or severity, at the proper moments. He was particularly clean in his person, and took a bath every evening. Besides a number of concubines, who were all daughters of persons of rank and quality, he had two lawful wives of royal extraction, whom, however, he visited secretly without any one daring to observe it, save his most confidential servants. He was perfectly innocent of any unnatural crimes. The dress he had on one day was not worn again until four days had elapsed. In the halls adjoining his own private apartments there was always a guard of 2000 men of quality, in waiting: with whom, however, he never held any conversation unless to give them orders or to receive some intelligence from them. Whenever for this purpose they entered his apartment, they had first to take off their rich costumes and put on meaner garments, though these were always neat and clean; and were only allowed to enter into his presence barefooted, with eyes cast down. No person durst look at him full in the face, and during the three prostrations which they were obliged to make before they could approach him, they pronounced these words: "Lord! my Lord! sublime Lord!" Everything that was communicated to him was to be said in few words, the eyes of the speaker being constantly cast down, and on leaving the monarch's presence he walked backwards out of the room. I also remarked that even princes and other great personages who come to Mexico respecting law-suits, or on other business from the interior of the country, always took off their shoes and changed their whole dress for one of a meaner appearance when they entered his palace. Neither were they allowed to enter the palace straightway, but had to show themselves for a considerable time outside the doors; as it would have been considered want of respect to the monarch if this had been omitted.

Above 300 kinds of dishes were served up for Motecusuma's dinner from his kitchen, underneath which were placed pans of porcelain filled with fire, to keep them warm. Three hundred dishes of various kinds were served up for him alone, and above 1000 for the persons in waiting. He sometimes, but very seldom, accompanied by the chief officers of his household, ordered the dinner himself, and desired that the best dishes and various kinds of birds should be called over to him. We were told that the flesh of young children as a very dainty bit, were also set before him sometimes by way of a relish. Whether there was any truth in this we could not possibly discover; on account of the great variety of dishes, consisting in fowls, turkeys, pheasants, partridges, quails, tame and wild geese, venison, musk swine, pigeons, hares, rabbits, and of numerous other birds and beasts; besides which there were various other kinds of provisions, indeed it would have been no easy task to call them all over by name.

I had almost forgotten to mention, that during dinner-time, two other young women of great beauty brought the monarch small cakes, as white as snow, made of eggs and other very nourishing ingredients, on plates covered with clean napkins; also a kind of long-shaped bread, likewise made of very substantial things, and some pachol, which is a kind of wafer-cake. They then presented him with three beautifully painted and gilt tubes, which were filled with liquid amber, and a herb called by the Indians tabaco. After the dinner had been cleared away and the singing and dancing done, one of the tubes was lighted, and the monarch took the smoke into his mouth, and after he had done this a short time, he fell asleep.

About this time a celebrated cazique [or cacique, a native Indian chief], whom we called Tapia, was Motecusuma's chief steward: he kept an account of the whole of Motecusuma's revenue, in large books of paper which the Mexicans call *Amatl*. A whole house was filled with such large books of accounts.

Motecusuma had also two arsenals filled with arms of every description, of which many were ornamented with gold and precious stones. These arms consisted in shields of different sizes, sabres, and a species of broadsword, which is wielded with both hands, the edge furnished with flint stones, so extremely sharp that they cut much better than our Spanish swords: further, lances of greater length than ours, with spikes at their end, full one fathom in length, likewise furnished with several sharp flint stones. The pikes are so very sharp and hard that they will pierce the strongest shield, and cut like a razor; so that the Mexicans even shave themselves with these stones. Then there were excellent bows and arrows, pikes with single and double points, and the proper thongs to throw them with; slings with round stones purposely made for them; also a species of large shield, so ingeniously constructed that it could be rolled up when not wanted: they are only unrolled on the field of battle, and completely cover the whole body from the head to the feet. Further, we saw here a great variety of cuirasses made of quilted cotton, which were outwardly adorned with soft feathers of different colours, and looked like uniforms. . . .

I will now, however, turn to another subject, and rather acquaint my readers with the skilful arts practised among the Mexicans: among which I will first mention the sculptors, and the gold and silversmiths, who were clever in working and smelting gold, and would have astonished the most celebrated of our Spanish goldsmiths: the number of these was very great, and the most skilful lived at a place called Ezcapuzalco, about four miles from Mexico. After these came the very skilful masters in cutting and polishing precious stones, and the calchihuis, which resemble the emerald. Then follow the great masters in painting, and decorators in feathers, and the wonderful sculptors. Even at this day there are living in Mexico three Indian artists, named Marcos de Aguino, Juan de la Cruz, and El Crespello, who have severally reached to such great proficiency in the art of painting and sculpture, that they may be compared to an Apelles, or our contemporaries Michael Angelo and Berruguete. . . .

The powerful Motecusuma had also a number of dancers and clowns: some danced in stilts, tumbled, and performed a variety of other antics for the monarch's entertainment: a whole quarter of the city was inhabited by these performers, and their only occupation consisted in such like performances. Last, Motecusuma had in his service great numbers of stone-cutters, masons, and carpenters who were solely employed in the royal palaces. Above all, I must not forget to mention here his gardens for the culture of flowers, trees, and vegetables, of which there were various kinds. In these gardens were also numerous baths, wells, basins, and ponds full of limpid water, which regularly ebbed and flowed. All this was enlivened by endless varieties of small birds, which sang among the trees. Also the plantations of medical plants and vegetables are well worthy of our notice: these were kept in proper order by a large body of gardeners. All the baths, wells, ponds, and buildings were substantially constructed of stonework, as also the theatres where the singers and dancers performed. There were upon the whole so many remarkable things for my observation in these gardens and throughout the whole town, that I can scarcely find words to express the astonishment I felt at the pomp and splendour of the Mexican monarch. . . .

We had already been four days in the city of Mexico, and neither our commander nor any of us had, during that time, left our quarters, excepting to visit the gardens and buildings adjoining the palace. Cortes now, therefore, determined to view the city, and visit the great market, and the chief temple of Huitzilopochtli. . . . The moment we arrived in this immense market, we were perfectly astonished at the vast numbers of people, the profusion of merchandise which was there exposed for sale, and at the good police and order that reigned throughout. The grandees who accompanied us drew our attention to the smallest circumstance, and gave us full explanation of all we saw. Every species of merchandise had a separate spot for its sale. We first of all visited those divisions of the market appropriated for the sale of gold and silver wares, of jewels, of cloths interwoven with feathers, and of other manufactured goods; besides slaves of both sexes. This slave market was upon as great a scale as the Portuguese market for negro slaves at Guinea. To prevent these from running away, they were fastened with halters about their neck, though some were allowed to walk at large. Next to these came the dealers in coarser wares—cotton, twisted, thread, and cacao. In short, every species of goods which New Spain produces were here to be found and everything put me in mind of my native town Medino del Campo during fair time, where every merchandise had a separate street assigned for its sale. In one place were sold the stuffs manufactured of nequen; ropes, and sandals; in another place, the sweet maguey root, ready cooked, and various other things made from this plant. In another division of the market were exposed the skins of tigers, lions, jackals, otters, red deer, wild cats, and of other beasts of prey, some of which were tanned. In another place were sold beans and sage, with other herbs and vegetables. A particular market was assigned for the merchants in fowls, turkeys, ducks, rabbits, hares, deer, and dogs; also for fruit-sellers, pastry-cooks, and tripe-sellers. Not far from these were exposed all manner of earthenware, from the large earthen cauldron to the smallest pitchers. Then came the dealers in honey and honey-cakes, and other sweetmeats. Next to these, the timber-merchants, furniture-dealers, with their stores of tables, benches, cradles, and all sorts of wooden implements, all separately arranged. What can I further add? If I am to note everything down, I must also mention human excrements, which are exposed for sale in canoes lying in the canals near this square, and is used for the tanning of leather; for, according to the assurances of the Mexicans, it is impossible to tan well without it. I can easily imagine that many of my readers will laugh at this; however, what I have stated is a fact, and, as further proof of this, I must acquaint the reader that along every road accommodations were built of reeds, straw, or grass, by which those who made use of them were hidden from the view of the passers-by, so that great care was taken that none of the last mentioned treasures should be lost. But why should I so minutely detail every article exposed for sale in this great market? If I had to enumerate everything singly, I should not so easily get to the end. And yet I have not mentioned the paper, which in this country is called amatl; the tubes filled with liquid amber and tobacco; the various sweet-scented salves, and similar things; nor the various seeds which were exposed for sale in the porticoes of this market, nor the medicinal herbs.

In this market-place there were also courts of justice, to which three judges and several constables were appointed, who inspected the goods exposed for sale. I had almost forgotten to mention the salt, and those who made the flint knives; also the fish, and a species of bread made of a kind of mud or slime collected from the surface of this lake, and eaten in that form, and has a similar taste to our cheese. Further, instruments of brass, copper, and tin; cups, and painted pitchers of wood; indeed, I wish I had completed the enumeration of all this profusion of merchandize. The variety was so great that it would occupy more space than I can well spare to note them down in; besides which, the market was so crowded with people, and the thronging so excessive in the porticoes, that it was quite impossible to see all in one day. . . .

On quitting the market, we entered the spacious yards which surrounded the chief temple. These appeared to encompass more ground than the market-place at Salamanca, and were surrounded by a double wall, constructed of stone and lime: these yards were paved with large white flag-stones, extremely smooth; and where these were wanting, a kind of brown plaster had been used instead, and all was kept so very clean that there was not the smallest particle of dust or straw to be seen anywhere.

Before we mounted the steps of the great temple, Motecusuma, who was sacrificing on the top to his idols, sent six papas and two of his principal officers to conduct Cortes up the steps. There were 114 steps to the summit. . . . Indeed, this infernal temple, from its great height, commanded a view of the whole surrounding neighbourhood. From this place we could likewise see the three causeways which led into Mexico,— that from Iztapalapan, by which we had entered the city four days ago; that from Tlacupa, along which we took our flight eight months after, when we were beaten out of the city by the new monarch Cuitlahuatzin; the third was that of Tepeaquilla. We also observed the aqueduct which ran from Chapultepec, and provided the whole town with sweet water. We could also distinctly see the bridges across the openings, by which these causeways were intersected, and through which the waters of the lake ebbed and flowed. The lake itself was crowded with canoes, which were bringing provisions, manufacturers, and other merchandize to the city. From here we also discovered that the only communication of the houses in this city, and of all the other towns built in the lake, was by means of drawbridges or canoes. In all these towns the beautiful white plastered temples rose above the smaller ones, like so many towers and castles in our Spanish towns, and this, it may be imagined, was a splendid sight.

After we had sufficiently gazed upon this magnificent picture, we again turned our eyes toward the great market, and beheld the vast numbers of buyers and sellers who thronged there. The bustle and noise occasioned by this multitude of human beings was so great that it could be heard at a distance of more than four miles. Some of our men, who had been at Constantinople and Rome, and travelled through the whole of Italy, said that they never had seen a marketplace of such large dimensions, or which was so well regulated, or so crowded with people as this one at Mexico.

On this occasion Cortes said to father Olmedo, who had accompanied us: "I have just been thinking that we should take this opportunity, and apply to Motecusuma for permission to build a church here."

To which father Olmedo replied, that it would, no doubt, be an excellent thing if the monarch would grant this; but that it would be acting overhasty to make a proposition of that nature to him now, whose consent would not easily be gained at any time.

Cortes then turned to Motecusuma, and said to him, by means of our interpretress, Doña Marina: "Your majesty is, indeed, a great monarch, and you merit to be still greater! It has been a real delight to us to view all your cities. I have now one favour to beg of you, that you would allow us to see your gods and teules."

To which Motecusuma answered, that he must first consult the chief papas, to whom he then addressed a few words. Upon this, we were led into a kind of small tower, with one room, in which we saw two basements resembling altars, decked with coverings of extreme beauty. On each of these basements stood a gigantic, fat-looking figure, of which the one on the right hand represented the god of war Huitzilopochtli. This idol had a very broad face, with distorted and furious-looking eyes, and was covered all over with jewels, gold, and pearls, which were stuck to it by means of a species of paste, which, in this country, is prepared from a certain root. Large serpents, likewise, covered with gold and precious stones, wound round the body of this monster, which held in one hand a bow, and in the other a bunch of arrows. Another small idol which stood by its side, representing its page, carried this monster's short spear, and its golden shield studded with precious stones. Around Huitzilopochtli's neck were figures representing human faces and hearts made of gold and silver, and decorated with blue stones. In front of him stood several perfuming pans with copal, the incense of the country; also the hearts of three Indians, who had that day been slaughtered, were now consuming before him as a burnt-offering. Every wall of this chapel and the whole floor had become almost black with human blood, and the stench was abominable.

Respecting the abominable human sacrifices of these people, the following was communicated to us: The breast of the unhappy victim destined to be sacrificed was ripped open with a knife made of sharp flint; the throbbing heart was then torn out, and immediately offered to the idol-god in whose honour the sacrifice had been instituted. After this, the head, arms and legs were cut off and eaten at their banquets, with the exception of the head, which was saved, and hung to a beam appropriated for that purpose. No other part of the body was eaten, but the remainder was thrown to the beasts which were kept in those abominable dens, in which there were also vipers and other poisonous serpents, and, among the latter in particular, a species at the end of whose tail there was a kind of rattle. This last mentioned serpent, which is the most dangerous, was kept in a cabin of a diversified form, in which a quantity of feathers had been strewed: here it laid its eggs, and it was fed with the flesh of dogs and of human beings who had been sacrificed. We were positively told that, after we had been beaten out of the city of Mexico, and had lost 850 of our men, these horrible beasts were fed for many successive days with the bodies of our unfortunate countrymen. Indeed, when all the tigers and lions roared together, with the howlings of the jackals and foxes, and hissing of the serpents, it was quite fearful, and you could not suppose otherwise than that you were in hell.

Our commander here said smilingly, to Motecusuma: "I cannot imagine that such a powerful and wise monarch as you are, should not have yourself discovered by this time that these idols are not divinities, but evil spirits, called devils. In order that you may be convinced of this, and that your papas may satisfy themselves of this truth, allow me to erect a cross on the summit of this temple; and, in the chapel, where stand your Huitzilopochtli and Tetzcatlipuca, give us a small space that I may place there the image of the holy Virgin; then you will see what terror will seize these idols by which you have been so long deluded."

Motecusuma knew what the image of the Virgin Mary was, yet he was very much displeased with Cortes' offer, and replied, in presence of two papas, whose anger was not less conspicuous, "Malinche, could I have conjectured that you would have used such reviling language as you have just done, I would certainly not have shown you my gods. In our eyes these are good divinities: they preserve our lives, give us nourishment, water, and good harvests, healthy and growing weather, and victory whenever we pray to them for it. Therefore we offer up our prayers to them, and make them sacrifices. I earnestly beg of you not to say another word to insult the profound veneration in which we hold these gods."

As soon as Cortes heard these words and perceived the great excitement under which they were pronounced, he said nothing in return, but merely remarked to the monarch with a cheerful smile: "It is time for us both to depart hence." To which Motecusuma answered, that he would not detain him any longer, but he himself was now obliged to stay some time to atone to his gods by prayer and sacrifice for having committed *gratlatlacol*, by allowing us to ascend the great temple, and thereby occasioning the affronts which we had offered them.

THE COLUMBIAN EXCHANGE

ALFRED W. CROSBY

Columbus was not the first European to step ashore in the Western hemisphere, but his voyage occasioned so many more exchanges across the Atlantic that it changed history. This is why Alfred Crosby, a modern historian, writes of a "Columbian exchange" of world-wide ecological implications. The ecologies of Europe, Africa, and the Americas were joined into a single system. In what ways were the "Old" and "New

Alfred W. Crosby, Jr., *The Columbian Exchange: Biological and Cultural Consequences of 1492* (Greenwood Press, Westport, CT, 1972), pp. 3–11. Copyright © 1972 by Alfred W. Crosby, Jr. Used by permission of the publisher.

*World" biologically different before 1492? What religious and philosoph-
ical problems did this difference cause Europeans? How did they "solve"
these problems?*

On the evening of October 11, 1492, Christopher Columbus, on board
the *Santa Maria* in the Atlantic Ocean, thought he saw a tiny light far in
the distance. A few hours later, Rodrigo de Triana, lookout on the
Pinta's forecastle, sighted land. In the morning a party went ashore.
Columbus had reached the Bahamas. The connection between the Old
and New Worlds, which for more than ten millennia had been no more
than a tenuous thing of Viking voyages, drifting fishermen, and shad-
owy contacts via Polynesia, became on the twelfth day of October 1492
a bond as significant as the Bering land bridge had once been.

The two worlds, which God had cast asunder, were reunited, and the
two worlds, which were so very different, began on that day to become
alike. That trend toward biological homogeneity is one of the most
important aspects of the history of life on this planet since the retreat of
the continental glaciers.

The Europeans thought they were just off the coast of Asia—back to
Eurasia again—but they were struck by the strangeness of the flora and
fauna of the islands they had discovered. The record kept by Columbus
is full of remarks like:

> I saw neither sheep nor goats nor any other beast, but I have been here but
> a short time, half a day; yet if there were any I couldn't have failed to see
> them. . . . There were dogs that never barked. . . . All the trees were as
> different from ours as day from night, and so the fruits, the herbage, the
> rocks, and all things.

The distinctiveness of the human inhabitants of these islands struck
Columbus, as well. He found the Indians unlike even black Africans, the
most exotic people he had ever met with before. The Indians' hair was
"not kinky, but straight and course like horsehair; the whole forehead
and head is very broad, more so than any other race that I have ever
seen." These Arawak Indians were so impressed with the Europeans—
their vessels, clothing, weapons, shapes, and colors—that they thought
them demigods and gathered around to kiss the Spaniards' "hands and
feet, marvelling and believing that they came from the sky . . . (and)
feeling them to ascertain if they were flesh and bones like themselves."

The differences between the life forms of the two worlds have amazed
men ever since 1492. Most nonbotanists are inclined to pay more
attention to animals than plants, so the contrast between the flora of the
eastern and western hemispheres has never excited as much interest as
that between the fauna, but the contrast is a marked one. It is not
absolute—some 456 species of plants, for instance, are indigenous to
both North America and Japan—but the uniqueness of American flora

must be acknowledged. Cacti, for instance, are exclusively American in origin. Despite hundreds of years of contact via shipping between the northeastern part of the United States and adjacent Canada and the rest of the world, only about 18 percent of the total number of plant species growing in this part of America are of non-American origin.

The pre-Columbian agriculturalists developed the American food plants from an assemblage of wild plants which was very different from that which the inventors of agriculture in the Old World had. Even the most optimistic of the early colonists of Virginia had to admit that the flora was alien more often than it was familiar. This difference becomes more and more pronounced as one moves south into Mexico and beyond. Jean de Léry, who was a member of the abortive French colony at Río de Janeiro in the 1550s, found only three plants with which he was familiar: purslane, basil, and a kind of fern. All the others were strange, leading to all sorts of difficulties. With no grapes, how were the Europeans to make the wine needed to celebrate the Lord's Supper? Was it better to forego the ceremony until wine could be obtained from Europe or to operate on the theory that Jesus used wine only because it was common in Palestine, and that, therefore, His sacrifice of Himself on the Cross could be commemorated with one of the local Indian beverages?

The contrast between the Old and New World fauna has impressed everyone who has ever crossed the Atlantic or Pacific. Some species are common to both worlds, especially in the northern latitudes, but sometimes this only serves to point up other contrasts. In South and Central America the biggest native quadruped is the tapir, an animal also present in southeast Asia, but by no means the most impressive animal there. The Old World elephant has a much more useful nose and is many times larger. Tropical America's four-legged carnivores are more impressive than the herbivorous tapir, but here, too, the strange disparity between New and Old World mammals appears. The jaguar is not an animal to treat with contempt, but compared to a lion or tiger, he is one of the middle-sized cats.

The early explorers wondered at the smallness of the American mammals they came upon in their early expeditions, most of which were limited to the torrid zone. It was the reptiles, snakes, birds, and insects that really impressed them. Europe has no reptile as big as the iguana; there is probably no animal quite as ugly. The iguana reminded Amerigo Vespucci of the flying serpent of legend, except for the lack of wings. Vespucci and his comrades reacted to the iguanas exactly as nature intended that the enemies of these harmless beasts should: "Their whole appearance," he wrote of the reptiles, "was so strange that we, supposing them to be poisonous, did not dare approach them." Many of the fellow jungle-dwellers of the iguanas were at least as strange, often as terrifying, and frequently a good deal more dangerous. In the rivers there were eels that defended themselves with electricity, and rays and piranhas. There were monkeys—no oddity in itself, but these swung by their tails! Who had ever seen a bird as strange as the toucan, who seemed more beak than body, and who had ever seen a land bird as large as the Andean condor actually fly? And who, outside of a nightmare, had ever seen bats that drank blood or a snake quite as long as the anaconda?

Europeans found the animals of temperate North America less alien than those of the lands to the south, but still very unlike the animals of Europe. The rivers contained more kinds of fish than had ever swum in the Ebro or Guadalquivir. One of the biggest kind swam in the Mississippi and had whiskers like a cat, "the third part of which was head, with gills from end to end and along the sides were great spines, like very sharp awls." There was a snake with a castanet on his tail (rattlesnake, no doubt) whose bite left the victim with enough time for his last confession, but for little more. Strangest of all, when Coronado rode onto the plains, he found no gold but a kind of huge cattle as numerous as fish in the sea (buffalo or bison). They were as large or larger than oxen and had short, thick horns and humps like camels and when they ran, they carried their tails erect like scorpions. The Spanish horses were frightened of them "for they have a narrow short face, the brow two palms across from eye to eye, the eyes sticking out at the side, so that, when they are running, they can see who is following them. They have very long beards, like goats, and when they are running they throw their heads back with the beard dragging on the ground."

Men returned from America with stories of mythical beasts—like that of the Mexican bird which never lands as long as it lives and even lays and hatches its eggs in the air—but there was no need to resort to fiction. American fauna is richer in species of unique animals than any imagination could devise. In the 1850s Philip L. Sclater, on the basis of what he knew about the geographic distribution of bird genera, decided that our planet is divided into six regions, each one with a characteristic bird population: two of these regions make up the New World. Twenty years later, Alfred Russel Wallace, co-originator with Darwin of the modern concept of evolution, saw that Sclater's six-part division of the planet is as valid for animals in general as for birds in particular. The animals of the six sections are prevented or at least inhibited from intermingling by oceans, mountain ranges, deserts, differences in temperature. The fauna of these regions are not absolutely distinctive—the tapir is native to both tropical America and tropical Asia; the cougar, rattlesnake, and hummingbird are native to both North and South America—but, to quote a modern zoo-geographer, "the animals in different parts of one faunal realm are on the whole more related to those of other parts of the same region than to those of other regions." To illustrate, although there are many similarities among the fauna of the Irrawaddy, lower

Niger, and Amazon valleys, a zoologist can differentiate between them at a glance.

South and Central America plus the West Indies and part of Mexico make up one of the Sclater-Wallace regions. The rest of Mexico, plus the United States, Canada, and Greenland make up another. Of the two, the southernmost is the richest zoologically, with forty-five families of backboned animals peculiar to it alone, according to Wallace. (Research since his time has shown that neither this southern region of the New World nor any of the other five regions is quite so clearly distinctive as he thought—accumulation of data always points up exceptions to any rule—but the general validity of the Sclater-Wallace system is still accepted.) It seems clear to the layman that southern America, with its unique anteaters, sloths, monkeys with prehensile tails, vampire bats, rodents as big as dogs, and wild profusion of insects and birds must rank as a separate region. Only Australia equals it in being truly exceptional.

Northern America is not nearly as distinctive. At most, Wallace grants only thirteen families of vertebrates as native to it exclusively, but it does have claim to uniqueness. A number of mammalian genera are peculiar to it, including several kinds of moles and species like the Rocky Mountain goat and the prong-buck. It shares with the region to the south the distinction of being home to the only marsupials outside of Australia and the only hummingbirds in the world. It is very rich in kinds of reptiles and amphibia, despite the fact that temperate and cold climates usually limit the numbers of such animals. And its peerless systems of lakes and rivers give it a wealth of fresh water mollusca and fish unequalled anywhere else on this planet.

Alfred Russel Wallace's careful accumulation of evidence and guarded generalities confirmed what Jean de Léry had guessed on the basis of one trip to Brazil more than three hundred years before: that America is so truly "different from Europe, Asia and Africa in the living habits of its people, the forms of its animals, and, in general, in that which the earth produces, that it can well be called the new world. . . ."

The contrasts between the two worlds piqued European curiosity. Not everything was different. American palms were quite like those of Africa, and the jaguar was very much like the leopard. But why even slight differences, and why the great ones? Why were there no horses or cattle anywhere in the Americas? Why were there no four-legged beasts bigger than a fox in the West Indies? Even those who had voyaged to Africa for slaves and to the Far East for spices found little in America that was familiar, and many things that were utterly strange.

The Europeans had emerged from the Middle Ages with intellectual systems, Christian and Aristotelian, claimed by the orthodox (and so few even guessed there was anything beyond orthodoxy) to explain everything from the first and last ticks of history to what happens in the egg prior to the hatching of the chick. These systems proved too cramped to accommodate the New World. Aristotle had quite logically supposed the equatorial zone of the earth so hot that life could not exist there. Joseph de Acosta crossed directly under the sun on his way to America in 1570 and "felt so great cold, as I was forced to go into the sunne to warme me: what could I else do then but laugh at Aristotle's Meteors and his philosophie. . . ." Pliny's *Natural History* contains thirty-seven books, and yet he did not mention the llama in any of them. The works of Hippocrates, Galen, and Avicenna occupied whole shelves of every good fifteenth-century library from Baghdad to Oxford to Timbuktu, but these three giants of medicine had not a word to say about syphilis. Ancient and medieval geographers had made fine maps of all the world, but the men of the Columbian generation discovered that "Ptolomeus, and others knewe not the halfe."

The ancient and medieval pronouncements on humans and human behavior seemed to leave Europeans little choice but to condemn the Indians as allies of the Devil. For instance, Christians agreed that heterosexual monogamy was the way to handle the sex relationship. The Indians, with a kind of abandon unmentioned in even the candid pages of the Old Testament, practiced promiscuity, polygamy, incest, and sodomy. The Europeans had either to conceive of the naturalness of cultural diversity and invent cultural toleration to go along with it, or to assume that Indians were in league with Hell. Most made the latter choice. The exception, of course, was Montaigne, who found nothing barbarous in what he heard of America, except insofar as "everyone gives the title barbarism to everything that is not according to his usage. . . ."

The Bible was the source of most wisdom, and the book of Genesis told all that one needed to know about the beginning of the heavens, earth, angels, plants, animals, and men. There was one God and there had been one Creation; when mankind had offended God, God caused a great flood in which all land creatures, including men, had perished, except those preserved in Noah's ark. This explanation seemed sufficiently broad to include within its bounds all the diversity of life—plant, animal, and human—which the European was obliged to acknowledge up to the end of the fifteenth century. Then da Gama and Columbus brought whole new worlds crashing into the area of European perception.

The problems of explaining Africa and Asia were difficult but surmountable. After all, it had always been known that they were there and, if Europeans had not seen elephants, they had at least always known about them. But America, who had ever dreamed of America? The uniqueness of the New World called into question the whole Christian cosmogony. If God had created all of the life forms in one week in one place and they had then spread out from there over the whole world, then why are the life forms in the eastern and western hemispheres so different? And if all land animals and men had drowned except for those in the ark, and all that now exist are descended from those chosen few, then why the different kinds of animals and men on either side of the Atlantic? Why are there no tree sloths in the African and Asian tropics, and why do the Peruvian heathens worship Viracocha instead of Baal or some other demon familiar to the ancient Jews? The effort to maintain the Hebraic version of the origin of life and man was to "put many learned Christians upon the rack to make it out."

The problem tempted a few Europeans to toy with the concept of multiple creations, but the mass of people clung to monogeneticism. They had to; it was basic to Christianity. For example, what would happen to the validity of the Pope's 1493 grant to Spain of "all islands and mainlands found and to be found, discovered, and to be discovered," in the western Atlantic unless their inhabitants were truly men and women and thus under papal jurisdiction? The famous Requirement of 1512, which the Spanish monarchs ordered the conquistadors to read to the Indians so that they would realize that their subsequent slaughter and subjugation were justified, opened with a statement that "the Lord our God, Living and Eternal, created Heaven and Earth, and one man and one woman, of whom you and I, and all the men of the world, were and are descendants. . . ." Being descendants of Adam and Eve, the American aborigines were subject to the Pope and, by his donation of America to Spain, to Ferdinand and Isabella.

If monogeneticism in this instance worked against the Indians, in 1537 it worked for them. The Pope denounced as satellites of the Devil those who claimed the Indians "should be treated as dumb brutes created for our service," a view common among the conquistadors. The Pope proclaimed "that the Indians are truly men, and that they are not only capable of understanding the Catholic faith but, according to our information, they desire exceedingly to receive it."

THE SLAVE TRADE

OLAUDAH EQUIANO

The consequences of the European arrival in the Americas were devastating for the human inhabitants of three continents: North America, South America, and Africa. The inhabitants of the Americas were decimated by diseases, especially smallpox, from which they had no immu-

From *The Interesting Narrative of Olaudah Equiano, or Gustavus Vasa, The African.* London: 1789. Reprinted in *Africa Remembered*, edited by Philip D. Curtin. Madison: University of Wisconsin Press, 1967.

*nities. The inhabitants of Africa, especially western Africa, were deci-
mated by the European slave trade.*

*This selection is part of the autobiography of one of the Africans who
was enslaved, Olaudah Equiano. He was born in 1745 in what is today
Nigeria, sold to British slavers at the age of eleven, and shipped off to the
British West Indies. In 1766 he was able to buy his freedom and became
involved in the antislavery movement in England. What was slavery in
Africa like, and how was it different from slavery in the Americas? For
those, like Equiano, who survived, what were the worst aspects of the
Atlantic slave trade? What do you think of Equiano's criticism of "nominal
Christians?"*

I hope the reader will not think I have trespassed on his patience in
introducing myself to him with some account of the manners and
customs of my country. They had been implanted in me with great care,
and made an impression on my mind, which time could not erase, and
which all the adversity and variety of fortune I have since experienced
served only to rivet and record; for, whether the love of one's country be
real or imaginary, or a lesson of reason, or an instinct of nature, I still
look back with pleasure on the first scenes of my life, though that
pleasure has been for the most part mingled with sorrow.

My father, besides many slaves, had a numerous family, of which
seven lived to grow up, including myself and a sister, who was the only
daughter. As I was the youngest of the sons, I became, of course, the
greatest favourite with my mother, and was always with her; and she
used to take particular pains to form my mind. I was trained up from my
earliest years in the arts of agriculture and war: my daily exercise was
shooting and throwing javelins; and my mother adorned me with
emblems, after the manner of our greatest warriors. In this way I grew
up till I was turned the age of eleven, when an end was put to my
happiness in the following manner:—Generally, when the grown people
in the neighbourhood were gone far in the fields to labour, the children
assembled together in some of the neighbour's premises to play; and
commonly some of us used to get up a tree to look out for any assailant,
or kidnapper, that might come upon us; for they sometimes took those
opportunities of our parents' absence, to attack and carry off as many as
they could seize. One day, as I was watching at the top of a tree in our
yard, I saw one of those people come into the yard of our next
neighbour but one, to kidnap, there being many stout young people in
it. Immediately, on this, I gave the alarm of the rogue, and he was
surrounded by the stoutest of them, who entangled him with cords, so
that he could not escape till some of the grown people came and secured
him. But alas! ere long, it was my fate to be thus attacked, and to be
carried off, when none of the grown people were nigh. One day, when

all our people were gone out to their works as usual, and only I and my dear sister were left to mind the house, two men and a woman got over our walls, and in a moment seized us both; and, without giving us time to cry out, or make resistance, they stopped our mouths, and ran off with us into the nearest wood. Here they tied our hands, and continued to carry us as far as they could, till night came on, when we reached a small house, where the robbers halted for refreshment, and spent the night. We were then unbound; but were unable to take any food; and, being quite overpowered by fatigue and grief, our only relief was some sleep, which allayed our misfortune for a short time. The next morning we left the house, and continued travelling all the day. For a long time we had kept the woods, but at last we came into a road which I believed I knew. I had now some hopes of being delivered; for we had advanced but a little way before I discovered some people at a distance, on which I began to cry out for their assistance; but my cries had no other effect than to make them tie me faster and stop my mouth, and then they put me into a large sack. They also stopped my sister's mouth, and tied her hands; and in this manner we proceeded till we were out of sight of these people. When we went to rest the following night they offered us some victuals; but we refused them; and the only comfort we had was in being in one another's arms all that night, and bathing each other with our tears. But alas! we were soon deprived of even the smallest comfort of weeping together. The next day proved a day of greater sorrow than I had yet experienced; for my sister and I were then separated, while we lay clasped in each other's arms: it was in vain that we besought them not to part us: she was torn from me, and immediately carried away, while I was left in a state of distraction not to be described. I cried and grieved continually; and for several days did not eat any thing but what they forced into my mouth. At length, after many days travelling, during which I had often changed masters, I got into the hands of a chieftain, in a very pleasant country. This man had two wives and some children, and they all used me extremely well, and did all they could to comfort me; particularly the first wife, who was something like my mother. Although I was a great many days journey from my father's house, yet these people spoke exactly the same language with us. This first master of mine, as I may call him, was a smith; and my principal employment was working his bellows, which were the same kind as I had seen in my vicinity. They were in some respects not unlike the stoves here in gentlemen's kitchens; and were covered over with leather; and in the middle of that leather a stick was fixed, and a person stood up, and worked it, in the same manner as is done to pump water out of a cask with a hand pump. I believe it was gold he worked, for it was of a lovely bright yellow colour, and was worn by the women on their wrists and ankles. . . .

Soon after this my master's only daughter and child by his first wife sickened and died, which affected him so much that for some time he was almost frantic, and really would have killed himself, had he not been watched and prevented. However, in a small time afterwards he recovered; and I was again sold. I was now carried to the left of the sun's rising, through many dreary wastes and dismal woods, amidst the hideous roarings of wild beasts. The people I was sold to used to carry me very often, when I was tired, either on their shoulders or on their backs. I saw many convenient well-built sheds along the roads, at proper distances, to accommodate the merchants and travellers, who lay in those buildings along with their wives, who often accompany them; and they always go well armed.

From the time I left my own nation I always found somebody that understood me till I came to the sea coast. The languages of different nations did not totally differ, nor were they so copious as those of the Europeans, particularly the English. They were therefore easily learned; and, while I was journeying thus through Africa, I acquired two or three different tongues. . . .

I came to a town called Timnah, in the most beautiful country I had yet seen in Africa. It was extremely rich, and there were many rivulets which flowed through it, and supplied a large pond in the centre of the town, where the people washed. Here I first saw and tasted cocoa nuts, which I thought superior to any nuts I had ever tested before; and the trees, which were loaded, were also interspersed amongst the houses, which had commodious shades adjoining, and were in the same manner as ours, the insides being neatly plastered and whitewashed. Here I also saw and tasted for the first time sugar-cane. Their money consisted of little white shells, the size of the fingernail: they were known in this country by the name of core.[1] I was sold here for one hundred and seventy-two of them by a merchant who lived and brought me there. I had been about two or three days at his house, when a wealthy widow, a neighbour of his, came there one evening, and brought with her an only son, a young gentleman about my own age and size. Here they saw me; and, having taken a fancy to me, I was bought of the merchant, and went home with them. Her house and premises were situated close to one of those rivulets I have mentioned, and were the finest I ever saw in Africa: they were very extensive, and she had a number of slaves to attend her. The next day I was washed and perfumed, and when mealtime came, I was led into the presence of my mistress, and eat and drank before her with her son. This filled me with astonishment; and I could scarce help expressing my surprise that the young gentleman should suffer me, who was bound, to eat with him who was free; and not only so, but that he would not at any time either eat or drink till I had taken first, because I

---

1. Cowrie, a sea shell obtained from the Maldive Islands and used as currency in many parts of West Africa.

was the eldest, which was agreeable to our custom. Indeed every thing here, and all their treatment of me, made me forget that I was a slave. The language of these people resembled ours so nearly, that we understood each other perfectly. They had also the very same customs as we. There were likewise slaves daily to attend us, while my young master and I, with other boys, sported with our darts and bows and arrows, as I had been used to do at home. In this resemblance to my former happy state, I passed about two months, and I now began to think I was to be adopted into the family, and was beginning to be reconciled to my situation, and to forget by degrees my misfortunes, when all at once the delusion vanished; for, without the least previous knowledge, one morning early, while my dear master and companion was still asleep, I was awakened out of my reverie to fresh sorrow, and hurried away even amongst the uncircumcised.

Thus, at the very moment I dreamed of the greatest happiness, I found myself most miserable; and it seemed as if fortune wished to give me this taste of joy only to render the reverse more poignant. The change I now experienced was as painful as it was sudden and unexpected. It was a change indeed from a state of bliss to a scene which is inexpressible by me, as it discovered to me an element I had never before beheld, and till then had no idea of, and wherein such instances of hardship and fatigue continually occurred as I can never reflect on but with horror.

• • •

The first object which saluted my eyes when I arrived on the coast was the sea, and a slaveship, which was then riding at anchor, and waiting for its cargo. These filled me with astonishment, which was soon converted into terror, which I am yet at a loss to describe, nor the then feelings of my mind. When I was carried on board I was immediately handled, and tossed up, to see if I were sound, by some of the crew; and I was now persuaded that I had got into a world of bad spirits, and that they were going to kill me. Their complexions too differing so much from ours, their long hair, and the language they spoke, which was very different from any I had ever heard, united to confirm me in this belief. Indeed, such were the horrors of my views and fears at the moment, that, if ten thousand worlds had been my own, I would have freely parted with them all to have exchanged my condition with that of the meanest slave in my own country. When I looked round the ship too, and saw a large furnace or copper boiling, and a multitude of black people of every description chained together, every one of their countenances expressing dejection and sorrow, I no longer doubted of my fate; and, quite over-powered with horror and anguish, I fell motionless on the deck and fainted. When I recovered a little, I found some black people about me, who I believed were some of those who brought me on board, and had been receiving their pay; they talked to me in order to cheer me, but all in vain. I asked them if we were not to be eaten by those white men with horrible looks, red faces, and long hair. They told me I was not; and one of the crew brought me a small portion of spirituous liquor in a wine-glass; but, being afraid of him, I would not take it out of his hand. One of the blacks therefore took it from him, and gave it to me, and I took a little down my palate, which, instead of reviving me, as they thought it would, threw me into the greatest consternation at the strange feeling it produced having never tasted any such liquor before. Soon after this, the blacks who brought me on board went off, and left me abandoned to despair. I now saw myself deprived of all chance of returning to my native country, or even the least glimpse of hope of gaining the shore, which I now considered as friendly; and I even wished for my former slavery, in preference to my present situation, which was filled with horrors of every kind, still heightened by my ignorance of what I was to undergo. I was not long suffered to indulge my grief; I was soon put down under the decks, and there I received such a salutation in my nostrils as I had never experienced in my life; so that, with the loathsomeness of the stench, and crying together, I became so sick and low that I was not able to eat, nor had I the least desire to taste any thing. I now wished for the last friend, death, to relieve me; but soon, to my grief, two of the white men offered me eatables; and, on my refusing to eat, one of them held me fast by the hands, and laid me across, I think, the windlass, and tied my feet while the other flogged me severely. I had never experienced any thing of this kind before; and, although not being used to the water, I naturally feared that element the first time I saw it; yet, nevertheless, could I have got over the nettings, I would have jumped over the side; but I could not; and, besides, the crew used to watch us very closely who were not chained down to the decks, lest we should leap into the water: and I have seen some of these poor African prisoners most severely cut for attempting to do so, and hourly whipped for not eating. This indeed was often the case with myself. In a little time after, amongst the poor chained men, I found some of my own nation, which in a small degree gave ease to my mind. I inquired of them what was to be done with us? they gave me to understand we were to be carried to these white people's country to work for them. I then was a little revived, and thought, if it were no worse than working, my situation was not so desperate: but still I feared I should be put to death, the white people looked and acted, as I thought, in so savage a manner; for I had never seen among any people such instances of brutal cruelty; and this not only shown towards us blacks, but also to some of the whites themselves. One white man in particular I saw, when we were permitted to be on deck, flogged[2] so unmercifully with a large rope near the foremast, that he died in consequence of it; and they tossed him over the side as they would have done a brute. This made me fear these people the more; and I expected nothing less than to be treated in the same manner. I could not help expressing my fears and apprehensions to some of my countrymen: I asked them if these people had no country, but lived in this hollow place the ship? they told me they did not, but came from a distant one. "Then," said I, "how comes it in all our country we never heard of them?" They told me, because they lived so very far off. I then asked, where were their women? had they any like themselves? I was told they had. "And why," said I, "do we not see them?" they answered, because they were left behind. I asked how the vessel could go? they told me they could not tell; but that there were cloth put upon the masts by the help of the ropes I saw, and then the vessel went on; and the white men had some spell or magic they put in the water when they liked in order to stop the vessel. I was exceedingly amazed at this account, and really thought they were spirits. I therefore wished much to be from amongst them, for I expected they would sacrifice me: but my wishes were vain; for we were so quartered that it was impossible for any of us to make our escape. While we staid on the coast I was mostly on deck; and one day, to my great astonishment, I saw one of these vessels coming in with the sails up. As soon as the whites saw it, they gave a great shout, at which we were amazed; and the more so as the vessel appeared larger by approaching nearer. At last she came to an anchor in my sight, and when the anchor was let go, I and my countrymen who saw it were lost in astonishment to observe the vessel stop; and were now convinced it was done by magic. Soon after this the other ship got her boats out, and they came on board of us, and the people of both ships seemed very glad to see each other. Several of the strangers also shook hands with us black people, and made motions with their hands, signifying, I suppose, we were to go to their country; but we did not understand them. At last, when the ship we were in had got in all her cargo, they made ready with many fearful noises, and we were all put under deck, so that we could not see how they managed the vessel. But this disappointment was the least of my sorrow. The stench of the hold while we were on the coast was so intolerably loathsome, that it was dangerous to remain there for any time, and some of us had been permitted to stay on the deck for the fresh air; but now that the whole ship's cargo were confined together, it became absolutely pestilential. The closeness of the place, and the heat of the climate, added to the number in the ship, which was so crowded that each had scarcely room to turn himself, almost suffocated us. This

2. Such brutal floggings were at this time considered essential to the maintenance of discipline in the British navy and on ships engaged in the slave trade.

produced copious perspirations, so that the air soon became unfit for respiration, from a variety of loathsome smells, and brought on a sickness amongst the slaves, of which many died, thus falling victims to the improvident avarice, as I may call it, of their purchasers. This wretched situation was again aggravated by the galling of the chains, now become insupportable; and the filth of the necessary tubs, into which the children often fell, and were almost suffocated. The shrieks of the women, and the groans of the dying, rendered the whole a scene of horror almost inconceivable. Happily perhaps for myself I was soon reduced so low here that it was thought necessary to keep me almost always on deck; and from my extreme youth I was not put in fetters. In this situation I expected every hour to share the fate of my companions, some of whom were almost daily brought upon deck at the point of death, which I began to hope would soon put an end to my miseries. Often did I think many of the inhabitants of the deep much more happy than myself; I envied them the freedom they enjoyed, and as often wished I could change my condition for theirs. Every circumstance I met with served only to render my state more painful, and heighten my apprehensions and my opinion of the cruelty of the whites. One day they had taken a number of fishes; and when they had killed and satisfied themselves with as many as they thought fit, to our astonishment who were on the deck, rather than give any of them to us to eat, as we expected, they tossed the remaining fish into the sea again, although we begged and prayed for some as well as we could, but in vain; and some of my countrymen, being pressed by hunger, took an opportunity, when they thought no one saw them, of trying to get a little privately; but they were discovered, and the attempt procured them some very severe floggings.

One day, when we had a smooth sea, and moderate wind, two of my wearied countrymen, who were chained together (I was near them at the time), preferring death to such a life of misery, somehow made through the nettings, and jumped into the sea; immediately another quite dejected fellow, who, on account of his illness, was suffered to be out of irons, also followed their example; and I believe many more would very soon have done the same, if they had not been prevented by the ship's crew, who were instantly alarmed. Those of us that were the most active were in a moment put down under the deck; and there was such a noise and confusion amongst the people of the ship as I never heard before, to stop her, and get the boat out to go after the slaves. However, two of the wretches were drowned, but they got the other, and afterwards flogged him unmercifully, for thus attempting to prefer death to slavery. In this manner we continued to undergo more hardships than I can now relate; hardships which are inseparable from this accursed trade. Many a time we were near suffocation, from the want of fresh air, which we were often without for whole days together. This, and the stench of the

necessary tubs, carried off many. During our passage I first saw flying
fishes, which surprised me very much: they used frequently to fly across
the ship, and many of them fell on the deck. I also now first saw the use
of the quadrant. I had often with astonishment seen the mariners make
observations with it, and I could not think what it meant. They at last
took notice of my surprise; and one of them, willing to increase it, as well
as to gratify my curiosity, made me one day look through it. The clouds
appeared to me to be land, which disappeared as they passed along. This
heightened my wonder: and I was now more persuaded than ever that
I was in another world, and that every thing about me was magic. At last,
we came in sight of the island of Barbadoes, at which the whites on board
gave a great shout, and made many signs of joy to us. We did not know
what to think of this; but, as the vessel drew nearer, we plainly saw the
harbour, and other ships of different kinds and sizes: and we soon
anchored amongst them off Bridge Town. Many merchants and planters now come on board, though it was in the evening. They put us in
separate parcels, and examined us attentively. They also made us jump,
and pointed to the land, signifying we were to go there. We thought by
this we should be eaten by these ugly men, as they appeared to us; and
when, soon after we were all put down under the deck again, there was
much dread and trembling among us, and nothing but bitter cries to be
heard all the night from these apprehensions, insomuch that at last the
white people got some old slaves from the land to pacify us. They told us
we were not to be eaten, but to work, and were soon to go on land where
we should see many of our country people. This report eased us much;
and sure enough, soon after we landed, there came to us Africans of all
languages. We were conducted immediately to the merchant's yard,
where we were all pent up together like so many sheep in a fold, without
regard to sex or age. As every object was new to me, everything I saw
filled me with surprise. What struck me first was, that the houses were
built with bricks, in stories, and in every other respect different from
those I have seen in Africa: but I was still more astonished on seeing
people on horseback. I did not know what this could mean; and indeed
I thought these people were full of nothing but magical arts. While I was
in this astonishment, one of my fellow prisoners spoke to a countryman
of his about the horses, who said they were the same kind they had in
their country. I understood them, though they were from a distant part
of Africa, and I thought it odd I had not seen any horses there; but
afterwards, when I came to converse with different Africans, I found
they had many horses amongst them, and much larger than those I then
saw. We were not many days in the merchant's custody, before we were
sold after their usual manner, which is this: on a signal given (as the beat
of a drum), the buyers rush at once into the yard where the slaves are
confined, and make choice of that parcel they like best. The noise and
clamour with which this is attended, and the eagerness visible in the

countenances of the buyers, serve not a little to increase the apprehension of the terrified Africans, who may well be supposed to consider them as the ministers of that destruction to which they think themselves devoted. In this manner, without scruple, are relations and friends separated, most of them never to see each other again. I remember in the vessel in which I was brought over, in the men's apartment, there were several brothers who, in the sale, were sold in different lots; and it was very moving on this occasion to see and hear their cries at parting. O, ye nominal Christians! might not an African ask you, learned you this from your God? who says unto you, Do unto all men as you would men should do unto you. Is it not enough that we are torn from our country and friends to toil for your luxury and lust of gain? Must every tender feeling be likewise sacrificed to your avarice? Are the dearest friends and relations, now rendered more dear by their separation from their kindred, still to be parted from each other, and thus preventing from cheering the gloom of slavery with the small comfort of being together, and mingling their sufferings and sorrows? Why are parents to love their children, brothers their sisters, or husbands their wives? Surely this is a new refinement in cruelty, which, while it has no advantage to atone for it, thus aggravates distress, and adds fresh horrors even to the wretchedness of slavery.

3. Asian Empires and Economic Expansion

ATLANTIC INFLATION AND OTTOMAN DECLINE

OMER LUTFI BARKAN

In 1500 few observers would have predicted that the future belonged to Europe. More likely candidates would have been the Islamic Ottoman Empire centered in modern Turkey or the Indian or Chinese empires. This chapter asks how all three of these great empires declined while Europe succeeded.

The decline of the Ottoman Empire at the end of the sixteenth and the beginning of the seventeenth century was as swift as the corresponding rise of Europe. This essay, by a modern historian, argues that the Ottoman Empire was undermined by a chain of events that included the European conquest of the African coast and the Americas, the importation of vast amounts of gold and silver and the resulting sixteenth-century price inflation, and the Ottoman inability to cope with the new economic, military, and political world.

How did the sixteenth-century price inflation affect the Ottoman economy? How did the European economy become stronger than the Ottoman? What prevented the Ottoman Empire from adapting to meet the new challenge? What should the Sublime Porte (as the Ottoman government was called) have done in order to maintain an equal footing with Europe?

The sixteenth century came to an end with the countries of the Ottoman Middle East falling into a grave economic and social crisis which presaged a decisive turning point in their history. The most symptomatic sign of what was, in fact, a structural crisis was a series of popular revolts which appeared most prominently among the Muslim Turkish population of Anatolia. Known as the Celali revolts, these uprisings developed

From "The Price Revolution of the Sixteenth Century: A Turning Point in the Economic History of the Near East," by Omer Lutfi Barkan, translated by Justin McCarthy. *International Journal of Middle East Studies*, Vol. 6, No. 1 (1974), Cambridge University Press. Reprinted by permission.

into open civil war against the forces of the Ottoman state, and in their first phase lasted approximately fifteen years, from 1595 to 1610. . . .

THE ECONOMIC STRUCTURE AND DOCTRINE
OF THE OTTOMAN EMPIRE

The economic system in effect in the first centuries of the Ottoman Empire was in many ways original and to a certain extent was in harmony with the conditions of its time. While it has been subjected to heavy criticism, one must remember that, during the first centuries of the Ottoman Empire, it permitted the rise of considerable economic prosperity in an area that before the Ottoman conquest had for centuries fallen into decay and impoverishment.

The Ottoman system was basically one of imperial self-sufficiency. In order systematically to exploit the vast sources of wealth within the empire and to preserve its political and economic integrity and unity, the Ottomans sought to establish a tightly closed economic order. They saw the need of bringing to an end the economic penetration and exploitation by European powers such as Venice and Genoa. At the same time they attempted to develop means by which the different economic zones of the Empire would complement one another, instead of developing the dangerous ruptures and disequilibrium that had brought economic crises and depressions in the past. To a great extent, the Ottomans were successful in these endeavors. The robust constitution and political power of the Empire in its first two centuries enabled it to pursue an economic policy that was highly favorable to it, and as a result to avoid entirely the kind of economic crises that had weakened its predecessors.

It was only when Europe began to develop its own political and economic power that the system was breached. The decline of the established Ottoman social and economic order began as the result of developments entirely outside the area dominated by the Porte, and in particular as a consequence of the establishment in Western Europe of an "Atlantic economy" of tremendous vitality and force. The economic system of the Empire decayed neither through a flaw inherent in its constitution, nor through an organic law, but because of immense historical changes that destroyed its equilibrium, arrested its natural economic evolution, and condemned its institutions to irreparable damage.

In the second half of the fifteenth century the major European nations began the intellectual and commercial development that was to eventually bring them to world domination. At that time, the expansion outside of Europe by the countries bordering the Atlantic began to reach a peak, extending first into Africa, and culminating in the discovery of entire new continents. The European nations were attracted to Africa primarily by the highly lucrative commerce in gold and slaves. It was not long before they had drained a substantial portion of the African gold supply. This gold had been the principal source of economic nourishment for the entire Mediterranean world, and by taking it the Europeans laid the foundation for the development of a highly profitable colonial system in the centuries to come. The African experience gave the colonial powers the experience and means to develop new techniques and a powerful economic and financial base which made it inevitable that they would proceed to the discovery of America (1492) and of the Cape of Good Hope (1498). These discoveries led them inevitably to conquest and exploitation in the heart of Asia.

The effects of these important geographic discoveries on the economic and social structures of Europe have only begun to be explored; their influence on non-European lands is even less known. The shift of the old international trade in silks and spices to the new all-water route was surely a severe blow to the economies and finances of the lands that controlled those routes. Here I examine less the overt facts of the trade shift and more the consequent "price revolution" that engulfed Europe as well as the Ottoman Empire during the sixteenth century.

Imperialist organization and colonial commerce produced incredible riches for certain European countries. After the initial phase of conquest and pillage, European powers quickly converted their colonial holdings into agrarian plantations and, perhaps more important, mines. Their rapidly developed efficient means of exploitation enabled them to bring Europe tremendous quantities of gold and silver; the amount rose to as much as three, five, or seven times that originally imported in 1495. The injection of the tremendous new supply of capital produced new activity in European commerce and industry and put at the Europeans' disposal new products whose profits could only be fully realized if new markets as well as new sources of investment could be found. At the same time, an inevitable result of this situation was an immense inflation throughout Europe, with vast repercussions in its social and political order.

While the European economy developed rapidly, with capital accretion, investment, and inflation feeding one another, the Ottoman closed economy, by its very nature, strongly resisted the temptation to follow a similar path. As a result, the economies of Western Europe and the Ottoman Empire moved farther and farther apart. The consequent increase in the prices paid for basic commodities in Europe gradually began a process by which those commodities were sucked out of Ottoman markets. Wheat, copper, wool, and the like, which had been the bases of the Ottoman economic strategy, now came into such short supply in the major centers of the Empire that here also was developed a rapid inflation of prices which soon endangered the equilibrium and security of the closed economic system. While the established system forbade the export of such basic commodities outside its boundaries, the lure of the profits to be found in the highly inflated European markets led Ottoman and foreign merchants alike to adopt all possible measures to smuggle these goods outside Ottoman territory.

This situation made it increasingly difficult for the Porte to fulfill its major function of arranging for sufficient supplies for the major cities of the Empire; at the same time the lack of raw materials produced a mounting crisis in Ottoman industry, which in turn led to ever greater discontent among the artisans, whose direct and indirect complaints found voice in the Ottoman administrative documents of the time. Of course, for them the situation was the result of the entry of the "accursed spirit of speculation and excessive gain" into the Empire, the abandonment of the older trade regulations and the corporate traditions among artisans and the indifference and corruption of the administrative authorities. They could not see that the situation was in fact created by economic developments outside the Empire, against which the traditional Ottoman administrative system found itself powerless to act. Traditional methods were naturally employed in an effort to counter the threat; controls on the export of "strategic" grains were augmented, violators were threatened with severe punishment, and goods seized in transit were expropriated by the state, but the profits to be gained from illicit smuggling of grains into the European market were so enormous that this traffic continued to attract participants who were able to find accomplices even among the most highly placed representatives of the state. This contraband commerce become for many persons in the Empire a normal trade and for some social classes a source of far more riches than they had ever been able to amass before. Ottoman agriculture, organized in great tax farms in the areas that were most conveniently located for participation in this clandestine trade, also began to feel the pressure of the inflated European prices on its own organic structure, and it began to orient itself toward an agrarian regime better adapted to massive commercialization of its products.

Archival materials from the time demonstrate that it was impossible to stem the flow resulting from the price differences between the hitherto integrated Ottoman zone and the "Atlantic economy." The penetration of the high pressure "dominant economy" into the Ottoman low tension economy was the inevitable result of the price difference between the two. It was accomplished in spite of all the resistance the Ottoman system could provide. Economic penetration produced a grave inflationary current in the Ottoman Empire which together with other, more internal factors, produced social and political changes that disturbed the social and economic security of the Empire, and in the end proved to be irreversible.

THE CRISIS IN OTTOMAN INDUSTRY

As the Empire's price system gradually fell under the influence of the "dominant economy," Ottoman industry was also undergoing disastrous changes which cannot be explained simply as the effects of European absorption of the reserve stocks of primary materials necessary for industry. In addition to the weapons of the price mechanism and the absorption of goods, the economy of the Atlantic zone threatened as well the traditional production and trade structures of the Empire.

In Europe, prodigious commercial expansion had given birth to a new capitalist industry, particularly in textiles and metallurgy, an industry working always for massive exportation. This new industry was concentrated in the hands of capitalist entrepreneurs and merchants—men free of all corporate restraint who worked with a new spirit, inventing new techniques, starting new fashions, and creating new needs. They inaugurated intensive methods of production and opened new markets in order to make their merchandise accessible to an increasingly far-flung clientele. In doing so, they completely changed international trade, giving it a new character—unlimited expansion.

The Ottoman craft industry was thus faced in the second half of the sixteenth century with a European industry rapidly evolving toward the conquest of the world's markets. The times had produced a vast change in traditional international commerce. For example, European commerce, represented by a small number of merchants, had previously exported a few luxury and specialty items to the Ottoman Empire. These imports represented no threat to local industry. On the contrary, they produced customs revenues and added to the pleasures of life for those classes privileged enough to afford them. Then again, the Europeans were good clients of the Ottoman luxury industries who bought as much, if not more, than they sold; their trade was actively sought and encouraged. European commerce was an indispensable part of Ottoman prosperity.

During the second half of the sixteenth century that picture changed. European commerce, sustained by strong commercial organization and encouraged by powerful nation-states, began to be a threat to local industry, a prime factor in economic decline. The new European national commerce intended to sell the greatest possible quantity of goods abroad, while restricting imports of any finished products. Thus it provided no market for local Ottoman export industry. The commerce of Levant changed to a "colonial commerce," turning Turkey into a client for the European industry which was itself to furnish only primary materials, no longer to export finished goods.

An example of this pattern is the silk industry of Bursa: Until the latter half of the sixteenth century, this city produced huge quantities of high quality silk cloth, most of it intended for the export market. Once the European silk industry was perfected, however, European merchants no longer bought anything from Bursa but silk thread, eagerly awaiting the day when they would only have to buy the cocoons. The same industrial evolution characterized the mohair (*sof*) industry of Ankara. Ankara had been renowned for its export-quality woven mohair cloth, but by the end of the sixteenth century it had fallen to the level of a thread center, a simple market for the hair of Angora [the former name of Ankara] goats. Like Bursa, it had become a supplier of primary material from which others now drew riches.

One can clearly see that the advent of the new European commerce began the stagnation of the Ottoman craft industry. Certainly the craft industry continued in many places to exist, but it never advanced or evolved. Faced with the continuously evolving European industry, Ottoman industry could not find the dynamism necessary to adapt to the new conditions of the world economy. As an even wider gap between it and European industry opened, the Ottoman system was condemned to degeneration.

The new European commerce must be included as one of the main causes of the sixteenth-century Ottoman economic stagnation. The shock produced by this commerce on local industry is one of the principal reasons for the progressive decline in the balance of trade. This in turn not only caused the loss of gold and silver, but made it impossible to redress the loss.

It is thus that, well before the use of steam as a source of energy in industry and transport and long before the Industrial Revolution, other, smaller economic revolutions in world commerce and industrial production had already given European commerce a crushing superiority in its drive for the conquest of world markets.

THE INDIAN MOGUL ECONOMY

FERNAND BRAUDEL

This survey of the Indian empire of the Moguls by a modern historian finds greater economic strength than we saw in the Ottoman Empire. The Indian empire, the author says, was the center of a vast Asian economy. What were the sources of strength in the Indian economy? In what ways was the Indian economy stronger than the European? What were its weaknesses? Were some of these weaknesses similar to those that undermined the Ottoman economy? What does this reading suggest about the relationship between economic growth and politics?

THE FAR EAST—GREATEST OF ALL
THE WORLD-ECONOMIES

The Far East taken as a whole, consisted of three gigantic world-economies: Islam, overlooking the Indian Ocean from the Red Sea and the Persian Gulf, and controlling the endless chain of deserts stretching across Asia from Arabia to China; India, whose influence extended throughout the Indian Ocean, both east and west of Cape Comorin; and China, at once a great territorial power—striking deep into the heart of Asia—and a maritime force, controlling the seas and countries bordering the Pacific. And so it had been for many hundreds of years.

But between the fifteenth and eighteenth centuries, it is perhaps permissible to talk of a *single* world-economy broadly embracing all three. Did the Far East, favoured by the regularity and the usefulness for shipping of the monsoon and the trade winds, actually combine to form a coherent whole, with a series of successive dominant centres, a network of long-distance trading connections and an inter-related series of prices? This combination—gigantic, fragile and intermittent—is the true subject of the following pages.

. . .

The Villages of India

India is made up of villages—thousands and thousands of them. It is more appropriate to use the plural than the singular which suggests a misleading image of "the typical" Indian village, enclosed in its little community, surviving as an intangible, unchanging and always self-sufficient unit, throughout the eventful history of India; and which also seems to suggest that by some second miracle, "the village" was the same throughout the huge sub-continent, despite the clear identities of different provinces. No doubt a self-sufficient village, producing its own food and clothing and entirely self-absorbed, could still be found in remote and backward regions even today. But it would be an exception.

As a rule, the village community was open to the outside world, subject to various authorities and to the markets which watched it closely, emptied it of its surpluses and forced upon it the convenience and the dangers of a money economy. This brings us close to the secret of the entire history of India: the vitality drawn up from the base to animate and nourish the great political and social corpus. In a very different context, the pattern is similar to that of the Russian economy at the same period.

Through recent studies, it is now possible to see how the machine functioned, fuelled as it was by harvests, rents and state-imposed taxes. The ubiquitous money economy was an excellent drive-belt, facilitating and increasing the number of transactions, including compulsory exchange. Credit for the creation of these circuits is only partly due to the government of the Mogul emperor. India had in fact been for centuries subject to a money economy, partly through her links with the Mediterranean world, which had since antiquity been acquainted with money, and indeed after a fashion had invented it and exported it abroad. If we can believe L.C. Jain, India already had bankers six centuries before Christ, a hundred years before the age of Pericles. The money economy had certainly penetrated Indian trade many centuries before the sultanate of Delhi.

The decisive contribution of the latter, in the fourteenth century, was a coercive administrative organization, with a hierarchy reaching down through the provincial and district authorities to the villages, which it kept under firm control. The weighty mechanisms of this state, inherited by the Mogul Empire in 1526, enabled the latter to stimulate and confiscate surplus output in the countryside. Consequently it encouraged the maintenance and expansion of such surpluses. For the Muslim despotism of the Moguls contained a measure of "enlightened despotism," a desire not to kill the goose that laid the golden eggs, a desire to encourage peasant "reproduction," to extend cultivation, to substitute a profitable crop for a less profitable one, to colonize virgin land, and to increase the possibilities of irrigation by wells and reservoirs.

To what extent then were the villages controlled from outside? This was certainly the aim of the provincial and district authorities, as it was that of the nobles, who had received from the emperor (theoretically the sole owner of the land) a share of the dues from the estates (*jagirs* or life-holdings); it was also the concern of the vigilant tax-collectors, the *zamindars* who had hereditary rights to land; and of the merchants, usurers and money-changers who bought, transported and sold harvests, and who also converted taxes and dues into cash so that their product could circulate more easily. The landlord would actually live at court in Delhi, keeping up his rank, and the *jagir* was granted him for a fairly short term, usually three years. He exploited it by flying visits quite shamelessly, from a distance; like the state, he preferred to receive his dues in cash rather than in kind. The conversion of crops into coin was therefore the cornerstone of the system. Not only were silver and gold both an object of and an encouragement to hoarding, they were also the indispensable mechanisms which made the whole great machine function, from its peasant base to the summit of society and the business world.

The village was, in addition, controlled from within by its own hierarchy and the caste system (embracing artisans and the proletariat of untouchables). It had a vigilant leader, the village headman, and an exclusive "aristocracy," the *khud-kashta*, a small minority of relatively wealthy or at any rate comfortably-off peasants, owners of the best land, possessors of four or five ploughs, four or five bullock or buffalo teams and in addition enjoying a favourable tax rating. These men effectively represented the famous village "community" about which so much has been written. In exchange for their privileges and the *individual* ownership of the fields they farmed themselves with family labour, they were *collectively* responsible to the state for the payment of taxes on behalf of the whole village. Indeed they received a share of the money collected. They enjoyed similar favours regarding the colonization of virgin lands and the creation of new villages. But they were closely watched by the authorities who viewed with suspicion the development of anything like tenant-farming or share-cropping which might benefit these village elders, or even of the introduction of wage-labour (which did exist but to a minimal extent)—that is of any form of land-tenure outside the norm, the extension of which might, in the hands of fiscally privileged individuals, eventually diminish the volume of taxation. As for the other peasants who did not own their fields, who came from elsewhere and might move on from time to time to another village taking their bullocks and ploughs, they were more heavily taxed than the elders.

The village also had its own artisans: wedded to their trades by the caste system, they received for their labour a share of the communal harvest, plus a plot of land to cultivate (although certain castes earned wages). The reader may think this a complicated system, but what peasant regime under the sun is simple? "While the peasant was not unfree or a serf, his status was definitely a dependent one." The share of his income confiscated by the state, by the lord of the *jagir* and other interested parties might be anything from a third to a half, or even more in fertile regions. So how was such a regime possible? How could the peasant economy support it, while at the same time maintaining a degree of expansion, since seventeenth-century India, despite her growing population, continued to produce enough food for her people, increased her industrial crops and even expanded the production of her many orchards to meet a higher demand for fruit and the new fashion among landowners?

Results like this must be put down to the modest living standards of the peasants and the high productivity of their agriculture.

For in 1600, rural India was farming only a portion of the available land: from the available statistics, it seems probable that in the Ganges basin for instance, only half the arable land under cultivation in the same region in 1900 was being farmed at all in the seventeenth century; in central India, the figure is between two-thirds and four-fifths; in southern India one may *conjecture* the figure was higher. So one thing is certain: almost everywhere in India between the fifteenth and the eighteenth century, only the best land was being farmed. And since there was no agricultural revolution here, since basic tools, methods and essential crops did not change until 1900, it can probably be assumed that the per capita output of the Indian peasant was higher in 1700 than 1900, particularly since land as yet uncultivated, on which new villages were built, offered the peasants extra space which could support more grazing and this in turn meant more draft animals, bullocks and buffaloes for ploughing, more dairy products and more ghee (melted butter used in Indian cookery). Irfan Habib has argued that in view of the two annual harvests, cereal yields in India were higher than those in Europe until the nineteenth century. But even with equivalent yields, India would still have had the advantage. In a hot climate, the needs of a labourer are fewer than in the temperate countries of Europe. The modest quantity subtracted from the harvest for the peasant's own subsistence left a larger surplus available for marketing.

A further source of the superiority of Indian agriculture, besides the two harvests a year (of rice, or of grain plus peas or chick peas, or oil-yielding plants), was the place occupied by cash-crops intended for export: indigo and cotton plants, sugar cane, opium poppies, tobacco (introduced to India in the early seventeenth century), the pepper-bush (a climbing plant which produced peppercorns between the third and the ninth years but which, contrary to popular belief, would not grow unless carefully tended). Such plants brought in more than millet, rye, rice or wheat. And in the case of the indigo plant for instance, "it is the practice among the Indians to cut it three times a year." Furthermore it required complicated industrial processes; so like sugar cane, and for similar reasons, the growing of indigo, which required substantial investment, was a *capitalist* venture very widespread in India, with active cooperation by large tax-farmers, merchants, representatives of the European companies and of the Mogul government which attempted to create a state monopoly by a policy of granting exclusive tenancy agreements.

None of this prevented visible poverty among the rural masses: poverty which was predictable given the general conditions of the system. What was more, the Delhi government levied in taxes a proportion of the harvest—in theory once it had been harvested, but in many regions, local administrators for the sake of convenience estimated the average yield of the land in advance and established a *fixed rate* of taxation on this basis, in kind or in cash, depending on the area under cultivation and the nature of the crop. This being the case, if the harvest did not come up to expectations, if there was a drought, if bullocks from the caravans or elephants from Delhi ravaged the cultivated fields, if prices rose or fell inopportunely, the burden was borne by the producer.

And the peasant's life was aggravated further by debt. With the complexity of land tenure systems, of ownership and taxation, depending on the province, the generosity of the local prince or on the presence of war or peace, any kind of variation could be expected—usually for the worse. On the whole, however, as long as the Mogul state remained strong, it was able to maintain the minimum level of peasant prosperity essential to its own prosperity. It was only in the eighteenth century that general decline began to affect the state, the obedience and loyalty of its officials and the security of transport. Peasant revolts became endemic.

Artisans and Industry

The other sufferers in India were the countless artisans present in all cities, towns and villages—some of which had been transformed into entire villages of artisans. This increase in the working population was inevitable if it is true that the seventeenth century saw a massive increase in the urban population of India, which some historians put at 20 per cent of the total: if they are right, the urban population of India was some 20 million inhabitants—roughly the equivalent of the total population of France in the seventeenth century. Even if this is an overestimate, the artisan population, augmented by an army of unskilled labourers, must still have represented millions of individuals working both for the domestic and the export market.

Rather than with the history of these countless artisans as such, Indian historians seeking to discover the situation of their country on the eve of the British conquest have been most concerned to discover the nature of India's ancestral industry, and in particular whether her industry was or was not comparable to that of Europe at the same time, whether it might have been capable on its own of engendering some kind of industrial revolution.

Industry, or rather proto-industry, encountered many obstacles in India. Some have been perhaps exaggerated and exist only in the minds of historians—in particular the trammels supposedly imposed by the caste system, which affected the whole of society, including of course the artisan population. Weberian analysis sees the caste system as preventing the advance of technology, stifling initiative among artisans and, since it confined a certain group of people to a single activity laid down once and for all, as inhibiting any new specialization or social mobility from generation to generation.

> There are good grounds (writes Irfan Habib) for throwing doubt on this entire theory. . . . First, the mass of ordinary or unskilled people formed a reserve from which new classes of skilled professions could be created when the need arose. Thus diamond miners in the (Carnatic) must have come from the ranks of the peasantry or agricultural labourers, for when some mines were abandoned, the miners "went back to their village." . . . More important

still, over a long period economic compulsions could bring about a radical transformation in the occupational basis of a caste. A well-documented case is that of the caste of tailors in Maharashtra, a section of which took to dyeing, and another to indigo-dyeing early in the eighteenth century.

Some flexibility among the work force cannot be denied. Indeed the ancient caste system had developed alongside the division of labour, since in Agra in the early seventeenth century more than a hundred different trades are recorded. And the workers could move about, as in Europe, in search of profitable work. The destruction of Ahmedabad stimulated a vigorous burst of growth in the Surat textile industry, in the second quarter of the eighteenth century. And the European Indies companies attracted to the areas round their branches weavers from the various provinces who, unless subject to specific prohibitions (some castes were forbidden to travel by sea for instance) could travel about to meet demand.

Other obstacles were more serious. Europeans were often astonished at the small number and rudimentary nature of the tools used by the Indian craftsmen—"a deficiency of tools" which, as Sonnerat explained with illustrations, meant that a sawyer took "three days to make a plank which would take our workmen but an hour." Who could fail to be surprised that "the fine muslins we seek so eagerly are made on looms composed of four pieces of wood stuck in the ground"? If the Indian craftsman nevertheless produced masterpieces, this was the result of extraordinary manual dexterity, further refined by extreme specialization: "A job that one man would do in Holland here passes through four men's hands before it is finished," remarked the Dutchman Pelsaert. Tools were made almost entirely of wood, unlike those of Europe which already contained a large proportion of iron even before the industrial revolution. And archaic methods prevailed: for example, the Indian version of the Persian-designed wheel for irrigation and pumping water used wooden gears, wooden cogwheels, leather bags, earthenware pots and was propelled by animal or human power until the nineteenth century. This was not so much for technical reasons, Irfan Habib thinks (since wooden mechanisms such as those used for spinning and weaving could often be sophisticated and ingenious) as for reasons of cost: the high price of European metal machinery would not have been compensated for by the savings made on labour—which was both plentiful and cheap.

Similarly, although the Indians were not well-versed in mining techniques (confining their efforts to the extraction of surface minerals only) they had succeeded in producing a crucible-fired steel of exceptional quality, which was exported at high prices to Persia and elsewhere. In this respect they were ahead of European metallurgy. They worked their own metal, producing ships' anchors, fine sidearms, swords and daggers of every design, good hand guns and respectable cannon (not cast but made of welded iron bars hooped together). So India was by no means hopelessly backward in technology. The Indian Mints, for example, were every bit as good as the European: 30,000 rupees were being turned out every day at the Surat Mint in 1660 for the English company alone.

Lastly, there was the wonder of wonders, the naval shipyards. According to a French report, the vessels built in Surat in about 1700 were "very good and extremely serviceable . . . and it would be most advantageous (for the French Indies Company) to have some built there," even if the price was the same as in France, since the teak wood from which they were made guaranteed them a lifetime at sea of forty years, "instead of ten, twelve or fourteen at most." During the first half of the nineteenth century, the Parsees in Bombay invested considerable sums in shipbuilding, having vessels constructed both on the spot and in other ports, especially Cochin. It was indeed in India that the finest Indianmen were built, vessels of enormous size for the time, which did the China run. In eastern waters, until the coming of the steamship in mid-nineteenth century, the English in fact relied exclusively on Indian-built ships. None of them sailed for Europe: indeed English ports were forbidden to them. In 1794, the war with France and the urgent need for transport ships was responsible for the ban being lifted for a few months. But the appearance of Indian ships and sailors caused such hostile reactions in London that English merchants quickly decided not to use their services.

India's remarkable textile production is so well known that I hardly need dwell on it. It possessed to the full the capacity so admired in the English cloth trade, to meet any increase in demand. It was to be found in the villages; it kept artisans busy in the towns; from Surat to the Ganges, it nourished a string of craft workshops producing for themselves or for the big export dealers; it was well entrenched in Kashmir; European companies tried, in vain, to introduce western working arrangements for the weaving trade, in particular the putting-out system. The clearest example occurred in Bombay, where thanks to belated immigration by Indian workers from Surat and elsewhere, the attempt could be started from scratch. But the traditional Indian system of advance payments and contracts remained the rule, at least until the conquest of Bengal, when its artisans were brought under direct supervision, in the last decades of the eighteenth century.

The textile industry was hard to take over for this very reason that it was not contained within a single network as in Europe. Different sectors and circuits governed the production and marketing of raw materials; the manufacture of cotton yarn (a long operation especially if the aim was a yarn both fine and strong, to make muslin for instance); weaving; bleaching and preparation of fabrics; and printing. Processes which in Europe were vertically linked (as in thirteenth-century Florence) were here organized in separate compartments. Buyers for the companies would sometimes go to the market where the weavers sold their wares but more often, when a large order was being placed (and orders grew steadily larger) it was better to strike a bargain with Indian merchants who had employees travelling through the production zones and themselves arranging contracts with the artisans. The middleman would undertake to deliver to a company servant on a specified date, at an agreed price, an agreed quantity of specified types of fabric. To the weaver he customarily made an advance payment in money, which was a kind of pledge of future purchase, enabling the worker to buy yarn and to maintain himself while he was working. When the piece of material was finished, the weaver would be paid the market price less the advance. Market prices, which were not fixed at the time of ordering, might vary according to the price of yarn or that of rice.

The merchant was thus shouldering a risk which would of course be reflected in his rate of profit. But the weaver was undoubtedly given a certain amount of leeway: he received his advance in money (not, as in Europe, in materials); and he could always resort directly to the market, something not open to the worker operating in the *Verlagssystem*. What was more, he could always default, change his place of work, even go on strike and give up the loom to return to the land or join the army. This being so, L.N. Chaudhuri finds it very difficult to explain the poverty of weavers, of which there is so much evidence. Could the reason be the antiquity of a social structure which condemned peasants and artisans to minimal remuneration? The huge increase in demand and production in the seventeenth and eighteenth centuries may have widened the range of choices for the artisan, without doing anything to alter the general low level of wages, despite the fact that production operated within a direct money economy.

On the whole this system made manufactories unnecessary, but some did exist, bringing together workers in large workshops—the *karkhanas*, which operated for their owners, the nobles or the emperor himself. The owners were not above letting these luxury goods go for export on occasion. Mandelslo (1638) speaks of a magnificent and very costly fabric of silk and cotton with gold-embroidered flowers, which the workshops had recently begun to manufacture in Ahmedabad when he was passing through, and "which was confined to (the use of) the Emperor; nevertheless foreigners are permitted to carry it out of the country."

In fact all India processed silk and cotton, sending an incredible quantity of fabrics, from the most ordinary to the most luxurious, all over the world, since through the Europeans even America received a large share of Indian textiles. The variety of materials can be conjectured from the descriptions left by travellers and the trade lists drawn up by the European companies. Here for example, without comment, is a list taken from a French memorandum on textiles from the different provinces:

Blue and unbleached cottons from Salem, blue guineas from Madure, bazeens from Gondelur, percales from Arni, table linens from Pondicherry, bettelles, chavonis, tarnatans, organdies, Steinkerques from the coast, cambays, nicannes, bejutapauts, papolis, korotes, brawles, boelans, lemanees, quilts, chittees, caddies, white dullees, handkerchief fabrics from Mazulipatam, sanees, muslins, terrindanis, durries (striped muslins), mulmuls, fine, embroidered in thread of gold or silver, common cottons from Patna seersuckers (mixed silk and cotton), baftas, hummums, cossaes, four-thread weaves, common bazeens, gazas, Permacody cottons, Yanaon guineas, conjoos.

But even this impressive list pales into insignificance beside the 91 varieties of textiles Chaudhuri lists as an appendix to his book.

There can be no doubt that until the English industrial revolution, the Indian cotton industry was the foremost in the world, both in the quality and quantity of its output and the scale of its exports.

A National Market

Every kind of commodity went into circulation in India, whether agricultural surpluses, raw materials or manufactured goods for export. The grain collected at village markets was conveyed by chains of local merchants, usurers and moneylenders, to small towns (*gasbahs*) then to the big cities through the offices of wholesalers who specialized in the transport of bulky goods—salt and grain in particular. This circulation was by no means perfect: it could be surprised by sudden outbreaks of famine which the great distances between one place and another only too often turned into disaster. But was this not equally true of colonial America or even of the Old World in Europe? And in India the circulation of goods employed every conceivable means, cutting through obstacles, linking distant regions of different cultures and living standards, thus enabling every kind of merchandise to travel, the everyday and the precious (the latter covered by insurance at comparatively low premiums).

The Significance of the Mogul Empire

When in 1526, the Mogul Empire replaced the sultanate of Delhi, it took over a well-tried organization; the combination of this inheritance with a rediscovered dynamism proved to be for many years a heavy but effective machine.

Its first achievement (the pioneering work of Akbar, 1556–1605) was to persuade the two religious communities, Hindu and Muslim, to cohabit without too much conflict, although in fact the latter faith, being that of the rulers, received most honour—so much so that Europeans, seeing the countless mosques in northern and central India, long assumed Islam to be the prevalent religion in India, and Hinduism, the religion of the merchants and peasants, a sort of idolatry on the way to extinction, like paganism in Europe before the spread of Christianity. European thought did not really discover Hinduism until the late eighteenth or early nineteenth century.

The second feat of the Moguls was to acclimatize and introduce to almost the whole of India a single civilization, borrowed from neighbouring Persia and ferrying its arts, literature and sensibility. Thus the two cultures present in the country came together and it was eventually the minority culture—that of Islam—which was on the whole absorbed by the Indian masses, though only after it had itself adopted many cultural borrowings. Persian remained the language of the rulers, of the upper, privileged classes: "I will have someone write to the Rajah in the Persian tongue," a Frenchman in difficulty in Benares informed the governor of Chandernagor on 19 March 1768. The administration used Hindustani, but its organization was also based on an Islamic model.

It is in the first place to the sultanate of Delhi, and then to the Mogul Empire, that responsibility must be attributed for the establishment in the provinces (*sarkars*) and the districts (*parganas*) of an ordered administration to handle the collecting of taxes and dues, but which also had the task of promoting agriculture—that is the basis of the fiscal system—as well as of developing irrigation and encouraging the spread of cash-crops for export. Its activities, backed up from time to time by state subsidies and propaganda missions, were often effective.

Central to the system, housed at the heart of the empire whose existence it guaranteed and from whose resources it lived, was the terrible strength of the army. The nobles around the emperor, the *mansabdars* or *omerahs*, numbering 8000 in 1647, were the commanders of this force. Depending on their rank, they recruited dozens, hundreds or thousands of mercenaries. The total size of the "standing army" in Delhi was considerable—it would have been unthinkable in Europe: almost 200,000 horsemen, plus over 40,000 matchlockmen or gunners. Both in Delhi and in Agra, the other capital, the departure of the army on campaign left behind a deserted city, inhabited only by the banyans. If one were to calculate the total numbers dispersed in garrisons all over the empire with reinforcements along the frontiers, the answer would probably be close on a million men. "There is no little village that has not at least two horsemen and four foot soldiers," detailed to keep order—and also to observe and spy on the population.

The army was itself the government, since the high offices of the regime were chiefly occupied by soldiers. The army was also the leading customer for luxury foreign fabrics, especially woollen cloth from Europe, which was not imported to make clothes in this hot climate but for "saddlebags and saddles for horses, elephants and camels, which the mighty have embroidered in embossed gold and silver, for palanquins, for gun-cases to protect them from the damp, and for the pomp of their foot soldiers." Up to 50,000 crowns' worth of cloth was being imported at this time (1724). The horses imported in large numbers from Persia or Arabia (for every cavalryman had several mounts) were themselves a luxury: the exhorbitant prices paid for them averaged four times those paid in England. At court, before the start of grand ceremonies, open "to great and humble alike," one of the pleasures of the emperor was to have parade "before his eyes a certain number of the finest horses in his stables," accompanied by "a few elephants, . . . their bodies well scrubbed and clean . . . painted black with the exception of two broad stripes of red paint," and decorated with embroidered cloths and silver bells.

The state kept by the *omerahs* was almost as grand as that of the emperor himself. Like him they possessed their own craft workshops, the *karkanahs*, manufactories whose refined products were reserved exclusively for their owners. Like him, they had a passion for building. Large suites of servants and slaves accompanied them everywhere and some *omerahs* amassed fabulous hoards of gold plate and jewels. It is not hard to imagine what a burden this aristocracy must have been on the Indian economy, living as it did from grants paid directly out of the imperial treasury, or from the dues paid by peasants on the *jagirs* granted to their masters by the empire, "to maintain their rank."

The mighty imperial machinery was by the eighteenth century showing signs of wear and fatigue. There is a wide choice of dates for the beginning of what is known as the decline of the Mogul Empire: 1739, the date of the capture and terrifying sack of Delhi by the Persians; 1757, the battle of Plassey, won by the English; 1761, the second battle of Paniput, when Afghans in medieval armours triumphed over the Mahrattas armed with modern weapons, at the very moment when the latter were preparing to reconstitute the Mogul Empire for their own benefit. Historians have generally accepted with little controversy the date of 1707, the year of Aurangzeb's death, as marking the end of the great days of Mogul India. If we accept their account, the empire died from within, rather than being done to death by outsiders, whether Persians, Afghans or English.

THE CHINESE ECONOMY

PING-TI HO

The period from 1500 to 1750 in China encompassed the end of the Ming dynasty (1368–1644) and the beginning of the Ch'ing or Manchu dynasty (1644–1912). In this selection a modern historian of China discusses the Chinese economy during this period. What were the strengths and weaknesses of the Chinese economy in this period? How were they similar to, or different from, those of India and the Ottoman empire? Why did China not undergo an industrial revolution?

Not only were increased means of livelihood provided by a vastly expanding and more intensive agriculture; the employment opportunities offered by an immense domestic trade, by a highly lucrative if somewhat limited foreign commerce, and by some newly rising industries and crafts throughout the later Ming and early Ch'ing were also considerable. Ever since the latter half of the eighth century the influence of money had been increasingly felt, at least in the Yangtze regions, which, thanks to an incomparable network of rivers, lakes, and canals, constituted a vast single trading area. The economic development of the Yangtze area was further stimulated by the continual influx of silver from the Europeans and the Japanese after the early sixteenth century. True, the Yangtze area and the southeast coast were not representative of the whole country. But when the southeast coast was brought into the sphere of a worldwide commercial revolution, the effects reached far into inland China. The commutation of labor services, which by 1600 had become nationwide, is one of the eloquent testimonials to the increasing influence of money. Although the majority of the people were engaged in subsistence farming, as they still are today, there were relatively few localities that did not depend to some extent on the supply of goods and products of neighboring or distant regions.

Whatever the institutional and ethical checks on the growth of capital, the late Ming period witnessed the rise of great merchants. The unusually observant Hsieh Chao-che, *chin-shih* [highest degree winner] of 1602, later governor of Kwangsi and author of the famous cyclopedia *Wu-tsa-tsu*, gives the following account:

Reprinted by permission of the publishers from *Studies on the Population of China, 1368–1953*, by Ping-ti Ho. Cambridge, Mass.: Harvard University Press, © 1959 by The President and Fellows of Harvard College.

The rich men of the empire in the regions south of the Yangtze are from Hui-chou (southern Anhwei), in the regions north of the river from Shansi. The great merchants of Hui-chou take fisheries and salt as their occupation and have amassed fortunes amounting to one million taels of silver. Others with a fortune of two or three hundred thousands can only rank as middle merchants. The Shansi merchants are engaged in salt, or silk, or reselling, or grain. Their wealth even exceeds that of the former.

In fact, many regions in later Ming times boasted resourceful long-distance merchants. People of the congested islands in the Tung-t'ing Lake in the heart of the lower Yangtze delta, for example, were driven by economic necessity to trade in practically every part of the country and for a time vied with the Hui-chou merchants in wealth. Merchants of the central Shensi area, while active in trading almost everywhere, specialized in transporting and selling grains to garrisons along the Great Wall, in the salt trade in the Huai River region, in the cotton cloth trade in southern Kiangsu, and in the tea trade with various vassal peoples along the thousand-mile western frontier stretching from Kokonor to the Szechwan-Tibet border. The southern Fukien ports, Ch'üan-chou and Chang-chou, which handled the bulk of the Sino-Portuguese trade in the sixteenth century, probably produced some of the largest individual fortunes.

As interregional merchants became more numerous, they gradually established guildhalls in commercial centers. In the early Ch'ing period there were guildhalls in Peking established by moneylenders from Shao-hsing in Chekiang, wholesale dye merchants from P'ing-yao in Shansi, large tobacco dealers from Chi-shan, Chiang-hsien, and Wen-hsi in Shansi, grain and vegetable-oil merchants from Lin-hsiang and Lin-fen in Shansi, silk merchants from Nanking, and Cantonese merchants who specialized in various exotic and subtropical products. From the late seventeenth century the accounts in local histories of guildhalls established by distant merchants became more and more common, which indicated the continual development of the interregional trade.

The dimensions of individual and aggregate merchant fortunes were growing along with the volume of interregional trade. It has been estimated that some of the Hui-chou salt merchants of the eighteenth century had individual fortunes exceeding 10,000,000 taels and that the aggregate profit reaped by some three hundred salt merchant families of the Yang-chou area in the period 1750–1800 was in the neighborhood of 250,000,000 taels. It was known to the Western merchant community in Canton during the early nineteenth century that the Wu family, under the leadership and management of the famous Howqua, had built up through foreign trade a fortune of 26,000,000 Mexican dollars. Commercial capital had made giant strides since China's first contacts with the Europeans.

A sampling of the biographies in the histories of Hui-chou prefecture reveals that the Hui-chou merchants, though their headquarters were in the cities along the lower Yangtze, carried on trade with various parts of north and central China, Yunnan, Kweichow, Szechwan, and even the remote aboriginal districts and Indochina. In the national capital alone there were 187 tea stores in 1789–1791 and 200 in 1801 which were owned and operated by merchants of She-hsien, the capital city of Hui-chou prefecture. So ubiquitous were the Hui-chou merchants that there was a common saying: "No market is without people of Hui-chou." The radius of the trading activities of these and other comparable merchant bodies is one indication of the increasingly mobile character of the national economy. The fact that it was trade as well as agriculture that sustained the local population and made its multiplication possible is well attested by various local histories, particularly those of the active trading areas, such as Hui-chou, a number of counties in Shansi, Shensi, and Kansu, the lower Yangtze counties, the Ningpo and Shao-hsing areas in Chekiang, Chang-chou and Ch'üan-chou in southern Fukien, and the Canton area. Even people of the poor and backward western Hupei highlands depended to a substantial degree on trading with Szechwan as a means of livelihood.

The interregional and local trade consisted of an exchange of a few staple commodities, like grains, salt, fish, drugs, timber, hardwares, potteries, and cloths, and of a number of luxury and artistic goods of quality for the consumption of the ruling classes. The quantity of internal trade in late Ming and early Ch'ing China, although not unusual according to modern Western standards, certainly left a profound impression upon the Jesuits of the seventeenth and eighteenth centuries. In fact, few modern scholars are in a better position to compare the dimensions of the domestic trade of early Ch'ing China with that of early modern Europe than were the Jesuits, who, knowing both about equally well, measured the Chinese economy with the standards of pre-industrial Europe.

Du Halde, whose famous description of China may well be regarded as the synthesis of seventeenth- and early eighteenth-century Jesuit works on China, said of Chinese commerce:

> The riches peculiar to each province, and the facility of conveying merchandise, by means of rivers and canals, have rendered the domestic trade of the empire always very flourishing. . . . The inland trade of China is so great that the commerce of all Europe is not to be compared therewith; the provinces being like so many kingdoms, which communicate to each other their respective productions. This tends to unite the several inhabitants among themselves, and makes plenty reign in all cities.

This generalization probably referred only to the vast Yangtze area, but it can nevertheless be applied to many other parts of China. The trade of mountainous Fukien during the late sixteenth century was described by the educational commissioner Wang Shih-mao:

> There is not a single day that the silk fabrics of Fu-chou, the gauze of Chang-chou, the indigo of Ch'üan-chou, the ironwares of Fu-chou and Yen-p'ing, the oranges of Fu-chou and Chang-chou, the lichee nuts of Fu-chou and Hsing-hua, the cane sugar of Ch'üan-chou and Chang-chou, and the paper products of Shun-ch'ang are not shipped along the watershed of P'u-ch'eng and Hsiao-kuan to Kiangsu and Chekiang like running water. The quantity of these things shipped by seafaring junks is still harder to reckon.

Wang's description of the large quantities of commodities shipped along the difficult mountain pass of northern Fukien is borne out by the later Jesuit testimony that in the watershed at P'u-ch'eng there were "eight or ten thousand porters attending to the barks, who get their livelihood by going continually backwards and forwards across these mountains." Wang's comment on the large coastal trade between Fukien ports and the lower Yangtze area is also corroborated by other sources. The demand of remote markets for Fukien sugar was so great that by the late sixteenth century a considerable percentage of the rice paddies in the Ch'üan-chou area had been turned into sugar-cane fields. Throughout the late Ming and early Ch'ing annually "hundreds and thousands of junks" discharged sugar in Shanghai and went back to southern Fukien ports with full loads of raw cotton which were made into cotton cloth locally.

Even in landlocked north China the interregional trade was very lively. Despite the lack of cheap water transportation in many northern areas, daily necessities as well as luxury goods from distant regions were carried by wheelbarrows, carts, mules, and asses. "The prodigious multitudes of people" and "astonishing multitudes of asses and mules" engaged in the shipping of commodities in north China never failed to impress those Jesuits commissioned by the K'ang-hsi Emperor as Imperial cartographers. Silk and cotton fabrics of various kinds and luxury goods from the lower Yangtze region and Chekiang were to be found in practically every northern provincial town, including the late Ming military posts along the Great Wall. Generally speaking, it was the technologically advanced southeast that supplied the inland Yangtze and northern provinces with finished products, for which the recipients paid in rice, cotton, and other raw materials. Even in westernmost Yunnan bordering Burma, trade in precious and common metals, ivory, precious stones and jades, silk and cotton fabrics was constantly going on during the late Ming. In fact, so great was the volume of China's interregional trade that for centuries it consistently impressed the Europeans.

This growing internal trade stimulated industries and crafts and made possible regional specialization in commercial crops. In the late Ming and early Ch'ing, rural industries and crafts of regional importance were so numerous that it is possible here to mention only a few outstanding ones. The pottery or porcelain industry of Ching-te-chen in northern Kiangsi expanded greatly during the sixteenth century, thanks to increasing government demand for high-quality porcelains and the investment of the Hui-chou merchants in privately owned kilns. By the K'ang-hsi period (1662–1722), when Chinese porcelain "had materially altered" the artistic tastes of the English aristocracy, the Ching-te borough had about five hundred porcelain furnaces working day and night to meet the national and foreign demand. At night, with its flame and smoke, this township, which stretched one and a half leagues along a river, looked like "a great city all on fire, or a vast furnace with a great many vent-holes." Since all the provisions and fuel had to be supplied by the surrounding districts, the cost of living in this industrial town was high. Yet, in the words of a contemporary Jesuit and longtime resident, "it is the refuge of an infinite number of poor families, who . . . find employment here for youths and weakly persons; there are none, even to the lame and blind, but get their living here by grinding colours."

Another outstanding industry was cotton textiles, in the Sung-chiang area, of which Shanghai was a rising city. Thanks to an early start and to its moist climate, Sung-chiang was the Lancashire of early modern China. Although an enormous quantity of cotton was grown locally, Sung-chiang in the seventeenth and eighteenth centuries depended on remote northern provinces like Honan and western Shantung for the supply of raw cotton. The Jesuits reckoned that in the late seventeenth century there were in the Shanghai area alone "200,000 weavers of calicoes." Since at least three spinners were needed to supply the yarn for one weaver, the total number of spinners must have been several times larger. Cloth of many grades and designs was made to meet the varied demands of the people of Shansi, Shensi, the Peking area, Hupei, Hunan, Kiangsi, Kwang-tung, and Kwangsi. Contemporaries remarked that Sung-chiang clothed and capped the whole nation. The Su-chou area was also an important textile center, supplying much of western Shantung with its finished products.

The area around Nanking, from which the name of the famous cotton fabric nankeen was derived, produced cloth of high quality which was exported to the West from Canton. Exports increased constantly until over one million pieces were being exported annually to Great Britain and the United States during the early nineteenth century. H.B. Morse, a New Englander and the famous historian of the Chinese Customs, said:

> Cotton manufactures in 1905 constituted 44 per cent of the value (excluding opium) of all (China's) foreign imports, but in this industry the West could compete with cheap Asiatic labor only after the development springing from the inventions of Richard Arkwright and Eli Whitney, and in the eighteenth and early nineteenth centuries the movement of cotton cloth was from China

to the West, in the shape of nankeens to provide small-clothes for our grandfathers.

From the late sixteenth century Sung-chiang was subject to increasing competition from the rising cotton textile centers in north China. The low plain area of north China could produce cotton at lower cost and in larger quantity than the densely populated lower Yangtze region. This increased production of raw cotton in turn stimulated spinning and weaving, which were becoming very important rural industries in north China. The rapid development of the cotton industry in southern Pei-chihli, or modern Hopei, greatly impressed the Christian prime minister Hsü Luang-ch'i (1562–1633), a native of Shanghai, who estimated that the cotton cloth produced by Su-ning county alone amounted to one tenth of the cloth produced by the entire Sung-chiang prefecture. In the course of the seventeenth century many northern districts became regionally famous for their finished cotton products, although few could vie with Sung-chiang in skill and quality. Toward the end of the seventeenth century the Hankow area had already deprived Sung-chiang of much of its old market in the northwest and the southwest.

Cotton cultivation, which had been extensive in the Ming period, further expanded under the repeated exhortations of the early Ch'ing emperors. Many counties in southern and western Chihli, western Shantung, Honan, the Wei River valley in Shensi, the Fen River valley in Shansi, the Hupei lowlands, and central Szechwan derived a major portion of their incomes from cotton. Cotton spinning and weaving became a common rural industry even in Yunnan and Kweichow. A great many people must have made their living partly or entirely on the growing of cotton or cotton spinning and weaving. . . .

A well-traveled European during the 1840s commented on the general state of commerce:

> One excellent reason why the Chinese care little about foreign commerce is that their internal trade is so extensive. . . . This trade consists principally in the exchange of grain, salt, metal, and other natural and artificial production of various provinces. . . . China is a country so vast, so rich, so varied, that its internal trade alone would suffice abundantly to occupy that part of the nation which can be devoted to mercantile operations. There are in all great towns important commercial establishments, into which, as into reservoirs, the merchandise of all the provinces discharges itself. To these vast store-houses people flock from all parts of the Empire, and there is a constant bustle going on about them—a feverish activity that would scarcely be seen in the most important cities of Europe.

From this and earlier Jesuit comments it becomes clear that the early Ch'ing economy, if somewhat less variegated than that of Europe, was reasonably complex and able to meet both the basic and the more sophisticated demands of the nation.

However, even during the period of steady economic growth there were inherent weaknesses in the traditional Chinese economy. It was capable of small gains but incapable of innovations in either the institutional or the technological sense. Institutionally, despite the availability of commercial capital on a gigantic scale (witness the Yang-chou salt merchants and the Canton Hong merchants), the traditional Chinese economy failed to develop a genuine capitalistic system such as characterized the Europe of the seventeenth and eighteenth centuries. The reasons were many and varied. In the first place, by far the easiest and surest way to acquire wealth was to buy the privilege of selling a few staples with universal demand, like salt and tea, which were under government monopoly. The activities of the Hong merchants, and of other powerful merchant groups, also partook of the nature of tax-farming rather than genuine private enterprise.

Secondly, the profit and wealth accruing to these merchant princes was not reinvested in new commercial or industrial enterprises but was diverted to various noneconomic uses. Ordinary commercial and industrial investments were less profitable than moneylending and tax-farming in the broad sense. Furthermore, the cultural and social values peculiar to the traditional Chinese society fostered this economic pattern. In a society where the primary standard of prestige was not money but scholarly attainment, official position, or literary achievement, rich merchants preferred to buy official ranks and titles for themselves, encourage their sons to become degree-holders and officials, patronize artists and men of letters, cultivate the expensive hobbies of the elite, or simply consume or squander their wealth in conspicuous ways. Consequently, up to a certain point wealth not only failed to beget more wealth; it could hardly remain concentrated in the same family for more than two or three generations.

Thirdly, the lack of primogeniture and the working of the clan system proved to be great leveling factors in the Chinese economy. The virtue of sharing one's wealth with one's immediate and remote kinsmen had been so highly extolled since the rise of Neo-Confucianism in the eleventh and twelfth centuries that few wealthy men in traditional China could escape the influence of this teaching. Business management, in the last analysis, was an extension of familism and was filled with nepotism, inefficiencies, and irrationalities. These immensely rich individuals not only failed to develop a capitalistic system; they seldom if ever acquired that acquisitive and competitive spirit which is the very soul of the capitalistic system.

Fourthly, the Confucian cultural and political system rewarded only the learned and studious. Technological inventions were viewed as minor contrivances unworthy of the dignity of scholars. Despite the budding scientific spirit in Chu Hsi's philosophy, China failed to develop a system of experimental science; moral philosophy always reigned supreme. Major technological inventions are seldom accidental and are necessarily based on scientific knowledge; hence traditional China could not produce a minor technological revolution, which depends as much on the application of scientific knowledge to practical industrial problems as on a coordination of various economic and institutional factors. By the last quarter of the eighteenth century there was every indication that the Chinese economy, at its prevailing technological level, could no longer gainfully sustain an ever increasing population without overstraining itself. The economy during the first half of the nineteenth century became so strained and the standard of living for the majority of the nation deteriorated so rapidly that a series of uprisings occurred, culminating in the Taiping Rebellion.

Finally, throughout the Ch'ing by far the most powerful control over the economy was exerted by the state, through the bureaucracy. Such key enterprises as the salt trade and foreign commerce were jointly undertaken by the bureaucracy and a few individuals who were resourceful enough to resume the financial responsibility demanded by the state. Even in the late Ch'ing and early Republican periods the few new industrial enterprises launched by the Chinese were almost invariably financed by bureaucratic capitalists. In the cotton textile industry, for example, out of a total of twenty-six mills established between 1890 and 1913, nine were established by active and retired high officials, ten by mixed groups of officials and individuals with official titles, and seven by the new breed of treaty-port compradores,* practically all of whom had official connections. It is common knowledge that after the founding of the Nationalist government in 1927 a few top-ranking bureaucrats who enjoyed Chiang Kai-shek's confidence exerted ever more powerful control over the modern sector of the national economy through the incomparably superior apparatus of four major modern banks. Genuine capitalism based on private enterprise never had a chance of success in modern China, which could only choose between bureaucratic capitalism and bureaucratic collectivism. . . .

---

* Chinese agents hired by foreigners to oversee Chinese employees and to act as intermediaries in business.—Ed.

4. The Scientific Revolution

THE SCIENTIFIC REVOLUTION IN THE WEST

FRANKLIN LE VAN BAUMER

This selection is a brief survey of the elements of the Western scientific revolution by a modern intellectual historian. What are the most important elements described here? What were some of the causes of the scientific revolution? What were some of the effects? Why might this essay be called a social or cultural history of science, instead of an internal history? Is this a revealing perspective?

In his book *The Origins of Modern Science* Professor Butterfield of Cambridge writes that the "scientific revolution" of the sixteenth and seventeenth centuries "outshines everything since the rise of Christianity and reduces the Renaissance and Reformation to the rank of mere episodes, mere internal displacements, within the system of medieval Christendom." "It looms so large as the real origin both of the modern world and of the modern mentality that our customary periodisation of European history has become an anachronism and an encumbrance."[1] This view can no longer be seriously questioned. The scientific achievements of the century and a half between the publication of Copernicus's *De Revolutionibus Orbium Celestium* (1543) and Newton's *Principia* (1687) marked the opening of a new period of intellectual and cultural life in the West, which I shall call the Age of Science. What chiefly distinguished this age from its predecessor was that science—meaning by science a body of knowledge, a method, an attitude of mind, a metaphysic (to be described below)—became the directive force of Western civilization, displacing theology and antique letters. Science made the world of the spirit, of Platonic Ideas, seem unreliable and dim by comparison with the material world. In the seventeenth century it drove revealed Christianity out of the physical universe into the region

From "The Scientific Revolution in the West" by Franklin Le Van Baumer, in *Main Currents of Western Thought,* fourth edition, edited by F. Le Van Baumer. New Haven: Yale University Press, 1978. Reprinted by permission of the publisher.
1. (London, 1950), p. viii.

of history and private morals; to an ever growing number of people in the two succeeding centuries it made religion seem outmoded even there. Science invaded the schools, imposed literary canons, altered the world-picture of the philosophers, suggested new techniques to the social theorists. It changed profoundly man's attitude toward custom and tradition, enabling him to declare his independence of the past, to look down condescendingly upon the "ancients," and to envisage a rosy future. The Age of Science made the intoxicating discovery that melioration depends, not upon "change from within" (St. Paul's birth of the new man), but upon "change from without" (scientific and social mechanics).

I

Some people will perhaps object that there was no such thing as "scientific revolution" in the sixteenth and seventeenth centuries. They will say that history does not work that way, that the new science was not "revolutionary," but the cumulative effect of centuries of trial and error among scientists. But if by "scientific revolution" is meant the occasion when science became a real intellectual and cultural force in the West, this objection must surely evaporate. The evidence is rather overwhelming that sometime between 1543 and 1687, certainly by the late seventeenth century, science captured the interest of the intellectuals and upper classes. Francis Bacon's ringing of a bell to call the wits of Europe together to advance scientific learning did not go unheeded. Note the creation of new intellectual institutions to provide a home for science— the *Academia del Cimento* at Florence (1661), the Royal Society at London (1662), the *Académie des Sciences* at Paris (1666), the Berlin Academy (1700), to mention only the most important. These scientific academies signified the advent of science as an organized activity. Note the appearance of a literature of popular science, of which Fontenelle's *Plurality of Worlds* is only one example, and of popular lectures on scientific subjects. Note the movement for educational reform sponsored by Bacon and the Czech John Amos Comenius, who denounced the traditional education for its exclusive emphasis upon "words rather than things" (literature rather than nature itself). Evidently, by the end of the seventeenth century the prejudice against "mechanical" studies as belonging to practical rather than high mental life had all but disappeared. Bacon complained in 1605 that "matters mechanical" were esteemed "a kind of dishonour unto learning to descend to inquiry or meditation upon." But the Royal Society included in its roster a number of ecclesiastics and men of fashion. The second marquis of Worcester maintained a laboratory and published a book of inventions in 1663. Not a few men appear to have been "converted" from an ecclesiastical to a scientific career, and, as Butterfield notes, to have carried the gospel into the byways, with all the zest of the early Christian missionaries.

To account historically for the scientific revolution is no easy task. The problem becomes somewhat more manageable, however, if we exclude from the discussion the specific discoveries of the scientists. Only the internal history of science can explain how Harvey, for example, discovered the circulation of the blood, or Newton the universal law of gravitation.

But certain extrascientific factors were plainly instrumental in causing so many people to be simultaneously interested in "nature," and, moreover, to think about nature in the way they did. Professor Whitehead reminds us that one of these factors was medieval Christianity itself and medieval scholasticism. Medieval Christianity sponsored the Greek, as opposed to the primitive, idea of a rationally ordered universe which made the orderly investigation of nature seem possible. Scholasticism trained western intellectuals in exact thinking. The Renaissance and the Protestant Reformation also prepared the ground for the scientific revolution—not by design, but as an indirect consequence of their thinking. As I have previously noted, humanism and Protestantism represented a movement toward the concrete. Erasmus preferred ethics to the metaphysical debates of the philosophers and theologians. The Protestants reduced the miraculous element in institutional Christianity and emphasized labor in a worldly calling. Furthermore, by attacking scholastic theology with which Aristotle was bound up, they made it easier for scientists to think about physics and astronomy in un-Aristotelian terms. As E.A. Burtt has noted of Copernicus, these men lived in a mental climate in which people generally were seeking new centers of reference. Copernicus, the architect of the heliocentric theory of the universe, was a contemporary of Luther and Archbishop Cranmer, who moved the religious center from Rome to Wittenberg and Canterbury. In the sixteenth century the economic center of gravity was similarly shifting from the Mediterranean to the English Channel and the Atlantic Ocean. The revival of ancient philosophies and ancient texts at the Renaissance also sharpened the scientific appetite. The Platonic and Pythagorean revival in fifteenth-century Italy undoubtedly did a good deal to accustom scientists to think of the universe in mathematical, quantitative terms. The translation of Galen and Archimedes worked the last rich vein of ancient science, and made it abundantly clear that the ancients had frequently disagreed on fundamentals, thus necessitating independent investigation. By their enthusiasm for natural beauty, the humanists helped to remove from nature the medieval stigma of sin, and thus to make possible the confident pronouncement of the scientific movement that God's Word could be read not only in the Bible but in the great book of nature.

But no one of these factors, nor all of them together, could have produced the scientific revolution. One is instantly reminded of Bacon's statement that "by the distant voyages and travels which have become frequent in our times, many things in nature have been laid open and discovered which may let in new light upon philosophy." The expansion of Europe, and increased travel in Europe itself, not only stimulated interest in nature but opened up to the West the vision of a "Kingdom of Man" upon earth. Much of Bacon's imagery was borrowed from the geographical discoveries: he aspired to be the Columbus of a new intellectual world, to sail through the Pillars of Hercules (symbol of the old knowledge) into the Atlantic Ocean in search of new and more useful knowledge. Bacon, however, failed to detect the coincidence of the scientific revolution with commercial prosperity and the rise of the middle class. Doubtless, the Marxist Professor Hessen greatly oversimplified when he wrote that "Newton was the typical representative of the rising bourgeoisie, and in his philosophy he embodies the characteristic features of his class." The theoretical scientists had mixed motives. Along with a concern for technology, they pursued truth for its own sake, and they sought God in his great creation. All the same, it is not stretching the imagination too far to see a rough correspondence between the mechanical universe of the seventeenth-century philosophers and the bourgeois desire for rational, predictable order. Science and business were a two-way street. If science affected business, so did business affect science—by its businesslike temper and its quantitative thinking, by its interest in "matter" and the rational control of matter.

II

The scientific revolution gave birth to a new conception of knowledge, a new methodology, and a new world-view substantially different from the old Aristotelian-Christian world-view. . . .

Knowledge now meant exact knowledge: what you know for certain, and not what may possibly or even probably be. Knowledge is what can be clearly apprehended by the mind, or measured by mathematics, or demonstrated by experiment. Galileo came close to saying this when he declared that without mathematics "it is impossible to comprehend a single word of (the great book of the universe)"; likewise Descartes when he wrote that "we ought never to allow ourselves to be persuaded of the truth of anything unless on the evidence of our Reason." The distinction between "primary" and "secondary qualities" in seventeenth-century metaphysics carried the same implication. To Galileo, Descartes, and Robert Boyle those mathematical qualities that inhered in objects (size, weight, position, etc.) were "primary," i.e., matters of real knowledge; whereas all the other qualities that our senses tell us are in objects (color, odor, taste, etc.) were "secondary," less real because less amenable to measurement. The inference of all this is plain: knowledge pertains to "natural philosophy" and possibly social theory, but not to theology or the older philosophy or poetry which involve opinion, belief, faith, but not knowledge. The Royal Society actually undertook to renovate the English language, by excluding from it metaphors and pulpit eloquence which conveyed no precise meaning. The "enthusiasm" of the religious man became suspect as did the "sixth sense" of the poet who could convey pleasure but not knowledge.

. . .

The odd thing about the scientific revolution is that for all its avowed distrust of hypotheses and systems, it created its own system of nature, or world-view. "I perceive," says the "Countess" in Fontenelle's popular dialogue of 1686, "Philosophy is now become very Mechanical." "I value (this universe) the more since I know it resembles a Watch, and the whole order of Nature the more plain and easy it is, to me it appears the more admirable." Descartes and other philosophers of science in the seventeenth century constructed a mechanical universe which resembled the machines—watches, pendulum clocks, steam engines—currently being built by scientists and artisans. However, it was not the observation of actual machines but the new astronomy and physics that made it possible to picture the universe in this way. The "Copernican revolution" destroyed Aristotle's "celestial world" of planets and stars which, because they were formed of a subtle substance having no weight, behaved differently from bodies on earth and in the "sublunary world." The new laws of motion formulated by a succession of physicists from Kepler to Newton explained the movement of bodies, both celestial and terrestrial, entirely on mechanical and mathematical principles. According to the law of inertia, the "natural" motion of bodies was in a straight line out into Euclidean space. The planets were pulled into their curvilinear orbits by gravitation which could operate at tremendous distances, and which varied inversely as the square of the distance.

Thus, the universe pictured by Fontenelle's Countess was very different from that of Dante in the thirteenth, or Richard Hooker in the sixteenth century. Gone was the Aristotelian-Christian universe of purposes, forms, and final causes. Gone were the spirits and intelligences which had been required to push the skies daily around the earth. The fundamental features of the new universe were numbers (mathematical quantities) and invariable laws. It was an economical universe in which nature did nothing in vain and performed its daily tasks without waste. In such a universe the scientist could delight and the bourgeois could live happily ever after—or at least up to the time of Darwin. The fact that nature appeared to have no spiritual purpose—

Descartes said that it would continue to exist regardless of whether there were any human beings to think it—was more than compensated for by its dependability. Philosophy had indeed become very mechanical. Descartes kept God to start his machine going, and Newton did what he could to save the doctrine of providence. But for all practical purposes, God had become the First Cause, "very well skilled in mechanics and geometry." And the rage for mechanical explanation soon spread beyond the confines of physics to encompass the biological and social sciences. Thus did Descartes regard animals as a piece of clockwork, Robert Boyle the human body as a "matchless engine."

Under the circumstances, one would logically expect there to have been warfare between science and religion in the seventeenth century. But such was not the case. To be sure, some theologians expressed dismay at the downfall of Aristotelianism, and the Roman Church took steps to suppress Copernicanism when Giordano Bruno interpreted it to mean an infinite universe and a plurality of worlds. But the majority of the scientists and popularizers of science were sincerely religious men— not a few were actually ecclesiastics—who either saw no conflict or else went to some lengths to resolve it. Science itself was commonly regarded as a religious enterprise. . . .

In the final analysis, however, the new thing in seventeenth-century thought was the dethronement of theology from its proud position as the sun of the intellectual universe. Bacon and Descartes and Newton lived in an age that was finding it increasingly difficult to reconcile science and religion. To save the best features of both they effected a shaky compromise. For all practical purposes they eliminated religious purpose from nature—thus allowing science to get on with its work, while leaving religion in control of private belief and morals. By their insistence that religious truth itself must pass the tests of reason and reliable evidence, John Locke and the rationalists further reduced theology's prerogatives. Bacon was prepared to believe the word of God "though our reason be shocked at it." But not Locke: " 'I believe because it is impossible,' might," he says, "in a good man, pass for a sally of zeal, but would prove a very ill rule for men to choose their opinions or religion by." Good Christian though Locke might be, his teaching had the effect of playing down the supernatural aspects of religion, of equating religion with simple ethics. . . .

THE PRINCIPLES OF PHILOSOPHY

RENE DESCARTES

Descartes (1596–1650) is one of the most important founders of modern science. It was Descartes who pointed the way to a scientific method based on quantification and measurement, a method, in short that could be checked and evaluated. The Cartesian method separated the measurable "primary" qualities of an object from its subjective "secondary" qualities by conceiving of nature as a mathematical machine.

Much of what Descartes says in this essay has become, with modern science, part of our "common sense." As you read it, try to imagine what people of the period must have thought for Descartes to feel he had to say this. There are also statements in this essay which you will find clearly absurd and wrong. Ask yourself why Descartes is saying these things. What does he mean? What accounts for such "absurd" statements?

PART II

I. The grounds on which the existence of material things may be known with certainty. . . . For we clearly conceive this matter as entirely distinct from God, and from ourselves, or our mind; and appear even clearly to discern that the idea of it is formed in us on occasion of objects existing out of our minds, to which it is in every respect similar. But since God cannot deceive us, for this is repugnant to his nature, as has been already remarked, we must unhesitatingly conclude that there exists a certain object extended in length, breadth, and thickness, and possessing all those properties which we clearly apprehend to belong to what is extended. And this extended substance is what we call body or matter. . . .

IV. That the nature of body consists not in weight, hardness, colour and the like, but in extension alone.

In this way we will discern that the nature of matter or body, considered in general, does not consist in its being hard, or ponderous, or coloured, or that which affects our senses in any other way, but simply in its being a substance extended in length, breadth, and depth. . . . In the same way, it may be shown that weight, colour, and all the other qualities of this sort, which are perceived in corporeal matter, may be

From "The Principles of Philosophy," in *Rene Descartes: The Meditation and Selections from The Principles of Philosophy*, translated by John Veitch. Edinburgh: Sutherland and Knox, 1853.

taken from it, itself meanwhile remaining entire: it thus follows that the nature of body depends on none of these.

XXII. It also follows that the matter of the heavens and earth is the same, and that there cannot be a plurality of worlds.

And it may also be easily inferred from all this that the earth and heavens are made of the same matter; and that even although there were an infinity of worlds, they would all be composed of this matter; from which it follows that a plurality of worlds is impossible, because we clearly conceive that the matter whose nature consists only in its being an extended substance, already wholly occupies all the imaginable spaces where these other worlds could alone be, and we cannot find in ourselves the idea of any other matter.

XXIII. That all the variety of matter, or the diversity of its forms, depends on motion.

There is therefore but one kind of matter in the whole universe, and this we know only by its being extended. All the properties we distinctly perceive to belong to it are reducible to its capacity of being divided and moved according to its parts; and accordingly it is capable of all those affections which we perceive can arise from the motion of its parts. For the partition of matter in thought makes no change in it; but all variation of it, or diversity of form, depends on motion.

PART III

II. That we ought to beware lest, in our presumption, we imagine that the ends which God proposed to himself in the creation of the world are understood by us.

The second is, that we should beware of presuming too highly of ourselves, as it seems we should do if we supposed certain limits to the world, without being assured of their existence either by natural reasons or by divine revelation, as if the power of our thought extended beyond what God has in reality made; but likewise still more if we persuaded ourselves that all things were created by God for us only, or if we merely supposed that we could comprehend by the power of our intellect the ends which God proposed to himself in creating the universe.

III. In what sense it may be said that all things were created for the sake of man.

For although, as far as regards morals, it may be a pious thought to believe that God made all things for us, seeing we may thus be incited to greater gratitude and love toward him; and although it is even in some sense true, because there is no created thing of which we cannot make some use, if it be only that of exercising our mind in considering it, and honouring God on account of it, it is yet by no means probable that all things were created for us in this way that God had no other end in their creation; and this supposition would be plainly ridiculous and inept in physical reasoning, for we do not doubt but that many things exist, or formerly existed and have now ceased to be, which were never seen or known by man, and were never of use to him.

PART IV

CXCVIII. That by our senses we know nothing of external objects beyond their figure (or situation), magnitude, and motion. . . . And we can easily conceive how the motion of one body may be caused by that of another, and diversified by the size, figure, and situation of its parts, but we are wholly unable to conceive how these same things (viz., size, figure, and motion), can produce something else of a nature entirely different from themselves, as, for example, those substantial forms and real qualities which many philosophers suppose to be in bodies; nor likewise can we conceive how these qualities or forms possess force to cause motions in other bodies. But since we know, from the nature of our soul, that the diverse motions of body are sufficient to produce in it all the sensations which it has, and since we learn from experience that several of its sensations are in reality caused by such motions, while we do not discover that anything besides these motions ever passes from the organs of the external senses to the brain, we have reason to conclude that we in no way likewise apprehend that in external objects, which we call light, colour, smell, taste, sound, heat or cold, and the other tactile qualities, or that which we call their substantial forms, unless as the various dispositions of these objects which have the power of moving our nerves in various ways.

CXCIX. That there is no phenomenon of nature whose explanation has been omitted in this treatise.

And thus it may be gathered, from an enumeration that is easily made, that there is no phenomenon of nature whose explanation has been omitted in this treatise; for beyond what is perceived by the senses, there is nothing that can be considered a phenomenon of nature. But leaving out of account motion, magnitude, figure, (and the situation of the parts of each body), which I have explained as they exist in body, we perceive nothing out of us by our senses except light, colours, smells, tastes, sounds, and the tactile qualities; and these I have recently shown to be nothing more, at least so far as they are known to us, than certain dispositions of the objects, consisting in magnitude, figure, and motion.

CHINA, TECHNOLOGY, AND CHANGE

LYNDA SHAFFER

In this selection a modern historian of China cautions against judging Chinese history by later events in Europe. What was the impact of the printing press, the compass, and gunpowder in Europe? What was the earlier impact of these inventions in China? To what extent were Chinese and European effects similar? To what extent were they different?

Francis Bacon (1561–1626), an early advocate of the empirical method, upon which the scientific revolution was based, attributed Western Europe's early modern take-off to three things in particular: the printing press, the compass, and gunpowder. Bacon had no idea where these things had come from, but historians now know that all three were invented in China. Since, unlike Europe, China did not take off onto a path leading from the scientific to the Industrial Revolution, some historians are now asking why these inventions were so revolutionary in Western Europe and, apparently, so unrevolutionary in China.

In fact, the question has been posed by none other than Joseph Needham, the foremost English-language scholar of Chinese science and technology. It is only because of Needham's work that the Western academic community has become aware that until Europe's take-off, China was the unrivaled world leader in technological development. That is why it is so disturbing that Needham himself has posed this apparent puzzle. The English-speaking academic world relies upon him and repeats him; soon this question and the vision of China that it implies will become dogma. Traditional China will take on supersociety qualities—able to contain the power of the press, to rein in the potential of the compass, even to muffle the blast of gunpowder.

The impact of these inventions on Western Europe is well known. The printing press not only eliminated much of the opportunity for human copying errors, it also encouraged the production of more copies of old books and an increasing number of new books. As written material became both cheaper and more easily available, intellectual activity increased. The printing press would eventually be held responsible, at least in part, for the spread of classical humanism and other ideas from

From the *World History Bulletin* (a publication of the World History Association, Drexel University, Philadelphia, PA), Fall/Winter 1986–7, volume 4, number 1.

the Renaissance. It is also said to have stimulated the Protestant Reformation, which urged a return to the Bible as the primary religious authority.

The introduction of gunpowder in Europe made castles and other medieval fortifications obsolete (since it could be used to blow holes in their walls) and thus helped to liberate Western Europe from feudal aristocratic power. As an aid to navigation the compass facilitated the Portuguese-and-Spanish sponsored voyages that led to Atlantic Europe's sole possession of the Western Hemisphere, as well as the Portuguese circumnavigation of Africa, which opened up the first all-sea route from Western Europe to the long-established ports of East Africa and Asia.

Needham's question can thus be understood to mean, Why didn't China use gunpowder to destroy feudal walls? Why didn't China use the compass to cross the Pacific and discover America, or to find an all-sea route to Western Europe? Why didn't China undergo a Renaissance or Reformation? The implication is that even though China possessed these technologies, it did not change much. Essentially Needham's question is asking, What was wrong with China?

Actually, there was nothing wrong with China. China was changed fundamentally by these inventions. But in order to see the changes, one must abandon the search for peculiarly European events in Chinese history, and look instead at China itself before and after these breakthroughs.

To begin, one should note that China possessed all three of these technologies by the latter part of the Tang dynasty (618–906)—between four and six hundred years before they appeared in Europe. And it was during just that time, from about 850, when the Tang dynasty began to falter, until 960, when the Song dynasty (960–1279) was established, that China underwent fundamental changes in all spheres. In fact, historians are now beginning to use the term revolution when referring to technological and commercial changes that culminated in the Song dynasty, in the same way that they refer to the changes in eighteenth- and nineteenth-century England as the Industrial Revolution. And the word might well be applied to other sorts of changes in China during this period.

For example, the Tang dynasty elite was aristocractic, but that of the Song was not. No one has ever considered whether the invention of gunpowder contributed to the demise of China's aristocrats, which occurred between 750 and 960, shortly after its invention. Gunpowder may, indeed, have been a factor although it is unlikely that its importance lay in blowing up feudal walls. Tang China enjoyed such internal peace that its aristocratic lineages did not engage in castle-building of the sort typical in Europe. Thus, China did not have many feudal fortifications to blow up.

The only wall of significance in this respect was the Great Wall, which was designed to keep steppe nomads from invading China. In fact, gunpowder may have played a role in blowing holes in this wall, for the Chinese could not monopolize the terrible new weapon, and their nomadic enemies to the north soon learned to use it against them. The Song dynasty ultimately fell to the Mongols, the most formidable force ever to emerge from the Eurasian steppe. Gunpowder may have had a profound effect on China—exposing a united empire to foreign invasion and terrible devastation—but an effect quite opposite to the one it had on Western Europe.

On the other hand, the impact of the printing press on China was in some ways very similar to its later impact on Europe. For example, printing contributed to a rebirth of classical (that is, preceding the third century A.D.) Confucian learning, helping to revive a fundamentally humanistic outlook that had been pushed aside for several centuries.

After the fall of the Han dynasty (206 B.C.–A.D. 220), Confucianism had lost much of its credibility as a world view, and it eventually lost its central place in the scholarly world. It was replaced by Buddhism, which had come from India. Buddhists believed that much human pain and confusion resulted from the pursuit of illusory pleasures and dubious ambitions: enlightenment and, ultimately, salvation would come from a progressive disengagement from the real world, which they also believed to be illusory. This point of view dominated Chinese intellectual life until the ninth century. Thus the academic and intellectual comeback of classical Confucianism was in essence a return to a more optimistic literature that affirmed the world as humans had made it.

The resurgence of Confucianism within the scholarly community was due to many factors, but the printing press was certainly one of the most important. Although the printing press was invented by Buddhist monks in China, and at first benefited Buddhism, by the middle of the tenth century, printers were turning out innumerable copies of the classical Confucian corpus. This return of scholars to classical learning was part of a more general movement that shared not only its humanistic features with the later Western European Renaissance, but certain artistic trends as well.

Furthermore, the Protestant Reformation in Western Europe was in some ways reminiscent of the emergence and eventual triumph of Neo-Confucian philosophy. Although the roots of Neo-Confucianism can be found in the ninth century, the man who created what would become its most orthodox synthesis was Zhu Xi (Chu Hsi, 1130–1200). Neo-confucianism was significantly different from classical Confucianism, for it had undergone an intellectual (and political) confrontation with Buddhism and had emerged profoundly changed. It is of the utmost importance to understand that not only was Neo-Confucianism new, it was also heresy, even during Zhu Xi's lifetime. It did not triumph until the thirteenth century, and it was not until 1313 (when Mongol conquerors ruled China) that Zhu Xi's commentaries on the classics became the single authoritative text against which all academic opinion was judged.

In the same way that Protestantism emerged out of a confrontation with the Roman Catholic establishment and asserted the individual Christian's autonomy, Neo-Confucianism emerged as a critique of Buddhist ideas that had taken hold in China, and it asserted an individual moral capacity totally unrelated to the ascetic practices and prayers of the Buddhist priesthood. In the twelfth century Neo-Confucianists lifted the work of Mencius (Meng Zi, 370–290 B.C.) out of obscurity and assigned it a place in the corpus second only to that of the *Analects of Confucius*. Many facets of Mencius appealed to the Neo-Confucianists, but one of the most important was his argument that humans by nature are fundamentally good. Within the context of the Song dynasty, this was an assertion that all men were morally equal, and that the Buddhist priests' withdrawal from life's mainstream did not bestow upon them any special virtue.

The importance of these philosophical developments notwithstanding, the printing press probably had its greatest impact on the Chinese political system. The origin of the civil service examination system in China can be traced back to the Han dynasty, but in the Song dynasty government-administered examinations became the most important route to political power in China. For almost a thousand years (except the early period of Mongol rule), China was governed by men who had come to power simply because they had done exceedingly well in examinations on the Confucian canon.

Of course, an examination system cannot be truly a measure of talent alone unless all the aspirants have equal access to study materials. At any one time thousands of students were studying for the exams, and thousands of inexpensive books were required. Without the printing press, the examination system would not have been possible.

The development of this alternative to aristocratic rule was one of the most radical changes in world history. Since the examinations were ultimately open to 98 percent of all males (actors were one of the few groups excluded), it was the most democratic system in the world prior to the development of representative democracy and popular suffrage in Western Europe in the eighteenth and nineteenth centuries. (There were some small-scale systems, such as the classical Greek city-states, which might be considered more democratic, but nothing comparable in size to Song China or even the modern nation-states of Europe.)

Finally we come to the compass. Suffice it to say that during the Song dynasty, China developed the world's largest and most technologically sophisticated merchant marine and navy. By the fifteenth century its ships were sailing from the north Pacific to the east coast of Africa. They could have made the arduous journey around the tip of Africa and on into Portuguese ports; however, they had no reason to do so. Although the Western European economy was prospering, it offered nothing that China could not acquire much closer to home at much less cost. In particular, wool, Western Europe's most important export, could easily be obtained along China's northern frontier.

Certainly, the Portuguese and the Spanish did not make their unprecedented voyages out of idle curiosity. They were trying to go to the Spice Islands, in what is now Indonesia, in order to acquire the most valuable commercial items of the time. In the fifteenth century these islands were the world's sole suppliers of the fine spices, such as cloves, nutmeg, and mace, as well as a source for the more generally available pepper. It was this spice market that lured Columbus westward from Spain and drew Vasco Da Gama around Africa and across the Indian Ocean.

China also wanted to go to the Spice Islands and, in fact, did go, regularly—but Chinese ships did not have to go around the world to get there. The Atlantic nations of Western Europe, on the other hand had to buy spices from Venice (which controlled the Mediterranean trade routes) or from other Italian city-states; or they had to find the Spice Islands. It was necessity that mothered those revolutionary routes that ultimately changed the world.

Gunpowder, the printing press, the compass—clearly these three inventions changed China as much as they changed Europe. And it should come as no surprise that changes wrought in China between the eighth and tenth centuries were different from changes wrought in Western Europe between the thirteenth and fifteenth centuries. It would, of course, be unfair and ahistorical to imply that something was wrong with Western Europe because the technologies appeared there later. It is equally unfair to ask why the Chinese did not accidentally bump into the Western Hemisphere while sailing east across the Pacific to find the wool markets of Spain.

II. THE WORLD OF THE WEST: 1750 TO 1914

A rare, 1855 photograph of Paris. (The Metropolitan Museum of Art, David H. McAlpin Fund, 1947.)

1750 —	
	Industrial Revolution begins (Europe)
	Hume writes about religion and miracles (Britain)
	France loses New World empire
	American Declaration of Independence; Smith's *Wealth of Nations* (Britain)
	French Revolution; U.S. Constitution written
1800 —	
	Louisiana Purchase
	Latin American revolutions
	Slavery abolished in British Empire
	First Opium War (China)
	European revolutions of 1848; Marx and Engels write *Communist Manifesto* (Germany)
1850 —	
	Admiral Perry in Japan
	Indian Mutiny
	Darwin develops evolution theory (Britain)
	U. S. Civil War
	Meiji Restoration (Japan)
	Suez Canal built
	European colonization of Africa
1900 —	Freud develops psychoanalytic theory (Vienna)
	Einstein works on relativity theory (Switzerland)
	Chinese Nationalist Revolution
	Panama Canal built
1914 —	World War I begins

5. Enlightenment and Revolution

ON MIRACLES

DAVID HUME

The European "Enlightenment" of the eighteenth century was the expression of a new class of intellectuals, independent of the clergy but allied with the rising middle class. Their favorite words were "reason," "nature," and "progress." They applied the systematic doubt of Descartes and the reasoning method of the scientific revolution to human affairs, including religion and politics. With caustic wit and good humor, they asked new questions and popularized new points of view that eventually revolutionized Western politics and culture. While the French philosophes *and Voltaire may be the best known, the Scottish philosopher David Hume (1711–1776) may have been the most brilliant. What is his argument in this selection? Does he prove his argument to your satisfaction? How does he use "reason" and "nature" to make his case? Is this scientific method incompatible with religion?*

I flatter myself that I have discovered an argument . . . , which, if just, will, with the wise and learned, be an everlasting check to all kinds of superstitious delusion, and consequently will be useful as long as the world endures; for so long, I presume, will the accounts of miracles and prodigies be found in all history, sacred and profane. . . .

A wise man proportions his belief to the evidence. . . .

A miracle is a violation of the laws of nature; and as a firm and unalterable experience has established these laws, the proof against a miracle, from the very nature of the fact, is as entire as any argument from experience can possibly be imagined. . . . Nothing is esteemed a miracle, if it ever happen in the common course of nature. It is no miracle that a man, seemingly in good health, should die on a sudden; because such a kind of death, though more unusual than any other, has yet been frequently observed to happen. But it is a miracle that a dead man should come to life; because that has never been observed in any age or country. There must, therefore, be an uniform experience against every miraculous event, otherwise the event would not merit that appellation. And as an uniform experience amounts to a proof, there is

From *The Philosophical Works of David Hume.* Edinburgh: A. Black & W. Tait, 1826.

here a direct and full *proof*, from the nature of the fact, against the existence of any miracle. . . .

(Further) there is not to be found, in all history, any miracle attested by a sufficient number of men, of such unquestioned good sense, education, and learning, as to secure us against all delusion in themselves; of such undoubted integrity, as to place them beyond all suspicion of any design to deceive others; of such credit and reputation in the eyes of mankind, as to have a great deal to lose in case of their being detected in any falsehood. . . . .

Secondly, We may observe in human nature a principle which, if strictly examined, will be found to diminish extremely the assurance, which we might, from human testimony, have in any kind of prodigy. . . . The passion of *surprise* and *wonder*, arising from miracles, being an agreeable emotion, gives a sensible tendency towards the belief of those events from which it is derived. . . .

With what greediness are the miraculous accounts of travellers received, their descriptions of sea and land monsters, their relations of wonderful adventures, strange men, and uncouth manners? But if the spirit of religion join itself to the love of wonder, there is an end of common sense; and human testimony, in these circumstances, loses all pretensions to authority. A religionist may be an enthusiast, and imagine he sees what has no reality: He may know his narrative to be false, and yet persevere in it, with the best intentions in the world, for the sake of promoting so holy a cause: Or even where this delusion has not place, vanity, excited by so strong a temptation, operates on him more powerfully than on the rest of mankind in any other circumstances; and self-interest with equal force. . . .

The many instances of forged miracles and prophecies and supernatural events, which, in all ages, have either been detected by contrary evidence, or which detect themselves by their absurdity, prove sufficiently the strong propensity of mankind to the extraordinary and marvellous, and ought reasonably to beget a suspicion against all relations of this kind. . . .

Thirdly, It forms a strong presumption against all supernatural and miraculous relations, that they are observed chiefly to abound among ignorant and barbarous nations; or if a civilized people has ever given admission to any of them, that people will be found to have received them from ignorant and barbarous ancestors, who transmitted them with that inviolable sanction and authority which always attend received opinions. . . .

I may add, as a *fourth* reason, which diminishes the authority of prodigies, that there is no testimony for any, even those which have not been expressly detected, that is not opposed by any infinite number of witnesses; so that not only the miracle destroys the credit of testimony, but the testimony destroys itself. To make this the better understood, let us consider, that in matters of religion, whatever is different is contrary;

and that it is impossible the religions of ancient Rome, of Turkey, of Siam, and of China, should all of them be established on any solid foundation. Every miracle, therefore, pretended to have been wrought in any of these religions, (and all of them abound in miracles), as its direct scope is to establish the particular system to which it is attributed; so has it the same force, though more indirectly, to overthrow every other system. In destroying a rival system, it likewise destroys the credit of those miracles on which that system was established, so that all the prodigies of different religions are to be regarded as contrary facts, and the evidences of these prodigies, whether weak or strong, as opposite to each other. . . .

Upon the whole, then, it appears, that no testimony for any kind of miracle has ever amounted to a probability, much less to a proof; and that, even supposing it amounted to a proof, it would be opposed by another proof, derived from the very nature of the fact which it would endeavour to establish. It is experience only which gives authority to human testimony; and it is the same experience which assures us of the laws of nature. When, therefore, these two kinds of experience are contrary, we have nothing to do but to subtract the one from the other, and embrace an opinion either on one side or the other, with that assurance which arises from the remainder. But according to the principle here explained, this subtraction with regard to all popular religions amounts to an entire annihilation; and therefore we may establish it as a maxim, that no human testimony can have such force as to prove a miracle, and make it a just foundation for any such system of religion.

WHAT IS ENLIGHTENMENT?
IMMANUEL KANT

Immanuel Kant (1724–1804), a university professor in the small town of Konigsberg, East Prussia (now the Soviet Union), was one of the most influential philosophers in European history. In this brief selection from his Critique of Practical Reason *he shows us how the Enlightenment's quest for scientific reason meant a demand, sometimes revolutionary, for political freedom. Do we, as Kant suggests, impose restrictions on our intellectual freedom? Do we need courage to use our own reason? What does he mean by "the freedom to make public use of one's reason"? Why is this so important?*

From Critique of Practical Reason by Immanuel Kant, translated by Lewis White Beck. Copyright © 1956, 1985 by Macmillan Publishing Company. Reprinted by permission of Macmillan Publishing Company.

Enlightenment is man's release from his self-incurred tutelage. Tutelage is man's inability to make use of his understanding without direction from another. Self-incurred is this tutelage when its cause lies not in lack of reason but in lack of resolution and courage to use it without direction from another. *Sapere aude!* "Have courage to use your own reason!"— that is the motto of enlightenment.

Laziness and cowardice are the reasons why so great a portion of mankind, after nature has long since discharged them from external direction, nevertheless remains under lifelong tutelage, and why it is so easy for others to set themselves up as their guardians. It is so easy not to be of age. If I have a book which understands for me, a pastor who has a conscience for me, a physician who decides my diet, and so forth, I need not trouble myself. I need not think, if I can only pay—others will readily undertake the irksome work for me.

That the step to competence is held to be very dangerous by the far greater portion of mankind (and by the entire fair sex)—quite apart from its being arduous—is seen to by those guardians who have so kindly assumed superintendence over them. After the guardians have first made their domestic cattle dumb and have made sure that these placid creatures will not dare take a single step without the harness of the cart to which they are confined, the guardians then show them the danger which threatens if they try to go alone. Actually, however, this danger is not so great, for by falling a few times they would finally learn to walk alone. But an example of this failure makes them timid and ordinarily frightens them away from all further trials.

For any single individual to work himself out of the life under tutelage which has become almost his nature is very difficult. He has come to be fond of this state, and he is for the present really incapable of making use of his reason, for no one has ever let him try it out. Statutes and formulas, those mechanical tools of the rational employment or rather mis-employment of his natural gifts, are the fetters of an everlasting tutelage. Whoever throws them off makes only an uncertain leap over the narrowest ditch because he is not accustomed to that kind of free motion. Therefore, there are only few who have succeeded by their own exercise of mind both in freeing themselves from incompetence and in achieving a steady pace.

But that the public should enlighten itself is more possible; indeed, if only freedom is granted, enlightenment is almost sure to follow. For there will always be some independent thinkers, even among the established guardians of the great masses, who, after throwing off the yoke of tutelage from their own shoulders, will disseminate the spirit of the rational appreciation of both their own worth and every man's vocation for thinking for himself. But be it noted that the public, which has first been brought under this yoke by their guardians, forces the guardians themselves to remain bound when it is incited to do so by some of the guardians who are themselves capable of some enlightenment—so harmful is it to implant prejudices, for they later take vengeance on their cultivators or on their descendants. Thus the public can only slowly attain enlightenment. Perhaps a fall of personal despotism or of avaricious or tyrannical oppression may be accomplished by revolution, but never a true reform in ways of thinking. Rather, new prejudices will serve as well as old ones to harness the great unthinking masses.

For this enlightenment, however, nothing is required but freedom, and indeed the most harmless among all the things to which this term can properly be applied. It is the freedom to make public use of one's reason at every point. But I hear on all sides, "Do not argue!" The officer says: "Do not argue but drill!" The tax-collector: "Do not argue but pay!" The cleric: "Do not argue but believe!" Everywhere freedom is restricted.

TWO REVOLUTIONARY DECLARATIONS

The American Declaration of Independence and the French Declaration of the Rights of Man and Citizen are similar products of the Enlightenment. Whether the French document of 1789 that served as a summary of the philosophy of the French Revolution was based on Thomas Jefferson's American Declaration of 1776, the debt of both to the Enlightenment ideas of John Locke, the French philosophes, and the emerging consensus of middle-class goals is evident. In what ways are the declarations similar and different? Have we broadened or lessened our idea of freedom since then?

1. THE AMERICAN DECLARATION OF INDEPENDENCE

In Congress, July 4, 1776 the Unanimous Declaration of the Thirteen United States of America

When in the course of human events, it becomes necessary for one people to dissolve the political bands which have connected them with another, and to assume among the powers of the earth, the separate and equal station to which the Laws of Nature and of Nature's God entitle them, a decent respect to the opinions of mankind requires that they should declare the causes which impel them to the separation.

We hold these truths to be self-evident, that all men are created equal, that they are endowed by their Creator with certain unalienable rights, that among these are life, liberty and the pursuit of happiness. That to secure these rights, governments are instituted among men, deriving their just powers from the consent of the governed. That whenever any form of government becomes destructive of these ends, it is the right of the people to alter or to abolish it, and to institute new government, laying its foundation on such principles and organizing its powers in such form, as to them shall seem most likely to effect their safety and happiness. Prudence, indeed, will dictate that governments long established should not be changed for light and transient causes; and accordingly all experience hath shown, that mankind are more disposed to suffer, while evils are sufferable, than to right themselves by abolishing the forms to which they are accustomed. But when a long train of abuses and usurpations, pursuing invariably the same object evinces a design to reduce them under absolute despotism, it is their right, it is their duty, to throw off such government, and to provide new guards for their future security. Such has been the patient sufferance of these Colonies; and such is now the necessity which constrains them to alter their former systems of government. The history of the present King of Great Britain is a history of repeated injuries and usurpations, all having in direct object the establishment of an absolute tyranny over these States. To prove this, let facts be submitted to a candid world.

He has refused his assent to laws, the most wholesome and necessary for the public good.

He has forbidden his Governors to pass laws of immediate and pressing importance, unless suspended in their operation till his assent should be obtained; and when so suspended, he has utterly neglected to attend to them.

He has refused to pass other laws for the accommodation of large districts of people, unless those people would relinquish the right of representation in the Legislature, a right inestimable to them and formidable to tyrants only.

He has called together legislative bodies at places unusual, uncomfortable, and distant from the depository of their public records, for the sole purpose of fatiguing them into compliance with his measures.

He has dissolved representative houses repeatedly, for opposing with manly firmness his invasions on the rights of the people.

He has refused for a long time, after such dissolutions, to cause others to be elected; whereby the legislative powers, incapable of annihilation, have returned to the people at large for their exercise; the State remaining in the meantime exposed to all the dangers of invasion from without and convulsions within.

He has endeavoured to prevent the population of these states; for that purpose obstructing the laws of naturalization of foreigners; refusing to pass others to encourage their migration hither, and raising the conditions of new appropriations of lands.

He has obstructed the administration of justice, by refusing his assent to laws for establishing judiciary powers.

He has made judges dependent on his will alone, for the tenure of their offices, and the amount and payment of their salaries.

He has erected a multitude of new offices, and sent hither swarms of officers to harass our people, and eat out their substance.

He has kept among us, in times of peace, standing armies without the consent of our legislatures.

He has affected to render the military independent of and superior to the civil power.

He has combined with others to subject us to a jurisdiction foreign to our constitution, and unacknowledged by our laws; giving his assent to their acts of pretended legislation:

For quartering large bodies of armed troops among us:

For protecting them, by a mock trial, from punishment for any murders which they should commit on the inhabitants of these States:

For cutting off our trade with all parts of the world:

For imposing taxes on us without our consent:

For depriving us in many cases, of the benefits of trial by jury:

For transporting us beyond seas to be tried for pretended offences:

For abolishing the free system of English laws in a neighbouring Province, establishing therein an arbitrary government, and enlarging its boundaries so as to render it at once an example and fit instrument for introducing the same absolute rule into these Colonies:

For taking away our Charters, abolishing our most valuable laws, and altering fundamentally the forms of our governments:

For suspending our own Legislatures, and declaring themselves invested with power to legislate for us in all cases whatsoever.

He has abdicated government here, by declaring us out of his protection and waging war against us.

He has plundered our seas, ravaged our coasts, burnt our towns, and destroyed the lives of our people.

He is at this time transporting large armies of foreign mercenaries to complete the works of death, desolation and tyranny, already begun with circumstances of cruelty and perfidy scarcely paralleled in the most barbarous ages, and totally unworthy the head of a civilized nation.

He has constrained our fellow citizens taken captive on the high seas to bear arms against their country, to become the executioners of their friends and brethren, or to fall themselves by their hands.

He has excited domestic insurrections amongst us, and has endeavoured to bring on the inhabitants of our frontiers, the merciless Indian savages, whose known rule of warfare, is an undistinguished destruction of all ages, sexes, and conditions.

In every state of these oppressions we have petitioned for redress in the most humble terms: our repeated petitions have been answered only by repeated injury. A prince whose character is thus marked by every act which may define a tyrant is unfit to be the ruler of a free people.

Nor have we been wanting in attention to our British brethren. We have warned them from time to time of attempts by their legislature to extend an unwarrantable jurisdiction over us. We have reminded them of the circumstances of our emigration and settlement here. We have appealed to their native justice and magnanimity, and we have conjured them by the ties of our common kindred to disavow these usurpations, which would inevitably interrupt our connections and correspondence. They too have been deaf to the voice of justice and of consanguinity. We must, therefore, acquiesce in the necessity, which denounces our separation, and hold them, as we hold the rest of mankind, enemies in war, in peace friends.

We, therefore, the Representatives of the United States of America, in General Congress assembled, appealing to the Supreme Judge of the world for the rectitude of our intentions, do, in the name, and by authority of the good people of these Colonies, solemnly publish and declare, That these United Colonies are, and of right ought to be Free and Independent States; that they are absolved from all allegiance to the British Crown, and that all political connection between them and the State of Great Britain, is and ought to be totally dissolved; and that as Free and Independent States, they have full power to levy war, conclude peace, contract alliances, establish commerce, and to do all other acts and things which Independent States may of right do. And for the support of this declaration, with a firm reliance on the protection of Divine Providence, we mutually pledge to each other our lives, our fortunes, and our sacred honor.

2. THE FRENCH DECLARATION OF THE RIGHTS OF MAN AND CITIZEN

The representatives of the French people, organized in National Assembly, considering that ignorance, forgetfulness, or contempt of the rights of man are the sole causes of public misfortunes and of the corruption of governments, have resolved to set forth in a solemn declaration the natural, inalienable, and sacred rights of man, in order that such declaration, continually before all members of the social body, may be a perpetual remainder of their rights and duties; in order that the acts of the legislative power and those of the executive power may constantly be

Reprinted with permission of Macmillan Publishing Company from *A Documentary Survey of the French Revolution* by John Hall Stewart. Copyright 1951, renewed 1979 by Macmillan Publishing Company.

compared with the aim of every political institution and may accordingly be more respected; in order that the demands of the citizens, founded henceforth upon simple and incontestable principles, may always be directed towards the maintenance of the Constitution and the welfare of all.

Accordingly, the National Assembly recognizes and proclaims, in the presence and under the auspices of the Supreme Being, the following rights of man and citizen.

1. Men are born and remain free and equal in rights; social distinctions may be based only upon general usefulness.

2. The aim of every political association is the preservation of the natural and inalienable rights of man; these rights are liberty, property, security, and resistance to oppression.

3. The source of all sovereignty resides essentially in the nation; no group, no individual may exercise authority not emanating expressly therefrom.

4. Liberty consists of the power to do whatever is not injurious to others; thus the enjoyment of the natural rights of every man has for its limits only those that assure other members of society the enjoyment of those same rights; such limits may be determined only by law.

5. The law has the right to forbid only actions which are injurious to society. Whatever is not forbidden by law may not be prevented, and no one may be constrained to do what it does not prescribe.

6. Law is the expression of the general will; all citizens have the right to concur personally, or through their representatives, in its formation; it must be the same for all, whether it protects or punishes. All citizens, being equal before it, are equally admissible to all public offices, positions, and employments, according to their capacity, and without other distinction than that of virtues and talents.

7. No man may be accused, arrested, or detained except in the cases determined by law, and according to the forms prescribed thereby. Whoever solicit, expedite, or execute arbitrary orders, or have them executed, must be punished; but every citizen summoned or apprehended in pursuance of the law must obey immediately; he renders himself culpable by resistance.

8. The law is to establish only penalties that are absolutely and obviously necessary; and no one may be punished except by virtue of a law established and promulgated prior to the offence and legally applied.

9. Since every man is presumed innocent until declared guilty, if arrest be deemed indispensable, all unnecessary severity for securing the person of the accused must be severely repressed by law.

10. No one is to be disquieted because of his opinions, even religious, provided their manifestation does not disturb the public order established by law.

11. Free communication of ideas and opinions is one of the most precious of the rights of man. Consequently, every citizen may speak, write, and print freely, subject to responsibility for the abuse of such liberty in the cases determined by law.

12. The guarantee of the rights of man and citizen necessitates a public force; such a force, therefore, is instituted for the advantage of all and not for the particular benefit of those to whom it is entrusted.

13. For the maintenance of the public force and for the expenses of administration a common tax is indispensable; it must be assessed equally on all citizens in proportion to their means.

14. Citizens have the right to ascertain, by themselves or through their representatives, the necessity of the public tax, to consent to it freely, to supervise its use, and to determine its quota, assessment, payment, and duration.

15. Society has the right to require of every public agent an accounting of his administration.

16. Every society in which the guarantee of rights is not assured or the separation of powers not determined has no constitution at all.

17. Since property is a sacred and inviolate right, no one may be deprived thereof unless a legally established public necessity obviously requires it, and upon condition of a just and previous indemnity.

THE U.S. BILL OF RIGHTS

The Bill of Rights are the first ten amendments to the U.S. Constitution. They were officially adopted in 1791, shortly after the Constitution went into effect. What rights are protected by these amendments? Why were they important? Are they still important? Compare the Bill of Rights with the declarations you have just read.

AMENDMENT I

Congress shall make no law respecting an establishment of religion, or prohibiting the free exercise thereof; or abridging the freedom of speech, or of the press; or the right of the people peaceably to assemble, and to petition the Government for a redress of grievances.

AMENDMENT II

A well regulated Militia, being necessary to the security of a free State, the right of the people to keep and bear Arms, shall not be infringed.

AMENDMENT III

No Soldier shall, in time of peace be quartered in any house, without the consent of the Owner, nor in time of war, but in a manner to be prescribed by law.

AMENDMENT IV

The right of the people to be secure in their persons, houses, papers, and effects, against unreasonable searches and seizures, shall not be violated, and no Warrants shall issue, but upon probable cause, supported by Oath or affirmation, and particularly describing the place to be searched, and the persons or things to be seized.

AMENDMENT V

No person shall be held to answer for a capital, or otherwise infamous crime, unless on a presentment or indictment of a Grand Jury, except in cases arising in the land or naval forces, or in the Militia, when an actual service in time of War or public danger; nor shall any person be subject for the same offence to be twice put in jeopardy of life or limb; nor shall be compelled in any criminal case to be a witness against himself, nor be deprived of life, liberty, or property, without due process of law; nor shall private property be taken for public use, without just compensation.

AMENDMENT VI

In all criminal prosecutions, the accused shall enjoy the right to a speedy and public trial, by an impartial jury of the State and district wherein the crime shall have been committed, which district shall have been previously ascertained by law, and to be informed of the nature and cause of the accusation; to be confronted with the witness against him; to have compulsory process for obtaining witness in his favor, and to have the Assistance of Counsel for his defence.

AMENDMENT VII

In Suits at common law, where the value in controversy shall exceed twenty dollars, the right of trial by jury shall be preserved, and no fact tried by a jury, shall be otherwise re-examined in any Court of the United States, than according to the rules of the common law.

AMENDMENT VIII

Excessive bail shall not be required, nor excessive fines imposed, nor cruel and unusual punishments inflicted.

AMENDMENT IX

The enumeration in the Constitution, of certain rights, shall not be construed to deny or disparage others retained by the people.

AMENDMENT X

The powers not delegated to the United States by the Constitution, nor prohibited by it to the States, are reserved to the States respectively, or to the people.

THE MANIFESTO OF THE EQUALS

GRACCHUS BABEUF

One of the ways in which ideas of freedom have broadened since 1789 can be seen in this example of the most radical thinking to emerge from the French Revolution. True equality, Babeuf argued in the 1790s, would mean common property as well as a common government. This may be the first socialist manifesto. Does it call for greater freedom or only greater equality? Were there economic limitations to the liberties of the American Declaration of Independence, the French Declaration of the Rights of Man and Citizen, and the U.S. Bill of Rights?

PEOPLE of FRANCE!—During fifteen ages you have lived slaves, and consequently unhappy. During six years you breathe with difficulty in the expectation of independence, of prosperity, and of equality.

EQUALITY!—first vow of nature, first want of man, and chief bond of all legitimate association! People of France! you have not been more favoured than the other nations which vegetate on this ill-fated globe!

From *Babeuf's Conspiracy for Equality* by Philippe Buonarroti, translated by Bronterre O'Brien. London: H. Hetherington, 1836. Reprinted by Augustus M. Kelley (New York: 1965).

Always and everywhere does the unfortunate human species, delivered over to cannibals more or less artful, serve for a plaything to all ambitions—for pasture to all tyrannies. Always and everywhere have men been fooled by fine words; never and nowhere have they obtained the *thing* with the word. From time immemorial we have been hypocritically told—*men are equal*; and from time immemorial does the most degrading and monstrous inequality insolently oppress the human race. Ever since the first existence of civil societies has the finest apanage of man been uncontradictedly *acknowledged*; but never, up to this moment, has it been once *realized*. Equality has never been other than a beautiful and barren fiction of law. Even now, when it is claimed with a stronger voice, we are answered, "Be silent, miserables!—absolute equality is but a chimaera; be content with conditional equality; you are all equal before law. Rabble! what more do you want?" what more do we want? Legislators, governors, rich proprietors—listen in your turn.

We are equal, are we not? This principle remains uncontested, because, without being self-convicted of folly, one cannot seriously say that it is night when it is day.

Well! we pretend henceforward to live and die equal, as we are born so. We desire real equality or death; behold what we want. And we shall have this real equality, no matter at what price. Woe to them who will interpose themselves between it and us! Woe to him who will offer resistance to so determined a resolve!

The French Revolution is but the forerunner of another revolution far more grand, far more solemn, and which will be the last. The people has marched over dead bodies against the kings and priests coalesced against it; it will do the same against the new tyrants—against the new political Tartuffes who have usurped the places of the old.

"What do we want," you ask, "more than equality of rights?" We want that equality not merely written in the "Declaration of the Rights of Man and of the Citizen;" we want it in the midst of us—under the roofs of our houses. We consent to everything for it—to become as *pliable wax, in order to have its characters engraven upon us*. Perish, if needs be, all the arts, provided real equality abides with us!

Legislators and governors, who are as destitute of genius as of honesty—you rich proprietors, without bowels of pity—in vain do you essay to neutralize our holy enterprise, by saying, "They are only re-producing the old Agrarian law, so often demanded already before them."

Calumniators! be silent in your turn; and in the silence of confusion hearken to our pretensions, dictated by nature herself, and based upon eternal justice. The Agrarian law, or partition of lands, was only the instantaneous wish of certain soldiers without principles—of certain small tribes, moved by instinct rather than by reason. We aim at something more sublime, and more equitable; we look to *common property, or the community of goods!* No more individual property in lands. *The earth belongs to no one.* We claim—we demand—we *will* the communal enjoyment of the fruits of the earth; *the fruits belong to all.*

We declare that we can no longer suffer that the great majority of men shall labour and sweat to serve and pamper the extreme minority. Long enough, and too long, have less than a million of individuals disposed of what belongs to more than twenty millions of men like themselves—of men in every respect their equals. Let there be at length an end to this enormous scandal, which posterity will scarcely credit. Away for ever with the revolting distinctions of rich and poor, of great and little, of masters and servants, of *governors and governed.*

Let there be no longer any other differences in mankind than those of age and sex. Since all have the same wants, and the same faculties, let all have accordingly the same education—the same nourishment. They are content with one sun, and the same air for all; why should not the like portion, and the same quality of food, suffice for each according to his wants?

But already do the enemies of an order of things, the most natural that can be imagined, declaim against us,—"Disorganizers, and seditionists," they exclaim, "you want but massacres and plunder."

PEOPLE of FRANCE! We will not waste our time to answer them; but we will tell you,—"the only enterprise we are organizing has no other object in view than to put an end to civil dissensions and to public disorder. Never was a more vast design conceived and put in execution. At distant intervals in the history of the world it has been talked of by some men of genius—by a few philosophers—but they spoke it with a low and trembling voice. Not one of them has had the courage to speak the entire truth.

The moment for great measures has arrived. Evil is at its height; it has reached its *maximum*, and covers the face of the earth. Chaos, under the name of politics, has too long reigned over it. Let everything revert to order, and resume its proper place. At the voice of equality, let the elements of justice and felicity be organized. The moment is come to found the REPUBLIC of EQUALS—the grand asylum open to all human kind. The days of general restitution are come. Weeping families, come and seat yourselves at the common table provided by nature for all her children.

PEOPLE of FRANCE! The purest of all earthly glories has been reserved for you—yes, 'tis you who are first destined to present the world with this touching spectacle.

Old habits, old prejudices, will again seek to oppose obstacles to the establishment of the REPUBLIC of EQUALS. The organization of real equality—the only one which satisfies all wants, without making victims, without costing sacrifices—will not, perhaps, at first please everybody. The egoist, the ambitious, will yell with rage. Those who possess unjustly, will raise the cry of injustice. Exclusive enjoyments, solitary pleasures, personal ease and privileges, will cause poignant regrets to some few individuals who are dead or callous to the pangs of others. The lovers of absolute power, the vile instruments of arbitrary authority, will feel it hard that their haughty chiefs should bend to the level of equality. Their short-sightedness will, with difficulty, penetrate into the future of public happiness, however near; but what can avail a few thousand malcontents against such a mass of human beings, all happy, and astonished at having been so long in quest of a felicity which they had within hands' reach. On the day that follows this real revolution, they will say to one another in amazement—"What—universal happiness depended on so little! We had but to will it. Ah, why had we not willed it sooner? Was it then necessary to have it told to us so often?" Yes, no doubt, a single man on the earth, more rich, more powerful, than his fellow man, than his equals, destroys the equilibrium, and crime and misfortune come on the world.

PEOPLE of FRANCE! By what sign then ought you henceforward to recognize the excellence of a constitution? . . . That which altogether reposes on actual, absolute equality, is the only one that can be suitable to you, and satisfy all your desires.

The aristocratic charters of 1791 and 1795 riveted your chains, instead of breaking them. That of 1793 was a great practical step towards real equality; never before was equality so nearly approached; but that Constitution did not yet touch the end, nor was it fully competent to attain general happiness, of which, however, it has solemnly consecrated the great principle.

PEOPLE of FRANCE! Open your eyes and hearts to the fulness of felicity; recognize and proclaim with us the REPUBLIC OF EQUALS!

6. Capitalism and the Industrial Revolution

THE WEALTH OF NATIONS

ADAM SMITH

The Wealth of Nations, published the year of the American Declaration of Independence, is also a work of the Enlightenment. Smith (1723–1790), applied scientific principles to economic behavior and came up with some startling conclusions for his age, and possibly ours too. Informing his conclusions was the conviction that people acted principally out of self-interest and that allowing them the freedom to do so resulted in a natural social harmony and economic productivity. "It is not from the benevolence of the butcher, the brewer, or the baker, that we expect our dinner," he says, "but from their regard of their own interest. We address ourselves not to their humanity, but to their self-love, and never talk to them of our own necessities, but of their advantage."

In the following selections, Smith discusses the division of labor, the market, the relation between labor and prices, supply and demand, money, and free trade. What does he say about these topics? How is his position different from that held by people in his day? Do most people today accept Smith's ideas?

BOOK I: OF THE CAUSES OF IMPROVEMENT IN THE PRODUCTIVE POWERS OF LABOUR, AND OF THE ORDER ACCORDING TO WHICH ITS PRODUCE IS NATURALLY DISTRIBUTED AMONG THE DIFFERENT RANKS OF THE PEOPLE

Chapter I: Of the Division of Labour

The greatest improvement in the productive powers of labour, and the greater part of the skill, dexterity, and judgment with which it is anywhere directed, or applied, seem to have been the effects of the division of labour.

The effects of the division of labour, in the general business of society,

From *The Wealth of Nations* by Adam Smith. London: Everyman's Library, J.M. Dent & Sons, Ltd., 1910.

will be more easily understood by considering in what manner it operates in some particular manufactures. It is commonly supposed to be carried furthest in some very trifling ones; not perhaps that it really is carried further in them than in others of more importance: but in those trifling manufactures which are destined to supply the small wants of but a small number of people, the whole number of workmen must necessarily be small; and those employed in every different branch of the work can often be collected into the same workhouse, and placed at once under the view of the spectator. In those great manufactures, on the contrary, which are destined to supply the great wants of the great body of the people, every different branch of the work employs so great a number of workmen that it is impossible to collect them all into the same workhouse. We can seldom see more, at one time, than those employed in one single branch. Though in such manufactures, there-fore, the work may really be divided into a much greater number of parts than in those of a more trifling nature, the division is not near so obvious, and has accordingly been much less observed.

To take an example, therefore, from a very trifling manufacture; but one in which the division of labour has been very often taken notice of, the trade of the pin-maker; a workman not educated to this business (which the division of labour has rendered a distinct trade), nor acquainted with the use of the machinery employed in it (to the invention of which the same division of labour has probably given occasion), could scarce, perhaps, with his utmost industry, make one pin in a day, and certainly could not make twenty. But in the way in which this business is now carried on, not only the whole work is a peculiar trade, but it is divided into a number of branches, of which the greater part are likewise peculiar trades. One man draws out the wire, another straights it, a third cuts it, a fourth points it, a fifth grinds it at the top for receiving the head; to make the head requires two or three distinct operations; to put it on is a peculiar business, to whiten the pins is another; it is even a trade by itself to put them into the paper; and the important business of making a pin is, in this manner, divided into about eighteen distinct operations, which, in some manufactories, are all performed by distinct hands, though in others the same man will sometimes perform two or three of them. I have seen a small manufac-tory of this kind where ten men only were employed, and where some of them consequently performed two or three distinct operations. But though they were very poor, and therefore but indifferently accommo-dated with the necessary machinery, they could, when they exerted themselves, make among them about twelve pounds of pins in a day. There are in a pound upwards of four thousand pins of a middling size. Those ten persons, therefore, could make among them upwards of forty-eight thousand pins in a day. Each person, therefore, making a tenth part of forty-eight thousand pins, might be considered as making four thousand eight hundred pins in a day. But if they had all wrought separately and independently, and without any of them having been educated to this peculiar business, they certainly could not each of them have made twenty, perhaps not one pin in a day; that is, certainly, not the two hundred and fortieth, perhaps not the four thousand eight hundredth part of what they are at present capable of performing, in consequence of a proper division and combination of their different operations.

In every other art and manufacture, the effects of the division of labour are similar to what they are in this very trifling one; though, in many of them, the labour can neither be so much subdivided, nor reduced to so great a simplicity of operation.

Chapter III: That The Division Of Labour Is Limited By The Extent Of The Market

As it is the power of exchanging that gives occasion to the division of labour, so the extent of this division must always be limited by the extent of that power, or, in other words, by the extent of the market. When the market is very small, no person can have any encouragement to dedicate himself entirely to one employment, for want of the power to exchange all that surplus part of the produce of his own labour, which is over and above his own consumption, for such parts of the produce of other men's labour as he has occasion for.

There are some sorts of industry, even of the lowest kind, which can be carried on nowhere but in a great town. A porter, for example, can find employment and subsistence in no other place. A village is by too much narrow a sphere for him.

Chapter V: Of The Real and Nominal Price Of Commodities, Or Their Price In Labour, and Their Price In Money

Every man is rich or poor according to the degree in which he can afford to enjoy the necessaries, conveniences, and amusements of human life. But after the division of labour has once thoroughly taken place, it is but a very small part of these with which a man's own labour can supply him. The far greater part of them he must derive from the labour of other people, and he must be rich or poor according to the quantity of that labour which he can command, or which he can afford to purchase. The value of any commodity, therefore, to the person who possesses it, and who means not to use or consume it himself, but to exchange it for other commodities, is equal to the quantity of labour which it enables him to purchase or command. Labour, therefore, is the real measure of the exchangeable value of all commodities.

The real price of everything, what everything really costs to the man who wants to acquire it, is the toil and trouble of acquiring it. What everything is really worth to the man who has acquired it, and who wants to dispose of it or exchange it for something else, is the toil and trouble which it can save to himself, and which it can impose upon other people. What is bought with money or with goods is purchased by labour as much as what we acquire by the toil of our own body. That money or those goods indeed save us this toil. They contain the value of a certain quantity of labour which we exchange for what is supposed at the time to contain the value of an equal quantity. Labour was the first price, the original purchase-money that was paid for all things. It was not by gold or by silver, but by labour, that all the wealth of the world was originally purchased; and its value, to those who possess it, and who want to exchange it for some new productions, is precisely equal to the quantity of labour which it can enable them to purchase or command.

.   .   .

Chapter VII: Of The Natural and Market Price Of Commodities

. . . When the quantity of any commodity which is brought to market falls short of the effectual demand, all those who are willing to pay the whole value of the rent, wages, and profit, which must be paid in order to bring it thither, cannot be supplied with the quantity which they want. Rather than want it altogether, some of them will be willing to give more. A competition will immediately begin among them, and the market price will rise more or less above the natural price, according as either the greatness of the deficiency, or the wealth and wanton luxury of the competitors, happen to animate more or less the eagerness of the competition. Among competitors of equal wealth and luxury the same deficiency will generally occasion a more or less eager competition, according as the acquisition of the commodity happens to be of more or less importance to them. Hence the exorbitant price of the necessaries of life during the blockade of a town or in a famine.

When the quantity brought to market exceeds the effectual demand, it cannot be all sold to those who are willing to pay the whole value of the rent, wages, and profit, which must be paid in order to bring it thither. Some part must be sold to those who are willing to pay less, and the low price which they give for it must reduce the price of the whole. The market price will sink more or less below the natural price, according as the greatness of the excess increases more or less the competition of the sellers, or according as it happens to be more or less important to them to get immediately rid of the commodity. The same excess in the importation of perishable, will occasion a much greater competition than in that of durable commodities; in the importation of oranges, for example, than in that of old iron.

When the quantity brought to market is just sufficient to supply the effectual demand, and no more, the market price naturally comes to be either exactly, or as nearly as can be judged of, the same with the natural price. The whole quantity upon hand can be disposed of for this price, and cannot be disposed of for more. The competition of the different dealers obliges them all to accept of this price, but does not oblige them to accept of less.

The quantity of every commodity brought to market naturally suits itself to the effectual demand. It is the interest of all those who employ their land, labour, or stock, in bringing any commodity to market, that the quantity never should exceed the effectual demand; and it is the interest of all other people that it never should fall short of that demand.

I thought it necessary, though at the hazard of being tedious, to examine at full length this popular notion that wealth consists in money, or in gold and silver. Money in common language, as I have already observed, frequently signifies wealth, and this ambiguity of expression has rendered this popular notion so familiar to us that even they who are convinced of its absurdity are very apt to forget their own principles, and in the course of their reasonings to take it for granted as a certain and undeniable truth. Some of the best English writers upon commerce set out with observing that the wealth of a country consists, not in its gold and silver only, but in its lands, houses, and consumable goods of all different kinds. In the course of their reasonings, however, the lands, houses, and consumable goods seem to slip out of their memory, and the strain of their argument frequently supposes that all wealth consists in gold and silver, and that to multiply those metals is the great object of national industry and commerce.

The produce of industry is what it adds to the subject or materials upon which it is employed. In proportion as the value of this produce is great or small, so will likewise be the profits of the employer. But it is only for the sake of profit that any man employs a capital in the support of industry; and he will always, therefore, endeavour to employ it in the support of that industry of which the produce is likely to be of the greatest value, or to exchange for the greatest quantity either of money or of other goods.

But the annual revenue of every society is always precisely equal to the exchangeable value of the whole annual produce of its industry, or rather is precisely the same thing with that exchangeable value. As every individual, therefore, endeavours as much as he can both to employ his capital in the support of domestic industry, and so to direct that industry that its produce may be of the greatest value; every individual necessarily labours to render the annual revenue of the society as great as he can. He generally, indeed, neither intends to promote the public interest, nor knows how much he is promoting it. By preferring the support of domestic to that of foreign industry, he intends only his own security; and by directing that industry in such a manner as its produce may be of the greatest value, he intends only his own gain, and he is in this, as in many other cases, led by an invisible hand to promote an end which was no part of his intention. Nor is it always the worse for the society that it was no part of it. By pursuing his own interest he frequently promotes that of the society more effectually than when he really intends to promote it. I have never known much good done by those who affected to trade for the public good. It is an affectation, indeed, not very common among merchants, and very few words need be employed in dissuading them from it.

What is the species of domestic industry which his capital can employ, and of which the produce is likely to be of the greatest value, every individual, it is evident, can, in his local situation, judge much better than any statesman or lawgiver can do for him. The statesman who should attempt to direct private people in what manner they ought to employ their capitals would not only load himself with a most unnecessary attention, but assume an authority which could safely be trusted, not only to no single person, but to no council or senate whatever, and which would nowhere be so dangerous as in the hands of a man who had folly and presumption enough to fancy himself fit to exercise it.

To give the monopoly of the home market to the produce of domestic industry, in any particular art or manufacture, is in some measure to direct private people in what manner they ought to employ their capitals, and must, in almost all cases, be either a useless or a hurtful regulation. If the produce of domestic can be brought there as cheap as that of foreign industry, the regulation is evidently useless. If it cannot, it must generally be hurtful. It is the maxim of every prudent master of a family never to attempt to make at home what it will cost him more to make than to buy. The tailor does not attempt to make his own shoes, but buys them of the shoemaker. The shoemaker does not attempt to make his own clothes, but employs a tailor. The farmer attempts to make neither the one nor the other, but employs those different artificers. All of them find it for their interest to employ their whole industry in a way in which they have some advantage over their neighbours, and to purchase with a part of its produce, or what is the same thing, with the price of a part of it, whatever else they have occasion for.

What is prudence in the conduct of every private family can scarce be folly in that of a great kingdom. If a foreign country can supply us with a commodity cheaper than we ourselves can make it, better buy it of them with some part of the produce of our own industry employed in a way in which we have some advantage. The general industry of the country, being always in proportion to the capital which employs it, will not thereby be diminished, no more than that of the above-mentioned artificers; but only left to find out the way in which it can be employed with the greatest advantage. It is certainly not employed to the greatest advantage when it is thus directed towards an object which it can buy cheaper than it can make.

THE FACTORY SYSTEM OF PRODUCTION

ANDREW URE

Andrew Ure was one of the leading spokesmen for the development of the factory system. Notice the way he describes, from the vantage of the 1830s, the factories of the early Industrial Revolution. Might some of the workers in these factories use different words to describe them? What are the advantages of factory production, according to Ure? Does he see any disadvantages? What does he think of Smith's comments on the division of labor? Will the factory continue to make use of the division of labor? What does he think of skilled workers? Who are the ideal workers for the factory, according to Ure?

The term *Factory System*, in technology, designates the combined operation of many orders of work-people, adult and young, in tending with assiduous skill a series of productive machines continuously impelled by a central power. This definition includes such organizations as cotton-mills, flax-mills, silk-mills, woollen-mills, and certain engineering works; but it excludes those in which the mechanisms do not form a connected series, nor are dependent on one prime mover. Of the latter class, examples occur in iron-works, dye-works, soap-works, brass-foundries, &c. Some authors, indeed, have comprehended under the title *factory*, all extensive establishments wherein a number of people cooperate towards a common purpose of art; and would therefore rank breweries, distilleries, as well as the workshops of carpenters, turners, coopers, &c., under the factory system. But I conceive that this title, in its strictest sense, involves the idea of a vast automaton, composed of various mechanical and intellectual organs, acting in uninterrupted concert for the production of a common object, all of them being subordinated to a self-regulated moving force. If the marshalling of human beings in

From "Factory System of Production" in *The Philosophy of Manufactures* by Andrew Ure. London: Charles Knight, 1835.

systematic order for the execution of any technical enterprise were allowed to constitute a factory, this term might embrace every department of civil and military engineering,—a latitude of application quite inadmissible.

In its precise acceptation, the Factory system is of recent origin, and may claim England for its birthplace. The mills for throwing silk, or making organizine, which were mounted centuries ago in several of the Italian states, and furtively transferred to this country by Sir Thomas Lombe in 1718, contained indeed certain elements of a factory, and probably suggested some hints of those grander and more complex combinations of self-acting machines, which were first embodied half a century later in our cotton manufacture by Richard Arkwright, assisted by gentlemen of Derby, well acquainted with its celebrated silk establishment. But the spinning of an entangled flock of fibres into a smooth thread, which constitutes the main operation with cotton, is in silk superfluous; being already performed by the unerring instinct of a worm, which leaves to human art the simple task of doubling and twisting its regular filaments. The apparatus requisite for this purpose is more elementary, and calls for few of those gradations of machinery which are needed in the carding, drawing, roving, and spinning processes of a cotton-mill.

. . .

In my recent tour, continued during several months, through the manufacturing districts, I have seen tens of thousands of old, young, and middle-aged of both sexes, many of them too feeble to get their daily bread by any of the former modes of industry, earning abundant food, raiment, and domestic accommodation, without perspiring at a single pore, screened meanwhile from the summer's sun and the winter's frost, in apartments more airy and salubrious than those of the metropolis in which our legislative and fashionable aristocracies assemble.

In those spacious halls the benignant power of steam summons around him his myriads of willing menials, and assigns to each the regulated task, substituting for painful muscular effort on their part, the energies of his own gigantic arm, and demanding in return only attention and dexterity to correct such little aberrations as casually occur in his workmanship. The gentle docility of this moving force qualifies it for impelling the tiny bobbins of the lace-machine with a precision and speed inimitable by the most dexterous hands, directed by the sharpest eyes. Hence, under its auspices, and in obedience to Arkwright's polity, magnificent edifices, surpassing far in number, value, usefulness, and ingenuity of construction, the boasted monuments of Asiatic, Egyptian, and Roman despotism, have, within the short period of fifty years, risen up in this kingdom, to show to what extent capital, industry, and science may augment the resources of a state, while they meliorate the condition of its citizens. Such is the factory system, replete with prodigies in mechanics and political economy, which promises in its future growth to become the great minister of civilization to the terraqueous globe, enabling this country, as its heart, to diffuse along with its commerce the life-blood of science and religion to myriads of people still lying "in the region and shadow of death."

When Adam Smith wrote his immortal elements of economics, automatic machinery being hardly known, he was properly led to regard the division of labor as the grand principle of manufacturing improvement; and he showed, in the example of pin-making, how each handicraftsman, being thereby enabled to perfect himself by practice in one point, became a quicker and cheaper workman. In each branch of manufacture he saw that some parts were, on that principle, of easy execution, like the cutting of pin wires into uniform lengths, and some were comparatively difficult, like the formation and fixation of their heads; and therefore he concluded that to each a workman of appropriate value and cost was naturally assigned. This appropriation forms the very essence of the division of labour, and has been constantly made since the origin of society. The ploughman, with powerful hand and skilful eye, has been always hired at high wages to form the furrow, and the ploughboy at low wages, to lead the team. But what was in Dr. Smith's time a topic of useful illustration, cannot now be used without risk of misleading the public mind as to the right principle of manufacturing industry. In fact, the division, or rather adaptation of labour to the different talents of men, is little thought of in factory employment. On the contrary, wherever a process requires peculiar dexterity and steadiness of hand, it is withdrawn as soon as possible from the *cunning* workman, who is prone to irregularities of many kinds, and it is placed in charge of a peculiar mechanism, so self-regulating, that a child may superintend it. . . .

Mr. Anthony Strutt, who conducts the mechanical department of the great cotton factories of Belper and Milford, has so thoroughly departed from the old routine of the schools, that he will employ no man who has learned his craft by regular apprenticeship; but in contempt, as it were, of the division of labour principle, he sets a ploughboy to turn a shaft of perhaps several tons weight, and never has reason to repent his preference, because he infuses into the turning apparatus a precision of action, equal, if not superior, to the skill of the most experienced journeyman.

An eminent mechanician in Manchester told me, that he does not choose to make any steam engines at present, because, with his existing means, he would need to resort to the old principle of the division of labour, so fruitful of jealousies and strikes among workmen; but he intends to prosecute that branch of business whenever he has prepared suitable arrangements on the equalization of labour, or automatic plan. On the graduation system, a man must serve an apprenticeship of many years before his hand and eye become skilled enough for certain mechanical feats; but on the system of decomposing a process into its constituents, and embodying each part in an automatic machine, a person of common care and capacity may be intrusted with any of the said elementary parts after a short probation, and may be transferred from one to another, on any emergency, at the discretion of the master. Such translations are utterly at variance with the old practice of the division of labour, which fixed one man to shaping the head of a pin, and another to sharpening its point, with most irksome and spirit-wasting uniformity, for a whole life. . . .

It is, in fact, the constant aim and tendency of every improvement in machinery to supersede human labour altogether, or to diminish its cost, by substituting the industry of women and children for that of men; or that of ordinary labourers for trained artisans. In most of the water-twist, or throstle cotton-mills, the spinning is entirely managed by females of sixteen years and upwards. The effect of substituting the self-acting mule for the common mule, is to discharge the greater part of the men spinners, and to retain adolescents and children. The proprietor of a factory near Stockport states, in evidence to the commissioners, that, by such substitution, he would save 50*l.* a week in wages, in consequence of dispensing with nearly forty male spinners, at about 25*s.* of wages each. This tendency to employ merely children with watchful eyes and nimble fingers, instead of journeymen of long experience, shows how the scholastic dogma of the division of labour into degrees of skill has been exploded by our enlightened manufacturers.

THE SADLER REPORT OF THE HOUSE OF COMMONS

Although children were among the ideal workers in the factories of the Industrial Revolution, according to Andrew Ure and many owners, their exploitation increasingly became a concern of the British Parliament. One important parliamentary investigation, chaired by Michael Sadler, took

From *The Sadler Report, Report from the Committee on the Bill to Regulate the Labour of Children in the Mills and Factories of the United Kingdom*. London: The House of Commons, 1832.

volumes of testimony from child workers and older people who had worked as children in the mines and factories. The following is only a brief, representative sample of the testimony gathered in the Sadler Report. The Report led to child-labor reform in the Factory Act of 1833.

How does Matthew Crabtree's experience of the factory compare with Andrew Ure's? What seem to be the causes of Crabtree's distress? How could it be alleviated?

FRIDAY, 18 MAY, 1832—MICHAEL THOMAS SADLER, ESQUIRE, IN THE CHAIR

Mr. Matthew Crabtree, *called in; and Examined.*

What age are you?—Twenty-two.

What is your occupation?—A blanket manufacturer.

Have you ever been employed in a factory?—Yes.

At what age did you first go to work in one?—Eight.

How long did you continue in that occupation?—Four years.

Will you state the hours of labour at the period when you first went to the factory, in ordinary times?—From 6 in the morning to 8 at night.

Fourteen hours?—Yes.

With what intervals for refreshment and rest?—An hour at noon.

Then you had no resting time allowed in which to take your breakfast, or what is in Yorkshire called your "drinking"?—No.

When trade was brisk what were your hours?—From 5 in the morning to 9 in the evening.

Sixteen hours?—Yes.

With what intervals at dinner?—An hour.

How far did you live from the mill?—About two miles.

Was there any time allowed for you to get your breakfast in the mill?—No.

Did you take it before you left your home?—Generally.

During those long hours of labour could you be punctual; how did you awake?—I seldom did awake spontaneously; I was most generally awoke or lifted out of bed, sometimes asleep, by my parents.

Were you always in time?—No.

What was the consequence if you had been too late?—I was most commonly beaten.

Severely?—Very severely, I thought.

In whose factory was this?—Messrs. Hague & Cook's, of Dewsbury.

Will you state the effect that those long hours had upon the state of your health and feelings?—I was, when working those long hours, commonly very much fatigued at night, when I left my work; so much so that I sometimes should have slept as I walked if I had not stumbled and started awake again; and so sick often that I could not eat, and what I did eat I vomited.

Did this labour destroy your appetite?—It did.

In what situation were you in that mill?—I was a piecener.

Will you state to this Committee whether piecening is a very laborious employment for children, or not?—It is a very laborious employment. Pieceners are continually running to and fro, and on their feet the whole day.

The duty of the piecener is to take the cardings from one part of the machinery, and to place them on another?—Yes.

So that the labour is not only continual, but it is unabated to the last?—It is unabated to the last.

Do you not think, from your own experience, that the speed of the machinery is so calculated as to demand the utmost exertions of a child supposing the hours were moderate?—It is as much as they could do at the best; they are always upon the stretch, and it is commonly very difficult to keep up with their work.

State the condition of the children toward the latter part of the day, who have thus to keep up with the machinery.—It is as much as they can do when they are not very much fatigued to keep up with their work, and toward the close of the day, when they come to be more fatigued, they cannot keep up with it very well, and the consequence is that they are beaten to spur them on.

Were you beaten under those circumstances?—Yes.

Frequently?—Very frequently.

And principally at the latter end of the day?—Yes.

And is it your belief that if you had not been so beaten, you should not have got through the work?—I should not if I had not been kept up to it by some means.

Does beating then principally occur at the latter end of the day, when the children are exceedingly fatigued?—It does at the latter end of the day, and in the morning sometimes, when they are very drowsy, and have not got rid of the fatigue of the day before.

What were you beaten with principally?—A strap.

Anything else?—Yes, a stick sometimes; and there is a kind of roller which runs on the top of the machine called a billy, perhaps two or three yards in length, and perhaps an inch and a half, or more in diameter; the circumference would be four or five inches; I cannot speak exactly.

Were you beaten with that instrument?—Yes.

Have you yourself been beaten, and have you seen other children struck severely with that roller?—I have been struck very severely with it myself, so much so as to knock me down, and I have seen other children have their heads broken with it.

You think that it is a general practice to beat the children with the roller?—It is.

You do not think then that you were worse treated than other children in the mill?—No, I was not, perhaps not so bad as some were.

In those mills is chastisement towards the latter part of the day going on perpetually?—Perpetually.

So that you can hardly be in a mill without hearing constant crying?—Never an hour, I believe.

Do you think that if the overlooker were naturally a humane person it would be still found necessary for him to beat the children, in order to keep up their attention and vigilance at the termination of those extraordinary days of labour?—Yes, the machine turns off a regular quantity of cardings, and of course they must keep as regularly to their work the whole of the day; they must keep with the machine, and therefore however humane the slubber may be, as he must keep up with the machine or be found fault with, he spurs the children to keep up also by various means but that which he commonly resorts to is to strap them when they become drowsy.

At the time when you were beaten for not keeping up with your work, were you anxious to have done it if you possibly could?—Yes; the dread of being beaten if we could not keep up with our work was a sufficient impulse to keep us to it if we could.

When you got home at night after this labour, did you feel much fatigued?—Very much so.

Had you any time to be with your parents, and to receive instruction from them?—No.

What did you do?—All that we did when we got home was to get the little bit of supper that was provided for us and go to bed immediately. If the supper had not been ready directly, we should have gone to sleep while it was preparing.

Did you not, as a child, feel it a very grievous hardship to be roused so soon in the morning?—I did.

Were the rest of the children similarly circumstanced?—Yes, all of them; but they were not all of them so far from their work as I was.

And if you had been too late you were under the apprehension of being cruelly beaten?—I generally was beaten when I happened to be too late; and when I got up in the morning the apprehension of that was so great, that I used to run, and cry all the way as I went to the mill.

That was the way by which your punctual attendance was secured?—Yes.

And you do not think it could have been secured by any other means?—No.

Then it is your impression from what you have seen, and from your own experience, that those long hours of labour have the effect of rendering young persons who are subject to them exceedingly unhappy?—Yes.

You have already said it had a considerable effect upon your health?—Yes.

Do you conceive that it diminished your growth?—I did not pay much attention to that; but I have been examined by some persons who said they thought I was rather stunted, and that I should have been taller if I had not worked at the mill.

What were your wages at that time?—Three shillings (per week).

And how much a day had you for overwork when you were worked so exeedingly long?—A halfpenny a day.

Did you frequently forfeit that if you were not always there to a moment?—Yes; I most frequently forfeited what was allowed for those long hours.

You took your food to the mill; was it in your mill, as is the case in cotton mills, much spoiled by being laid aside?—It was very frequently covered by flues from the wool; and in that case they had to be blown off with the mouth, and picked off with the fingers before it could be eaten.

So that not giving you a little leisure for eating your food, but obliging you to take it at the mill, spoiled your food when you did get it?—Yes, very commonly.

And that at the same time that this overlabour injured your appetite?—Yes.

Could you eat when you got home?—Not always.

What is the effect of this piecening upon the hands?—It makes them bleed; the skin is completely rubbed off, and in that case they bleed in perhaps a dozen parts.

The prominent parts of the hand?—Yes, all the prominent parts of the hand are rubbed down till they bleed; every day they are rubbed in that way.

All the time you continue at work?—All the time we are working. The hands never can be hardened in that work, for the grease keeps them soft in the first instance, and long and continual rubbing is always wearing them down, so that if they were hard they would be sure to bleed.

It is attended with much pain?—Very much.

Do they allow you to make use of the back of the hand?—No; the work cannot be so well done with the back of the hand, or I should have made use of that.

7. Free Trade Empires

THE IMPERIALISM OF
FREE TRADE

JOHN GALLAGHER AND
RONALD ROBINSON

The period from 1840 to 1880 in Britain (the mid-Victorian period) was one in which the doctrine of "free trade" was very popular. Groups like the "Manchester school" and economic liberals (influenced by Adam Smith) advocated "free trade" as against tariffs, protection, and political empire. That fact has led many historians to interpret British policy in this period as anti-imperialist.

Nonsense, say these modern authors. The British did not oppose empire in this period. They just did not want to own one. They believed that Britain could dominate the rest of the world, without having to pay for the occupation and administration of colonies, through free trade. If Britain could convince the weak governments of Asia, Africa, and South America to eliminate trade barriers, the superiority of British industry would bring Britain cheaper "informal empire." How do Robinson and Gallagher support this argument? Are you convinced?

It ought to be a commonplace that Great Britain during the nineteenth century expanded overseas by means of "informal empire" as much as by acquiring dominion in the strict constitutional sense. For purposes of economic analysis it would clearly be unreal to define imperial history exclusively as the history of those colonies coloured red on the map. Nevertheless, almost all imperial history has been written on the assumption that the empire of formal dominion is historically comprehensible in itself and can be cut out of its context in British expansion and world politics. The conventional interpretation of the nineteenth-century empire continues to rest upon study of the formal empire alone, which is rather like judging the size and character of icebergs solely from the parts above the water-line.

The most striking fact about British history in the nineteenth century, as Seeley pointed out, is that it is the history of an expanding society. The exports of capital and manufacturers, the migration of citizens, the

From "The Imperialism of Free Trade" by John Gallagher and Ronald Robinson, in *The Economic Review* (August 1953), 2d Series, VI, No. 1.

dissemination of the English language, ideas and constitutional forms, were all of them radiations of the social energies of the British peoples. Between 1812 and 1914 over twenty million persons emigrated from the British Isles, and nearly 70 per cent of them went outside the Empire. Between 1815 and 1880, it is estimated, £1,187,000,000 in credit had accumulated abroad, but no more than one-sixth was placed in the formal empire. Even by 1913, something less than half of the £3,975,000,000 of foreign investment lay inside the Empire. Similarly, in no year of the century did the Empire buy much more than one-third of Britain's exports. The basic fact is that British industrialization caused an ever-extending and intensifying development of overseas regions. Whether they were formally British or not, was a secondary consideration.

As the British industrial revolution grew, so new markets and sources of supply were linked to it at different times, and the degree of imperialist action accompanying that process varied accordingly. Thus mercantilist techniques of formal empire were being employed to develop India in the mid-Victorian age at the same time as informal techniques of free trade were being used in Latin America for the same purpose. It is for this reason that attempts to make phases of imperialism correspond directly to phases in the economic growth of the metropolitan economy are likely to prove in vain. The fundamental continuity of British expansion is only obscured by arguing that changes in the terms of trade or in the character of British exports necessitated a sharp change in the process.

From this vantage point the many-sided expansion of British industrial society can be viewed as a whole of which both the formal and informal empires are only parts. Both of them then appear as variable political functions of the extending pattern of overseas trade, investment, migration and culture. If this is accepted, it follows that formal and informal empires are essentially interconnected and to some extent interchangeable. Then not only is the old, legalistic, narrow idea of empire unsatisfactory, but so is the old idea of informal empire as a separate, non-political category of expansion. A concept of informal empire which fails to bring out the underlying unity between it and the formal empire is sterile. Only within the total framework of expansion is nineteenth-century empire intelligible.

Let us now attempt, tentatively, to use the concept of the totality of British expansion described above to restate the main themes of the history of modern British expansion. We have seen that interpretations of this process fall into contradictions when based upon formal political criteria alone. If expansion both formal and informal is examined as a single process, will these contradictions disappear?

The growth of British industry made new demands upon British policy. It necessitated linking undeveloped areas with British foreign trade and, in so doing, moved the political arm to force an entry into markets closed by the power of foreign monopolies.

British policy . . . was active in this way before the American colonies had been lost, but its greatest opportunities came during the Napoleonic Wars. The seizure of the French and Spanish West Indies, the filibustering expedition to Buenos Aires in 1806, the taking of Java in 1811, were all efforts to break into new regions and to tap new resources by means of political action. But the policy went further than simple house-breaking, for once the door was opened and British imports with their political implications were pouring in, they might stop the door from being shut again. Raffles,* for example, temporarily broke the Dutch monopoly of the spice trade in Java and opened the island to free trade. Later, he began the informal British paramountcy over the Malacca trade routes and the Malay peninsula by founding Singapore. In South America, at the same time, British policy was aiming at indirect political hegemony over new regions for the purposes of trade. The British navy carried the Portuguese royal family to Brazil after the breach with Napoleon, and the British representative there extorted from his grateful clients the trade treaty of 1810 which left British imports paying a lower tariff than the goods of the mother country. The thoughtful stipulation was added "that the Present Treaty shall be unlimited in point of duration, and that the obligations and conditions expressed or implied in it shall be perpetual and immutable.". . .

In both the formal and informal dependencies in the mid-Victorian age there was much effort to open the continental interiors and to extend the British influence inland from the ports and to develop the hinterlands. The general strategy of this development was to convert these areas into complementary satellite economies, which would provide raw materials and food for Great Britain, and also provide widening markets for its manufactures. This was the period, the orthodox interpretation would have us believe, in which the political arm of expansion was dormant or even withered. In fact, that alleged inactivity is seen to be a delusion if we take into account the development in the informal aspect. Once entry had been forced into Latin America, China and the Balkans, the task was to encourage stable governments as good investment risks, just as in weaker or unsatisfactory states it was considered necessary to coerce them into more co-operative attitudes.

The types of informal empire and the situations it attempted to exploit were as various as the success which it achieved. Although commercial and capital penetration tended to lead to political co-operation and hegemony, there are striking exceptions. In the United

---

* Sir Thomas Stamford Bingley Raffles (1781–1826), an administrator of the British East India Company.—Ed.

States, for example, British business turned the cotton South into a colonial economy, and the British investor hoped to do the same with the Mid-West. But the political strength of the country stood in his way. It was impossible to stop American industrialization, and the industrialized sections successfully campaigned for tariffs, despite the opposition of those sections which depended on the British trade connexion. In the same way, American political strength thwarted British attempts to establish Texas, Mexico and Central America as informal dependencies.

Conversely, British expansion sometimes failed, if it gained political supremacy without effecting a successful commercial penetration. There were spectacular exertions of British policy in China, but they did little to produce new customers. Britain's political hold upon China failed to break down Chinese economic self-sufficiency. The Opium War of 1840, the renewal of war in 1857, widened the inlets for British trade but they did not get Chinese exports moving. Their main effect was an unfortunate one from the British point of view, for such foreign pressures put Chinese society under great strains as the Taiping Rebellion unmistakably showed. It is important to note that this weakness was regarded in London as an embarrassment, and not as a lever for extracting further concessions. In fact, the British worked to prop up the tottering Pekin regime, for as Lord Clarendon put it in 1870, "British interests in China are strictly commercial, or at all events only so far political as they may be for the protection of commerce." The value of this self-denial became clear in the following decades when the Pekin government, threatened with a scramble for China, leaned more and more on the diplomatic support of the honest British broker.

The simple recital of these cases of economic expansion, aided and abetted by political action in one form or other, is enough to expose the inadequacy of the conventional theory that free trade could dispense with empire. We have seen that it did not do so. Economic expansion in the mid-Victorian age was matched by a corresponding political expansion which has been overlooked because it could not be seen by that study of maps which, it has been said, drives sane men mad. It is absurd to deduce from the harmony between London and the colonies of white settlement in the mid-Victorian age any British reluctance to intervene in the fields of British interests. The warships at Canton are as much a part of the period as responsible government for Canada; the battlefields of the Punjab are as real as the abolition of suttee.

Far from being an era of "indifference," the mid-Victorian years were the decisive stage in the history of British expansion overseas, in that the combination of commercial penetration and political influence allowed the United Kingdom to command those economies which could be made to fit best into her own. A variety of techniques adapted to diverse conditions and beginning at different dates were employed to effect this domination. A paramountcy was set up in Malaya centred on Singapore;

a suzerainty over much of West Africa reached out from the port of Lagos and was backed up by the African squadron. On the east coast of Africa British influence at Zanzibar, dominant thanks to the exertions of Consul Kirk, placed the heritage of Arab command on the mainland at British disposal.

But perhaps the most common political technique of British expansion was the treaty of free trade and friendship made with or imposed upon a weaker state. The treaties with Persia of 1836 and 1857, the Turkish treaties of 1838 and 1861, the Japanese treaty of 1858, the favours extracted from Zanzibar, Siam and Morocco, the hundreds of anti-slavery treaties signed with crosses by African chiefs—all these treaties enabled the British government to carry forward trade with these regions.

BRITISH RULE IN INDIA

JAWAHARLAL NEHRU

British rule in India was an example of how what began as "informal" commercial administration (that of the East India Company) became increasingly a matter of formal, government policy. Finally the shock of the Indian mutiny in 1857 forced the government to take over officially.

Jawaharlal Nehru was a leader in the Indian struggle for independence and became India's first prime minister. The Discovery of India, from which this selection was taken, was written from prison in 1946, the year before Indian independence. This is obviously a work written in the heat of the struggle. That gives it a directness and clarity but also an uncompromising sharpness. Do you find it convincing, or overstated? Can you explain why?

Looking back over (the 18th century), it almost seems that the British succeeded in dominating India by a succession of fortuitous circumstances and lucky flukes. With remarkably little effort, considering the glittering prize, they won a great empire and enormous wealth which helped to make them the leading power in the world. It seems easy for a slight turn in events to have taken place which would have dashed their hopes and ended their ambitions. They were defeated on many occasions—by Haider Ali and Tipu, by the Marathas, by the Sikhs and by the Gurkhas. A little less of good fortune and they might have lost their

From *The Discovery of India* by Jawaharlal Nehru. New York: John Day Company, 1941.

foothold in India, or at the most, held on to certain coastal territories only.

And yet a closer scrutiny reveals, in the circumstances then existing, a certain inevitability in what happened. Good fortune there certainly was, but there must be an ability to profit by good fortune.

India was then exporting her manufactured products to Europe and other countries. Her banking system was efficient and well organized throughout the country, and the hundis or bills of exchange issued by the great business or financial houses were honored everywhere in India, as well as in Iran, and Kabul and Herat and Tashkent and other places in central Asia. Merchant capital had evolved, and there was an elaborate network of agents, jobbers, brokers, and middlemen. The shipbuilding industry was flourishing; one of the flagships of an English admiral during the Napoleonic wars had been built by an Indian firm in India. India was, in fact, as advanced industrially, commercially, and financially as any country prior to the Industrial Revolution. No such development could have taken place unless the country had enjoyed long periods of stable and peaceful government and the highways were safe for traffic and trade.

Foreign adventurers originally came to India because of the excellence of her manufacturers, which had a big market in Europe. The chief business of the British East India Company in its early days was to trade with Indian goods in Europe, and very profitable trading it was, yielding enormous dividends. So efficient and highly organized were Indian methods of production, and such was the skill of India's artisans and craftsmen, that they could compete successfully even with the higher techniques of production which were being established in England. When the big machine age began in England, Indian goods continued to pour in and had to be stopped by very heavy duties, and in some cases by outright prohibition.

Clive described Murshidabad in Bengal in 1757, the very year of Plassey,* as a city "as extensive, populous, and rich as the city of London, with this difference that there are individuals in the first possessing infinitely greater property than in the last." The city of Dacca in eastern Bengal was famous for its fine muslins. These two cities, important as they were, were near the periphery of Hindustan. All over the vast land there were greater cities and large numbers of big manufacturing and trading centers, and a very rapid and ingenious system of communicating news and market prices had been evolved. The great business houses often received news, even of the wars that were going on, long before dispatches reached the officials of the East India Company. The economy of India had thus advanced to as high a stage as it could reach prior

---

* Robert Clive gained control of the West Bengal state of Plassey in 1757, thus clearing the way for British rule in north India.—Ed.

to the Industrial Revolution. Whether it had the seeds of further progress in it or was too much bound up with the rigid social structure, it is difficult to say. It seems quite possible, however, that under normal conditions it would have undergone that change and begun to adapt itself, in its own way, to the new industrial conditions. And yet, though it was ripe for a change, that change itself required a revolution within its own framework. Perhaps some catalytic agent was necessary to bring about that change. It is clear that howsoever highly organized and developed its preindustrial economy was, it could not compete for long with the products of industrialized countries. It had to industrialize itself or submit to foreign economic penetration, which would have led to political interferences. As it happened, foreign political domination came first and this led to a rapid destruction of the economy she had built up, without anything positive or constructive taking its place. The East India Company represented both British political power and British vested interests and economic power. It was supreme, and being a company of merchants, it was intent on making money. Just when it was making money with amazing rapidity and in fantastic quantities, Adam Smith wrote about it in *The Wealth of Nations* in 1776: "The government of an exclusive company of merchants is perhaps the worst of all governments for any country whatever."

Though the Indian merchant and manufacturing classes were rich and spread out all over the country, and even controlled the economic structure, they had no political power. Government was despotic and still largely feudal. In fact, it was probably more feudal than it had been at some previous stages of Indian history. Hence there was no middle class strong enough to seize power, or even consciously of thinking of doing so, as in some Western countries. The people generally had grown apathetic and servile. There was thus a gap which had to be filled before any revolutionary change could take place. Perhaps this gap had been produced by the static nature of Indian society which refused to change in a changing world, for every civilization which resists change declines. That society, as constituted, had no more creative part to play. A change was overdue.

The British, at that time, were politically much more advanced. They had had their political revolution and had established the power of Parliament over that of the king. Their middle classes, conscious of their new power, were full of the impulse to expand. That vitality and energy, proof of a growing and progressive society, are indeed very evident in England. They show themselves in many ways, and most of all in the inventions and discoveries which heralded the Industrial Revolution.

The chief business of the East India Company in its early period, the very object for which it was started, was to carry Indian manufactured goods—textiles, etc., as well as spices and the like—from the East to Europe, where there was a great demand for these articles. With the developments in industrial techniques in England a new class of industrial capitalists rose there demanding a change in this policy. The British market was to be closed to Indian products and the Indian market opened to British manufacturers. The British parliament, influenced by this new class, began to take a greater interest in India and the working of the East India Company. To begin with, Indian goods were excluded from Britain by legislation, and as the company held a monopoly in the Indian export business, this exclusion influenced other foreign markets also. This was followed by vigorous attempts to restrict and crush Indian manufactures by various measures and internal duties which prevented the flow of Indian goods within the country itself. British goods meanwhile had free entry. The Indian textile industry collapsed, affecting vast numbers of weavers and artisans. The process was rapid in Bengal and Bihar; elsewhere it spread gradually with the expansion of British rule and the building of railways. It continued through the nineteenth century, breaking up other old industries also, shipbuilding, metalwork, glass, paper, and many crafts.

To some extent this was inevitable as the older manufacturing came into conflict with the new industrial technique. But it was hastened by political and economic pressure, and no attempt was made to apply the new techniques to India. Indeed every attempt was made to prevent this happening, and thus the growth of the new industry prevented. Machinery could not be imported into India. A vacuum was created in India which could only be filled by British goods, and which also led to rapidly increasing unemployment and poverty. The classic type of modern colonial economy was built up, India becoming an agricultural colony of industrial England, supplying raw materials and providing markets for England's industrial goods.

The liquidation of the artisan class led to unemployment on a prodigious scale. What were all these scores of millions, who had so far been engaged in industry and manufacture, to do now? Where were they to go? Their old profession was no longer open to them; the way to a new one was barred. They could die of course; that way of escape from an intolerable situation is always open. They did die in tens of millions. The English governor-general of India, Lord Bentinck, reported in 1834 that "the misery hardly finds a parallel in the history of commerce. The bones of the cotton-weavers are bleaching the plains of India."

But still vast numbers of them remained, and these increased from year to year as British policy affected remoter areas of the country and created more unemployment. All these hordes of artisans and craftsmen had no jobs, no work, and all their ancient skill was useless. They drifted to the land, for the land was still there. But the land was fully occupied and could not possibly absorb them profitably. So they became a burden on the land and the burden grew, and with it grew the poverty of the country, and the standard of living fell to incredibly low levels. This compulsory back-to-the-land movement of artisans and craftsmen led to an ever-growing disproportion between agriculture and industry; agriculture became more and more the sole business of the people because of the lack of occupations and wealth-producing activities.

India became progressively ruralized. In every progressive country there has been, during the past century, a shift of population from agriculture to industry; from village to town; in India this process was reversed, as a result of British policy. The figures are instructive and significant. In the middle of the nineteenth century about 55 per cent of the population is said to have been dependent on agriculture; recently this proportion was estimated to be 74 per cent. This is a prewar figure. Though there has been greater industrial employment during the war, those dependent on agriculture actually went up in the census of 1941, owing to increase of population. The growth of a few large cities (chiefly at the expense of the smaller towns) is apt to mislead the superficial observer and give him a false idea of Indian conditions.

This, then, is the real, the fundamental cause of the appalling poverty of the Indian people, and it is of comparatively recent origin. Other causes that contribute to it are themselves the result of this poverty and chronic starvation and undernourishment—like diseases and illiteracy. Excessive population is unfortunate and steps should be taken to curb it wherever necessary; but the density in India still compares favorably with that of many industrialized countries. It is only excessive for a predominantly agricultural community, and under a proper economic system the entire population can be made productive and should add to the wealth of the country. As a matter of fact, great density of population exists only in special areas, like Bengal and the Gangetic valley, and vast areas are still sparsely populated. It is worth remembering that Great Britain is more than twice as densely populated as India.

• • •

Then there was the Indian Army, consisting of British and Indian troops but officered entirely by Englishmen. This was reorganized repeatedly, especially after the mutiny of 1857, and ultimately became organizationally linked up with the British Army. This was so arranged as to balance its different elements and keep the British troops in key positions. "Next to the grand counterpoise of a sufficient European force, comes the counterpoise of natives against natives," says the official report on reorganization in 1858. The primary function of these forces was to serve as an army of occupation—"Internal Security Troops" they were called, and a majority of these were British. The Frontier Province served as a training ground for the British Army at India's expense. The field army (chiefly Indian) was meant for service abroad and it took part in numerous British imperial wars and expeditions, India always bearing the cost. Steps were taken to segregate Indian troops from the rest of the population.

Thus India had to bear the cost of her own conquest, and then of her transfer (or sale) from the East India Company to the British crown, and for the extension of the British empire to Burma and elsewhere, and expeditions to Africa, Persia, etc., and for her defense against Indians themselves. She was not only used as a base for imperial purposes, without any reimbursement for this, but she had further to pay for the training of part of the British Army in England—"capitation" charges these were called. Indeed India was charged for all manner of other expenses incurred by Britain, such as the maintenance of British diplomatic and consular establishments in China and Persia, the entire cost of the telegraph line from England to India, part of the expenses of the British Mediterranean fleet, and even the receptions given to the sultan of Turkey in London.

The building of railways in India, undoubtedly desirable and necessary, was done in an enormously wasteful way. The government of India guaranteed 5 per cent interest on all capital invested, and there was no need to check or estimate what was necessary. All purchases were made in England.

The civil establishment of government was also run on a lavish and extravagant scale, all the highly paid positions being reserved for Europeans. The process of indianization of the administrative machine was very slow and only became noticeable in the twentieth century. This process, far from transferring any power to Indian hands, proved yet another method of strengthening British rule. The really key positions remained in British hands, and Indians in the administration could only function as the agents of British rule.

To all these methods must be added the deliberate policy, pursued throughout the period of British rule, of creating divisions among Indians, of encouraging one group at the cost of the other. This policy was openly admitted in the early days of their rule, and indeed it was a natural one for an imperial power. With the growth of the nationalist movement, that policy took subtler and more dangerous forms, and though denied, functioned more intensively than ever.

Nearly all our major problems today have grown up during British rule and as a direct result of British policy: the princes; the minority problem; various vested interests, foreign and Indian; the lack of industry and the neglect of agriculture; the extreme backwardness in the social services; and, above all, the tragic poverty of the people. . . .

The modern type of finance imperialism added new kinds of economic exploitation which were unknown in earlier ages. The record of British rule in India during the nineteenth century must necessarily depress and anger an Indian, and yet it illustrates the superiority of the

British in many fields, not least in their capacity to profit by our disunity and weaknesses. A people who are weak and who are left behind in the march of time invite trouble and ultimately have only themselves to blame. If British imperialism with all its consequences was, in the circumstances, to be expected in the natural order of events, so also was the growth of opposition to it inevitable, and the final crisis between the two.

THE LETTER OF COMMISSIONER LIN TO QUEEN VICTORIA

One of the darkest hours of European commercial imperialism was the British insistence that the Chinese open their ports to the trade of British opium, harvested and shipped from British India. The Chinese Emperor sent Lin Tse-hsu, a distinguished scholar-official who had already proved his ability to halt opium smuggling in his area of jurisdiction, and two other officials to the port of Canton in 1839 to deal with British demands. In the following letter to Queen Victoria, Commissioner Lin and his colleagues tried to explain the reasons for the Chinese ban on opium importation. What reasons do they give? Do you find them convincing? What do you think was the response of the queen and her government?

Lin, high imperial commissioner, a president of the Board of War, viceroy of the two Keäng provinces, &c., Tang, a president of the Board of War, viceroy of the two Kwang provinces, &c., and E, a vice-president of the Board of War, lieut.-governor of Kwangtung, &c., hereby conjointly address this public dispatch to the queen of England for the purpose of giving her clear and distinct information (on the state of affairs) &c.

It is only our high and mighty emperor, who alike supports and cherishes those of the Inner Land, and those from beyond the seas— who looks upon all mankind with equal benevolence—who, if a source of profit exists anywhere, diffuses it over the whole world—who, if the tree of evil takes root anywhere, plucks it up for the benefit of all nations:— who, in a word, hath implanted in his breast that heart (by which beneficent nature herself) governs the heavens and the earth! You, the

From *Modern Asia and Africa,* edited by William H. McNeill and Mitsuko Iriye. Copyright © 1971 by Oxford University Press, Inc. Reprinted by permission.

queen of your honorable nation, sit upon a throne occupied through successive generations by predecessors, all of whom have been styled respectful and obedient. Looking over the public documents accompanying the tribute sent (by your predecessors) on various occasions, we find the following—"All the people of my (i.e. the king of England's) country, arriving at the Central Land for purposes of trade, have to feel grateful to the great emperor for the most perfect justice, for the kindest treatment," and other words to that effect. Delighted did we feel that the kings of your honorable nation so clearly understood the great principles of propriety, and were so deeply grateful for the heavenly goodness (of our emperor):—therefore, it was that we of the heavenly dynasty nourished and cherished your people from afar, and bestowed upon them redoubled proofs of our urbanity and kindness. It is merely from these circumstances, that your country—deriving immense advantage from its commercial intercourse with us, which has endured now two hundred years—has become the rich and flourishing kingdom that it is said to be!

But, during the commercial intercourse which has existed so long, among the numerous foreign merchants resorting hither, are wheat and tares, good and bad; and of these latter are some, who, by means of introducing opium by stealth, have seduced our Chinese people, and caused every province of the land to overflow with that poison. These then know merely to advantage themselves, they care not about injuring others! This is a principle which heaven's Providence repugnates; and which mankind conjointly look upon with abhorrence! Moreover, the great emperor hearing of it, actually quivered with indignation, and especially dispatched me, the commissioner, to Canton, that in conjunction with the viceroy and lieut.-governor of the province, means might be taken for its suppression!

Every native of the Inner Land who sells opium, as also all who smoke it, are alike adjudged to death. Were we then to go back and take up the crimes of the foreigners, who, by selling it for many years have induced dreadful calamity and robbed us of enormous wealth, and punish them with equal severity, our laws could not but award to them absolute annihilation! But, considering that these said foreigners did yet repent of their crime, and with a sincere heart beg for mercy; that they took 20,283 chests of opium piled up in their store-ships, and through Elliot, the superintendent of the trade of your said country, petitioned that they might be delivered up to us, when the same were all utterly destroyed, of which we, the imperial commissioner and colleagues, made a duly prepared memorial to his majesty;—considering these circumstances, we have happily received a fresh proof of the extraordinary goodness of the great emperor, inasmuch as he who voluntarily comes forward, may yet be deemed a fit subject for mercy, and his crimes be graciously remitted him. But as for him who again knowingly violates the laws, difficult indeed will it be thus to go on repeatedly pardoning! He or they shall alike be doomed to the penalties of the new statute. We presume that you, the sovereign of your honorable nation, on pouring out your heart before the altar of eternal justice, cannot but command all foreigners with the deepest respect to reverence our laws! If we only lay clearly before your eyes, what is profitable and what is destructive, you will then know that the statutes of the heavenly dynasty cannot but be obeyed with fear and trembling!

We find that your country is distant from us about sixty or seventy thousand miles, that your foreign ships come hither striving the one with the other from our trade, and for the simple reason of their strong desire to reap a profit. Now, out of the wealth of our Inner Land, if we take a part to bestow upon foreigners from afar, it follows, that the immense wealth which the said foreigners amass, ought properly speaking to be portion of our own native Chinese people. By what principle of reason then, should these foreigners send in return a poisonous drug, which involves in destruction those very natives of China? Without meaning to say that the foreigners harbor such destructive intentions in their hearts, we yet positively assert that from their inordinate thirst after gain, they are perfectly careless about the injuries they inflict upon us! And such being the case, we should like to ask what has become of that conscience which heaven has implanted in the breasts of all men?

We have heard that in your own country opium is prohibited with the utmost strictness and severity:—this is a strong proof that you know full well how hurtful it is to mankind. Since then you do not permit it to injure your own country, you ought not to have the injurious drug transferred to another country, and above all others, how much less to the Inner Land! Of the products which China exports to your foreign countries, there is not one which is not beneficial to mankind in some shape or other. There are those which serve for food, those which are useful, and those which are calculated for resale;—but all are beneficial. Has China (we should like to ask) ever yet sent forth a noxious article from its soil? Not to speak of our tea and rhubarb, things which your foreign countries could not exist a single day without, if we of the Central Land were to grudge you what is beneficial, and not to compassionate your wants, then wherewithal could you foreigners manage to exist? And further, as regards your woolens, camlets, and longells, were it not that you get supplied with our native raw silk, you could not get these manufactured! If China were to grudge you those things which yield a profit, how could you foreigners scheme after any profit at all? Our other articles of food, such as sugar, ginger, cinnamon, &c., and our other articles for use, such as silk piece-goods, chinaware, &c., are also many necessaries of life to you; how can we reckon up their number! On the other hand, the things that come from your foreign countries are only calculated to make presents of, or serve for mere amusement. It is quite the same to us if we have them, or if we have them not. If these are of no material consequence to us of the Inner Land, what difficulty would there be in prohibiting and shutting our market against them? It is only that our heavenly dynasty most freely permits you to take off her tea, silk, and other commodities, and convey them for consumption everywhere, without the slightest stint or grudge, for no other reason, but that where a profit exists, we wish that it be diffused abroad for the benefit of all the earth!

Your honorable nation takes away the products of our central land, and not only do you thereby obtain food and support for yourselves, but moreover, by re-selling these products to other countries you reap a threefold profit. Now if you would only not sell opium, this threefold profit would be secured to you: how can you possibly consent to forgo it for a drug that is hurtful to men, and an unbridled craving after gain that seems to know no bounds! Let us suppose that foreigners came from another country, and brought opium into England, and seduced the people of your country to smoke it, would not you, the sovereign of the said country, look upon such a procedure with anger, and in your just indignation endeavor to get rid of it? Now we have always heard that your highness possesses a most kind and benevolent heart, surely then you are incapable of doing or causing to be done unto another, that which you should not wish another to do unto you! We have at the same time heard that your ships which come to Canton do each and every of them carry a document granted by your highness' self, on which are written these words "you shall not be permitted to carry contraband goods;" this shows that the laws of your highness are in their origin both distinct and severe, and we can only suppose that because the ships coming here have been very numerous, due attention has not been given to search and examine; and for this reason it is that we now address you this public document, that you may clearly know how stern and severe are the laws of the central dynasty, and most certainly you will cause that they be not again rashly violated!

Moreover, we have heard that in London the metropolis where you dwell, as also in Scotland, Ireland, and other such places, no opium whatever is produced. It is only in sundry parts of your colonial kingdom of Hindostan, such as Bengal, Madras, Bombay, Patna, Malwa, Benares, Malacca, and other places where the very hills are covered with the opium plant, where tanks are made for the preparing of the drug; month by month, and year by year, the volume of the poison increases, its unclean stench ascends upwards, until heaven itself grows angry, and the very gods thereat get indignant! You, the queen of the said honorable nation, ought immediately to have the plant in those parts plucked up by the very root! Cause the land there to be hoed up afresh, sow in its stead the five grains, and if any man dare again to plant in these grounds a single poppy, visit his crime with the most severe punishment. By a truly benevolent system of government such as this, will you indeed reap advantage, and do away with a source of evil. Heaven must support you, and the gods will crown you with felicity! This will get for yourself the blessing of long life, and from this will proceed the security and stability of your descendants!

In reference to the foreign merchants who come to this our central land, the food that they eat, and the dwellings that they abide in, proceed entirely from the goodness of our heavenly dynasty:—the profits which they reap, and the fortunes which they amass, have their origin only in that portion of benefit which our heavenly dynasty kindly allots them: and as these pass but little of their time in your country, and the greater part of their time in our's, it is a generally received maxim of old and of modern times, that we should conjointly admonish, and clearly make known the punishment that awaits them.

Suppose the subject of another country were to come to England to trade, he would certainly be required to comply with the laws of England, then how much more does this apply to us of the celestial empire! Now it is a fixed statute of this empire, that any native Chinese who sells opium is punishable with death, and even he who merely smokes it, must not less die. Pause and reflect for a moment: if you foreigners did not bring the opium hither, where should our Chinese people get it to re-sell? It is you foreigners who involve our simple natives in the pit of death, and are they alone to be permitted to escape alive? If so much as one of those deprive one of our people of his life, he must forfeit his life in requital for that which he has taken:—how much more does this apply to him who by means of opium destroys his fellowmen? Does the havoc which he commits stop with a single life? Therefore it is that those foreigners who now import opium into the Central Land are condemned to be beheaded and strangled by the new statute, and this explains what we said at the beginning about plucking up the tree of evil, wherever it takes root, for the benefit of all nations.

THE AUTOBIOGRAPHY OF YUKICHI FUKUZAWA

Japan learned wisely from the humiliation of China. In order to avoid a similar fate, the Japanese sought to imitate the West, to learn from it

From *The Autobiography of Yukichi Fukuzawa*, translated by Elichi Kiyooka. Copyright © 1966 Columbia University Press. Reprinted by permission.

rather than surrender to it. Within seven years of the arrival of U.S. Commander Perry's "Black Ship" of steam, Japan had opened its ports to foreign trade, signed a "Treaty of Amity and Commerce" with the United States, and sent a ship across the Pacific to San Francisco. Yukichi Fukuzawa (1835–1901) was on that ship in 1860.

Fukuzawa was one of the leading Japanese scholars of Western civilization. His books sold in millions of copies, he established a newspaper to voice his opinions, and he founded a school to train young Japanese. It is now Keio University, one of the finest universities in Japan.

What does the account of Fukuzawa's childhood tell you about life in traditional Japan? How was this changed by Admiral Perry's arrival? What things surprised Fukuzawa about America? What do these surprises tell you about Japan in 1860?

My father, Fukuzawa Hyakusuke, was a samurai belonging to the Okudaira Clan of Nakatsu on the island of Kyūshū. My mother, called O-Jun as her given name, was the eldest daughter of Hashimoto Hamaemon, another samurai of the same clan. In social order, my father was barely high enough to have a formal audience with the lord. He was a few ranks above the common soldier (*ashigaru*), but he was of the lower order among the samurai. In today's society his position would probably correspond to *hanninkan*, the lowest rank of government officials.

My father had been made "securer of the foundation" (*motojimeyaku*), or in other words the overseer of the treasury. Consequently he had to spend much of his time at his lord's storage office and headquarters in the city of Ōsaka.

Therefore all of us children were born in Ōsaka, five in all—first a boy, then three girls, and then myself, the youngest. I was born on the twelfth of December in the fifth year of the Tempō era (according to the modern calendar, January 10, 1835) when my father was forty-three years old and my mother thirty-one.

A year and a half later, in June, my father died. At that time, my brother was only eleven, and I was a mere infant, so the only course for our mother to follow was to take her children back with her to her original feudal province of Nakatsu, which she did.

What I seem to remember best about Nakatsu is the fact that we children never quite mixed with other children there. Though we had dozens of cousins, and there were flocks of children in the neighborhood, we never seemed to get along with any of them, or play with them, as we did among ourselves. There was no real reason for this, but, having a different Ōsaka dialect, we children grew self-conscious even in saying "yes" and "no" to our neighbors. Moreover, my mother, although she was a native of Nakatsu, had accustomed herself to the life of Ōsaka, then the most prosperous city in Japan, and so the way she dressed us and arranged our hair made us seem queer in the eyes of these people in a secluded town on the coast of Kyūshū. And having nothing else to wear but what we had brought from Ōsaka, we naturally felt more comfortable to stay at home and play among ourselves.

I must mention a very important characteristic of our family. My father was really a scholar. And the scholars of the time, different from the Western scholars of today, disdained to spend any thought on money, or even to touch it. My father always longed for a quiet scholarly life with his books and the noble philosophy of the ancient sages. Yet he was forced to attend to the most worldly affairs, for it was his duty as treasury overseer to associate with merchants, and to count money, and to negotiate loans for his lord. Sometimes when his lord was in difficulty, my father had to bargain with the rich men like Kajimaya and Kōnoike of Ōsaka.

In this work he was unhappy, and so when it came to bringing up his children, he tried, it seems to me, to give them what he thought was an ideal education. For instance, he once sent them to a teacher for calligraphy and general education. The teacher lived in the compound of the lord's storage office, but, having some merchants' children among his pupils, he naturally began to train them in numerals: "Two times two is four, two times three is six, etc." This, today, seems a very ordinary thing to teach, but when my father heard this, he took his children away in a fury.

"It is abominable," he exclaimed, "that innocent children should be taught to use numbers—the tool of merchants. There is no telling what the teacher may do next."

I counted myself twenty-one years old (my exact age, nineteen years and three months) when in February of the first year of Ansei (1854) I set out to Nagasaki.

At that time there was not a single one in our town who could understand the "strange letters written sideways," nor was there even a man who had looked at the forms of those letters, though in larger cities there had been students of the Dutch language for a hundred years or longer.

But it was a few months after the coming of Commodore Perry. And the news of the appearance of the American fleet in Yedo had already made its impression on every remote town in Japan. At the same time the problem of national defense and the modern gunnery had become the foremost interest of all the samurai. Now, all those who wanted to study gunnery had to do so according to the instruction of the Dutch who were the only Europeans permitted to have intercourse with Japan after the seventeenth century.

One day my brother told me that anyone who wanted to learn Western gunnery must study *gensho*.

"What is *gensho*?" I asked.

"*Gensho* means books published in Holland with letters printed sideways," he replied. "There are some translations in Japanese, but if one wishes to study this Western science seriously, one must do so in the original language. Are you willing to learn the Dutch language?"

As I had had no trouble in learning Chinese, I had some confidence in myself. So I answered, "I will study Dutch or any other language. If other people can learn it, I think I can too."

And so the next time my brother had business in Nagasaki, I went with him, and there began my first study of the A B C's. Nowadays the European letters are seen everywhere in the country; they are even on the labels of beer bottles, and no ones sees any strangeness in them. But to me those odd looking letters were very strange. It took me a full three days to learn the twenty-six letters of the alphabet.

I JOIN THE FIRST MISSION TO AMERICA

The year after I was settled in Yedo—the sixth year of Ansei (1859)—the government of the Shōgun made a great decision to send a ship-of-war to the United States, an enterprise never before attempted since the foundation of the empire. On this ship I was to have the good fortune of visiting America.

I am willing to admit my pride in this accomplishment for Japan. The facts are these: It was not until the sixth year of Laei (1853) that a steamship was seen for the first time; it was only in the second year of Ansei (1855) that we began to study navigation from the Dutch in Nagasaki; by 1860, the science was sufficiently understood to enable us to sail a ship across the Pacific. This means that about seven years after the first sight of a steamship, after only about five years of practice, the Japanese people made a trans-Pacific crossing without help from foreign experts. I think we can without undue pride boast before the world of this courage and skill. As I have shown, the Japanese officers were to receive no aid from Captain Brooke throughout the voyage. Even in taking observations, our officers and the Americans made them independently of each other. Sometimes they compared their results, but we were never in the least dependent on the Americans.

As I consider all the other peoples of the Orient as they exist today, I feel convinced that there is no other nation which has the ability or the courage to navigate a steamship across the Pacific after a period of five years of experience in navigation and engineering. Not only in the Orient would this feat stand as an act of unprecedented skill and daring. Even Peter the Great of Russia, who went to Holland to study navigation, with all his attainments could not have equalled this feat of the Japanese. Without doubt, the famous emperor was a man of genius, but his people did not respond to his leadership in the practice of science as did our Japanese in this great adventure.

As soon as our ship came into the port of San Francisco, we were greeted by many important personages who came on board from all over the country.

Along the shores thousands of people were lined up to see the strange newcomers. It had been decided that the Americans on shore should fire a salute. If this were done, our Kanrin-maru would have to respond with a return salute. There is an amusing anecdote in this connection.

Second in command under Captain Kimura was Katsu Rintarō, but Katsu proved a very poor sailor—he did not leave his cabin during the whole voyage across. But now that we were in port, he appeared again to take charge of various operations. When the question of the salute came up, Katsu demurred: "That will be difficult. If we should not fire it off properly, it would bring shame on us. I think it wiser not attempt it."

To this the First Officer, Sasakura Kiritarō, replied: "Who says we cannot fire our ordnance properly? I myself will take charge of it, if you won't."

"Don't be a fool!" returned Katsu. "You don't know anything about firing a cannon. If you can do it, I'll pledge you my head."

Thus taunted, Sasakura was roused. He swore he would fire off a salute. He ordered the sailors to make ready and load the gun. Then using an hourglass for timing, he brought off a salute beautifully. Sasakura naturally swelled with pride. He declared that the head of the sub-captain was his, but that, as long as the voyage lasted, the head had better remain on the man as it would be needed. It made a big story all over the ship.

Our welcome on shore was certainly worthy of a friendly people. They did everything for us, and they could not have done more. The feeling on their part must have been like that of a teacher receiving his old pupil several years after graduation, for it was their Commodore Perry who had effected the opening of our country seven years before, and now here we were on our first visit to America.

As soon as we came on shore, we found we were to be driven off in carriages to a hotel. While we were resting in the hotel, city officials and various dignitaries came to offer entertainment. We were given quarters in the official residence of the Navy station on Mare Island. Our hosts knew that we Japanese were accustomed to a different diet, so they arranged that our food, instead of being served, should be prepared by our own cook. But the officials being very kind, and desiring to satisfy the Japanese love for seafood, sent fish every day. Also, on learning the Japanese custom of bathing frequently, they had baths prepared daily. Our ship had been damaged by the passing storms, so it was put in dry dock to be repaired—all expressions of American hospitality. This generous treatment in every way brought to mind an old expression of ours—"as if our host had put us on the palm of his hand to see that we lacked nothing."

On our part there were many confusing and embarrassing moments, for we were quite ignorant of the customs of American life. For instance, we were surprised even by the carriages. On seeing a vehicle with horses attached to it, we should easily have guessed what it was. But really we did not identify our mode of conveyance until the door had been opened, we were seated inside, and the horses had started off. Then we realized we were riding in a carriage behind horses.

All of us wore the usual pair of swords at our sides and the hemp sandals. So attired, we were taken to the modern hotel. There we noticed, covering the interior, the valuable carpets which in Japan only the more wealthy could buy from importers' shops at so much a square inch to make purses and tobacco pouches with. Here the carpet was laid over an entire room—something quite astounding—and upon this costly fabric walked our hosts wearing the shoes with which they had come in from the streets! We followed them in our hemp sandals.

Immediately bottles were brought in. Suddenly an explosion—the popping of champagne. When the glasses were passed around, we noticed strange fragments floating in them—hardly did we expect to find *ice* in the warm spring weather. Some of the party swallowed these floating particles; others expelled them suddenly; others bravely chewed them. This was an adventure—finding out that they were ice.

I wanted to have a smoke, but seeing no "tobacco tray" such as in Japan is placed before the smoker to hold the burning charcoal brazier and the bamboo ash-receiver, I took a light from the open fireplace. Perhaps there was an ash-tray and a box of matches on the table, but I did not recognize them as such. I finished my smoke, but finding no ash receiver, I took out some of the tissue paper which we carry in place of handkerchiefs, and wrapping the ashes in it, crushed them very carefully, and placed the ball in my sleeve. After a while I took out the paper to have another smoke; some wisps of smoke were trickling from my sleeve. The light that I thought I had crushed out was quietly setting me afire!

After all these embarrassing incidents, I thought I could well sympathize with the Japanese bride. Her new family welcome her and do everything to make her comfortable.

One laughs with her; another engages her in conversation—all happy with the new addition to the family. In the midst of all this the bride has to sit trying to look pleasant, but in her efforts she goes on making mistakes and blushes every time.

Before leaving Japan, I, the independent soul—a care-free student who could look the world in the face—had feared nothing. But on arriving in America, I was turned suddenly into a shy, selfconscious, blushing "bride." The contrast was indeed funny, even to myself.

One evening our host said that some ladies and gentlemen were having a dancing party and that they would be glad to have us attend it. We went. To our dismay we could not make out what they were doing. The ladies and gentlemen seemed to be hopping about the room together. As funny as it was, we knew it would be rude to laugh, and we controlled our expressions with difficulty as the dancing went on. These were but a few of the instances of our bewilderment at the strange customs of American society.

A certain Dutch physician was living then in a place called Vallejo near Mare Island. Since he knew that Holland had maintained the earliest and longest association with Japan, the doctor wished to show some courtsey towards the captain and officers of our ship. The home of the Dutch doctor was a fine dwelling showing his success in that region, but the strange behavior of the household puzzled us. While the mistress of the house stayed constantly in the drawing-room entertaining the guests, the doctor, the supposed master, was moving in and out of the room, directing the servants. This was the reverse of the domestic custom in our country. How strange, we thought. Then, when the dinner was served, came a real shock. On a dish was brought in a whole pig, roasted—head, legs, tail and all. We at once thought of the fabled land of Adachiga Hara where lived a cruel witch who indulged in gruesome feasts. Still, it tasted very good.

When we were taking leave, our host and hostess kindly offered us horses to ride home on. This pleased us, for a chance to ride horseback again was a relief. Especially did Captain Kimura enjoy this, for he was an accomplished horseman who used to ride every day in Yedo. We touched whip to the horses and rode back to our quarters at a trot. The Americans watched us and exclaimed at the Japanese ability in riding. So neither of us really knew much about the other after all.

Our hosts in San Francisco were very considerate in showing us examples of modern industry. There was as yet no railway laid to the city, nor was there any electric light in use. But the telegraph system and also Galvani's electroplating were already in use. Then we were taken to a sugar refinery and had the principle of the operation explained to us quite minutely. I am sure that our hosts thought they were showing us something entirely new, naturally looking for our surprise at each new device of modern engineering. But on the contrary, there was really nothing new, at least to me. I knew the principle of the telegraphy even if I had not seen the actual machine before; I knew that sugar was bleached by straining the solution with bone-black, and that in boiling down the solution, the vacuum was used to better effect than heat. I had been studying nothing else but such scientific principles ever since I had entered Ogata's school.

Rather, I was surprised by entirely different things in American life. First of all, there seemed to be an enormous waste of iron everywhere. In garbage piles, on the sea-shores—everywhere—I found lying old oil tins, empty cans, and broken tools. This was remarkable to us, for in Yedo, after a fire, there would appear a swarm of people looking for nails in the ashes.

Then too, I was surprised at the high cost of daily commodities in California. We had to pay a half-dollar for a bottle of oysters, and there were only twenty or thirty in the bottle at that. In Japan the price of so many would be only a cent or two.

Things social, political, and economic proved most inexplicable. One day, on a sudden thought, I asked a gentleman where the descendants of George Washington might be. He replied, "I think there is a woman who is directly descended from Washington. I don't know where she is now, but I think I have heard she is married." His answer was so very casual that it shocked me.

Of course, I knew that America was a republic with a new president every four years, but I could not help feeling that the family of Washington would be revered above all other families. My reasoning was based on the reverence in Japan for the founders of the great lines of rulers—like that for Ieyasu of the Tokugawa family of Shōguns, really deified in the popular mind. So I remember the astonishment I felt at receiving this indifferent answer about the Washington family. As for scientific inventions and industrial machinery, there was no great novelty in them for me. It was rather in matters of life and social custom and ways of thinking that I found myself at a loss in America.

A certain officer at the naval base on Mare Island, a Captain McDougall, was a collector of coins, and he one day requested our commanding officer to show him some Japanese coins. Captain Kimura must have been anticipating just such a request, for he had a number of both new and old coins arranged in sequence. These he sent to Captain McDougall. In expressing their gratitude, both the officer and his wife were emphatic over their uniqueness, but they showed no sign of having received a gift that had monetary value. The next morning the wife of the officer brought some flowers to Captain Kimura, thanking him again for the uncommon gift she had received the day before. As I received the lady and carried her message to my commandant, I was much moved by her act which had a touch of nobility. I wished that everyone could be like this American lady who thanked one for the gift of gold and silver with a bouquet of flowers.

I have already described the generosity of our hosts and the people in San Francisco. Not only did they repair the damaged parts of our vessel, but they were thoughtful enough to build lockers in convenient places on board for the use of the crew. When the ship was ready and we were preparing to sail on the homeward voyage, we inquired how much we should have to pay for the repair of our ship and other expenses. We were met with a kindly smile. And we were obliged to sail away with our obligations unpaid.

Before we sailed, the interpreter, Nakahama, and I each bought a copy of Webster's dictionary. This, I know, was the very first importation of Webster's into Japan. Once I had secured this valuable work, I felt no disappointment on leaving the new world and returning home again.

8. Workers of the World

THE COMMUNIST MANIFESTO

KARL MARX AND
FRIEDRICH ENGELS

The impact of the Communist Manifesto *was slight when it was first published by Karl Marx and Friedrich Engels in the midst of the revolutionary upheaval in Europe in 1848, but it has since become the most influential revolutionary declaration in the world. As you read the* Manifesto, *you might notice the differences in tone, content, and style, between it and the earlier declarations of the American and French revolutions. What accounts for some of these differences?*

Among other things, the Manifesto *is an interpretation of history. What is that interpretation? What do the authors mean when they say that the history of past societies is the history of class struggle? How is that different from other interpretations? What, according to them, are the most distinctive features of modern society, and how did this modern society come about? What do you think of their characterization of modern bourgeois society? Where do you agree or disagree with their descriptions of bourgeois society? What, according to Marx and Engels, are the forces which will destroy bourgeois society?*

A specter is haunting Europe—the specter of communism. All the powers of old Europe have entered into a holy alliance to exorcise this specter: Pope and Czar, Metternich and Guizot, French Radicals and German police spies.

Where is the party in opposition that has not been decried as communistic by its opponents in power? Where the Opposition that has not hurled back the branding reproach of communism, against the more advanced opposition parties, as well as against its reactionary adversaries?

Two things result from this fact: I. Communism is already acknowledged by all European powers to be itself a power.

II. It is high time that Communists should openly, in the face of the whole world, publish their views, their aims, their tendencies, and meet

From *Manifesto of the Communist Party* by Karl Marx and Friedrich Engels, reprinted in the Crofts Classics Series. Arlington Heights, IL: Harlan Davidson, 1955.

their nursery tale of the specter of communism with a manifesto of the party itself.

To this end, Communists of various nationalities have assembled in London and sketched the following manifesto, to be published in the English, French, German, Italian, Flemish, and Danish languages.

BOURGEOIS AND PROLETARIANS[1]

The history of all hitherto existing society is the history of class struggles.

Freeman and slave, patrician and plebeian, lord and serf, guildmaster and journeyman, in a word, oppressor and oppressed, stood in constant opposition to one another, carried on an uninterrupted, now hidden, now open fight, a fight that each time ended, either in a revolutionary reconstitution of society at large, or in the common ruin of the contending classes.

In the earlier epochs of history, we find almost everywhere a complicated arrangement of society into various orders, a manifold gradation of social rank. In ancient Rome we have patricians, knights, plebeians, slaves; in the Middle Ages, feudal lords, vassals, guild-masters, journeymen, apprentices, serfs; in almost all of these classes, again, subordinate gradations.

The modern bourgeois society that has sprouted from the ruins of feudal society, has not done away with class antagonisms. It has but established new classes, new conditions of oppression, new forms of struggle in place of the old ones.

Our epoch, the epoch of the bourgeoisie, possesses, however, this distinctive feature: It has simplified the class antagonisms. Society as a whole is more and more splitting up into the two great hostile camps, into two great classes directly facing each other—bourgeoisie and proletariat.

From the serfs of the Middle Ages sprang the chartered burghers of the earliest towns. From these burgesses the first elements of the bourgeoisie were developed.

The discovery of America, the rounding of the Cape, opened up fresh ground for the rising bourgeoisie. The East-Indian and Chinese markets, the colonization of America, trade with the colonies, the increase in the means of exchange and in commodities generally, gave to commerce, to navigation, to industry, an impulse never before known, and

---

In French *bourgeois* means a town-dweller. "Proletarian" comes from the Latin, *proletarius*, which meant a person whose sole wealth was his offspring (*proles*).
(Note by Engels) By "bourgeoisie" is meant the class of modern capitalists, owners of the means of social production and employers of wage-labor; by "proletariat," the class of modern wage-laborers who, having no means of production of their own, are reduced to selling their labor power in order to live.

thereby, to the revolutionary element in the tottering feudal society, a rapid development.

The feudal system of industry, in which industrial production was monopolized by closed guilds, now no longer sufficed for the growing wants of the new markets. The manufacturing system took its place. The guild-masters were pushed aside by the manufacturing middle class; division of labor between the different corporate guilds vanished in the face of division of labor in each single workshop.

Meantime the markets kept ever growing, the demand ever rising. Even manufacture[2] no longer sufficed. Thereupon, steam and machinery revolutionized industrial production. The place of manufacture was taken by the giant, modern industry, the place of the industrial middle class, by industrial millionaires—the leaders of whole industrial armies, the modern bourgeois.

Modern industry has established the world market, for which the discovery of America paved the way. This market has given an immense development to commerce, to navigation, to communication by land. This development has, in its turn, reacted on the extension of industry; and in proportion as industry, commerce, navigation, railways extended, in the same proportion the bourgeoisie developed, increased its capital, and pushed into the background every class handed down from the Middle Ages.

We see, therefore, how the modern bourgeoisie is itself the product of a long course of development, of a series of revolutions in the modes of production and of exchange.

Each step in the development of the bourgeoisie was accompanied by a corresponding political advance of that class. An oppressed class under the sway of the feudal nobility, it became an armed and self-governing association in the medieval commune; here independent urban republic (as in Italy and Germany), there taxable "third estate" of the monarchy (as in France); afterwards, in the period of manufacture proper, serving either the semifeudal or the absolute monarchy as a counterpoise against the nobility, and, in fact, cornerstone of the great monarchies in general—the bourgeoisie has at last, since the establishment of modern industry and of the world market, conquered for itself, in the modern representative state, exclusive political sway. The executive of the modern state is but a committee for managing the common affairs of the whole bourgeoisie.

The bourgeoisie has played a most revolutionary role in history.

The bourgeoisie, wherever it has got the upper hand, has put an end

---

2. By *manufacture* Marx meant the system of production which succeeded the guild system but which still relied mainly upon direct human labor for power. He distinguished it from modern industry which arose when machinery driven by water and steam was introduced.

to all feudal, patriarchal, idyllic relations. It has pitilessly torn asunder the motley feudal ties that bound man to his "natural superiors," and has left no other bond between man and man than naked self-interest, than callous "cash payment." It has drowned the most heavenly ecstasies of religious fervor, of chivalrous enthusiasm, of philistine sentimentalism, in the icy water of egotistical calculation. It has resolved personal worth into exchange value, and in place of the numberless indefeasible chartered freedoms, has set up that single, unconscionable freedom—Free Trade. In one word, for exploitation, veiled by religious and political illusions, it has substituted naked, shameless, direct, brutal exploitation.

The bourgeoisie has stripped of its halo every occupation hitherto honored and looked up to with reverent awe. It has converted the physician, the lawyer, the priest, the poet, the man of science, into its paid wage-laborers.

The bourgeoisie has torn away from the family its sentimental veil, and has reduced the family relation to a mere money relation.

The bourgeoisie has disclosed how it came to pass that the brutal display of vigor in the Middle Ages, which reactionaries so much admire, found its fitting complement in the most slothful indolence. It has been the first to show what man's activity can bring about. It has accomplished wonders far surpassing Egyptian pyramids, Roman aqueducts, and Gothic cathedrals; it has conducted expeditions that put in the shade all former migrations of nations and crusades.

The bourgeoisie cannot exist without constantly revolutionizing the instruments of production, and thereby the relations of production, and with them the whole relations of society. Conservation of the old modes of production in unaltered form, was, on the contrary, the first condition of existence for all earlier industrial classes. Constant revolutionizing of production, uninterrupted disturbance of all social conditions, everlasting uncertainty and agitation distinguish the bourgeois epoch from all earlier ones. All fixed, fast-frozen relations, with their train of ancient and venerable prejudices and opinions, are swept away, all new-formed ones become antiquated before they can ossify. All that is solid melts into air, all that is holy is profaned, and man is at last compelled to face with sober senses his real conditions of life and his relations with his kind.

The need of a constantly expanding market for its products chases the bourgeoisie over the whole surface of the globe. It must nestle everywhere, settle everywhere, establish connections everywhere.

The bourgeoisie has through its exploitation of the world market given a cosmopolitan character to production and consumption in every country. To the great chagrin of reactionaries, it has drawn from under the feet of industry the national ground on which it stood. All old-established national industries have been destroyed or are daily being destroyed. They are dislodged by new industries, whose introduction becomes a life and death question for all civilized nations, by industries that no longer work up indigenous raw material, but raw material drawn from the remotest zones; industries whose products are consumed, not only at home, but in every quarter of the globe. In place of the old wants, satisfied by the production of the country, we find new wants, requiring for their satisfaction the products of distant lands and climes. In place of the old local and national seclusion and self-sufficiency, we have intercourse in every direction, universal interdependence of nations. And as in material, so also in intellectual production. The intellectual creations of individual nations become common property. National one-sidedness and narrow-mindedness become more and more impossible, and from the numerous national and local literatures there arises a world literature.

The bourgeoisie, by the rapid improvement of all instruments of production, by the immensely facilitated means of communication, draws all nations, even the most barbarian, into civilization. The cheap prices of its commodities are the heavy artillery with which it batters down all Chinese walls, with which it forces the barbarians' intensely obstinate hatred for foreigners to capitulate. It compels all nations, on pain of extinction, to adopt the bourgeois mode of production; it compels them to introduce what it calls civilization into their midst, i.e., to become bourgeois themselves. In a word, it creates a world after its own image.

The bourgeoisie has subjected the country to the rule of the towns. It has created enormous cities, has greatly increased the urban population as compared with the rural, and has thus rescued a considerable part of the population from the idiocy of rural life. Just as it has made the country dependent on the towns, so it has made barbarian and semibarbarian countries dependent on the civilized ones, nations of peasants on nations of bourgeois, the East on the West.

More and more the bourgeoisie keeps doing away with the scattered state of the population, of the means of production, and of property. It has agglomerated population, centralized means of production, and has concentrated property in a few hands. The necessary consequence of this was political centralization. Independent, or but loosely connected provinces, with separate interests, laws, governments and systems of taxation, became lumped together into one nation, with one government, one code of laws, one national class interest, one frontier and one customs tariff.

The bourgeoisie, during its rule of scarce one hundred years, has created more massive and more colossal productive forces than have all preceding generations together. Subjection of nature's forces to man, machinery, application of chemistry to industry and agriculture, steam-navigation, railways, electric telegraphs, clearing of whole continents for cultivation, canalization of rivers, whole populations conjured out of the ground—what earlier century had even a presentiment that such productive forces slumbered in the lap of social labor?

We see then that the means of production and of exchange, which served as the foundation for the growth of the bourgeoisie, were generated in feudal society. At a certain stage in the development of these means of production and of exchange, the conditions under which feudal society produced and exchanged, the feudal organization of agriculture and manufacturing industry, in a word, the feudal relations of property became no longer compatible with the already developed productive forces; they became so many fetters. They had to be burst asunder; they were burst asunder.

Into their place stepped free competition, accompanied by a social and political constitution adapted to it, and by the economic and political sway of the bourgeois class.

A similar movement is going on before our own eyes. Modern bourgeois society with its relations of production, of exchange and of property, a society that has conjured up such gigantic means of production and exchange, is like the sorcerer who is no longer able to control the powers of the nether world whom he has called up by his spells. For many a decade past the history of industry and commerce is but the history of the revolt of modern productive forces against modern conditions of production, against the property relations that are the conditions for the existence of the bourgeoisie and of its rule. It is enough to mention the commercial crises that by their periodical return put the existence of the entire bourgeois society on trial, each time more threateningly. In these crises a great part not only of the existing products, but also of the previously created productive forces, are periodically destroyed. In these crises there breaks out an epidemic that, in all earlier epochs, would have seemed an absurdity—the epidemic of overproduction. Society suddenly finds itself put back into a state of momentary barbarism; it appears as if a famine, a universal war of devastation had cut off the supply of every means of subsistence; industry and commerce seem to be destroyed. And why? Because there is too much civilization, too much means of subsistence, too much industry, too much commerce. The productive forces at the disposal of society no longer tend to further the development of the conditions of bourgeois property; on the contrary, they have become too powerful for these conditions, by which they are fettered, and no sooner do they overcome these fetters than they bring disorder into the whole of bourgeois society, endanger the existence of bourgeois property. The conditions of bourgeois society are too narrow to comprise the wealth created by them. And how does the bourgeoisie get over these crises? On the one hand by enforced destruction of a mass of productive forces; on the other, by the conquest of new markets, and by the more thorough exploitation of the old ones. That is to say, by paving the way for more

extensive and more destructive crises, and by diminishing the means
whereby crises are prevented.

The weapons with which the bourgeoisie felled feudalism to the
ground are now turned against the bourgeoisie itself.

But not only has the bourgeoisie forged the weapons that bring death
to itself; it has also called into existence the men who are to wield those
weapons—the modern working class—the proletarians.

LABOR ON THE MOVE

ERIC WOLF

"Workers of the world, unite!" was the concluding call of the Communist
Manifesto. *In fact, the call of capitalism might have been "workers of the
world, disperse." The great age of capitalist industrialization (the last two
hundred years) has witnessed one of the greatest mass population
movements in world history. Marx and Engels would not have been
surprised. The great labor migrations were part of the establishment of
the single world market that they described.*

*Here a modern anthropologist gives us a sense of the enormous
dimensions of those population transfers. We in the United States are
particularly aware of the story of North American immigration, but this
selection reminds us that it was part of a global story. What, according to
the author, are the three stages of migration? Are any of these stages still
continuing? What was the relationship between immigration to and the
industrialization of the United States? In what ways was South African
immigration similar to that of the United States? Why were there so many
Indian and Chinese migrants? Was there any connection between migration and the "free trade empires" discussed in the previous chapter?*

People may move for religious, political, ecological, or other reasons; but
the migrations of the nineteenth and twentieth centuries were largely
labor migrations, movements of the bearers of labor power. These labor
migrations, of course, carried with them newspaper editors to publish
papers for Polish miners or German metalworkers, shopkeepers to
supply their fellow migrants with pasta or red beans, religious specialists
to minister to Catholic or Buddhist souls, and others. Each migration
involved the transfer to the new geographical location not only of

From *Europe and the People Without History* by Eric R. Wolf. Copyright © 1982 The University of
California Press. Reprinted by permission of the publisher.

manpower but also of services and resources. Each migratory wave generated, in turn, suppliers of services at the point of arrival, whether these were labor agents, merchants, lawyers, or players of percussion instruments.

In the development of capitalism, three waves of migration stand out, each a response to critical changes in the demand for labor, each creating new working classes. The first of these waves was associated with the initial period of European industrialization. Beginning in England, these initial movements toward capitalist industry covered only short distances, since industrial development was itself still localized and limited. Thus, in the cotton town of Preston in Lancashire, where roughly half the population consisted of immigrants in 1851, over 40 percent had come less than ten miles from their birthplaces and only about 30 percent had come more than thirty miles. Fourteen percent of all immigrants had been born in Ireland, however, and came to Preston as part of the rising tide of Irish immigration in the 1840s. Localized as such movements were, they made Lancashire the most urbanized county in Britain by the middle of the nineteenth century, with more than half the people of the county living in fourteen towns with populations of more than 10,000.

Belgium followed Britain in the movement of workers from the countryside, as the industrial towns of the Walloon-speaking southern provinces burgeoned in the 1820s. In the 1830s the Prussian provinces of Westphalia, Rhine, Berlin, and Brandenburg initiated their industrial expansion, attracting a large-scale flow of population from Prussia's eastern agricultural regions. This flow intensified greatly in the last quarter of the century, as dependent cultivators were displaced by the consolidation and mechanization of the large Junker estates.

While the first wave of labor migration under capitalism carried people toward the industrial centers within the European peninsula, a second flow sent Europeans overseas. An estimated 50 million people left Europe permanently between 1800 and 1914. The most important destination of this movement was the United States, which between 1820 and 1915 absorbed about 32 million immigrants, most of them of European origins. This influx of people provided the labor power that underwrote the industrialization of the United States.

A third wave of migration carried contract laborers of diverse origins to the expanding mines and plantations of the tropics. This flow represents a number of developments, such as the establishment of a migratory labor force for the South African mines, the growth of the trade in Indian and Chinese contract labor, and the sponsored migration of Italian laborers to the coffee regions of Brazil. These movements not only laid the basis for a large increase in tropical production but also played a major part in creating an infrastructure of transport and communication, prerequisites for a further acceleration of capitalist development.

THE UNITED STATES

While Britain, Belgium, and Germany recruited their working classes largely through internal and intracontinental migration, the United States imported its working class by sailboat and steamship. Such reliance on immigrant labor, of course, predates the onset of industrialization in the United States. We have discussed the forced movement of Africans to the New World, including the area that was to become, under the impact of British textile development, the Cotton South. European migration before the American War of Independence also included many people who accepted the temporary bondage of indenture in the hope of establishing themselves in the New World; these indentured laborers may have comprised as many as two-thirds of all early migrants. Later in the eighteenth century, there came a quarter of a million Scotch-Irish, transplanted first from the Scottish Lowlands to Ulster, and then forced by rack-renting and rising tithes to abandon Ulster for America. Another group that came in the nineteenth century were Scottish Highlanders, displaced by sheep or driven by rising rents; they were led by their "tacksmen," heads of cadet lines of the chiefly *clann*, who acted as intermediaries between chief and commoners. Another quarter of a million migrants arrived from southwestern Germany, an area of impoverished and parcelized agriculture. Mass immigration into the United States, however, began only after the cessation of the Napoleonic wars.

In the 1820s, 151,000 immigrants came to the United States; in the decade of the 1830s, the number tripled to 599,000. It increased again to 1,713,000 in the 1840s, and to 2,314,000 in the 1850s. The main factors pushing these people out of Europe were the spread of industrial capitalism and the commercialization of agriculture. As industrial capitalism spread, it displaced artisans and destroyed the domestic putting-out system. Transformations in agriculture burdened Irish and southwestern German cultivators with increased rents, mortgages, and indebtedness, and drove Scottish, English, and Scandinavian cultivators off the land to make way for sheep or cattle. In the period between 1820 and 1860, therefore, the main contingents of immigrants came from Ireland (2 million), southwestern Germany (1.5 million), and the British Isles (750,000). Of course, the United States was not the only target of such migrations. Between 1818 and 1828, 250,000 Germans settled in southern Russia. Others went to Brazil, while Irishmen settled in Canada and the Maritime Provinces, or sought new homes in Australia. In the United States, the advent of the new immigrants speeded up capitalist industrialization. "Neither the factory system," says Maldwyn Jones, "nor the great canal and railroad development of the period could have come into existence so quickly without the reservoir of cheap labor provided by immigration." The role of the Irish immigrants, who quickly developed a new monopoly on unskilled labor in construction work and factory employment in this period, in fierce competition with American Blacks, proved especially important in this regard.

More Englishmen, Swedes, and Germans from east of the Elbe arrived between 1860 and 1890. Again, many of them were displaced agriculturalists driven off the land by the disintegration of English, Swedish, and German wheat production between 1865 and 1875, a result of the importation of low-priced American and Russian grain. The Great Depression also affected German and English coal mining, iron and steel production, and textiles; miners, metalworkers, spinners, and weavers came to seek employment in the New World. The cultivators among them could take advantage of land grants offered by the advancing railroads and by the midwestern and western states and territories.

Around 1890 the area of migrant supply shifted from northern and western Europe to southern and eastern Europe. The new immigrants were largely displaced peasants and agricultural laborers from southern Italy, the Austro-Hungarian empire, and the Balkans. In addition, there were Poles, Jews, and Volga-Germans from the Russian empire; Russians themselves migrated mostly to Siberia. The newcomers quickly replaced their predecessors in a number of industrial locations and occupations. The coal miners in Pennsylvania had been largely of British or German origin before 1890, but after that time they were mainly Poles, Slovaks, Italians, and Hungarians. Whereas the New England textile mills had been manned primarily by French-Canadians, English, and Irish, the new textile workers were Portuguese, Greeks, Poles, and Syrians. In the garment trades, Russian Jews and Italians took over from Germans, Czechs, and Irish.

This large-scale influx of European labor had a marked influence on the direction of American technological development. During the first half of the nineteenth century, capitalist entrepreneurs were faced with a relative shortage of labor. There was land available to those who wanted to farm, and there were opportunities for artisan employment, both of which attracted newcomers away from industrial work. Wages were relatively high for all categories of workers. This appears to have fostered the development of labor-saving devices and their early introduction into industry. The later influx of industrially unskilled workers from southern and eastern Europe, in turn, favored the further development of machinery and of rationalized processes of production that did not rely on mechanical skills. In 1908 the U.S. Immigration Commission noted that the new migrants were often drawn into highly capitalized industries, despite their lack of skills:

As a consequence their employment in the mines and manufacturing plants of the country has been made possible only by the invention of mechanical devices and processes which have eliminated the skill and experience formerly recognized in a large number of occupations.

Most of the foreign-born workers entered the unskilled, lower-paid levels of industrial occupations. While their new employment yielded remuneration substantially higher than they would have earned in Europe, the combination of mechanization and unskilled immigrant labor permitted American entrepreneurs to keep wages down. Without the Italian, Slav, Greek, Portuguese, French-Canadian, and Russian Jewish workers who furnished the bulk of the labor for the leading American industries by 1900, the industrial expansion that took place between 1880 and 1900 would not have been possible.

LABOR FOR THE MINES: SOUTH AFRICA

We have seen that at about the same time the United States moved toward full industrialization, a takeoff into capitalist development also took hold in southern Africa. There, diamonds and gold were discovered in the last third of the nineteenth century, in the areas north of the Orange and Vaal rivers. The core area of South African development shifted correspondingly to these inland areas. At first diamonds and gold were both mined by surface diggers. Sometimes particular tasks were contracted to White entrepreneurs who organized work gangs. While some Africans paid the license fees needed to become full-time diggers, by 1876 the higher-paid skilled jobs were monopolized by White diggers, and African laborers were contracted only for short periods of about three months. By 1892 the skilled workers had formed a trade union to defend their position against any attempt of management to lower labor costs by using African laborers or by sponsoring further immigration from England.

War between Britain and the Afrikaaners for political control of South Africa disrupted mining operations between 1899 and 1902, and cut the available working force in half. By 1906, however, the mines were again in full production, with a labor force of 18,000 Whites, 94,000 Africans, and 51,000 Chinese indentured servants. In 1907 there was a strike of White skilled workers who opposed management plans to increase Chinese immigration and to replace White with Black labor. It was broken when unemployed Afrikaaners were brought in as strikebreakers. The lasting outcome, however, was the repatriation of Chinese miners and a reinforcement of the color bar in employment.

Most of the White miners, as of 1912, came from outside South Africa—from Britain, Australia, the United States, and elsewhere. These Whites made up the skilled labor force. The Africans, in contrast, were unskilled migratory workers, on contracts from six to eighteen months' duration, who received a tenth of the wages paid to the Whites.

The idea of employing Africans as temporary laborers became established in the first decade of mining. In the 1880s it was combined with the notion of confining Africans to residential compounds for their contractual period. This practice took root first in the Kimberley diamond mines, in part to stop the illicit sale of diamonds by African miners to dealers, in part to control desertion. This "closed" compound has remained a feature of the diamond mines ever since. Local traders initially protested the company stores set up by the mining companies for their shut-in work force. When the gold mines adopted the compound system somewhat later, compounds were set up in an "open" rather than "closed" form to meet the objections of local storekeepers.

LABOR FOR THE PLANTERS: EAST INDIANS

While Britain, northwestern continental Europe, and the high South African *veld* were importing labor to man the new industrial machinery, other regions of the world were seeking new sources of agricultural labor. The "old" areas of plantation agriculture, most of them growing sugar cane, had lost their supply of slave labor with abolition. On some of the small islands of the Caribbean, such as Barbados and St. Kitts, the freed slaves had no alternative but to work for their former masters. But on the larger islands like Trinidad and Jamaica, and in the mainland sugar colony of Guyana (then Demarara), the ex-slaves could and did take up land beyond the confines of the plantation, and they resisted further work on the old estates. Facing potential ruin, the planters began to agitate for new sources of labor. Sometimes the British intercepted slave ships going to Brazil, nominally freed the slaves, and then sent them to the West Indian sugar islands.

These proved to be only stopgap measures. To the cry for replacement of the old labor supply was soon added the demand for more and more labor as the scale of commercial agriculture expanded. Beyond the old sugar areas, there were sometimes political reasons for importing laborers. In Malaya, for example, the British decided to maintain intact the Malay peasantry and its tributary relationship with village headmen and ruling nobles. The need for plantation labor was therefore met through the organized migration of indentured laborers from India and of contract labor from China.

Whereas Chinese labor came to be utilized primarily in mining and construction work, Indian indentured labor was deployed mainly in plantations, specifically plantations located within the British empire. Already under the Mughals groups of men had taken service as bearers and on ships, and by the end of the eighteenth century there were

Indian laborers—hired for periods of two to three years—in all the ports of southeast Asia. Yet the great stimulus for the development of what Tinker has called "the second slavery" came with the abolition of the slave trade in 1808 and the sudden need for cheap and tractable labor, especially on the sugar-producing plantations of the tropics.

Guyana asked for Indian laborers, as did Jamaica and Trinidad from 1836 on. (At present, East Indians make up more than 50 percent of the population in Guyana, about 40 percent in Trinidad, and about 2 percent in Jamaica.) East Indian labor migration to Mauritius began in 1835; by 1861 East Indians constituted about two-thirds of the population of the island. In 1860 the tea plantations in Assam and Bhutan began to compete for migrants, and between 1870 and the end of the century 700,000–750,000 laborers were recruited for work there. The demand for East Indians in Fiji began in 1879; today, Indians there outnumber native Fijians. After the 1870s Ceylon became a main area of demand; in the 1880s, Burma; after the turn of the century, Malaya. Natal in South Africa began importing East Indian contract labor for its sugar plantations around 1870. All together, Tinker estimates, "over a million Indian laborers went overseas to tropical plantations in the forty years before 1870; though the figure could be as high as two million."

LABOR FOR THE PLANTERS: EUROPEANS

Another major source of agricultural labor was European. We have already made mention of the Polish workers who began to replace German tenant-laborers on the Junker estates of eastern Germany after 1870. In the coffee belt of Brazil, the end of slavery also created a labor crisis. It proved impossible to tap the labor of Luso-Brazilian small-scale cultivators, most of whom were held fast in relationships of dependency upon local landlords and other powerholders. For a time, some Brazilian political leaders harbored plans to bring in indentured "Asiatics." Finally, the problem was solved by importing Italian laborers. The government paid for their voyage, and the local planter advanced a year's wages and a subsistence plot, thus subsidizing "free" Italian labor.

The Italian emigration was prompted largely by the crisis of agriculture within Italy beginning in the 1870s. The sale of public-domain land and church holdings had created a situation in which large landowners were able to add to their holdings, while small cultivators were being squeezed out by falling prices for agricultural products. This price decline was in considerable part the result of competition from Russian and American wheat. The increasing flood of manufactured goods also disrupted local handicrafts, while the phylloxera blight destroyed vineyards. Wealthy landowners began to move their liquid wealth into industry but smallholders and laborers could escape the squeeze only by moving elsewhere, either seasonally, temporarily, or permanently.

At first, in the 1860s, Italians took up work in France, Switzerland, Germany, and Austria-Hungary, but only 16,000 emigrated permanently in that decade. In the 1870s the stream of permanent emigration grew to 360,000, with some 12,000 now going to Argentina and Brazil. Then, between 1881 and 1901, the number of permanent emigrants rose sixfold to more than 2 million. In all, more than 4 million left Italy permanently between 1861 and 1911. The majority came from southern Italy, where the agricultural crisis hit most heavily. Four-fifths were agricultural laborers and construction workers. In the 1800s and 1890s South America was the major target of migration: three times as many went to Brazil and Argentina as went to the United States. By 1901, however, the trend was reversed. In the first decade of the twentieth century, more than twice as many went to the United States as to South America; in the second decade, more than three times as many. By that time, however, the new labor supply had permitted Brazil's coffee planters to lay the basis for rapid industrial growth, with the Brazilian government paying the transportation costs for the new work force.

THE TRADE IN CHINESE LABOR

China proved to be another source of labor for the outside world. In Southeast Asia there had been Chinese before the European expansion. Moslem Chinese of mixed Han, Persian, Arabic, and Central Asian origins, called Hwei or Hui, moved into the southwestern Chinese borderlands during the Mongol period of the thirteenth and fourteenth centuries; many carried on the overland trade to southern Asia. Chinese trading colonies also settled in the islands at this time. In the fifteenth century, however, the Chinese state throttled foreign commerce and created an unpopulated no-man's-land along the coastal fringe in order to prevent foreign contracts with the Han population. This stemmed out-migration. Nevertheless, Chinese laborers were exported by the Portuguese through Macao, while the Dutch East India Company captured Chinese along the China coast in order to populate its headquarters town of Batavia.

The conclusion of treaties at the end of the Opium War in 1842 removed the barrier to emigration and permitted foreign entrepreneurs to tap the Chinese labor market directly through the establishment of the "coolie" trade. Political disorders and economic crises in China, such as the Taiping rebellion, drove many to accept labor contracts abroad. Soon a sophisticated apparatus of traders grew up to facilitate this movement. If an entrepreneur wanted Chinese laborers for use in Malaya, he could contact a "coolie broker" in Singapore or Penang. The coolie broker, in turn, issued the orders for labor to "eating-house" keepers in Swatow, Amoy, Hong Kong, or Macao. The eating-house keepers then contacted "headmen" (*khah-taus*), who recruited laborers on the village level. Laborers either paid for their own transportation or else indentured themselves to a "credit-ticket" broker who paid the cost of their travel.

The laborers who had paid their own fare could move about freely in search of work after arrival. The "unpaid passengers," however, were in debt to the broker and indentured to him for the duration of their debt. In Malaya, such indentured arrivals were housed in depots, where they were guarded by "depot keepers" employed by the coolie broker. Coolie brokers and depot keepers usually held positions in powerful secret societies, which also furnished the depot guards. The secret societies developed a dual function in the context of the labor trade. They maintained social control and coercion over the dependent Chinese population, while at the same time they defended the interests of the Chinese enclave against the dictates and strategies of local governments. The depot system lasted in Malaya until the onset of World War I in 1914.

SINGAPORE

One of the great hubs of this Chinese labor migration was Singapore. Singapore provides an apt example of the ways that the labor trade fitted into the other activities of a major port and commercial center in Asia.

Singapore had been founded in 1819, when England received rights to the site—then inhabited by a few Malay and Chinese fishermen. By 1900 the city had 229,000 inhabitants—two-thirds of them Chinese, the remainder Malays—drawn mainly from the Malay peninsula but also from the island archipelago as far east as Borneo and the Philippines.

From 1867 on, Singapore became a pivot of the British efforts to govern in the peninsula, using British officials, Malay adjutants, and Chinese and Tamil clerks. The British also managed the agency houses charged with handling the European-based trade. Alongside the European traders stood the Chinese merchants, headed by the prestigious Baba families and closely interlinked through kinship ties. As non-Malays they were barred from any access to the formal positions of political authority, but they held much of the real power over capital and men in the city. They advanced money to planters and miners. They managed the labor trade through which workers were funneled to the tin mines of Perak and Selangor and to the plantations. They dominated the powerful secret societies that controlled the immigrant laborers and offered protection and assistance in return for loyalty and service. The British, in turn, used the heads of these secret societies as "captains of the Chinese" to control the Chinese population, until the secret societies themselves accumulated too much power and were declared illegal in 1889. Their place was taken by associations based on common dialect or surname, patterned on the regional associations found in China and fulfilling similar functions of support and welfare. These associations also functioned as religious bodies. In the setting of Singapore, they both embodied the anti-Manchu political stance of the secret societies and offered unorthodox religious expression of individual needs through spirit-medium cults.

Capital in the city thus flowed mainly through British and Chinese hands, while most of the labor was furnished by Chinese.

CHINESE LABOR: OTHER DESTINATIONS

Malaya was not the only destination of Chinese labor. Some 90,000 indentured Chinese laborers were sent to Peru between 1849 and 1874, mostly through Macao, to replace Hawaiians who had died working in the guano beds. Some of these Chinese were assigned to work in the cotton fields of coastal Peru when demand for cotton rose in the wake of the scarcity created by the war between the Union and the Confederacy. Others were employed in railroad construction.

Another 200,000 Chinese were sent to California between 1852 and 1875, where they were employed in fruit growing and processing, in panning for gold, and in building railroads. In the 1860s some 10,000 to 14,000 Chinese laborers built the Central Pacific Railroad of California, which by 1885 linked the West Coast with eastern Utah and thus completed the transcontinental railroad. Five thousand more workers were taken from Hong Kong to Victoria to build the Canadian Pacific Railroad, which opened up the gold placer beds of British Columbia.

In California the movement of Chinese labor was controlled by merchant-brokers who hired out the laborers as needed, while retaining control over them through the operations of secret societies. The secret societies, in turn, were interlinked with the so-called Six Companies, named for their districts of origin in Kwantung province and patterned after the regional associations that developed in China during the Manchu Ch'ing regime. As in Singapore, the Six Companies defended Chinese interests in an antagonistic environment. At the same time, they exercised control over the Chinese population on the West Coast. The Pacific Steamship Company cooperated with them by agreeing not to allow any man to return to China who had not cleared his debts. After the cessation of the labor trade, the Six (later Seven) Companies continued as political, educational, and welfare associations of the Chinese community in the United States.

Gold was discovered not only in California and British Columbia but also in Australia (1853). By 1854 there were 2,000 Chinese miners in the Australian gold fields, with 42,000 there by 1859. Other areas also entered the Chinese labor trade. Cuba contracted for 800 Chinese in 1847, and for some 8,000 to 15,000 in 1852. Between 1856 and 1867, 19,000 Chinese left Hong Kong under contract, of whom 6,630 went to the British West Indies (mostly Guyana), 4,991 to Cuba, 2,370 to Bombay in India, 1,609 to Dutch Guiana, and 1,035 to Tahiti, Hawaii, and other Pacific islands.

In addition to Chinese laborers who stayed abroad only until their contracts expired, there were also migrants who went in search of permanent settlement. One of the major areas of such settlement was Southeast Asia, where the Chinese population in the 1970s was more than 12 million. Early migrant groups were often traders who in time formed a mercantile aristocracy, such as the Babas of Malacca and the Peranakans of Indonesia. Later comers frequently had to contend for power with the earlier arrivals.

Often Chinese merchants would, in their new homeland, build up a dependable following by calling on kinsmen or people from the same home region in China. In employment, close kin were preferred to more distant kin, more distant kin to speakers of the same Chinese dialect, members of the same dialect category to other Chinese, and Chinese to non-Chinese. Such a following, built up on kin or quasi-kin ties, would engage in many different activities, often centering around operations that connected the primary producers in the hinterland with Western commercial enterprises. Chinese were widely active as middlemen, to the point where Indonesians began calling them *bangsa tengah*, "the middle race." Chinese merchants also advanced the credit necessary to oil the circuits of commerce. "The native peasant is in debt to the Chinese trader, the trader to the wholesaler, the wholesaler to the export-import firm. Debt obligations connect all the steps of trade with each other." Unsurprisingly, these middleman and credit functions have often made the Chinese creditor-merchant the target of political attack and persecution in Southeast Asia, where their position has often been compared to that of the Jews in Eastern Europe.

The Chinese laborers, too, faced hostility from workers in the areas to which they were brought. In 1882 the United States passed the Chinese Exclusion Act under presure from the Knigths of Labor, who had even insisted on the ejection of Chinese from the laundry business. The anti-Chinese agitations that broke out on the West Coast of the United States were not merely a California problem but part of an emergent racism in the United States. Restrictions on Chinese immigration constitute merely one phase in a larger movement to divide employment opportunities along racial lines. Similar efforts at excluding the Chinese were made in Australia after their employment in the gold fields came to an end, and in South Africa, where 43,296 Chinese contract laborers worked on the Rand in 1904, only to be repatriated in 1907.

CHINA MEN

MAXINE HONG KINGSTON

In this selection the modern writer Maxine Hong Kingston recreates her great-grandfather's migration from China to Hawaii. Most of the Chinese who emigrated in the nineteenth century came, like Bak Goong, from cities like Canton in southern China. They settled throughout Southeast Asia, the Pacific, and the Americas. Most intended to return to China. Many, again like Bak Goong, actually did.

Why, according to the author, were "ocean people" more likely to migrate? Why did Bak Goong leave? How was he changed by his experiences in Hawaii (Sandalwood Mountain)? What were some of the possibilities and hardships of the new immigrant?

Ocean people are different from land people. The ocean never stops saying and asking into ears, which don't sleep like eyes. Those who live by the sea examine the driftwood and glass balls that float from foreign ships. They let scores of invisible imps loose out of found bottles. In a scoop of salt water, they revive the dead blobs that have been beached in storms and tides: fins, whiskers, and gills unfold; mouths, eyes, and colors bloom and spread. Sometimes ocean people are given to understand the newness and oldness of the world; then all morning they try to keep that boundless joy like a little sun inside their chests. The ocean also makes its people know immensity.

They wonder what continents contain the ocean on its other side, what people live there. Hong Kong off the coast tugged like a moon at the Cantonese; curiosity had a land mass to fasten upon, and beyond Hong Kong, Taiwan, step by step a leading out. Cantonese travel, and they gamble.

But China has a long round coastline, and the northern people enclosed Peiping, [Bejing], only one hundred miles from the sea, with walls and made roads westward across the loess. The Gulf of Chihli has arms, and beyond, Korea, and beyond that, Japan. So the ocean and hunger and some other urge made Cantonese people explorers and Americans.

Bak Goong, Great Grandfather, came to Hawai'i at the invitation of the Royal Hawaiian Agricultural Society. Their agent, who had been born in our district and spoke like us, came straight into the village and talked about how he got to be a recruiter. Even today the family trusts any insurance, encyclopedia, or gadget salesman who talks like us, our language a music that charms away common sense. The family knew the growing habits of cane; a stand grew in the courtyard. Convoys used to relay lichee and sugarcane from Canton to the Imperial palace. A few times a year, on a holiday or a birthday, Grandmother cut a stalk and divided it into small chunks, one for each person. The sweet taste affected Bak Goong. The recruiter told his fellow villagers, Chinese were the first sugarmakers in Hawai'i; they brought the first millstones and vats in 1802. "Right now," said the agent, "we're offering free passage, free food, free clothing, and housing. In fact, we're advancing you six dollars. Here. See. I have six dollars right here. Here, Grandma. We'll let Po Po hold it; she can return it to me if she wants to. Couldn't you use six dollars before you've even begun to work? You repay it with just six weeks' work. After six weeks, clear profit. Figure it out. You're joining us at a lucky time. The pay just went up again. You're getting an instant raise. We need every kind of labor. You inexperienced kids can be house servants for two dollars a month. Now, once you secure this fine job, you'll want to protect it, right? You're thinking, What if I get to the Sandalwood Mountains, and they fire me? Well, listen to this. We can't fire you. We protect you against firing. We can't fire you because you sign this three-year contract, and for more protection, this five-year contract." "Mm," said the family. "Of course, there'll be some hardships, but that's life, isn't it? You'll be traveling with a shipload of fellow Chinese, with whom you'll be sharing free housing. You'll have people to discuss things with. We're giving you a dormitory just like going to college. And did you know that the Sandalwood Mountains are very close to the Gold Mountain? You get free passage as far as the Sandalwood Mountains, where you can stay as long as you want, and you invest a little of your profits in passage to California. You'll get there before the Gold Rush is over. Why, in Hawai'i, you're already halfway there. Figure: You start with nothing. You already have six dollars' advance. Three years from today, home with riches."

Impressed by the agent's homely dialect, his suit, his title, and his philosophic bent, Bak Goong muttered what Confucius taught on the occasion of breaking a promise to his captors. "'Heaven doesn't hear an oath which is forced on one,'" and made his X.

He told his family that he would be back in three years. Traveling alone, he watched armies march or straggle by, close calls, he on a cliff, an army in the ravine; he behind a waterfall, an army drinking at the river; he flattened like a shadow on the earth, an army silhouetted against the moon. He spied British demons with big noses and guns. He was walking on dangerous and sick land. In the north, the Yellow River had reversed its course overnight; it reared up, coiled in the air, and slapped down backwards to run the other way, south instead of north. It troughed new watercourses and flooded four provinces before settling on its route. Winds collided. The Yangtze also flooded. Eels hung from ceilings, and red worms curled inside wells and jars. Migrating from lakes of drowned crops and trees, farmers came to fields of dust where drought cracked the ground, the land was burned, and there were no fishing boats on the rivers. New monsters were appearing on the earth, barbarians everywhere; the British demons opened the seaports to opium and soldiers. . . .

Bak Goong recognized a century-size upheaval; he shook his head and walked away, turned his back and walked away. He arrived in Canton without being conscripted, and signed on a schooner as a crewman to make extra money while traveling. He would jump ship in Hawai'i if he wasn't allowed to quit there.

. . .

After three months at sea, Bak Goong smelled in the wind a sweetness like a goddess visiting. Whenever the hatches and doors opened in the right combinations, the men below also smelled it. "It's sandalwood," Bak Goong said, looking for land on the horizon. The smell of boxes and chests of drawers, statues, castanets and fans, incenses and powders must have inspired him to come here. Chinese had followed that essence to India, where sandalwood grew in phoenix-shaped roots in the caves of lions, and to Persia, where it congealed in the Eastern Ocean as a cicada. And now they followed sandalwood to its home here.

One day Bak Goong opened the hatches for the men below, who stumbled through the passageways and up ladders to the topdeck, where they blinked in the sunlight. A demon from shore counted and re-counted the China Men. There were three or four fewer live ones than when they began the journey. The demon strung a tab about each neck. Bak Goong climbed down to the longboat, past the weeds that had grown like skirts on the ship's sides.

On shore among crates, burlap bags, barrels, haystacks, they waited for their bosses, some of whom were China Men. The men with no papers signed anything that was handed them; most made a cross like the ideograph *ten*; "The Word Ten," they called their signatures. A pair of horses, which delighted Bak Goong, pulled a wagon to the dock, but only a few workers rode to those fields close enough to Honolulu to be reached by roads. Bak Goong's group was to walk, led by a demon boss on a horse. He bade good-byes to friends he had made on the ship. Walking after rolling on the sea confused his legs, but with his seabag across his back, he edged quickly to the front of the group. He buffered himself in case the demon used his whip on men.

They walked out of the town and up a mountain road so narrow that the demon dismounted and led the horse. The trail led upward among banana trees. Bak Goong ate bananas to his heart's content, throwing away the peels instead of scraping their insides and eating the fibers; there were that many bananas, hands of them, overripe fruit rotting on the ground. He ate fruit and nuts he had never seen before. And mangos like in China. He wished he could give his wife some. With a handful of rice a day, he could live here without working. Five-petaled flowers spun from the trees, pink stars, white stars, yellow stars, striped red and white stars. At one beautiful spot, white trumpet flowers hung above his head like hats. He walked on ground royally carpeted with jacaranda. When the sun became hot, a tall rain fell and made two rainbows across the sky, the colors of the top one in the opposite order of the bottom one, "Aiya," said the men. "Beautiful. Beautiful." "Is that a good omen or a bad omen?" "How does it happen?" "It has to be a good omen." The rainbows moved ahead of them. Before they became too wet, the rain stopped; the sun and breeze dried them. Bak Goong memorized all this to tell his wife.

·   ·   ·

They descended another side of the mountain and walked along the sea all day, and at last came to the place where they were to work. They had arrived in the middle of the workday, and were to start at once. There was no farm, no sugarcane ready to tend. It was their job to hack a farm out of the wilderness, which they were to level from the ocean to the mountain. To do this, Bak Goong was given a machete, a saw, an ax, and a pickax. The green that had looked like grass at a distance was a tangle of trees so thick that they shut out sunlight. Leaves grew only on their tops and bent backs. They were not tall trees, branch having wrestled branch into a knot that gnarled for miles. It may have been one tree that had replanted itself tighter and tighter. A criminal dropped into the midst of the webwork would be imprisoned forever. Beginning anywhere, Bak Goong chopped into the edge of this strange forest. He could not take hold of the branches because of the thorns on them. Dust shook down. Coughing, alarmed at how quickly he grew hot, tired, and thirsty in the intervals between the water-and-tea man's rounds, he shook a silver ball from the flat glass bottle he carried in his pocket and swallowed it for thirst. He gave pills to the boys working on either side of him. Though he chopped, hacked, and sawed with all his might, the knot of trees did not seem smaller. Black birds with flashes of white wings flew easily straight through the maze.

After work, though he could get sick and die from mixing cold water with hot sweat—open pores draw in the cold—he ran with the others into the ocean, and let it wash him. In the water rushing away from him, he held on to his body and mind with effort. The horizon seemed to be up in the air. He would have gone to sleep right there on the beach, but the ones who had arrived earlier had established an eating system, "Eh, China Man, come eat," the China Men invited. They had already organized the food, decided who would cook and on what terms. "Eh, China Man, come eat," Bak Goong imitated their English. So he got to sit down to a good dinner on plank tables. They passed around candy before dinner; it was a regular welcome party. The few Hawaiian workers passed around salt. Chinese take a bit of sugar to remind them in times of bitter struggle of the sweetness of life, and Hawaiians take a few grains of salt on the tongue because it tastes like the sea, like the earth, like human sweat and tears. Some fishermen and surfers and a demon traveler also ate with them, as did the other great grandfather, Bak Sook Goong, who was not yet related. (They would have called one another Bak and Sook in any case—Uncles.) These strangers ate like a family, drank from the same soup tureen, ate from the same plates of accompaniments to the rice. They did not gobble directly from the center dishes to the mouth but first touched the meat or vegetable to the rice. Bak Goong was lucky to have fallen among the civilized in the wild Sandalwood Mountains. He ate chunks of coconut wet in its milk and the fruit they had gathered on the way that morning. The hot tea on the hot day cooled him.

In the talk-story time after dinner, young men gave advice to young men. There were no old men in the Sandalwood Mountains. "Mind your own business, and work like an ox." "Don't gamble." "Keep your machete sharp, and hold it like so when you smell a demon near you." "Wrap your queue around your head or tuck it inside your shirt." "If you have the opium habit, you can ask for your wages by the week." Bak Goong congratulated himself on what a good ear he had; he could understand much of what these unusual men were saying. He had traveled to the middle of the ocean and was getting along with the people he found. He spoke to the most foreign, barbarous-looking China Men. When a storyteller lost him with apocopations,* he wondered whether a puff of opium would help him understand language more clearly, but "No," he said politely, "I'd not be able to repay you." The men who had come earlier also said that the plantation had a rule

---

* Losing of sounds or letters at the end of a word.—Ed.

that they not talk at work, but this rule was so absurd, he thought he must have misheard tones.

. . .

On their "day offu," the China Men went into Honolulu to spend their pay. The could ride cane and mill wagons as far as they had built roads, and they walked until there was another road, where they could catch another wagon for a few cents more. A family could eat for a week on that fare. They dressed for town in their black silk suits and yellow straw boaters with the black band and forked streamers; their braids hung between the swallowtails. "I'm going to town," Bak Goong sang and sang *town* as if Honolulu were his own village. A family man, he walked the entire way and reached town by noon. He went directly to the general store, where he bought a money order for his wife and dictated a letter about how well and lighthearted he was in this Sandalwood paradise. The leftover money was his to keep or spend on careful gambling (more for the companionship than the money), a restaurant meal with a shot of whiskey, and a yearly picture taken at the photo studio. Unlike Bak Sook Goong, the other great grandfather, he did not spend money on Sandalwood Mountain women. He wandered about on the wooden sidewalks creaking underfoot and sat in the stores. "Come in and sit awhile," the store owners said as if inviting him into their own houses in China, and he was a real uncle or brother.

Most of the men were young enough to have their entire lives changed on a day off. A farmer could come to town, change his name, and become a merchant. Bak Goong met men who had forgotten the names of their Chinese family or the name and location of their Chinese village. They kept shaking their heads when he named village after village. They had lost a last piece of paper or a letter with the address on it. The gambling men played with fate for a new life. They bought chances. It was no work at all to throw the dice, flip a card, or pick a word in the pigeon lottery. In one Sunday, a lucky man could buy a farm or take a ship home or to California, stand up from the gambling table and walk to the harbor. Or he could sign his years away, mortgage his labor and future, not go home yet, ever. Two poor men gamble and one becomes a rich man. The other becomes a fleaman. A day in town was full of possibilities.

. . .

The next day the men plowed, working purposefully, but they dug a circle instead of straight furrows. They dug a wide hole. They threw down their tools and flopped on the ground with their faces over the edge of the hole and their legs like wheel spokes.

"Hello down there in China!" they shouted. "Hello, Mother." "Hello, my heart and my liver."

"I miss you." "What are you doing right now?" "Happy birthday. Happy birthday for last year too."

"I've been working hard for you, and I hate it."

"Sometimes I forget my family and go to clubs. I drink all night." "I lost all the money again." "I've become an opium addict." "I don't even look Chinese any more." "I'm sorry I ate it all by myself."

". . . and I fell to my knees at the sight of twenty waterfalls." "I saw only one sandalwood tree."

They said any kind of thing. "Blonde demoness." "Polynesian demoness."

"I'm coming home by and by." "I'm not coming home." "I'm staying here in the Sandalwood Mountains."

"I want to be home," Bak Goong said.

"I'm bringing her home," said Bak Sook Goong.

They had dug an ear into the world, and were telling the earth their secrets.

"I want home," Bak Goong yelled, pressed against the soil, and smelling the earth. "I want my home," the men yelled together. "I want home. Home. Home. Home. Home."

Talked out, they buried their words, planted them. "Like cats covering shit," they laughed.

"That wasn't a custom," said Bak Goong. "We made it up. We can make up customs because we're the founding ancestors of this place."

They made such a noise that the demons could have come charging upon them and the hole fill with the sounds of battle. But the demons hid, the China Men so riled up, who knows what they were up to?

From the day of the shout party, Bak Goong talked and sang at his work, and did not get sent to the punishment fields. In cutting season, the demons no longer accompanied the knife-wielding China Men into deep cane.

Soon the new green shoots would rise, and when in two years the cane grew gold tassels, what stories the wind would tell.

Bak Goong, the great grandfather with a good memory, kept his promises and so chose to go back to China. Bak Sook Goong also went back, though the king and queen of the Sandalwood Mountains had ruled that a China Man who married a Hawaiian would be called Hawaiian, and many another Paké godfather stayed. Bak Sook Goong brought his Sandalwood Mountain wife back with him. She would become sister of his other two wives. He would abandon none of them. So these two great grandfathers made their lives of a piece.

9. The New Imperialism

THE TOOLS OF EMPIRE

DANIEL R. HEADRICK

The "imperialism of free trade" that characterized much European expansion from 1840 to 1860 was followed, especially after 1880, by more aggressive and popular policies calling for actual possession of colonies, especially in Africa. The reasons for the "new imperialism" of military conquest and occupation have been widely debated. Marxists and socialists pointed to the financial panic of 1873, the troubled Western economies in the 1870s, shrinking domestic markets, and the need for raw materials. Others have seen the change in the growth of popular antiforeign sentiment and racism at the end of the nineteenth century.

In this essay, Daniel Headrick, a modern historian of technology, suggests that we look at the technological developments of the late nineteenth century as well. What technological innovations does he mention? How would they have made military conquest, colonization, and occupation easier?

The history of European imperialism in the nineteenth century still contains a number of paradoxes, which an understanding of technology can help elucidate. One of them is the expansion of Britain in the mid-century, a world power claiming to want no more imperial responsibilities yet reluctantly acquiring territories "in a fit of absent-mindedness." Was this really a case, as Fieldhouse put it, of "a metropolitan dog being wagged by its colonial tail"? A more appropriate metaphor might be the pseudonym Macgregor Laird used in writing to *The Spectator:* Cerberus, the many-headed dog.

For the imperialist drive did not originate from only one source. In the outposts of empire, and most of all in Calcutta and Bombay, were eager imperialists, adventurous and greedy for territory. They lacked, however, the industry to manufacture the tools of conquest. Had they been able to create the instruments appropriate to their ambitions, they might well have struck out on their own, like the settlers in the Thirteen Colonies of North America. But against Burma, China, the Middle East, and Africa they needed British technology.

In Britain, meanwhile, the politicians were at times reluctant; the lengthy delay in occupying Egypt is an example of this. But the creators of the tools of empire—people like Peacock, the Lairds, the arms manufacturers—were provisioning the empire with the equipment that the peripheral imperialists required. The result was a secondary imperialism, the expansion of British India, sanctioned, after the fact, by London.

Imperialism in the mid-century was predominantly a matter of British tentacles reaching out from India toward Burma, China, Malaya, Afghanistan, Mesopotamia, and the Red Sea. Territorially, at least, a much more impressive demonstration of the new imperialism was the scramble for Africa in the last decades of the century. Historians generally agree that from a profit-making point of view, the scramble was a dubious undertaking. Here also, technology helps explain events.

Inventions are most easily described one by one, each in its own technological and socioeconomic setting. Yet the inner logic of innovations must not blind us to the patterns of chronological coincidence. Though advances occurred in every period, many of the innovations that proved useful to the imperialists of the scramble first had an impact in the two decades from 1860 to 1880. These were the years in which quinine prophylaxis made Africa safer for Europeans; quick-firing breechloaders replaced muzzle-loaders among the forces stationed on the imperial frontiers; and the compound engine, the Suez Canal, and the submarine cable made steamships competitive with sailing ships, not only on government-subsidized mail routes, but for ordinary freight on distant seas as well. Europeans who set out to conquer new lands in 1880 had far more power over nature and over the people they encountered than their predecessors twenty years earlier had; they could accomplish their tasks with far greater safety and comfort.

Few of the inventions that affected the course of empire in the nineteenth century were indispensable; quinine prophylaxis comes closest, for it is unlikely that many Europeans would willingly have run the risks of Africa without it. The muzzle-loaders the French used in Fighting Abd-el Kader could also have defeated other non-Western peoples; but it is unlikely that any European nation would have sacrificed for Burma, the Sudan, or the Congo as much as France did for Algeria.

Today we are accustomed to important innovations being so complex—computers, jet aircraft, satellites, and weapons systems are but a few examples—that only the governments of major powers can defray their research and development costs; and generally they are eager to do so. In the nineteenth century European governments were preoccupied with many things other than imperialism. Industrialization, social conflicts, international tensions, military preparedness, and the striving for a balanced budget all competed for their attention. Within the ruling circles of Britain, France, Belgium, and Germany, debates raged on the need for colonies and the costs of imperialism.

What the breechloader, the machine gun, the steamboat and steam-ship, and quinine and other innovations did was to lower the cost, in both financial and human terms, of penetrating, conquering, and exploiting new territories. So cost-effective did they make imperialism that not only national governments but lesser groups as well could now play a part in it. The Bombay Presidency opened the Red Sea Route; the Royal Niger Company conquered the Caliphate of Sokoto; even individuals like Macgregor Laird, William Mackinnon, Henry Stanley, and Cecil Rhodes could precipitate events and stake out claims to vast territories which later became parts of empires. It is because the flow of new technologies in the nineteenth century made imperialism so cheap that it reached the threshold of acceptance among the peoples and governments of Europe, and led nations to become empires. Is this not as important a factor in the scramble for Africa as the political, diplomatic, and business motives that historians have stressed?

All this only begs a further question. Why were these innovations developed, and why were they applied where they would prove useful to imperialists? Technological innovations in the nineteenth century are usually described in the context of the Industrial Revolution. Iron shipbuilding was part of the growing use of iron in all areas of engineering; submarine cables resulted from the needs of business and the development of the electrical industry. Yet while we can (indeed, we must) explain the invention and manufacture of specific new technologies in the context of general industrialization, it does not suffice to explain the transfer and application of these technologies to Asia and Africa. To understand the diffusion of new technologies, we must consider also the flow of information in the nineteenth century among both Western and non-Western peoples.

In certain parts of Africa, people are able to communicate by "talking drums" which imitate the tones of the human voice. Europeans inflated this phenomenon into a great myth, that Africans could speak to one another across their continent by the throbbing of tom-toms in the night. This myth of course reflected the Westerners' obsession with long-range communication. In fact, nineteenth-century Africans and Asians were quite isolated from one another and ignorant of what was happening in other parts of the world. Before the Opium War, the court of the Chinese emperor was misinformed about events in Canton and ignorant of the ominous developments in Britain, Burma, and Nigeria. People living along the Niger did not know where the river came from, nor where it went. Stanley encountered people in the Congo who had never before heard of firearms or white men. Throughout Africa, warriors learned from their own experiences but rarely from those of their neighbours.

To be sure, there were cases in which Africans or Asians adopted new technologies. Indian princes hired Europeans to train their troops. The Ethiopian Bezbiz Kasa had an English sergeant make cannons for him, while Samori Touré sent a blacksmith to learn gunsmithing from the French. Mehemet Ali surrounded himself with European engineers and officers in a crash program to modernize his country. What is remarkable about these efforts is their rarity and, in most cases, their insufficiency. In the nineteenth century, only Japan succeeded in keeping abreast of Western technological developments.

In contrast, Western peoples—whether Europeans or descendants of Europeans settled on other continents—were intensely interested in events elsewhere, technological as well as otherwise. Physicians in Africa published their findings in France and Britain. American gun manufacturers exhibited their wares in London, British experts traveled to America to study gunmaking, and General Wolseley paid a visit to the American inventor Hiram Maxim to offer suggestions. Macgregor Laird was inspired by news of events on the Niger to try out a new kind of ship. Dutch and British botanists journeyed to South America to obtain plants to be grown in Asia. Scientists in Indonesia published a journal in French and German for an international readership. The latest rifles were copied in every country and sent to the colonies for testing. The mails and cables transmitted to and from the financial centers of Europe up-to-date information on products, prices, and quantities of goods around the world. And the major newspapers, especially the London *Times*, sent out foreign correspondents and published detailed articles about events in faraway lands. Then, as now, people in the Western world were hungry for the latest news and interested in useful technological innovations. Thus what seemed to work in one place, whether iron river steamers, quinine prophylaxis, machine guns, or compound engines, was quickly known and applied in other places. In every part of the world, Europeans were more knowledgeable about events on other continents than indigenous peoples were about their neighbors. It is the Europeans who had the "talking drums."

European empires of the nineteenth century were economy empires, cheaply obtained by taking advantage of new technologies, and, when the cost of keeping them rose a century later, quickly discarded. In the process, they unbalanced world relations, overturned ancient ways of life, and opened the way for a new global civilization.

The impact of this technologically based imperialism on the European nations who engaged in it is still hotly debated. The late nineteenth and early twentieth centuries were a time of overweening national pride, of frantic, often joyful, preparations for war. The cheap victories on the imperial frontiers, the awesome power so suddenly acquired over the forces of nature and over whole kingdoms and races, were hard to reconcile with the prudence and compromises which the delicate European balance required.

The era of the new imperialism was also the age in which racism reached its zenith. Europeans, once respectful of some non-Western peoples—especially the Chinese—began to confuse levels of technology with levels of culture in general, and finally with biological capacity. Easy conquests had warped the judgment of even the scientific elites.

Among Africans and Asians the legacy of imperialism reflects their assessment of the true value of the civilization that conquered them. Christianity has had little impact in Asia, and its spread in Africa has been overshadowed by that of Islam. Capitalism, that supposed bedrock of Western civilization, has failed to take root in most Third World countries. European concepts of freedom and the rule of law have fared far worse. The mechanical power of the West has not brought, as Macgregor Laird had hoped, "the glad tidings of 'peace and good will toward men' into the dark places of the earth which are now filled with cruelty."

The technological means the imperialists used to create their empires, however, have left a far deeper imprint than the ideas that motivated them. In their brief domination, the Europeans passed on to the peoples of Asia and Africa their own fascination with machinery and innovation. This has been the true legacy of imperialism.

THE PARTITION OF AFRICA

L. S. STAVRIANOS

The division of Africa into territories ruled by European powers is the most striking example of the "new imperialism." Here L. S. Stavrianos, a modern historian, puts this development in the context of European economic history. What was the conflict between African agricultural producers and European merchants that Stavrianos refers to? Why was government and military intervention more likely after 1870? Was the conquest of Africa motivated purely by economic causes or were there other factors at work?

The partition of Africa was, as we all recognize, due primarily to the economic necessity of increasing the supplies of raw materials and food to meet the needs of the industrialized nations of Europe.

Lord Lugard

What have these big companies done for the country? Nothing. The concessions were given with the hope that the companies would develop the country. They have exploited it, which is not the same thing as development; they have bled and squeezed it like an orange whose skin is sooner or later discarded.

André Gide

The transition from the free-trade imperialism of the early nineteenth century to the global colonialism of the latter part of the century was demonstrated most dramatically in the continent of Africa, and particularly by the activities of Henry Morton Stanley. In 1871 Stanley found Livingstone on the banks of Lake Tanganyika in one of the most memorable episodes of African exploration. In 1879 Stanley appeared on the Congo River, but this time he was functioning as an agent for King Leopold of Belgium rather than as an explorer. The age of exploration had given way to the age of African partition. By the First World War the Great Powers of Europe had divided among themselves the entire continent, the only exceptions being the precarious states of Liberia and Ethiopia. With the partition of Africa, the way was clear for the economic penetration of the continent—for the full-scale integration of Africa into the global market economy.

PARTITION OF AFRICA

During the early nineteenth century the trade in slaves gradually was replaced by a flourishing trade in West African natural resources—palm oil, palm kernels, groundnuts, gold, timber, ivory and cotton. The terms of trade were favorable for West Africa until the 1850s, when economic conditions deteriorated sharply. The resulting economic tensions between European companies and native traders combined with changing Great Power diplomatic relationships to precipitate a scramble for African lands and the speedy partitioning of the continent.

After the 1850s, palm-oil prices dropped sharply because of the competition from oil fields opened in the United States in 1860; from groundnuts being imported from India; and from Australian tallow that was being transported profitably to Western Europe after the opening of the Suez Canal in 1869. The effect of this growing competition was accentuated by the shrinking European demand for oils and fats during the Great Depression of the last quarter of the nineteenth century. European firms now received lower prices in Europe for their West African goods and tried to pass on the reductions to the African producers. This started an economic power struggle in which each side indulged in malpractices such as diluting the palm oil and misrepresenting the quality and length of cloth. Demarcation disputes also arose over their respective functions and areas of operation. Some European firms established bases inland to buy commodities more cheaply from the producers by eliminating the African middlemen, and the latter often responded by destroying the company bases. Conversely, some African wholesalers tried to bypass the companies by selling directly in Europe, and they also attempted to keep up prices by withholding supplies.

European firms called on their governments to use force to beat down what they considered to be unreasonable obstructionism by native growers and merchants. Colonial officials often supported this demand for an "active policy" viewing it as a means for advancing their own careers. Furthermore, activism was becoming more feasible and appealing with the vastly increased power made available to Europeans by the Industrial and Scientific revolutions.

Advances in tropical medicine, especially the use of quinine for combating malaria, freed Europeans from the staggering mortality rates they had hitherto suffered. Also, the invention of the Gatling and Maxim machine guns shifted the military balance of power decisively against the Africans. So long as muskets were the standard firearms, a reasonable military balance prevailed between the two sides, especially since the Africans purchased huge numbers of muskets and even some cannon. But with the advent of repeating rifles and machine guns, the Africans were almost as badly outclassed as the Aztecs and the Incas had been by the Spaniards with their muskets. Other technological advances effected during the Industrial Revolution further facilitated penetration of the African continent, including river steamers, railways and telegraphic communications. When the first British steamship appeared in the Niger in 1857, it was foreordained that a decade later the first British consul should be appointed in the interior, at Lokaja.

This increasing power available to Europeans stimulated demand to make use of it to gain certain objectives. One was to lower the cost of goods reaching the coast by eliminating African middlemen and the tolls levied by African states. Another was to build railways into the interior, which it was believed would transform the economy of Africa as it had that of Europe. The most far-reaching objective was outright annexation, which was urged in order to assure law and order, maximize business opportunities and keep out European rivals. To rationalize their demands, the new merchants who wished to penetrate inland (as against those who wanted to safeguard their traditional operations on the coast) began using phrases such as "the regeneration of Africa," "the redemption of the savage" and the "preaching of the Gospel on the Banks of the Niger." But, as Dike observes, "The battle between the two groups was predominantly economic, not ideological." So far as the

British government was concerned it was ready to protect them in whatever regions they extended their operations. "Where there is money to be made," wrote a Foreign Office official, William Wylde, in 1876, "our merchants will be certain to intrude themselves, and . . . if they establish a lucrative trade, public opinion in this country practically compels us to protect them."

Outstanding among the annexationists in West Africa was Sir George Goldie. "My dream as a child," this masterful builder once said, "was to colour the map red." He found his opportunity in the Niger Valley, where competing British companies had enabled African leaders such as Ja Ja to preserve their independence. In 1879 these companies under Goldie's direction combined to form the United African Company, which later absorbed French competitors in the upper Niger and was renamed the National African Company. Goldie was quite clear in his mind as to the role of his company in the Niger basin: "With old established markets closing to our manufacturers, with India producing cotton fabrics not only for her own use but for export, it would be suicidal to abandon to a rival power the only great remaining undeveloped opening for British goods."

With his customary vigor, Goldie set out to gain mastery over the Niger delta and to present the British government with a *fait accompli*. He established over 100 trading posts in the interior, and backed them up with some 237 treaties, which his agents concluded by 1886 with African chiefs. These documents invariably ceded to the National African Company "the whole of the territories of the signatories," along with the right to exclude foreigners and to monopolize the trade of the involved territories. To deal with those African leaders who were unwilling to submit, the Company constructed twenty gunboats of shallow draft that were capable of navigating the Niger during the dry as well as the rainy season. Attacks upon company posts were countered by devastating naval bombardments. Thus the Company became the *de facto* government of the Nigerian hinterland before it was claimed by Britain at the 1884–85 Berlin African Conference.

It was not only West Africa that was partitioned between 1880 and 1900. During those same decades other parts of the continent also were annexed, even though they were not generating any large-scale trade of the sort that was causing frictions in West Africa. It is necessary, therefore, to take into account also the background forces engendered by the Industrial Revolution that culminated in the partitioning not only of Africa but also of virtually the entire globe. Entire continents were subjected to either outright colonial status, as in Africa, India and Southeast Asia, or into semicolonial status, as in the Ottoman, Persian and Chinese empires, as well as all of Latin America.

In the case of Africa the partition process was triggered by new intruding powers that annexed choice but unclaimed African regions, thereby precipitating a chain reaction of pre-emptive partitioning by all the Great Powers. King Leopold of Belgium started the partitioning process in Africa by hiring the explorer Henry Stanley to acquire territory in the rich Congo Basin. In 1879–80 Stanley gained title to over nine hundred thousand square miles (over seventy-six times the entire area of Belgium) from local chiefs who could not comprehend the meaning of the scraps of paper they were signing in return for baubles such as cases of gin and rum, and brightly colored coats, caps and handkerchiefs. With their communal landholding traditions, the notion of selling title to tribal lands was as preposterous to these chiefs as it would be for an American city mayor to sell title to his courthouse or city hall. Yet this was done all over Africa—not only by Stanley for Belgium but also by Count de Brazza for France (north of the Congo), by Dr. Karl Peters for Germany (East Africa) and by other adventurers in the service of other powers.

The race for colonies was under way, so the Berlin African Conference was held in 1884–85 to set down ground rules for future acquisitions of African lands. It was agreed that notice of intent should be given, that claims had to be legitimized by effective occupation and that disputes were to be settled by arbitration. This treaty cleared the way for the greatest land grab in history. In 1879 the only colonies in Africa were those of France in Algeria and Senegal, of Britain along the Gold Cost and at the Cape, and of Portugal in Angola and Mozambique. By 1914 the entire continent had been partitioned, except for Ethiopia and Liberia, as indicated in the following table:

Political Division in Africa in 1914

	SQUARE MILES
French (Tunisia, Algeria, Morocco, French West Africa, French Congo, French Somaliland, Madagascar)	4,086,950
British (Union of South Africa, Basutoland, Bechuanaland, Nyasaland, Rhodesia, British East Africa, Uganda, Zanzibar, Somaliland, Nigeria, Gold Coast, Sierra Leone, Gambia, Egypt, Anglo-Egyptian Sudan)	3,701,411
German (East Africa, South-West Africa, Cameroon, Togoland)	910,150
Belgian (Congo State)	900,000
Portuguese (Guinea, West Africa, East Africa)	787,500
Italian (Eritrea, Italian Somaliland, Libya)	600,000
Spanish (Rio de Oro, Muni River Settlements)	79,800
Independent States (Liberia, Ethiopia)	393,000
TOTAL	11,458,811

The table is my compilation, published earlier in my *The World Since 1500* (Englewood Cliffs, N.J.: Prentice-Hall, 1971), p. 380.

ROOTS OF AMERICAN EXPANSION

JAMES C. THOMSON, JR., PETER W. STANLEY, AND JOHN CURTIS PERRY

While Africa was carved up by European powers, the United States also participated in the territorial expansion of the "new imperialism," especially in the Pacific and Latin America. Here the "roots" of American expansion are explored by three modern historians. What were these roots? What do you think of the assertion that the United States has always been an expansive nation? Was American expansion similar to European? Did American expansion also change after 1870? Has it continued since?

The United States has always been an expansive, assertive nation. From its earliest days, founding fathers such as Franklin and Washington conceived of it explicitly as an empire—a "rising empire," as Washington put it in 1783—with an inherent right to expand wherever its destiny or needs might direct.

For roughly the first century after independence, this expansion took two forms. The first, westward movement across the continent, was pivotal: it both expressed and fueled the dynamism at the heart of American society. The result of this was the vast nation of almost incalculable resources, with its imagery of individualism and struggle, that we know today.

The second, overseas commercial, cultural, and evangelical expansion, was peripheral in every sense. Such expansion had its uses: supplying certain specific lacks, providing a market of varying importance for excess agricultural production, and venting some of the most grandiose and least realistic psychological drives of the society. Moreover, it affected the history of certain other peoples, notably the Japanese. With the exception of the large export trade in southern cotton to Great Britain, however, it was relatively unimportant to the development of the United States. Expansionism, even imperialism, was in the genes of American civilization. But until well after the Civil War, it appeared that a maritime empire of the British or French type was not.

Late in the nineteenth century, this began to change. By then, it was becoming clear that the continental limits of the United States had been reached with the Gadsden Purchase of 1853 and the acquisition of Alaska in 1867—1868. Enormous possibilities for growth and development remained within the country's existing boundaries, but henceforth there would be no more new expansion into contiguous territory. No one but buccaneers wanted to annex more of Mexico; and the rise of Canadian nationalism combined with the power of the British fleet to block expansion to the north. Only the ocean frontiers remained open.

So, with the renovation of the United States Navy, the annexation of the Philippines and Puerto Rico, the promulgation of the Open Door notes, and the appearance of big-power diplomacy under Theodore Roosevelt, America turned its expansive energies toward the overseas world.

This new stage of American expansionism differed from its predecessor in more than geographic focus. It had a character of its own that reflected important changes in the domestic society, economy, and politics of the country.

The most obvious of these changes was the elimination of slavery. Between roughly 1820 and 1865, few Americans had recognized that expansion was an issue in its own right, with moral and constitutional consequences of the first order. Instead, expansion had been subsumed under the debate over the extension of slavery and the maintenance of a balance of power between slave states and free. Proposals to annex new territory turned principally upon such considerations as whether the land in question was suitable for plantation slavery and whether its organization as a state would augment the Northern or the Southern voting bloc in Congress. With the end of slavery and its especially rigid type of political sectionalism, expansion was debated on its own merits for the first time since the days of Thomas Jefferson.

More subtly, the experience of the Civil War and Reconstruction changed American attitudes toward two closely related moral questions that arose inescapably in connection with territorial expansion: whether, to be true to its origins and principles, the United States must respect the inherent sovereignty of other political societies—their right to create, by revolution if necessary, a government of their own choosing; and whether it was justifiable morally for the United States to extend its sovereignty over others by conquest.

Prior to the Civil War, most Americans were sympathetic toward nationalist revolutions—especially if the nationalists were white, republican, and respectful toward the rights of property owners. In the 1820s, for example, popular support for the Latin American revolutions against Spain compelled John Quincy Adams and James Monroe to abandon diplomatic discretion and promptly recognize the new republics to the south. In 1848, sympathy for revolutionaries in Hungary and elsewhere in Europe was so widespread that American politicians such as

Daniel Webster and Stephen Douglas competed to identify themselves with the issue.

This kind of identification with nationalist revolutions was inevitably a constraint upon American expansion, although, to be sure, it did nothing to save the American Indians. In the popular and political mythology of the time, America's continental expansion was conceived of as an "empire for liberty," an "extension of the area of freedom." This is a faith impossible to reconcile with the dispatch of over half the United States Army several decades later to extinguish the independence of the Philippines, seven thousand miles away.

In the interval, however, the Civil War had changed Americans' attitudes toward revolution, conquest, and political self-determination. Whatever else it may have been, the Civil War was plainly a forcible denial of the South's right to self-determination. To justify to themselves the fratricidal horror of one of the most murderous and destructive wars in modern history, Americans had to conclude that the right to revolution and self-determination were not absolute—that they were, in fact, less important than the unity of an existing nation, the continuity of institutions, and the rights of an oppressed minority. Moreover, to explain to themselves what General Sherman was doing in Georgia, they had to concede the legitimacy of wars of conquest.

The result was the shattering of what had been one of the nation's central myths. Americans emerged from the Civil War hardened to mass violence and alienated from the revolutionary tradition. More than that; they emerged with a growing sense of identification with the great monarchical empires of the age. When Polish nationalists revolted against Tsarist tyranny in 1865, a conspicuous body of American opinion—liberal as well as conservative—backed the Russians. America, said Herman Melville approvingly, stood before the world with "law on her brow and empire in her eyes."

Concomitantly, the international competition for empire changed between the middle and the end of the nineteenth century. In the era of Manifest Destiny, when the United States annexed Texas, California, and Oregon, the Western world's conception of empire was in flux. Since Adam Smith and the American Revolution, mercantilist colonial empires of the seventeenth-and eighteenth-century type had been largely repudiated as expensive, inefficient, and corrupting. Although commercial (and even territorial) expansion continued, there was a relative hiatus in the conquest of new colonies. Symptomatically, our term "imperialism," connoting a dynamic, aggressive, exploitative process, did not yet exist. The word itself first obtained currency later in the century as a sarcastic description of the posturing of Napoleon III.

By the final decades of the century, on the other hand, imperialism, in the modern sense had become normal for the major Western powers—and even Japan. In the thirty years between 1870 and 1900, European nations acquired sovereignty over one-fifth of the earth's land area and one-tenth of its population. This was an intensely self-conscious process on the part of the various governments, and it was accompanied by the appearance of both popular and theoretical literature celebrating conquest and expansion as measures of national greatness. This gave American thought about overseas expansion a competitive impetus and a focused intensity lacking in the earlier part of the century.

The most important change underlying the creation of what many people have called America's "new empire" appears, on the surface, to have been economic. One of the most dramatic developments in the United States between the middle and the end of the nineteenth century was the emergence of an industrial, urban economy. In one sense, this was a success story: industrial development and technological innovation brought with them profits, employment, and greater productivity. The face of the nation changed, for the better, many people felt; and by the turn of the century, there was genuine pride in America's identification with progress, its achievement of first place among the industrial powers of the world.

On the other hand, industrialism and urbanization caused terrible, soul-racking problems. Major depressions struck the country in 1873 and 1893, and there was a serious recession in the mid-1880s. Contemporaries said that half the years between the Civil War and the Spanish-American War fell in either a depression or a recession, and that 95 percent of all capitalists went bankrupt sooner or later. Partly for this reason, employers drove their workers hard and paid them little. It was the era of ten-hour days, six-day weeks, unsanitary buildings, and dangerous machinery.

Even Herbert Spencer, advocate of Social Darwinism and the survival of the fittest, recoiled from the "repulsive" pollution and stench of the American factory. "Six months residence here," he said after viewing the Carnegie steel works in Pittsburgh, "would justify suicide." The normal wage for unskilled laborers in such places was between $1.25 and $1.50 per day. When there was work to be had, that is. At its worst, the unemployment rate during the depression of the 1880s reached 20 percent, and for the whole period 1893–1898 it averaged more than 9 percent. For those out of work, there was no insurance or public welfare.

These dilemmas of poverty, failure, unemployment, and insecurity were intensified by the social environment in which they occurred. Influxes of immigrants and rural Americans overtaxed the facilities and political institutions of the cities. In the two decades between 1880 and 1900, for example, the population of New York City grew from roughly 2 million to 3.5 million; Chicago tripled in size; Detroit, Cleveland, and Milwaukee doubled. The population density of the tenth ward in New York in 1898 was 747 people per acre, probably the highest in the world at the time.

In the face of such an explosion, housing and public services lagged far behind the need for them. As late as 1900, two-thirds of the streets of Chicago were unpaved; most of the streets of Baltimore and New Orleans and over one-third of those in Philadelphia, St. Louis, and Atlanta lacked underground sewers; better than half the streets of Atlanta had no water mains. The inevitable effects of such conditions were aggravated by the inexperience of most of the newcomers with the requirements of life in cities, or America, or both. Vice, corruption, violence, and exploitation rose; and public health plummeted. At the turn of the century, rural death rates in the United States were 20 percent lower than those in the cities. When New York introduced effective street cleaning and garbage collection in 1885, the death rate there fell 27 percent within two years.

Americans of many motives and persuasions agreed that the malfunctioning of the economy, the demoralization of the cities, and the corruption and ineffectuality of government cried out for rectification. Eventually, broad alliances would be struck between them to attack specific issues under the banner of progressivism. The earliest attempts to deal with such problems, however, were primitive and fragmented. Among them, two stand out, Populism and expansionism. Where the former looked to internal purification as a remedy, the latter sought an external escape.

The new expansionism of the 1890s arose at least partly because many people blamed America's economic troubles on overproduction. Too much investment in the industrial economy, it was said, had created excess productive capacity in relation to the purchasing power of the American public. The resulting failure of the American market to consume the output of its own factories, people concluded, lay behind the high incidence of depression and recession, the general decline of profits and price levels characteristic of the age, and the impoverishment of the working class. The more fearful of the nation's political and economic leaders worried that unless a remedy were found, American capitalism might destroy itself and produce a social revolution. Rather than encourage the government to intervene and redistribute wealth, so as to create a larger effective market within the country, they looked to increased exports to end the glut and keep up profits and employment.

The emphasis upon exports made sense, because by the last quarter of the nineteenth century, American industry had achieved sufficient maturity and efficiency to compete successfully with British and German rivals for the markets of the world. Apart from cyclical fluctuations, industrial exports had grown steadily since the Civil War; and by the end of the century several industries relied upon foreign sales for a significant part of their business. Exports of iron and steel, for example, took between 7 and 15 percent of total output, depending upon the year; exports of agricultural implements and machinery sometimes as much as 16 percent. More than half of the illuminating oil refined in the United States and about one-quarter of the sewing machines made here were sold abroad. So was roughly half of the copper mined in this country. With examples like these in mind, it was plausible to suppose that, if overproduction were indeed at the root of the economy's troubles, the way out was to increase exports.

By the same token, some Americans hoped that exporting capital would relieve the pressure on the domestic economy. Investing in another country was much riskier, however, than simply trying to sell goods there. Its greatest appeal—and that a rather desperate one—was to minor leaguers in the financial world who could not compete at home with the likes of Morgan, Harriman, Henry Lee Higginson, or Kuhn, Loeb and Company. Consequently, while verbal speculation flourished over such esoterica as Chinese and Russian railways, relatively little actual investment occurred outside the North American continent and its adjacent territory. It took the recession of 1907 and the gathering attack on investment bankers in the progressive era to shake the faith of major European and American investors in the long-term attraction of the American economy. As late as 1900, there was still more than five times as much European capital invested in the United States as there was American capital invested in the whole rest of the world.

Those who argued for overseas markets did not necessarily want the United States to conquer and rule a great colonial empire on the Victorian model. Despite the lessons of the Civil War, many Americans still found that a course difficult to reconcile with their own constitution and Declaration of Independence. More important, however, the businessmen with most to gain from commercial expansion opposed anything, such as wars and colonies, that would increase the costs and power of government. It is true that those in the coal, steel, and armaments industries stood to gain from naval construction; and the makers of cheap clothing, blankets, and tents profited from increased recruitments. But for most businessmen, gains of this sort were more than offset by higher taxes, the disruption of commerce, dislocations in the labor and capital markets, and increased social agitation. In an age of depressions, living in fear of anarchy and socialism, they wanted less excitement and more predictability.

For the most part, therefore, the emphasis was simply upon using American foreign policy to create favorable trading conditions. This took various forms, including improving the consular service, negotiating reciprocal tariffs, recognizing and supporting governments sympathetic to American trade, and building a navy competent to protect trade routes and overawe local troublemakers. The Open Door policy in China was the principal Asian expression of this emphasis in policy: a formal commitment by the United States government to the desire of business interests for what they called a "fair field and no favor."

By the same token, the territorial acquisitions of 1898 suited the needs of economic expansionists. Hawaii and the new protectorate in Cuba offered safe, attractive investment opportunities and valuable raw materials. Puerto Rico, Hawaii, and the Philippines established an American strategic presence along key trade routes. The Philippines had the potential to become the base of operations for American economic penetration of the Asian market, an American equivalent of Hong Kong.

It would be mistaken, however, to conclude from this that late-nineteenth-century American expansionism was wholly—or even primarily—economic in motivation. The returns are not yet in from the historiographical debate over this question. For every scholar who ranks economic causes first, there is another who finds the picture more complicated. No one denies that the condition of the American economy influenced the thought and action that led to expansionism. Indeed, the evidence is overwhelming that many people, including men of great political and economic power, sought expansion to relieve the pressure of overproduction. But the promotion of foreign trade and investment was not, *in itself*, the essence of the expansionism of this era.

For one thing, the fear of overproduction cannot successfully explain what was new in turn-of-the-century American expansionism.

Morally, politically, and strategically, the heart of the new expansionism was the acquisition of a large colonial empire, the projection of American military and naval power into Asia and Latin America on a permanent basis, and the deliberate emergence of the United States as one of the key forces in the international balance of power. The turn of the century was a transitional moment for America in all these respects. Where previously the initiative had lain with private interests, the government simply playing the role of a rather unreliable enabling agent, now *the United States government itself was the expansive force*. This was the truly imperial dimension that changed not just the weight but the character of American intervention in the lives, the rights, and even the economies of other peoples. Without it, the pursuit of commercial advantage would have made only a diffuse impact upon the rest of the world. Yet, as we have seen, this went far beyond what business advocates of exports desired.

10.   Culture and Change

THE ORIGIN OF SPECIES

CHARLES DARWIN

Modern consciousness begins with Darwin, Marx, and Freud. It is difficult to think about any important issue in modern life without having to confront one of the ideas of these seminal thinkers. In agreement or disagreement, we are their students. Our science, the questions we ask, even much of our "common sense" reflects their work.

As often happens in cases like this, however, the thinker or work becomes a code word for shaking heads. Everyone has an opinion. Few actually read what was said.

What did Darwin say in the following excerpts from The Origin of the Species, *published in 1859? Why was he writing? What occasion prompted his book? What did he think he proved? What was the difference between the idea of evolution and the idea of independent creation of species? Did he think his ideas were irreligious? Do you?*

When on board H.M.S. "Beagle," as naturalist, I was much struck with certain facts in the distribution of the organic beings inhabiting South America, and in the geological relations of the present to the past inhabitants of that continent. These facts, as will be seen in the latter chapters of this volume, seemed to throw some light on the origin of species—that mystery of mysteries, as it has been called by one of our greatest philosophers. On my return home, it occurred to me, in 1837, that something might perhaps be made out on this question by patiently accumulating and reflecting on all sorts of facts which could possibly have any bearing on it. After five years' work I allowed myself to speculate on the subject, and drew up some short notes; these I enlarged in 1844 into a sketch of the conclusions, which then seemed to me probable: from that period to the present day I have steadily pursued the same object. I hope that I may be excused for entering on these personal details, as I give them to show that I have not been hasty in coming to a decision.

My work is now (1859) nearly finished; but as it will take me many more years to complete it, and as my health is far from strong, I have been urged to publish this Abstract. I have more especially been induced

From *The Origin of Species by Means of Natural Selection* by Charles Darwin. London: 1859. Reprinted in *Darwin*, edited by Philip Appleman. New York: Norton, 1979.

to do this, as Mr. [Alfred Russel] Wallace, who is now studying the natural history of the Malay archipelago, has arrived at almost exactly the same general conclusions that I have on the origin of species. In 1858 he sent me a memoir on this subject, with a request that I would forward it to Sir Charles Lyell, who sent it to the Linnean Society, and it is published in the third volume of the Journal of that society. Sir C. Lyell and Dr. Hooker, who both knew of my work—the latter having read my sketch of 1844—honoured me by thinking it advisable to publish, with Mr. Wallace's excellent memoir, some brief extracts from my manuscripts.

This Abstract, which I now publish, must necessarily be imperfect. I cannot here give references and authorities for my several statements; and I must trust to the reader reposing some confidence in my accuracy. No doubt errors will have crept in, though I hope I have always been cautious in trusting to good authorities alone. I can here give only the general conclusions at which I have arrived, with a few facts in illustration, but which, I hope, in most cases will suffice. No one can feel more sensible than I do of the necessity of hereafter publishing in detail all the facts, with references, on which my conclusions have been grounded; and I hope in a future work to do this. For I am well aware that scarcely a single point is discussed in this volume on which facts cannot be adduced, often apparently leading to conclusions directly opposite to those at which I have arrived. A fair result can be obtained only by fully stating and balancing the facts and arguments on both sides of each question; and this is here impossible.

In considering the Origin of Species, it is quite conceivable that a naturalist, reflecting on the mutual affinities of organic beings, on their embryological relations, their geographical distribution, geological succession, and other such facts, might come to the conclusion that species had not been independently created, but had descended, like varieties, from other species. Nevertheless, such a conclusion, even if well founded, would be unsatisfactory, until it could be shown how the innumerable species inhabiting this world have been modified, so as to acquire that perfection of structure and coadaptation which justly excites our admiration. Naturalists continually refer to external conditions, such as climate, food, &c., as the only possible source of variation. In one limited sense, as we shall hereafter see, this may be true; but it is preposterous to attribute to mere external conditions, the structure, for instance, of the woodpecker, with its feet, tail, beak, and tongue, so admirably adapted to catch insects under the bark of trees. In the case of the mistletoe, which draws its nourishment from certain trees, which has seeds that must be transported by certain birds, and which has flowers with separate sexes absolutely requiring the agency of certain insects to bring pollen from one flower to the other, it is equally preposterous to account for the structure of this parasite, with its relations to several distinct organic beings, by the effects of external conditions, or of habit, or of the volition of the plant itself.

It is, therefore, of the highest importance to gain a clear insight into the means of modification and coadaptation. At the commencement of my observations it seemed to me probable that a careful study of domesticated animals and of cultivated plants would offer the best chance of making out this obscure problem. Nor have I been disappointed; in this and in all other perplexing cases I have invariably found that our knowledge, imperfect though it be, of variation under domestication, afforded the best and safest clue.

From these considerations, I shall devote the first chapter of this Abstract to Variation under Domestication. We shall thus see that a large amount of hereditary modification is at least possible; and, what is equally or more important, we shall see how great is the power of man in accumulating by his Selection successive slight variations. I will then pass on to the variability of species in a state of nature; but I shall, unfortunately, be compelled to treat this subject far too briefly, as it can be treated properly only by giving long catalogues of facts. We shall, however, be enabled to discuss what circumstances are most favourable to variation. In the next chapter the Struggle for Existence amongst all organic beings throughout the world, which inevitably follows from the high geometrical ratio of their increase, will be considered. This is the doctrine of Malthus, applied to the whole animal and vegetable kingdoms. As many more individuals of each species are born than can possibly survive; and as, consequently, there is a frequently recurring struggle for existence, it follows that any being, if it vary however slightly in any manner profitable to itself, under the complex and sometimes varying conditions of life, will have a better chance of surviving, and thus be *naturally selected*. From the strong principle of inheritance, any selected variety will tend to propagate its new and modified form.

This fundamental subject of Natural Selection will be treated at some length in the fourth chapter; and we shall then see how Natural Selection almost inevitably causes much Extinction of the less improved forms of life, and leads to what I have called Divergence of Character. In the next chapter I shall discuss the complex and little known laws of variation. In the five succeeding chapters, the most apparent and gravest difficulties in accepting the theory will be given: namely, first, the difficulties of transitions, or how a simple being or a simple organ can be changed and perfected into a highly developed being or into an elaborately constructed organ; secondly, the subject of Instinct, or the mental powers of animals; thirdly, Hybridism, or the infertility of species and the fertility of varieties when intercrossed; and fourthly, the imperfection of the Geological Record. In the next chapter I shall consider the geological succession of organic beings throughout time; in the twelfth and thirteenth, their geographical distribution throughout space; in the fourteenth, their classification or mutual affinities, both when mature and in an embryonic condition. In the last chapter I shall give a brief recapitulation of the whole work, and a few concluding remarks.

No one ought to feel surprise at much remaining as yet unexplained in regard to the origin of species and varieties, if he make due allowance for our profound ignorance in regard to the mutual relations of the many beings which live around us. Who can explain why one species ranges widely and is very numerous, and why another allied species has a narrow range and is rare? Yet these relations are of the highest importance, for they determine the present welfare and, as I believe, the future success and modification of every inhabitant of this world. Still less do we know of the mutual relations of the innumerable inhabitants of the world during the many past geological epochs in its history. Although much remains obscure, and will long remain obscure, I can entertain no doubt, after the most deliberate study and dispassionate judgment of which I am capable, that the view which most naturalists until recently entertained, and which I formerly entertained—namely, that each species has been independently created—is erroneous. I am fully convinced that species are not immutable; but that those belonging to what are called the same genera are lineal descendants of some other and generally extinct species, in the same manner as the acknowledged varieties of any one species are the descendants of that species. Furthermore, I am convinced that Natural Selection has been the most important, but not the exclusive, means of modification.

I see no good reason why the views given in this volume should shock the religious feelings of any one. It is satisfactory, as showing how transient such impressions are, to remember that the greatest discovery ever made by man, namely, the law of the attraction of gravity, was also attacked by Leibnitz, "as subversive of natural, and inferentially of revealed, religion." A celebrated author and divine has written to me that "he has gradually learnt to see that it is just as noble a conception of the Deity to believe that He created a few original forms capable of self-development into other and needful forms, as to believe that He required a fresh act of creation to supply the voids caused by the action of His laws."

Why, it may be asked, until recently did nearly all the most eminent living naturalists and geologists disbelieve in the mutability of species? It cannot be asserted that organic beings in a state of nature are subject to no variation; it cannot be proved that the amount of variation in the course of long ages is a limited quality; no clear distinction has been, or can be, drawn between species and well-marked varieties. It cannot be maintained that species when intercrossed are invariably sterile, and varieties invariably fertile; or that sterility is a special endowment and sign of creation. The belief that species were immutable productions was almost unavoidable as long as the history of the world was thought to be of short duration; and now that we have acquired some idea of the lapse of time, we are too apt to assume, without proof, that the geological record is so perfect that it would have afforded us plain evidence of the mutation of species, if they had undergone mutation.

But the chief cause of our natural unwillingness to admit that one species has given birth to clear and distinct species, is that we are always slow in admitting great changes of which we do not see the steps. The difficulty is the same as that felt by so many geologists, when Lyell first insisted that long lines of inland cliffs had been formed, the great valleys excavated, by the agencies which we see still at work. The mind cannot possibly grasp the full meaning of the term of even a million years; it cannot add up and perceive the full effects of many slight variations, accumulated during an almost infinite number of generations.

Although I am fully convinced of the truth of the views given in this volume under the form of an abstract, I by no means expect to convince experienced naturalists whose minds are stocked with a multitude of facts all viewed, during a long course of years, from a point of view directly opposite to mine. It is so easy to hide our ignorance under such expressions as the "plan of creation," "unity of design," &c., and to think that we give an explanation when we only re-state a fact. Any one whose disposition leads him to attach more weight to unexplained difficulties than to the explanation of a certain number of facts will certainly reject the theory. A few naturalists, endowed with much flexibility of mind, and who have already begun to doubt the immutability of species, may be influenced by this volume; but I look with confidence to the future,— to young and rising naturalists, who will be able to view both sides of the question with impartiality. Whoever is led to believe that species are mutable will do good service by conscientiously expressing his conviction; for thus only can the load of prejudice by which this subject is overwhelmed be removed.

Authors of the highest eminence seem to be fully satisfied with the view that each species has been independently created. To my mind it accords better with what we know of the laws impressed on matter by the Creator, that the production and extinction of the past and present inhabitants of the world should have been due to secondary causes, like those determining the birth and death of the individual. When I view all beings not as special creations, but as the lineal descendants of some few beings which lived long before the first bed of the Cambrian system was deposited, they seem to me to become ennobled. Judging from the past, we may safely infer that not one living species will transmit its unaltered likeness to a distant futurity. And of the species now living very few will transmit progeny of any kind to a far distant futurity; for the manner in which all organic beings are grouped, shows that the greater number of species in each genus, and all the species in many genera, have left no descendants, but have become utterly extinct. We can so far take a prophetic glance into futurity as to foretell that it will be the common and widely-spread species, belonging to the larger and dominant groups within each class, which will ultimately prevail and procreate new and dominant species. As all the living forms of life are the lineal descendants of those which lived long before the Cambrian epoch, we may feel certain that the ordinary succession by generation has never once been broken, and that no cataclysm has desolated the whole world. Hence we may look with some confidence to a secure future of great length. And as natural selection works solely by and for the good of each being, all corporeal and mental endowments will tend to progress towards perfection.

It is interesting to contemplate a tangled bank, clothed with many plants of many kinds, with birds singing on the bushes, with various insects flitting about, and with worms crawling through the damp earth, and to reflect that these elaborately constructed forms, so different from each other, and dependent upon each other in so complex a manner, have all been produced by laws acting around us. These laws, taken in the largest sense, being Growth with Reproduction; Inheritance which is almost implied by reproduction; Variability from the indirect and direct action of the conditions of life, and from use and disuse: a Ratio of Increase so high as to lead to a Struggle for Life, and as a consequence to Natural Selection, entailing Divergence of Character and the Extinction of less-improved forms. Thus, from the war of nature, from famine and death, the most exalted object which we are capable of conceiving, namely, the production of the higher animals, directly follows. There is grandeur in this view of life, with its several powers, having been originally breathed by the Creator into a few forms or into one; and that, whilst this planet has gone cycling on according to the fixed law of gravity, from so simple a beginning endless forms most beautiful and most wonderful have been, and are being evolved.

THE PSYCHOPATHOLOGY
OF EVERYDAY LIFE

SIGMUND FREUD

Maybe Freud, working in Vienna, Austria, at the turn of the twentieth century, did not "invent" psychology, the unconscious, or self-analysis, but he certainly left the world with a much deeper understanding of the human psyche than it had before. After Freud, nothing, not the most casual remark nor most typical dream, could be taken at face value. Everything could mean something else, often its opposite.

Freud's revelations about the human mind were the product of his scientific work and his medical practice, but they were also the product of the most intense personal analysis he ever conducted—that on himself. Freud endlessly posed questions and searched for deeper meanings. The following fragment is only a brief example of his method. Notice how a general question leads to specific cases, including his own. Does his analysis seem right? If such clearly convoluted investigations do lead to real truths, what does that say about the complexity of the human psyche? Can you reconstruct a dream or an experience of your own in this way?

How far back into childhood do our memories reach? I am familiar with some investigations on this questions by V. and C. Henri and Potwin. They assert that such examinations show wide individual variations, inasmuch as some trace their reminiscences to the sixth month of life, while others can recall nothing of their lives before the end of the sixth or even the eighth year. But what connection is there between these variations in the behaviour of childhood reminiscences, and what signification may be ascribed to them? It seems that it is not enough to procure the material for this question by simple inquiry, but it must later be subjected to a study in which the person furnishing the information must participate.

I believe we accept too indifferently the fact of infantile amnesia—that is, the failure of memory for the first years of our lives—and fail to find in it a strange riddle. We forget of what great intellectual accomplishments and of what complicated emotions a child of four years is capable. We really ought to wonder why the memory of later years has, as a rule, retained so little of these psychic processes, especially as we have every reason for assuming that these same forgotten childhood activities have

From *The Psychopathology of Everyday Life*, in *The Basic Writings of Sigmund Freud*, translated and edited by Dr. A. A. Brill. New York: The Modern Library, 1938. Reprinted by permission.

not glided off without leaving a trace in the development of the person, but that they have left a definite influence for all future time. Yet in spite of this unparalleled effectiveness they were forgotten! This would suggest that there are particularly formed conditions of memory (in the sense of conscious reproduction) which have thus far eluded our knowledge. It is quite possible that the forgetting of childhood may give us the key to the understanding of those amnesias which, according to our newer studies, lie at the basis of the formation of all neurotic symptoms.

Of these retained childhood reminiscences, some appear to us readily comprehensible, while others seem strange or unintelligible. It is not difficult to correct certain errors in regard to both kinds. If the retained reminiscences of a person are subjected to an analytic test, it can be readily ascertained that a guarantee for their correctness does not exist. Some of the memory pictures are surely falsified and incomplete, or displaced in point of time and place. The assertions of persons examined, that their first memories reach back perhaps to their second year, are evidently unreliable. Motives can soon be discovered which explain the disfigurement and the displacement of these experiences, but they also demonstrate that these memory lapses are not the result of a mere unreliable memory. Powerful forces from a later period have molded the memory capacity of our infantile experiences, and it is probably due to these same forces that the understanding of our childhood is generally so very strange to us.

The recollection of adults, as is known, proceeds through different psychic material. Some recall by means of visual pictures—their memories are of a visual character; other individuals can scarcely reproduce in memory the most paltry sketch of an experience; we call such persons "*auditifs*" and "*moteurs*" in contrast to the "*visuels*," terms proposed by Charcot. These differences vanish in dreams; all our dreams are preponderatingly visual. But this development is also found in the childhood memories; the latter are plastic and visual, even in those people whose later memory lacks the visual element. The visual memory, therefore, preserves the type of the infantile recollections. Only my earliest childhood memories are of a visual character; they represent plastically depicted scenes, comparable only to stage settings.

In these scenes of childhood, whether they prove true or false, one usually sees his own childish person both in contour and dress. This circumstance must excite our wonder, for adults do not see their own persons in their recollections of later experiences. It is, moreover, against our experiences to assume that the child's attention during his experiences is centered on himself rather than exclusively on outside impressions. Various sources force us to assume that the so-called earliest childhood recollections are not true memory traces but later elaborations of the same, elaborations which might have been subjected to the influences of many later psychic forces. Thus the "childhood reminiscences" of individuals altogether advance to the signification of "concealing memories," and thereby form a noteworthy analogy to the childhood reminiscences as laid down in the legends and myths of nations.

Whoever has examined mentally a number of persons by the method of psychoanalysis must have gathered in this work numerous examples of concealing memories of every description. However, owing to the previously discussed nature of the relations of the childhood reminiscences to later life, it becomes extraordinarily difficult to report such examples. For, in order to attach the value of the concealing memory to an infantile reminiscence, it would be often necessary to present the entire life-history of the person concerned. Only seldom is it possible, as in the following good example, to take out from its context and report a single childhood memory.

A twenty-four-year-old man preserved the following picture from the fifth year of his life: In the garden of a summer-house he sat on a stool next to his aunt, who was engaged in teaching him the alphabet. He found difficulty in distinguishing the letter m from n and he begged his aunt to tell him how to tell one from the other. His aunt called his attention to the fact that the letter m had one whole portion (a stroke) more than the letter n. There was no reason to dispute the reliability of this childhood recollection; its meaning, however, was discovered only later, when it showed itself to be the symbolic representation of another boyish inquisitiveness. For just as he wanted to know the difference between m and n at that time, so he concerned himself later about the difference between boy and girl, and he would have been willing that just this aunt should be his teacher. He also discovered that the difference was a similar one; that the boy again had one whole portion more than the girl, and at the time of this recognition his memory awoke to the corresponding childish inquisitiveness.

I would like to show by one more example the sense that may be gained by a childhood reminiscence through analytic work, although it may seem to contain no sense before. In my forty-third year, when I began to interest myself in what remained in my memory of my own childhood, a scene struck me which for a long time, as I afterwards believed, had repeatedly come to consciousness, and which through reliable identification could be traced to a period before the completion of my third year. I saw myself in front of a chest, the door of which was held open by my half-brother, twenty years my senior: I stood there demanding something and screaming; my mother, pretty and slender, then suddenly entered the room, as if returning from the street.

In these words I formulated this scene so vividly seen, which, however, furnished no other clue. Whether my brother wished to open or lock the chest (in the first explanation it was a "cupboard"), why I cried, and what bearing the arrival of my mother had, all these questions were dim to me; I was tempted to explain to myself that it dealt with the memory of a hoax by my older brother, which was interrupted by my mother. Such misunderstandings of childhood scenes retained in memory are not uncommon; we recall a situation, but it is not centralized; we do not know on which of the elements to place the psychic accent. Analytic effort led me to an entirely unexpected solution of the picture. I missed my mother and began to suspect that she was locked in this cupboard or chest, and therefore demanded that my brother should unlock it. As he obliged me, and I became convinced that she was not in the chest, I began to cry; this is the moment firmly retained in the memory, which was directly followed by the appearance of my mother, who appeased my worry and anxiety.

But how did the child get the idea of looking for the absent mother in the chest? Dreams which occurred at the same time pointed dimly to a nurse, concerning whom other reminiscences were retained; as for example, that she conscientiously urged me to deliver to her the small coins which I received as gifts, a detail which in itself may lay claim to the value of a concealing memory for later things. I then concluded to facilitate for myself this time the task of interpretation, and asked my now aged mother about that nurse. I found out all sorts of things, among others the fact that this shrewd but dishonest person had committed extensive robberies during the confinement of my mother, and that my half-brother was instrumental in bringing her to justice.

This information gave me the key to the scene from childhood, as through a sort of inspiration. The sudden disappearance of the nurse was not a matter of indifference to me; I had just asked this brother where she was, probably because I had noticed that he had played a part in her disappearance, and he, evasive and witty as he is to this day, answered that she was "boxed in." I understood this answer in the childish way, but asked no more, as there was nothing else to be discovered. When my mother left me shortly thereafter I suspected that the naughty brother had treated her in the same way as he did the nurse, and therefore pressed him to open the chest.

I also understand now why in the translation of the visual childhood scene my mother's slenderness was accentuated; she must have struck me as being newly restored. I am two and a half years older than the sister born at that time, and when I was three years of age I was separated from my half-brother.

IMMIGRANT WOMEN AND THE MOVIES

STEWART AND ELIZABETH EWEN

The ideas of Darwin and Freud encouraged a revolution in the way educated Europeans and Americans at the beginning of the twentieth century thought about history, society, and the individual. It is true that most common people could not or did not read Darwin and Freud. Still, their own ideas were changing. New instructors, replacing the time-honored ones such as parents, family, religion, and tradition, were preparing people for a vastly changed and changing world, and were themselves bringing about those changes. Among these new educators were department stores, ready-made clothing, advertising billboards, and—perhaps most effectively—the new moving pictures. The movies turned peasants into Italians or Frenchmen. They also turned immigrants into Americans. Silent films were particularly effective in bridging the barriers of different dialects or languages. The following reading, by two modern historians, discusses this phenomenon.

What particular role did American silent films play for immigrant women? How did movies replace or undermine the authority of fathers and families? What new ideas of femininity did the early movies teach?

From 1890 to 1920, over twenty-three million people from eastern Europe and southern Italy came to the United States and settled in primarily urban centers. Though they were to labor in and populate a maturing industrial society, they emerged from semi-industrial peasant and artisan backgrounds where the social institutions of family and community organized and maintained a customary culture. For these people, the migration represented an unraveling of the fabric of their lives, felt most deeply in the home and the family, the customary realm of women. The new urban world undercut the basis of traditional womanhood, forcing women to look in two directions simultaneously: to the past for strength to sustain life in the present and to the future to find new means of survival. This split impinged directly on family life and created strains on the customary expectations of the mother-daughter relationship. One generation, the mothers, had grown to maturity in European society. Urban life challenged the sense of survival and perception they had brought with them when they migrated to the

United States. The next generation, the daughters, although touched by the experience of the Old World, were much more the children of the metropolis. Their lives were caught up in social dynamics beyond the frame of old-world understandings.

In the cities new cultural images—billboards, signs, advertising, the electric lights of Broadway—pressed themselves on people's attention and created a new visual landscape of possibility. An urban and distinctly American culture proclaimed itself in image form, demanding response and notice, as strange to small-town Americans as it was to incoming immigrants. Viola Paradise of the Immigrant Protective League analyzed the social complexity of this new cultural formation:

> The very things which strike the native born [Americans] as foreign seem to her [the new immigrant] as distinctly American: the pretentiousness of signs and advertisements, the gaudy crowded shop windows, the frequency of fruit stands and meat markets, her own countrymen in American clothes . . . she sums it all up as "America."

One of the most powerful components of this new urban culture was the development of moving pictures. For immigrants in a world of constant language barriers, the silent film was compelling and accessible. Silent pictures spoke primarily to urban immigrant audiences of women and children, themselves caught up in the social drama of transformation.

· · ·

While immigrant parents resisted their daughters' participation in most of the recreational opportunities of the city, *everyone* went to the movies, which were the one American institution that had the possibility of uniting generations and was cross-generational in its appeal. Most film historians agree that the first audiences for motion pictures came primarily from the immigrant working-class neighborhoods of America's largest cities. The movies were a welcome diversion from the hardships of daily life in the communities. By 1909, New York City alone had over 340 movie houses and nickelodeons with a quarter of a million people in daily attendance and a half million on Sundays. *Survey* magazine, the journal of social work, observed that "in the tenement districts the motion picture has well nigh driven other forms of entertainment from the field" and that "it was the first cheap amusement to occupy the economic plane that the saloon [had] so exclusively controlled." Like the saloon, it was cheap: a nickel per person, twenty-five cents for the whole family. Unlike the saloon, it was not sex-defined; anyone who had a nickel could enter. There, for a low price, families could be enveloped in a new world of perception, a magical universe of madness and motion.

The movies became for immigrants a powerful experience of the American culture otherwise denied to them, surrounding them with images, fantasies, and revelations about the New World: "More vividly than any other social agency, they revealed the social typography of America to the immigrant, to the poor. . . . From the outset, the movies were, besides a commodity and a developing craft, a social agency." In *Sons of Italy*, Antonio Mangano described the effects of motion pictures on the typical recently arrived Italian: "Moving pictures were a great attraction, and he went every day to see what new pictures there were on the billboards. . . . Cold chills crept up and down his back as he witnessed thrilling scenes of what he thought was *really* American life." The movies became a translator of the social codes of American society, which could now be unraveled, looked at, interpreted, made fun of, understood. They formed a bridge between an older form of culture inadequate to explain the present and a social world of new kinds of behavior, values, and possibilities; their images and fantasies were a text of explanation, a way of seeing. Like their audience, early movies had not yet found a voice. Silent movies spoke in a more comprehensible language of silence, image, sign, and gesture.

The movies also presented themselves as a release from daily troubles, a world where the realities of daily life were rendered empathetically in comedic or melodramatic form. Movie advertisements pitched themselves to working-class audiences in a tone of compassion:

> If you're tired of life, go to the movies
> If you're sick of trouble rife, go to the picture show
> You'll forget your unpaid bills, rheumatism and other ills
> If you'll stop your pills and go to the picture show.

In a sense, movies were a form of community. Families went together; local merchants advertised on the screen; people sang along and read or translated captions out loud; the organ played. Moreover, as one observer commented: "Visit a motion picture show on a Saturday night below 14th Street when the house is full and you will soon be convinced of the real hold this new amusement has on its audience. Certain houses have become genuine social centers where neighborhood groups may be found . . . where regulars stroll up and down the aisles between acts and visit friends." The *Jewish Daily Forward* in 1908 commented on the growing popularity of this medium for women and children during the day. "Hundreds of people wait on line. . . . A movie show lasts a half an hour. If it's not too busy you can see it several times. They open at one in the afternoon and customers, mainly women and children, gossip, eat fruit and nuts and have a good time."

The content of some early films bore a direct relationship to the historical experience of its audience. Some films depicted a landscape outside of immigration; these brought American history and culture, in the form of westerns, news clips, and costume dramas, to ethnic eyes. Some movies were nativist, racist, and sexist. But many early movies showed the difficult and ambiguous realities of urban tenement life in an idiom that spoke directly to immigrant women. The new medium attracted many immigrant and working-class entrepreneurs into its ranks. Before Hollywood took center stage, the movies were created in primarily urban settings. As Lewis Jacobs, the film historian, observed, "The central figure of adventure comedies was always a common man or woman—the farmer, fireman, policeman, housewife, stenographer, clerk, servant, cook. . . . Such characters were selected because the audience and filmmakers alike were of this class and because of the growing popular interest in the everyday person." From 1903 to 1915, he argues, poverty and the struggle for existence were "favorite dramatic themes." In films with such titles as *The Eviction, The Need for Gold, She Won't Pay Her Rent, Neighbors Who Borrow, The Miser's Hoard, Bertha, The Sewing Girl,* and *The Kleptomaniac,* everyday situations were depicted, the causes of poverty were held to be environmental, and economic injustice was deplored.

. . .

Early movies existed outside of the moral universe of correct and respectable middle-class society. Comedies also mocked respectable ruling elites and looked at authority, social conventions, and wealth with a jaundiced eye. In the Sennett and Chaplin comedies, the artifacts of the new consumer culture became objects of ridicule. Mack Sennett explained the attraction of his films:

> Their approach to life was earthy and understandable. They whaled the daylights out of pretension. . . . They reduced convention, dogma, stuffed shirts and Authority to nonsense and then blossomed into pandemonium. . . . I especially like the reduction of authority to absurdity, the notion that Sex could be funny, and the bold insults hurled at Pretension.

Yet, despite the affinities between audience and early film, the movies were primarily an institution of the larger society, subject to its shifts and pulls. If some of the silent movies registered, to some degree, the social and economic problems of urban life, others spoke increasingly to the social and sexual dynamics, the ideological superstructure of an evolving consumer culture. The outlines of this development are to be seen in the contradictory experiences of immigrant daughters and their interaction with the silent screen. The concerns and experiences of immigrant daughters, as opposed to those of their more homebound mothers, led in some cases to active participation in the trade-union movement, political life, and involvement in the suffrage movement. For others, contact with American culture was mainly involved with educational aspirations and cultural transformations.

For many, contact with American culture at work or at school created compelling new definitions of femininity, which spoke to a sense of independence from the constriction of family bonds; ready-made clothes, makeup, dance halls, amusement parks all symbolized a cultural environment that assumed greater individual freedom and less formal relations with the opposite sex. As one social worker noted at the time:

> Inevitably, the influences of her new work life, in which she spends nine hours a day, begin to tell on her. Each morning and evening as she covers her head with a crocheted shawl and walks to and from the factory, she passes the daughters of her Irish and American neighbors in their cheap waists in the latest smart styles, their tinsel ornaments and gay hair bows; a part of their pay envelopes go into the personal expenses of these girls. Nor do they hurry through the streets to their homes after working hours, but linger with a boy companion "making dates" for a movie or affair.

While most immigrant mothers became reconciled to the fact that their daughters would leave home to go to work or school, they still expected their daughters to obey and adopt their own standards of sexual deportment. For the second generation, the gap between home life and work life was acute: "It wasn't that we [the younger generation] wanted to be Americans as much as we wanted to be like other people. . . . We gradually accepted the notion that we were Italians at home and Americans elsewhere. Instinctively, we all sensed the necessity of adapting ourselves to two different worlds." A social worker noted: "The old standards can scarcely be maintained in a modern community where girls work in factories side by side with men. . . . It was impossible for the parents to supervise young women in school or at work . . . the girl naturally thinks that if she can take care of herself at work, she is equally able to do so at play."

•   •   •

While the old family ways of understanding seemed inadequate as a guide to industrial culture, the movies seemed more shaped to the tempo of urban life. Increasingly, the social authority of the media of mass culture replaced older forms of family authority and behavior. The authority of this new culture organized itself around the premise of freedom from customary bonds as a way of turning people's attention to the consumer marketplace as a source of self-definition. This new cultural thrust took on the culture of Victorian America as much as that of first-generation immigrant parents.

The movies became less identified with family entertainment as young people increasingly turned to them for a place away from family life, a place to escape, to use a hard-won allowance, to sneak a date. As True observed:

> There is a signal of restlessness beneath the surface. . . . Into her nature are surging for the first time the insistent needs and desires of her womanhood. She is the daughter of the people, the child of the masses. Athletics, sports, discussions, higher education will not be hers to divert this deep craving. . . . The city bristles with the chances she longs for—"to have fun and see the fellows."

Because of these needs and the limited options for their expression, "the control of a little money is far more essential to these girls in their search for enjoyment than to girls in another class. There are many doors which a very small coin will open for her."

One of these doors was the movies, where "flashing gaudy posters lined the entrances. . . . These supply the girls with a 'craze.' These same needs send them . . . to the matinees. There pictures spread out showing adventure and melodrama which are soul-satisfying." Filomena Ognibene, an Italian garment worker brought up by strict parents, claimed that "the one place I was allowed to go by myself was the movies. I went to the movies for fun. My parents wouldn't let me go out anywhere else, even when I was twenty-four. I didn't care. I wasn't used to going out, going anywhere outside of going to the movies. I used to enjoy going to the movies two or three times a week. But I would always be home by nine o'clock." Sometimes the movies were used to subvert the watchful eye of parental supervision. Grace Gello recounted that she met her future husband in 1918 through her father. "We kept company for a year and a half. We weren't allowed to go out alone, even with groups of people. My father or mother always accompanied us. But we did meet on the sly. Occasionally, we would take the afternoon off to go to the movies. We didn't do this too much because we were afraid of my father. He would say, 'If I catch you, I'll break you neck.' "

By 1915, the year of D. W. Griffith's *Birth of a Nation*, the movie industry had expanded its initial audience to include middle-class patrons, had moved to the remote environs of Hollywood, and had established the studio and star systems. The thematic content showed the transition; the earlier images depicting the urban housewife embattled by the economic forces of the New World were increasingly displaced by images of women in flight from or redefining the meaning of home, family, sexual behavior, and social codes. The first female "stars" of the industry were cast in new roles: the vamp, the gamine, and, of lesser significance, the virgin. Through the creation of these feminine archetypes, the silent screen began to raise sexual issues and develop imagistic fantasies that spoke directly to the confusing sexual experiences of immigrant daughters.

The vamp was the symbol of the war between passion and respectability. Theda Bara, born Theodosia Goodman, daughter of a Jewish garment worker from Cincinnati, was created by Fox Studios as one of America's first movie stars. In over forty films from 1915 to 1919, she played the vamp, the woman who flaunts men and social convention to get what she wants. In the American lexicon, the archetype of the sexual woman was European, a woman who used her beauty and passion "to lure some helpless and completely dumb man to his ruin." Underneath this image was a new consciousness about sexual relations. In Theda Bara's own words, "Believe me, for every woman vamp there are ten men of the same . . . men who take everything from women, love, devotion, youth, beauty and give nothing in return. *V* stands for Vampire and it stands for Vengeance too. The vampire that I play is the vengeance of my sex on its exploiters. You see . . . I have the face of a vampire, perhaps, but the heart of a 'feministe.' " For example, in *A Fool There Was* (1914), Bara portrayed a woman who reduced respectable middle-class men to bumbling idiots, leaving a trail of madness and suicide along the way. Its imagery depicts a woman who has broken with social convention, who drinks and smokes with abandon, and who reverses the traditional assumptions of the male-female relationship. In doing so, her image points to a clear critique of the double standard.

The gamine, epitomized by Mary Pickford, was an archetype of female adolescence whose pluck and determination allowed her to create a more independent future. Born Gladys Smith into a poor family and forced at an early age to become "father" to her family, Mary Pickford often played a battling tomboy "provoked by a sense of injustice and motivated by the attempt to bring happiness to others." In her many films, she took on repressive fathers, ministers, and moralistic community values and defined for herself her own space. While she was part sweetness, she was also part "hellion . . . morally and physically committed to all-out attacks against the forces of bigotry and malicious snobbery that sought to frustrate the proper denouement of a triumphant lovely girl." Playing a spirited adolescent girl in such movies as *Rags* and *Little Annie Rooney*, she was an appealing example for women attempting their own fights against barriers. Although Mary Pickford occasionally played adult roles, her screen projection of independence was usually circumscribed by childhood. She herself stated the irony of her position. For Mary Pickford, "the longing for motherhood was to some extent filled by the little children I played on the screen. Through my professional creations, I became, in a sense, my own baby."

While the vamp and the gamine projected images of sexual freedom and social independence, the virgin—the Griffith heroine—was, in many ways, the last holdout of the patriarchal tradition. The virgin, played by Lillian Gish, was the good woman firmly devoted to the protection of her virtue against the menace of male passion. While the virgin, as the male symbol of American womanhood, registered the existence of the new sexual wilderness, she recoiled against it, seeking protection from its claims through patriarchal solutions.

The history of these transitional female archetypes parallels the social and sexual struggles of the immigrant daughters. If they were torn between fresh notions of sexuality and constricting family structures, the vamp and the gamine, who seemed to point the way to new definitions of femininity, were locked into a constricting star system, which severely limited their expression and development. Their images were used by the new studios as building blocks of an expanding industry. By 1919–20, the movie industry had become a major corporate enterprise, committed to a national rather than a class audience. To create this audience, some movies opted for images from the consumer marketplace. Some of the content and form of postwar movies revealed a new definition of "Americanization," the consumer society as an ideal way of life. Perhaps early movies had shown an ambivalence toward urban industrial society, but by 1920 American capitalism's consumer culture was in full force.

. . .

Some early films spoke sympathetically to the confused cultural experience of uprooted women—to the tasks of maintaining home and community in a world threatening to tear them apart. They helped to unify generations caught up in the divisive experiences of urban life. To the daughters, also the children of cultural transformation, film spoke differently. As themes of traditional family and community began to fade, the cinema spoke increasingly in the idiom of an urban, individualized culture. At first, these films briefly revealed new archetypes of feminine possibility that bore a relationship to the dynamics of cultural change. Yet in affirming the daughters' break from the traditions of family life, these films also pointed, as teachers and guides, to a mode of existence predicated on a commitment to individual survival and satisfaction within the social relationships defined by the consumer marketplace.

. . .

Nonetheless, moving pictures were the most universal form of cheap and satisfying entertainment in urban immigrant communities. As escape, education, or pleasure, they constituted a major source of new ideas and social experience. For immigrant women, motion pictures were a community-sanctioned form of urban mass culture, beguiling in its presentation of dress, manners, freedom, and sexual imagery. They provided an escape, but they also extended the world as a visual universe of magic and illusion.

III. THE MODERN WORLD: 1914 TO THE PRESENT

Chinese workers doing their daily exercises. (UPI/Bettman Newsphotos.)

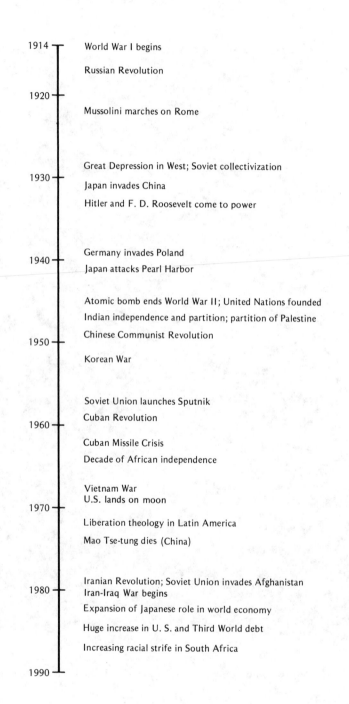

1914	World War I begins
	Russian Revolution
1920	Mussolini marches on Rome
1930	Great Depression in West; Soviet collectivization
	Japan invades China
	Hitler and F. D. Roosevelt come to power
1940	Germany invades Poland
	Japan attacks Pearl Harbor
	Atomic bomb ends World War II; United Nations founded
	Indian independence and partition; partition of Palestine
	Chinese Communist Revolution
1950	Korean War
	Soviet Union launches Sputnik
	Cuban Revolution
1960	Cuban Missile Crisis
	Decade of African independence
	Vietnam War
	U.S. lands on moon
1970	Liberation theology in Latin America
	Mao Tse-tung dies (China)
1980	Iranian Revolution; Soviet Union invades Afghanistan
	Iran-Iraq War begins
	Expansion of Japanese role in world economy
	Huge increase in U. S. and Third World debt
	Increasing racial strife in South Africa
1990	

11. World War I and the Russian Revolution

WORLD WAR I IN WORLD HISTORY

K. M. PANIKKAR

From an Asian perspective, according to this Indian historian and diplomat, World War I was a European civil war. But the involvement of African and Asian soldiers and colonial subjects made the war a major turning point in world history. In what ways were Africans and Asians involved in the war? How did that involvement change life in the colonies? Who were perceived as the anticolonial forces of the First World War? Who were they after the war?

The Great War of 1914–8 was from the Asian point of view a civil war within the European community of nations. The direct participation of Asian countries, during some stages of this conflict, was at the invitation and by the encouragement of one of the parties, the *entente* Powers, and was greatly resented by the Germans. It is necessary to emphasize this internal character of the European conflict to realize its full significance on the development of events in Asia.

We have already noticed that at the beginning of the twentieth century the European nations, in the enjoyment of unprecedented economic prosperity and political prestige, remained unshakably convinced that they had inherited the earth, and that their supremacy in Asia was permanent and was something in the nature of a predetermined Divine Order. It was the age of Kipling and the white man's burden, and it seemed the manifest destiny of the white race to hold the East in fee.

In 1914, when the German invaders had reached the Marne, divisions of the Indian Army under British officers had been rushed to France and had helped at the critical moment to stem the German tide. Later, they were extensively used in the defence of the Suez Canal and the Middle East and in campaigns elsewhere in Africa. In 1917, Siam declared war on Germany. An Indo-Chinese labour force had been recruited and was working in France. On August 14, 1917, China also joined the Allies. Thus all the nations of Asia were brought into the European civil war. However, opinion in India, China and even in Japan was at the time more pro-German than pro-Ally. In India, except among the ruling princes, there was no pro-British feeling, and public opinion rejoiced at every report of German victory and felt depressed when the Allies were winning. China declared war only with the greatest reluctance and for the express purpose of checkmating Japanese plans of aggression. In Japan itself, after the Shantung Campaign, feeling against the Allies was most marked, and a Press campaign of great virulence was conducted against Britain at the end of 1916. Actually, though the Asian countries fought on the side of the Allies, public opinion in the East looked upon the conflict as a civil war in which neither party had a claim to the friendship of the peoples of Asia, and if any party could appeal to the sympathy of Asians it was the Germanic alliance which had no tradition of Asian conquest and was allied with the chief Muslim Power, Turkey.

But the participation of Asian people in the war had far-reaching consequences. The Indian soldier who fought on the Marne came back to India with other ideas of the *Sahib* than those he was taught to believe by decades of official propaganda. Indo-Chinese Labour Corps in the South of France returned to Annam with notions of democracy and republicanism which they had not entertained before. Among the Chinese who went to France at the time was a young man named Chou En-lai, who stayed on to become a Communist and had to be expelled for activities among the members of the Chinese Labour Corps.

More important than these influences was the fact that the French and British administrations in Asia had to appeal to their subjects for moral support. To ask Indians and Indo-Chinese to subscribe to war loans for the defence of democracy and to prevent the world being overwhelmed by German *Kultur*, would have sounded as strange and callous irony unless accompanied by promises of democracy for themselves and freedom for their own cultures. When, besides subscriptions for war loans, Indians and Indo-Chinese were pressed to join up and fight to save democracy, the contradictions of the position became too obvious even for the colonial administrators. In India the demand was made openly by the nationalist leaders that prior agreement on political problems was necessary before support of the war could be considered a national programme.

Politically, a further weakening of the colonial and imperialist position came about as a result of President Wilson's declaration of fourteen points. In 1917, the doctrine of the "self-determination of peoples" had the ring of a new revelation. Whatever its effect was on the suppressed nationalities of Europe, in Asia it was acclaimed as a doctrine of liberation. As every Allied Power hastened to declare its faith in the new formula of Wilson (and it was soon raised to the position of an accepted "war aim" in the propaganda campaign against the Germans), the colonial Powers found it difficult to oppose openly or resist publicly the claims of Asian nations based on this formula. It became difficult to proclaim self-determination of people as a great ideal for the establishment of which Asian peoples should co-operate with Europeans and fight and lose their lives in distant battlefields, but which, however excellent, could not be applied to themselves. Self-government for colonial countries had thus to be accepted, and the claim to it could no longer be brushed aside as premature or stigmatized as sedition.

Apart from these political considerations economic forces generated by the war were also helping to undermine the supremacy of the West. Japan utilized the four years of war for a planned expansion of her trade in the East. German competition had been eliminated. Britain and France, engaged in a mortal struggle when their entire resources of production had to be directed towards victory, had also left the field fairly open. India gained her first major start on the industrial road and, with the strain on British economy, Indian national capital was placed in a position of some advantage. In fact the full results of the weakening of European capitalism became evident only after the war when the pre-eminence of London was challenged by America, and British capital, though still powerful, began to be on the defensive in India. The growth of capitalist enterprise in India, and the development of industries and participation by Indian capital in spheres so far monopolistically held by Britain, like jute [a plant fiber used in making burlap], resulted directly from the weakening of the economic position of Britain.

Two other results of a general character may be indicated. The first, the growth of a powerful left-wing movement in the countries of Western Europe had a direct effect on shaping events in the Eastern Empire. The Labour Party in England during the days of its growth had been closely associated with the nationalist movement in India. In fact, Ramsay MacDonald, the leader of the Socialist Party after the war, had been one of its champions from the earliest days. Similarly, Annamite nationalism had worked hand in hand with left-wing parties in France. In the period that immediately followed the war these parties had come to possess considerable influence in national affairs and, as we shall see, were instrumental in giving effect to policies which loosened the old bonds of political domination.

The second factor was, of course, the influence of the Russian Revolution. Imperialism meant something totally different after Lenin's definition of it as the last phase of capitalism and his insistence that the liberation of subject peoples from colonial domination was a part of the struggle against capitalism. Also, Russia's call for and practice of racial equality, abolition of the special privileges that Tsarist Russia had acquired in Persia and China, and her acceptance, in the first flush of revolutionary enthusiasm, of the independence of countries which had been previously annexed to Russia, made it difficult for Western nations which had so long claimed to stand for liberty and progress to deny the claims of Eastern nations.

Finally, the war had accelerated the pace of movements everywhere. For example, in India, the movement for independence which was confined to the intelligentsia in 1914 became a mass movement of immense proportions in 1919. Everywhere the case was similar. The *tempo* of events had acquired a momentum which few had foreseen and none had forecast in 1918. The war, on the world scale it was conducted in 1914–18, was in itself a great world revolution, and an impenetrable chasm has been created between the days preceding August 1914 and those following November 11, 1918.

One fact which stands out clear and illustrates this chasm in thought is the lack of faith in imperialist ideals in the period that followed the war. With the solitary exception of Churchill, there was not one major figure in any of the British parties who confessed to a faith in the white man's mission to rule. Successive Viceroys of India, Liberal, Conservative and non-party, professed publicly their adherence to the cause of Indian freedom. Secretaries of State from Edwin Montagu (1917–22) to Pethick Lawrence, including such stalwarts of Conservatism as Sir Samuel Hoare (Lord Templewood), claimed that they were working for the freedom of the Indian people and not for the maintenance of British rule. The French were no doubt more brave in their words, but the faith had gone out of them also.

Nowhere did this come out more clearly than in the treatment of China. Incidents which previously would have been dealt with sternly and for which territories and indemnities would have been exacted, were now only the subjects of a mild protest. Chiang Kai-shek's armies occupied the concessions at Hankow, and for months Hong Kong was subjected to an intensive trade boycott; these events would earlier have immediately led to a display of overwhelming naval strength. Britain in 1926 was prepared patiently to negotiate. Even the "old China hands," who had watched with regret the sudden eclipse of European prestige, though they acted the Blimps in their clubs, never seriously felt that Western authority could be re-established over China by the use of gunboats. There was no conviction left of the European's superiority or sense of vision.

WOODROW WILSON'S FOURTEEN POINTS

Woodrow Wilson (1856–1924) was President of the United States during the First World War. He presented these "Fourteen Points" to Congress in January 1918 as a basis for a just peace treaty to end the war.

You may wish to compare these proposals with the actual peace settlement. Only points VII, VIII, X, and XIV were realized. Point IV was applied only to the defeated nations. The Versailles Treaty, which the defeated Germans were forced to sign on June 28, 1919, contained much harsher terms, including the famous "war guilt" clause (Article 231):

The Allied and Associated Governments affirm and Germany accepts the responsibility of Germany and her allies for causing all the loss and damage to which the Allied and Associated Governments and their nationals have been subjected as a consequence of the war imposed upon them by the aggression of Germany and her allies.

Why do you think there was such a gap between Wilson's ideals and the actual treaty? How might Wilson have improved on these "Fourteen Points"? Could he reasonably expect all of them to be accepted?

It will be our wish and purpose that the processes of peace, when they are begun, shall be absolutely open, and that they shall involve and permit henceforth no secret understandings of any kind. The day of conquest and aggrandizement is gone by; so is also the day of secret covenants entered into in the interest of particular Governments and likely at some unlooked-for moment to upset the peace of the world. It is this happy fact, now clear to the view of every public man whose thoughts do not still linger in an age that is dead and gone, which makes it possible for every nation whose purposes are consistent with justice and the peace of the world to avow now or at any other time the objects it has in view.

We entered this war because violations of right had occurred which touched us to the quick and made the life of our own people impossible unless they were corrected and the world secured once for all against their recurrence. What we demand in this war, therefore, is nothing peculiar to ourselves. It is that the world be made fit and safe to live in; and particularly that it be made safe for every peace-loving nation which, like our own, wishes to live its own life, determine its own institutions, be assured of justice and fair dealing by the other peoples of

Woodrow Wilson, *War & Peace: Presidential Messages, Addresses and Public Papers (1917–1924)*, I, edited by Ray Stannard Baker and William E. Dodd. New York: Harper Brothers, 1927.

the world as against force and selfish aggression. All the peoples of the world are in effect partners in this interest, and for our own part we see very clearly that unless justice be done to others it will not be done to us. The program of the world's peace, therefore, is our program; and that program, the only possible program, as we see it, is this:

I. Open covenants of peace, openly arrived at, after which there shall be no private international understandings of any kind but diplomacy shall proceed always frankly and in the public view.

II. Absolute freedom of navigation upon the seas, outside territorial waters, alike in peace and in war, except as the seas may be closed in whole or in part by international action. . . .

III. The removal, so far as possible, of all economic barriers and the establishment of an equality of trade conditions among all the nations consenting to the peace and associating themselves for its maintenance.

IV. Adequate guarantees given and taken that national armaments will be reduced to the lowest point consistent with domestic safety.

V. A free, open-minded, and absolutely impartial adjustment of all colonial claims, based upon a strict observance of the principle that in determining all such questions of sovereignty the interests of the populations concerned must have equal weight with the equitable claims of the government whose title is to be determined.

VI. The Evacuation of all Russian territory and such a settlement of all questions affecting Russia as will secure the best and freest cooperation of the other nations of the world in obtaining for her an unhampered and unembarrassed opportunity for the independent determination of her own political development and national policy and assure her of a sincere welcome into the society of free nations under institutions of her own choosing; and, more than a welcome, assistance also of every kind that she may need and may herself desire. The treatment accorded Russia by her sister nations in the months to come will be the acid test of their good will, of their comprehension of her needs as distinguished from their own interests, and of their intelligent and unselfish sympathy.

VII. Belgium, the whole world will agree, must be evacuated and restored, without any attempt to limit the sovereignty which she enjoys in common with all other free nations. No other single act will serve to restore confidence among the nations in the laws which they have themselves set and determined for the government of their relations with one another. Without this healing act the whole structure and validity of international law is forever impaired.

VIII. All French territory should be freed and the invaded portions restored, and the wrong done to France by Prussia in 1871 in the matter of Alsace-Lorraine, which has unsettled the peace of the world for nearly fifty years, should be righted, in order that peace may once more be made secure in the interest of all.

IX. A readjustment of the frontiers of Italy should be effected along clearly recognizable lines of nationality.

X. The peoples of Austria-Hungary, whose place among the nations we wish to see safeguarded and assured, should be accorded the freest opportunity of autonomous development.

XI. Rumania, Serbia, and Montenegro should be evacuated; occupied territories restored; Serbia accorded free and secure access to the sea; and the relations of the several Balkan states to one another determined by friendly counsel along historically established lines of allegiance and nationality; and international guarantees of the political and economic independence and territorial integrity of the several Balkan states should be entered into.

XII. The Turkish portions of the present Ottoman Empire should be assured a secure sovereignty, but the other nationalities which are now under Turkish rule should be assured an undoubted security of life and an absolutely unmolested opportunity of autonomous development, and the Dardanelles should be permanently opened as a free passage to the ships and commerce of all nations under international guarantees.

XIII. An independent Polish state should be erected which should include the territories inhabited by indisputably Polish populations, which should be assured a free and secure access to the sea, and whose political and economic independence and territorial integrity should be guaranteed by international covenant.

XIV. A general association of nations must be formed under specific covenants for the purpose of affording mutual guarantees of political independence and territorial integrity to great and small states alike.

In regard to these essential rectifications of wrong and assertions of right we feel ourselves to be intimate partners of all the governments and peoples associated together against the Imperialists. We cannot be separated in interest or divided in purpose. We stand together until the end.

For such arrangements and covenants we are willing to fight and to continue to fight until they are achieved; but only because we wish the right to prevail and desire a just and stable peace such as can be secured only by removing the chief provocations to war, which this program does remove. We have no jealousy of German greatness, and there is nothing in this program that impairs it. We grudge her no achievement or distinction of learning or of pacific enterprise such as have made her record very bright and very enviable. We do not wish to injure her or to block in any way her legitimate influence or power. We do not wish to fight her either with arms or with hostile arrangements of trade if she is willing to associate herself with us and the other peace-loving nations of the world in covenants of justice and law and fair dealing. We wish her only to accept a place of equality among the peoples of the world,—the new world in which we now live—instead of a place of mastery.

Neither do we presume to suggest to her any alteration or modification of her institutions. But it is necessary, we must frankly say, and necessary as a preliminary to any intelligent dealings with her on our part, that we should know whom her spokesmen speak for when they speak to us, whether for the Reichstag majority or for the military party and the men whose creed is imperial domination. We have spoken now, surely, in terms too concrete to admit of any further doubt or question. An evident principle runs through the whole program I have outlined. It is the principle of justice to all peoples and nationalities, and their right to live on equal terms of liberty and safety with one another, whether they be strong or weak. Unless this principle be made its foundation no part of the structure of international justice can stand. The people of the United States could act upon no other principle; and to the vindication of this principle they are ready to devote their lives, their honor, and everything that they possess. The moral climax of this the culminating and final war for human liberty has come, and they are ready to put their own strength, their own highest purpose, their own integrity and devotion to the test.

STATE AND REVOLUTION

V. I. LENIN

Perhaps the most significant outcome of World War I was the Russian Revolution of 1917. Without the war the revolution might not have occurred at all; perhaps not even the mild, liberal phase of March and certainly not the radical, soviet stage in November which brought Lenin (1870–1924) and the Bolsheviks to power. In the summer of 1917, as the liberal government led by Alexander Kerensky was falling apart under the pressure of hunger, demands for land distribution, and the war, Lenin wrote State and Revolution. *Here he argued that, although Marx had spoken of the "withering away of the state" under communism, Marx also envisioned a necessary "dictatorship of the proletariat" as the immediate consequence of revolution. First the working class majority would have to deprive the capitalists of their power; only then could the state wither away.*

As you read this selection from State and Revolution, *notice how Lenin makes his case. What does he seem to mean by such words as "the state," "democracy," and "communism"? Would freedom decrease under "the dictatorship of the proletariat," according to Lenin? Why was Lenin saying these things?*

THE ECONOMIC BASE OF THE WITHERING AWAY OF THE STATE

Formulation of the Question by Marx

The whole theory of Marx is an application of the theory of evolution—in its most consistent, complete, well-considered and fruitful form—to modern capitalism. It was natural for Marx to raise the question of applying this theory both to the *coming* collapse of capitalism and to the *future* evolution of *future* Communism.

On the basis of what *data* can the future evolution of future Communism be considered?

On the basis of the fact that *it has its origin* in capitalism, that it develops historically from capitalism, that it is the result of the action of a social force to which capitalism *has given birth*. There is no shadow of an attempt on Marx's part to conjure up a Utopia, to make idle guesses about that which cannot be known. Marx treats the question of Communism in the same way as a naturalist would treat the question of the evolution of, say, a new biological species, if he knew that such and such was its origin, and such and such the direction in which it changed.

The first fact that has been established with complete exactness by the whole theory of evolution, by science as a whole—a fact which the Utopians forgot, and which is forgotten by the present-day opportunists who are afraid of the Socialist revolution—is that, historically, there must undoubtedly be a special state or epoch of *transition* from capitalism to Communism.

Transition from Capitalism to Communism

Marx writes:

> Between capitalist and Communist society lies the period of the revolutionary transformation of the former into the latter. To this also corresponds a political transition period, in which the state can be no other than the revolutionary dictatorship of the proletariat.

This conclusion Marx bases on an analysis of the role played by the proletariat in modern capitalist society, on the data concerning the evolution of this society, and on the irreconcilability of the opposing interests of the proletariat and the bourgeoisie.

Earlier the question was put thus: to attain its emancipation, the proletariat must overthrow the bourgeoisie, conquer political power and establish its own revolutionary dictatorship.

Now the question is put somewhat differently: the transition from capitalist society, developing towards Communism, towards a Communist society, is impossible without a "political transition period," and the state in this period can only be the revolutionary dictatorship of the proletariat.

What, then, is the relation of this dictatorship to democracy?

We have seen that the *Communist Manifesto* simply places side by side the two ideas: the "transformation of the proletariat into the ruling class" and the "establishment of democracy." On the basis of all that has been said above, one can define more exactly how democracy changes in the transition from capitalism to Communism.

In capitalist society, under the conditions most favourable to its development, we have more or less complete democracy in the democratic republic. But this democracy is always bound by the narrow framework of capitalist exploitation, and consequently always remains, in reality, a democracy for the minority, only for the possessing classes, only for the rich. Freedom in capitalist society always remains just about the same as it was in the ancient Greek republics: freedom for the slaveowners. The modern wage-slaves, owing to the conditions of capitalist exploitation, are so much crushed by want and poverty that "democracy is nothing to them," "politics is nothing to them"; that, in the ordinary peaceful course of events, the majority of the population is debarred from participating in social and political life.

The correctness of this statement is perhaps most clearly proved by Germany, just because in this state constitutional legality lasted and remained stable for a remarkably long time—for nearly half a century (1871–1917)—and because Social-Democracy in Germany during that time was able to achieve far more than in other countries in "utilising legality," and was able to organise into a political party a larger proportion of the working class than anywhere in the world.

What, then, is this largest proportion of politically conscious and active wage-slaves that has so far been observed in capitalist society? One million members of the Social-Democratic party—out of fifteen million wage-workers! Three million organised in trade unions—out of fifteen million.

Democracy for an insignificant minority, democracy for the rich—that is the democracy of capitalist society. If we look more closely into the mechanism of capitalist democracy, everywhere, both in the "petty"— so-called petty—details of the suffrage (residential qualification, exclusion of women, etc.), and in the technique of the representative institutions, in the actual obstacles to the right of assembly (public buildings are not for "beggers"!), in the purely capitalist organisation of the daily press, etc., etc.—on all sides we see restriction after restriction upon democracy. These restrictions, exceptions, exclusions, obstacles for the poor, seem slight, especially in the eyes of one who has never been in close contact with the oppressed classes in their mass life (and nine-tenths, if not ninety-nine hundredths, of the bourgeois publicists and politicians are of this class), but in their sum total these restrictions exclude and squeeze out the poor from politics and from an active share in democracy.

Marx splendidly grasped this *essence* of capitalist democracy, when, in analysing the experience of the Commune, he said that the oppressed were allowed, once every few years, to decide which particular representatives of the oppressing class should be in parliament to represent and repress them.

But from this capitalist democracy—inevitably narrow, subtly rejecting the poor, and therefore hypocritical and false to the core—progress does not march onward, simply, smoothly and directly, to "greater and greater democracy," as the liberal professors and petty-bourgeois opportunists would have us believe. No, progress marches onward, i.e., towards Communism, through the dictatorship of the proletariat; it cannot do otherwise, for there is no one else and no other way to *break the resistance* of the capitalist exploiters.

But the dictatorship of the proletariat—i.e., the organisation of the vanguard of the oppressed as the ruling class for the purpose of crushing the oppressors—cannot produce merely an expansion of democracy. *Together* with an immense expansion of democracy which *for the first time* becomes democracy for the poor, democracy for the people, and not democracy for the rich folk, the dictatorship of the proletariat produces a series of restrictions of liberty in the case of the oppressors, the exploiters, the capitalists. We must crush them in order to free humanity from wage-slavery; their resistance must be broken by force; it is clear that where there is suppression there is also violence, there is no liberty, no democracy.

. . .

Again, during the *transition* from capitalism to Communism, suppression is *still* necessary; but it is the suppression of the minority of exploiters by the majority of exploited. A special apparatus, special machinery for suppression, the "state," is *still* necessary, but this is now a transitional state, no longer a state in the usual sense, for the suppression of the minority of exploiters, by the majority of the wage slaves of *yesterday*, is a matter comparatively so easy, simple and natural that it will cost far less bloodshed than the suppression of the risings of slaves, serfs or wage laborers, and will cost mankind far less. This is compatible with the diffusion of democracy among such an overwhelming majority of the population, that the need for *special machinery* of suppression will begin to disappear. The exploiters are, naturally, unable to suppress the people without a most complex machinery for performing this task; but *the people* can suppress the exploiters even with very simple "machinery," almost without any "machinery," without any special apparatus, by the simple *organisation of the armed masses* (such as the Soviets of Workers' and Soldiers' Deputies, we may remark, anticipating a little).

Finally, only Communism renders the state absolutely unnecessary, for there is *no one* to be suppressed—"no one" in the sense of a *class*, in the sense of a systematic struggle with a definite section of the population. We are not Utopians, and we do not in the least deny the possibility and inevitability of excesses on the part of *individual persons*, nor the need to suppress *such* excesses. But, in the first place, no special machinery, no special apparatus of repression is needed for this; this will be done by the armed people itself, as simply and as readily as any crowd of civilised people, even in modern society, parts a pair of combatants or does not allow a woman to be outraged. And, secondly, we know that the fundamental social cause of excesses which consist in violating the rules of social life is the exploitation of the masses, their want and their poverty. With the removal of this chief cause, excesses will inevitably begin to "*wither away.*" We do not know how quickly and in what succession, but we know that they will wither away. With their withering away, the state will also *wither away.*

Without going into Utopias, Marx defined more fully what can *now* be defined regarding this future, namely, the difference between the lower and higher phases (degrees, stages) of Communist society.

12. Communism and Nazism

STALIN

ROBERT GOLDSTON

Here a modern historian gives us a picture of Soviet dictator Joseph Stalin (1879–1953). What kind of man was Stalin? How did he become so powerful? What problems did he confront? How did he deal with those problems? What was the purpose of Stalin's Five Year Plans?

The picture which emerges of Joseph Stalin [in the first years after the revolution] is one of a man of undoubted courage and determination, but with little imagination and almost no personal theoretical capabilities. It is a picture of a man who has chosen the revolution as his profession, the picture of the perfect bureaucrat. And as the perfect bureaucrat, in the days following 1917, of the consolidation of Bolshevik power in Russia, by serving the party he served himself. A ruthless administrator with a capacious appetite for detail, he used the burgeoning government bureaucracy to build for himself a personal following among bureaucrats as uninspired but as devoted to the acquisition and administration of power as himself. When, following Lenin's death in 1924, a struggle for leadership commenced, Stalin had little difficulty in using his party "machine" to secure power for himself. Slowly, over subsequent years, he exiled or murdered almost all of the Old Bolsheviks who might have contested his supremacy. Trotsky, for example, was driven into foreign exile at the end of the twenties and, when this failed to silence him, he was murdered by a Stalinist agent in 1940.

But it is not really necessary to seek the seeds of totalitarian dictatorship in the personality of Stalin. We have seen that the Bolshevik party (it was renamed the Communist party in 1920) was organized as a totalitarian apparatus. If Lenin's personal restraint and political good sense mitigated its tyranny during the years of his leadership, there was no built-in guarantee that a successor might not wield the party like a weapon to gain absolute personal power. Years before, Trotsky had warned: "The organization of the party will take the place of the party; the Central Committee will take the place of the organization; and finally, the dictator will take the place of the Central Committee." This

From Robert Goldston, *Communism: A Narrative History.* New York: Fawcett, 1972.

was exactly what happened—and it would undoubtedly have happened no matter who succeeded in winning power after 1924.

The transformation of the Leninist revolutionary dictatorship into a permanent party and personal dictatorship in Russia depended not only on the inherent tyrannical aspect of party organization, but also on objective exterior factors. Prime among these was the fact that the socialist revolutions which Lenin had so eagerly awaited in the West never transpired. True, as we have seen, socialist power in Western Europe was sufficient to prevent the military strangulation of the infant Soviet state by capitalist countries. But it was not sufficient to provide the industrial aid, to furnish the international industrial base upon which the Russian revolution, according to Lenin's revision of Marx, ought to have depended. Thus Russia, after 1917, found itself both ruined and isolated. Lenin had attempted to resolve the problems of revitalizing Russian industry through his New Economic Policy, through a tactical retreat into small-scale capitalism at home and tentative cooperation with capitalist industrialized states abroad. Stalin, however, declared that Russia would have to "build communism in one country." To follow Lenin's New Economic Policy might open the way for Russia to slip back into capitalism; to liquidate the New Economic Policy would be to alienate foreign capital.

So be it! Stalin declared. A communist Russia would industrialize itself with the capital available—the labor power of the Russian people. Like all good Marxists, Stalin devoted not a little time to reinterpreting Marx and Lenin in order to find theoretical support for his position. His principal work along these lines was *Foundations of Leninism*, a massive book he published after Lenin's death. The unimaginative, dry, and repetitious text (in which the catechismical training of Stalin's years at the Seminary in Tiflis is evident) enshrined certain of Lenin's teachings as dogma—just as Lenin had enshrined Marx. But Lenin's teachings had been largely political, so such tactical conceptions as party discipline and centralized organization now became universal and permanent theoretical laws.

· · ·

Having established himself in power through the murder or exile of those older associates of Lenin who would not cooperate, Stalin, in 1927, began to reshape Russia in his own image. His solution to the agricultural problem, to the scarcity of food, was the industrialization of agriculture, its mechanization through the introduction of machinery. But such mechanization could only be carried out efficiently on a large scale, collectively. Therefore he reduced some 25 million individual peasant farms to 200,000 collective farms. The peasants, who had just won their land a few years before, resisted their transformation into agricultural laborers on state property by burning their fields, killing their livestock, and even fighting pitched battles with police and Army units sent to enforce the new decrees. Stalin's response was to starve, kill, and exile all who opposed his plans. It has been estimated that between 1927 and 1929 no less than 5 million peasants were killed through military action or enforced starvation, and another 10 million deported to the icy wastes of Siberia. Not since the time of the Mongol Khans had such wholesale massacre descended on the Russian land.

Russian workers found themselves as regimented as Russian farmers. They were tied to their jobs as completely as the old serfs had been tied to their masters' estates. Inefficiency on the job, absenteeism, were classified now as treason and could be punished by exile to Siberia or incarceration in one of the many dreadful labor camps established by Stalin's secret police. This reign of terror was supplemented in the mid-thirties by an incentive program known as the "Stakhanov Movement." Named for a worker (Stakhanov) who had overfulfilled his production norms, the program offered better rations, higher pay, medals, and even, on occasion a trip to Moscow to shake hands with the top government officials, to workers who exceeded their expected daily output.

Beginning in 1928, Stalin introduced the first of a series of Five-Year Plans for the expansion of Russian industry and the mechanization of Russian agriculture. Typically, Stalin found his first plan amid the dusty files of the old tsarist regime. Sprucing it up and claiming it for his own, he used it not only as a political weapon in his rise to absolute power. During the thirties Five-Year Plan succeeded Five-Year Plan (sometimes overlapping) with bewildering rapidity. By the beginning of World War II three had been put into effect. The first Five-Year Plan concentrated on the construction of new factories, hydroelectric stations, and transportation networks; the second on improving labor productivity by rationalizing production methods; the third was intended to coordinate the growth of mechanized agriculture with the new needs of an emerging industrial society, but it failed. One of the reasons it failed was because by 1937, when it was introduced, Russia lay in the grip of widespread terror as Stalin instituted his Great Purges.

STALIN'S INDUSTRIALIZATION PROGRAM AND PURGES

J. P. NETTL

In this reading, another historian looks at Soviet life in the 1930s to evaluate the impact of Stalinism. In what ways was Soviet life better in the 1930s than it had been in czarist times? In what ways was it worse? Was Stalinist industrialization a failure or a success? Were Stalin's Five Year Plans after 1928 more or less effective than Lenin's earlier, more "capitalist" New Economic Policy (NEP)? Why did the purges occur? What was their effect?

What was life like for ordinary people in the 1930s? The answer must be: grim and grey. If you were not a Party member for whom the present was made luminous by the logic of historical necessity and the conviction of being on the side of the future, if you were not a manager, technician or shockworker* with special privileges, the pressures must at times have seemed well-nigh intolerable. At the bottom of the process of industrialization, life is hard under any system, but even more so when all the basic received certainties of life—religion, friendship, tradition— were being questioned and changed at the same time. The myth of the good times under Lenin and NEP grew up in this period, particularly in the countryside. Some people even thought nostalgically of pre-war Russia, though of course they did not dare to say so. This was above all a period of dislocation, of movement into new regions and towns. Housing was in desperately short supply, and not high on the order of official priorities. Around many of the major cities of the Soviet Union, both in the old industrial Russia of the west and in the new towns in the centre and east, there grew a ring of improvised dwellings, often no more than holes in the ground, in which whole families crowded together. The provision of an adequate apartment was in fact one of the rewards for deserving workers and technicians, and therefore a major incentive. The hours of work were long. When they were over, social

From *The Soviet Achievement*, J. P. Nettl. Reprinted by permission of Harcourt Brace Jovanovich, Inc., 1967.
* "Shockworkers" were laborers who accomplished much more than the required norm. The model was Stakhanov, a coal miner who in 1931 produced 102 tons of coal with two assistants in a five-and-three-quarter-hour work shift. Shockworkers in the mid 1930s ran the risk of being killed by their workmates. See p. 217.—Ed.

and political obligations started: meetings of factory groups or cells, trade union meetings and other activities in which Party and government plans were explained and—in an increasingly formalized manner—discussed. Informal social life virtually disappeared from the Soviet Union, for by the time all obligations of formal society had been discharged, only one's immediate family could enjoy the little energy and time that was left. Nevertheless, in spite of the fact that almost all women worked, and that the state assumed ever greater responsibilities for children, the family was the residual beneficiary; even more than in western Europe family ties were actually strengthened in this period. For every son who denounced his father to the police or the schoolteacher during the purges, a thousand failed to do so. The only successful splitters of the family in this era were the Nazis in Germany.

In general the Party was everywhere. Behind it, once the great purges began, stood the Secret Police. You learnt to trust no one. The naturally open nature of the Russians, to whom long and inconclusive conversations about the problems of life, and the offer of intimate confidences to almost complete strangers, were a normal part of life, gradually became enclosed in the new official culture of silence. The class enemy, one was constantly reminded, lurked everywhere, waiting and watching. With household names like Trotsky, Zinoviev and Bukharin [prominent Soviet leaders whom Stalin killed] suddenly revealed as bourgeois agents, English spies, whom could you trust? Did not Stalin called for incessant vigilance, which made surveillance of your neighbour a social duty? Whatever else the purges did, they taught the Russians the need for extreme reserve.

In the countryside things were worse, though for different reasons. The economic discrimination against agriculture made itself felt on all levels. The Communist Party made little headway among the collective farmers. Recreation, medical services, education hardly existed except on posters. The idiocy of rural life (Marx's phrase) found a grimmer realization in the Soviet Union. The depletion of the human and cultural as well as economic resources of the countryside in favour of the new industrial towns was only made worse by the absolute refusal of the leadership to acknowledge it—even though official policy was directly responsible.

Any objective evaluation of the Soviet standard of living during these years must take into account the substantial benefits supplied by the state to sections of the population who had hitherto been almost completely deprived. During the period of industrialization, there was an enormous expansion of medical and health services. Already by 1940 there were more doctors per thousand of population than in the United States, Britain, Germany or France. The system of polyclinics, whatever its medical pros and cons, certainly made access to facilities more readily available to greater numbers of people—especially since some of the sociological inhibitions which prevent people from visiting doctors were largely removed. It was in this period that relatively general sick-pay benefits were instituted, though an attempt to reduce the excessive labour turnover in the late 1930s tied these to a minimum period of service in any one enterprise. Sport became professionalized. Footballers, athletes, and above all chess players (the Russian national game *par excellence*) were induced to treat their performance as part of their plan fulfilment. Outstanding excellence was equivalent to the achievements of the shock-worker in industry. More important, however, was the popularization of these events in terms of mass participation. The commitment to the performance of teams and individuals, which still marks the Soviet Union today, is thus a compound of the natural loyalties of most *aficionados* for their favourite performers with the identification of support for sporting performance as a social duty.

The system of paid holidays also dates from the mid-1930s. Naturally the facilities in no way expanded as rapidly as the demand, but the principle had at any rate been established, and was to survive as a sheet-anchor of the Soviet approach to labour problems. It is significant that recent investigations into comparative job satisfaction in the Soviet Union, on the one hand, and the United States and the West on the other, show clearly how important a part of the general attitude to work paid and organized holidays have become, and above all to what extent this institution is regarded as a fundamental and original aspect of Soviet life.

· · ·

To us and our contemporaries in the Soviet Union today, preoccupied with welfare and rising standards of living, these times must in retrospect seem grim indeed. What was achieved? Let the unadorned figures speak once more. In general the year 1928, just prior to the first Five Year Plan, showed a level of industrial production very similar to the Russia of 1913 (adjusted for loss of territories after 1918). The enormous ravages of six years of foreign and civil war had been made good at last. By 1940 Soviet industrial output had trebled. The annual growth rate in these twelve years was almost 9 per cent per annum, compared to present British growth rates of less than 3 per cent. The beginning of Soviet industrialization, and the period of the first Five Year Plan, coincided with the great depression in other parts of the world, when output in the United States fell by almost a third. By 1940 the Soviet Union was a major industrial power. Yet at the same time the rate of growth, impressive as it appeared, was not significantly higher than during the recovery period of NEP from 1921 to 1927. We are therefore faced with two obvious questions, only one of which historians have really tried to answer. This concerns the means chosen to achieve full-scale industrialization in the Soviet Union. Could NEP have been continued and still have attained the levels of industrial output and the growth rates of the Stalin period? Not surprisingly historians divide ideologically over this question. Pointing to the growth rates of NEP, many Western economists and historians maintain that the system was "taking off" in any event. The partial market factors of "limited" socialism under NEP might have allocated resources more rationally, they say; there would have been more consumer goods, and more efficient use of resources. Soviet historians naturally take a contrary view. Only the absolute priority for basic industries made possible the further growth rates of the post-Second World War period, and the attainment of the superior technological sophistication of the present day. Moreover they consider the question itself largely absurd. Socialism requires this order of priorities, the transformation of the economy from individual small-scale procedures to collective and integrated large-scale production. This problem had already been discussed in the early 1920s. Only fully controlled industrialization justifies planning, and *vice versa*—only full-scale planning can solve the problems of socialist industrialization.

This leads to the second question: why was the process of industrialization in this form begun in 1928? Was it a purposeful execution of a rational and deliberate decision, or did it just happen? It is still not possible to answer this question with any real authority, but I think that within the context of a desire to accelerate production and tighten the planning process, Soviet industrialization was to a considerable extent self-generated, feeding on itself politically and economically just as collectivization had done. However much Stalin covered his actions with explanations of historical and logical inevitability, he was a far less acute theorist and thinker than Lenin. His explanations were always retrospective rather than programmatic. The squeeze on the *kulaks* [better-off peasants] may have started as an attempt to obtain grain, but once the class-war justification for it had been articulated, a more fundamental solution to the problem developed mainly under its own steam, and this self-reinforcement was fed back up the line into the political process to become official policy. Similarly the dramatic switch from indicative planning to a full command economy became self-generating, with official explanations and justification hurrying alongside. Once the process was under way, the Soviet leaders embraced it wholeheartedly. The vision of a long next step towards socialism and finally communism opened out in the early 1930s, and transformed a series of particular policies into a fundamental philosophy.

There was one field especially to which Stalin had devoted a great deal of time and effort—Party manipulation and control. Both collectivization and the first Five Year Plan meant a greatly strengthened role for the Party, which was wholly in line with the wishes and intentions of the communist leaders. In the course of the economic upheaval the Party was to become formally integrated into Soviet life at every level—except in the agricultural countryside—in a way which hitherto had been impossible. By the time things had settled down after the purges and just before the Second World War, the Party was installed literally everywhere. Those who controlled the Party really controlled the Soviet Union rather than merely ruling it.

The great purges from 1934 to 1938 seem to be in flagrant contradiction to the demands of forced industrialization. If the Party was to lead society in its enormous production drive, it would surely need to be cohesive and united. But there are always two approaches to cohesion and unity: consensus or discipline, persuasion or terror. Stalin chose the latter alternative. Society and Party were galvanized simultaneously. Terror was applied to production. Its threat was a spur to fulfilment, and its victims were often reintegrated into the bottom of the production process as slave labourers who consumed only a fraction of what they produced—the ideal form of surplus accumulation. How then to galvanize the Party? Hitherto the struggle among the leadership in the late 1920s had had relatively little effect on the middle and lower Party levels. By 1929 the simple and gross condemnation of Trotskyism had worked its way right through, and following on the leaders the lower echelons were being purged as well—no longer because they were unsuitable, but because they were deviationists. By the mid-1930s recantation of error no longer made re-admission possible. Between 1928 and 1933 industrialization brought an influx of new recruits; the Party grew from one and a half to three and a half million members and candidates. But the numbers declined again sharply during the continuous purge of the next three years, and this time the mass purge preceded that of the élite. By the beginning of 1937 numbers were down to just below two million. The purge had got out of hand. Most important, the character of the Party was completely changed during these years; it became on average substantially younger, and though the proportion of workers or sons of workers was still overwhelming, they were themselves increasingly members of the new intelligentsia, the product of Soviet schools and Komsomol [the Party youth organization].

. . .

By the end of 1936 a wave of arrests with and without subsequent trial was swamping the Soviet Union. The most distinguished old Bolsheviks were being arraigned and executed in batches. Perhaps a formal trial was the only concession to their rank; for every one of these, hundreds and thousands of people simply disappeared into the prisons and labour camps of the secret police and thence all too often to the grave. No one really knew how it had all started, and certainly no one knew how it was going to end. Safety of a very uncertain kind lay in denouncing others, and so the gruesome immolation went on for two years. The record, like all records of such enormity, loses its impact by the sheer quantity of well-known men who died: in August 1936 the trial of Zinoviev, Kamenev and fourteen others on capital charges, in September 1936 the suicide of Tomsky, in January 1937 the suicide of Ordzhonikidze, hitherto one of Stalin's closest collaborators (according to Khrushchev once more, he was forced to shoot himself). In June 1937 the secret trial and execution of Tukhachevsky with a galaxy of the most senior Red Army commanders—German spies all. In March 1938 the trial of Bukharin, Rykov, Yagoda and eighteen others on capital charges. Each time the arch-villain was Trotsky, grinning behind the scenes and manipulating corrupt Bolsheviks into their treacherous practices. By the time the last trial had taken place even the solid Stalinist majority of the Central Committee of 1934 had been almost wholly liquidated; the leadership of the army, of the Komsomol, and of every other major institution of the Soviet Union had been turned upside-down.

Then, quite suddenly, the fury of the terror died down to a dreadful whisper. As in the case of collectivization, the purge was rotting away the foundations of those very sectors of society which it had meant to cleanse and strengthen. The Party hierarchy was running out of replacements. In January 1938 the new Central Committee met and issued a stern warning against excesses. It was time to make an end. By December 1938 Ezhov, whose name has become notorious in Russia through the word *"Ezhovshchina"* by which the great purges are usually referred to, had quietly disappeared. The men now around Stalin, with a few exceptions, were relatively unknown: Molotov, Zhdanov, Khrushchev and Beria, Kaganovich and Mikoyan. The aftermath of the purges was in fact truly Thermidorean*: the liquidation of the secret police, a purge of the purgers. In the meantime, however, the prison population, especially of the labour camps, had swollen to the size and importance of a state within a state, and went on making its contribution to socialist accumulation. People began to wonder if the growth rate and the whole system could in fact survive without them, whether the real reason for the purges was not the need for a cheap supply of non-consuming labour.

---

* "Thermidorean" means a reversal of a revolution, like that which ended the terror of the French Revolution in the month of Thermidor (July) 1794.—Ed.

HOPE AGAINST HOPE

NADEZHDA MANDELSTAM

Nadezhda Mandelstam (1899–1980) was the wife of the great Russian poet Osip Mandelstam (1891–1938?). During the Stalin era, the poet was persecuted and twice arrested, and he eventually died in prison in Siberia. In her memoirs Mrs. Mandelstam offers a heartrending, tough-minded, yet at times witty account of her life with her husband and of how innocent people suffered during Stalin's purges. Taking advantage of the relative "thaw" that followed Stalin's death in 1953, Mrs. Mandelstam devoted the remainder of her life to trying to clear her husband's name and to have his work published in the Soviet Union. The first volume of the English translation of her memoirs is called Hope Against Hope; *note that in Russian* nadezhda *means "hope." Why, according to the author, did the Stalinist terror last? What were its effects? How did it affect her own life? What does she mean by the "favor" of her husband's death certificate and the "good tidings" of his death? Why does she say, "The sooner he died, the better?"*

When life becomes absolutely intolerable, you begin to think the horror will never end. In Kiev during the bombardment I understood that even the unbearable can come to an end, but I was not yet fully aware that it often does so only at death. As regards the Stalinist terror, we always knew that it might wax or wane, but that it might end—this we could never imagine. What reason was there for it to end? Everybody seemed intent on his daily round and went smilingly about the business of carrying out his instructions. It was essential to smile—if you didn't, it meant you were afraid or discontented. This nobody could afford to admit—if you were afraid, then you must have a bad conscience. Everybody who worked for the State—and in this country even the humblest stall-keeper is a bureaucrat—had to strut around wearing a cheerful expression, as though to say: "What's going on is no concern of mine, I have very important work to do, and I'm terribly busy. I am trying to do my best for the State, so do not get in my way. My conscience is clear—if what's-his-name had been arrested, there must be good reason." The mask was taken off only at home, and then not always— even from your children you had to conceal how horror-struck you were; otherwise, God save you, they might let something slip in school. . . . Some people had adapted to the terror so well that they knew how to profit from it—there was nothing out of the ordinary about denouncing a neighbor to get his apartment or his job. But while wearing your smiling mask, it was important not to laugh—this could look suspicious to the neighbors and make them think you were indulging in sacrilegious mockery. We have lost the capacity to be spontaneously cheerful, and it will never come back to us. . . .

The principles and aims of mass terror have nothing in common with ordinary police work or with security. The only purpose of terror is intimidation. To plunge the whole country into a state of chronic fear, the number of victims must be raised to astronomical levels, and on every floor of every building there must always be several apartments from which the tenants have suddenly been taken away. The remaining inhabitants will be model citizens for the rest of their lives—this will be true for every street and every city through which the broom has swept. The only essential thing for those who rule by terror is not to overlook the new generations growing up without faith in their elders, and to keep on repeating the process in systematic fashion. Stalin ruled for a long time and saw to it that the waves of terror recurred from time to time, always on an even greater scale than before. But the champions of terror invariably leave one thing out of account—namely, that they can't kill everyone, and among their cowed, half-demented subjects there are always witnesses who survive to tell the tale. . . .

The only link with a person in prison was the window through which one handed parcels and money to be forwarded to him by the authorities. Once a month, after waiting three or four hours in line (the number of arrests was by now falling off, so this was not very long), I went up to the window and gave my name. The clerk behind the window thumbed through his list—I went on days when he dealt with the letter "M"—and asked me for my first name and initial. As soon as I replied, a hand stretched out of the window and I put my identity papers and some money into it. The hand then returned my papers with a receipt and I went away. Everybody envied me because I at least knew that my husband was alive and where he was. It happened only too often that the man behind the window barked: "No record. . . . Next!" All questions were useless—the official would simply shut his window in your face and one of the uniformed guards would come up to you. Order was immediately restored and the next in line moved up to the window. If anybody ever tried to linger, the guard found ready allies among the other people waiting.

.   .   .

The women who stood in line with me tried not to get drawn into conversation. They all, without exception, said that their husbands had been arrested by mistake and would soon be released. Their eyes were red from tears and lack of sleep, but I don't recall anyone ever crying while we stood in line. When they left their homes, they composed their features by some effort of the will and tried to look their best. Most of them came to hand in their parcels during working hours—they got off on some pretext or other—and on returning to their offices they had to be very careful not to show their feelings. Their faces had become masks.

. . .

After several months of standing in line at the window on the Sophia Embankment I was told one day that M. had been transferred to Butyrki. This was the prison in which people were held before being sent off in prison trains to the forced-labor camps. I rushed there to find out on what days they dealt with inquiries about people whose names began with the letter "M." In Butyrki I was only once able to hand over something for M.; the second time I tried, I was told that he had been sent to a camp for five years by decision of the Special Tribunal.[1]

This was confirmed to me in the Prosecutor's Office after I had stood in line there endlessly. There were special windows through which requests for information were handed, and I did the same as everybody else. Exactly a month after putting in a request, one was always informed that it had been turned down. This was the usual routine for a prisoner's wife—if she was lucky enough not to have been sent to a camp herself. In the smooth, impregnable wall against which we beat our heads they had cut these little windows through which we handed in parcels or requests for information. I was considered particularly lucky because I got a letter—the only one—from M. and thus learned where he was. I immediately sent a package to him there, but it was returned to me and I was told that the addressee was dead. A few months after this, M.'s brother Alexander Emilievich was given a document to certify his death. I know of no other prisoner's wife who ever received a certificate like this. I cannot imagine why such a favor was shown to me.

Nobody has said he actually saw M. dead. Nobody claims to have washed his body or put it in the grave. For those who went through the camps, life was like a delirium in which the sequence of time was lost and fact became mixed with fantasy. What these people have to say is no more reliable than similar accounts of any other calvary. Those few who survived to bear witness, including such people as Dombrovski, had no chance to check their facts at the time, let alone to weigh hypotheses about them.

1. Established in 1934 to deal with "socially dangerous persons," the Special Tribunal was composed of high-ranking NKVD [the predecessor of the KGB] and militia officials and could impose sentences of exile or confinement to forced-labor camps.

I can be certain of only one thing: that somewhere M.'s sufferings ended in death. Before his death, he must have lain dying on his bunk, like others around him. Perhaps he was waiting for a parcel—a parcel which never came in time and was sent back to me. For us its return was a sign that he had died. He, on the other hand, may have concluded from its non-arrival that something had happened to us: this because some well-fed official in military uniform, a trained killer, weary of searching through endless, constantly changing lists of prisoners for one unpronounceable name, had simply scrawled on the accompanying form the simplest thing that came into his head: "Addressee Dead"— and I, who had prayed for the merciful release of my husband, received these last, inevitable good tidings from a girl clerk in a Moscow post office.

And after his death— or even before it, perhaps—he lived on in camp legend as a demented old man of seventy who had once written poetry in the outside world and was therefore nicknamed "The Poet." And another old man—or was it the same one?—lived on in the transit camp at Vtoraya Rechka, waiting to be shipped to Kolyma,* and was thought by many people to be Osip Mandelstam—which, for all I know, he may have been.

That is all I have been able to find out about the last days, illness and death of Mandelstam. Others know very much less about the death of their dear ones.

ONE FINAL ACCOUNT

But there is still a little more to tell. The transport which took M. to Vladivostok left Moscow on September 9, 1938. Another person who was on it is a physicist called L. He does not wish to be identified because, as he says, "things are all right just now, but who knows what may happen later?" During the terror he worked in a Moscow technical college whose staff was completely decimated because one of its members was the son of a man hated by Stalin. L. was taken to join this transport from the Taganka prison. Others were brought from Butyrki, to which they had been transferred from the Lubianka** just before the transport was due to leave. As the train was traveling east, L. learned from another prisoner that M. was there, too. The other prisoner had learned this after he had fallen ill and been put in the sick bay, where he had met M. He reported to L. that M. just lay on his bunk all the time, his head covered with a blanket. He still had a little money and the guards sometimes bought bread rolls for him at stations. . . .

---

* A notoriously brutal prison camp in Siberia.—Ed.
** Another large Moscow prison.—Ed.

When he left the infirmary L. heard that M. had died. This must have been between December 1938 and April 1939—in April L. was transferred to a work camp. He met no witnesses of M.'s death and knew about it only from hearsay. L.'s story seems to bear out what Kazarnovski had told me—namely, that M. died early. I also conclude from L.'s account that, since all typhus cases were taken to the infirmary, then M., who was found not to have it, must have died in quarantine. This means that he did not even die in his own bunk, covered by his own miserable convict's blanket.

There is nowhere I can make inquiries and nobody who will tell me anything. Who is likely to search through those grisly archives just for the sake of Mandelstam, when they won't even publish a volume of his work? Those who perished are lucky if they have been posthumously rehabilitated, or if, at any rate, their cases have been "discontinued for lack of evidence." . . .

All I can do, therefore, is to gather what meager evidence there is and speculate about the date of his death. As I constantly tell myself: the sooner he died, the better. There is nothing worse than a slow death. I hate to think that at the moment when my mind was set at rest on being told in the post office that he was dead, he may actually have been still alive and on his way to Kolyma. The date of death has not been established. And it is beyond my power to do anything more to establish it.

THE RISE OF HITLER

JOACHIM C. FEST

The rise of Adolf Hitler (1889–1945), this historian shows, was not a trick sprung on the unsuspecting German people. Hitler seemed to be what many Germans (and non-Germans) wanted. Why was this? What popular yearnings did Hitler seem to satisfy? To what groups of people did he appeal? Would there have been other ways of satisfying these needs? Do these needs still exist anywhere today? Can you recognize yourself in this portrait of Germany in the 1920s?

From *Hitler* by Joachim Fest. Copyright © 1973 by Verlag Ullsten; English translation copyright © 1974 by Harcourt Brace Jovanovich, Inc. Reprinted by permission of Harcourt Brace Jovanovich, Inc.

At the end of the First World War the victory of the democratic idea seemed beyond question. Whatever its weaknesses might be, it rose above the turmoil of the times, the uprisings, the dislocations, and the continual quarrels among nations as the unifying principle of the new age. For the war had not only decided a claim to power. It had at the same time altered a conception of government. After the collapse of virtually all the governmental structures of Central and Eastern Europe many new political entities had emerged out of turmoil and revolution. And these for the most part were organized on democratic principles. In 1914 there had been only three republics alongside of seventeen monarchies in Europe. Four years later there were as many republics as monarchies. The spirit of the age seemed to be pointing unequivocally toward various forms of popular rule.

Only Germany seemed to be opposing this mood of the times, after having been temporarily gripped and carried along by it. Those who would not acknowledge the reality created by the war organized into a fantastic swarm of *völkisch* (racist-nationalist) parties, clubs, and free corps. To these groups the revolution had been an act of treason; parliamentary democracy was something foreign and imposed from without, merely a synonym for "everything contrary to the German political will," or else an "institution for pillaging created by Allied capitalism."

Germany's former enemies regarded the multifarious symptoms of nationalistic protest as the response of an inveterately authoritarian people to democracy and civic responsibility. To be sure, the Germans were staggering beneath terrible political and psychological burdens: there was the shock of defeat, the moral censure of the Versailles Treaty, the loss of territory and the demand for reparations, the impoverishment and spiritual undermining of much of the population. Nevertheless, the conviction remained that a great moral gap existed between the Germans and most of their neighbours. Full of resentment, refusing to learn a lesson, this incomprehensible country had withdrawn into its reactionary doctrines, made of them a special virtue, adjured Western rationality and humanity, and in general set itself against the universal trend of the age. For decades this picture of Germany dominated the discussion of the reasons for the rise of National Socialism.

But the image of democracy victorious was also deceptive. The moment in which democracy seemed to be achieving historic fulfillment simultaneously marked the beginning of its crisis. Only a few years later the idea of democracy was challenged in principle as it had never been before. Only a few years after it had celebrated its triumph it was overwhelmed or at least direly threatened by a new movement that had sprung to life in almost all European countries.

This movement recorded its most lasting successes in countries in which the war had aroused considerable discontent or made it conscious of existing discontent, and especially in countries in which the war had been followed by leftist revolutionary uprisings. In some places these movements were conservative, harking back to better times when men were more honorable, the valleys more peaceable, and money had more worth; in others these movements were revolutionary and vied with one another in their contempt for the existing order of things. Some attracted chiefly the petty bourgeois elements, others the peasants, others portions of the working class. Whatever their strange compound of classes, interests, and principles, all seemed to be drawing their dynamic force from the less conscious and more vital lower strata of society. National Socialism was merely one variant of this widespread European movement of protest and opposition aimed at overturning the general order of things.

National Socialism rose from provincial beginnings, from philistine clubs, as Hitler scornfully described them, which met in Munich bars over a few rounds of beer to talk over national and family troubles. No one would have dreamed that they could ever challenge, let alone outdo, the powerful, highly organized Marxist parties. But the following years proved that in these clubs of nationalistic beer drinkers, soon swelled by disillusioned homecoming soldiers and proletarianized members of the middle class, a tremendous force was waiting to be awakened, consolidated, and applied.

In Munich alone there existed, in 1919, nearly fifty more or less political associations, whose membership consisted chiefly of confused remnants of the prewar parties that had been broken up by war and revolution.

They had such names as New Fatherland, Council of Intellectual Work, Siegfried Ring, Universal League, Nova Vaconia, League of Socialist Women, Free Union of Socialist Pupils, and Ostara League. The German Workers' Party was one such group. What united them all and drew them together theoretically and in reality was nothing but an overwhelming feeling of anxiety.

First of all, and most immediate, there was the fear of revolution, that *grande peur* which after the French Revolution had haunted the European-bourgeoisie throughout the nineteenth century. The notion that revolutions were like forces of nature, elemental mechanisms operating without reference to the will of the actors in them, following their own logic and leading perforce to reigns of terror, destruction, killing, and chaos—that notion was seared into the public mind. That was the unforgettable experience, not Kant's belief that the French Revolution had also shown the potentiality for betterment inherent in human nature. For generations, particularly in Germany, this fear stood in the way of any practical revolutionary strivings and produced a mania for keeping things quiet, with the result that every revolutionary proclamation up to 1918 was countered by the standard appeal to law and order.

This old fear was revived by the pseudorevolutionary events in Germany and by the menace of the October Revolution in Russia. Diabolical traits were ascribed to the Reds. The refugees pouring into Munich described bloodthirsty barbarians on a rampage of killing. Such imagery had instant appeal to the nationalists. The following article from one of Munich's racist newspapers is a fair example of the fears of the period and the way these were expressed:

> Dreadful times in which Christian-hating, circumcised Asiatics everywhere are raising their bloodstained hands to strangle us in droves! The butcheries of Christians by the Jew Issachar Zederblum, alias Lenin, would have made even a Genghis Khan blush. In Hungary his pupil Cohn, alias Béla Kun, marched through the unhappy land with a band of Jewish terrorists schooled in murder and robbery, to set up, among brutal gallows, a mobile machine gallows and execute middle-class citizens and peasants on it. A splendidly equipped harem served him, in his stolen royal train, to rape and defile honorable Christian virgins by the dozen. His lieutenant Samuely has had sixty priests cruelly butchered in a single underground room. Their bellies are ripped open, their corpses mutilated, after they have been plundered to their blood-drenched skin. In the case of eight murdered priests it has been established that they were first crucified on the doors of their own churches! The very same atrocious scenes are . . . now reported from Munich.

This threat dominated Hitler's speeches of the early years. In garish colors he depicted the ravages of the "Red squads of butchers," the "murderous communists," the "bloody morass of Bolshevism." In Russia, he told his audiences, more than thirty million persons had been murdered, "partly on the scaffold, partly by machine guns and similar means, partly in veritable slaughterhouses, partly, millions upon millions, by hunger; and we all know that this wave of hunger is creeping on . . . and see that this scourge is approaching, that it is also coming upon Germany." The intelligentsia of the Soviet Union, he declared, had been exterminated by mass murder, the economy utterly smashed. Thousands of German prisoners-of-war had been drowned in the Neva or sold as slaves. Meanwhile, in Germany the enemy was boring away at the foundations of society "in unremitting, ever unchanging undermining work." The fate of Russia, he said again and again, would soon be ours! And years later, when he was already in power, he spoke again of "the horror of the Communist international hate dictatorship" that had preyed on his mind at the beginning of his career: "I tremble at the thought of what would become of our old, overcrowded continent if the chaos of the Bolshevistic revolution were to be successful."

National Socialism owed a considerable part of its emotional appeal, its militancy, and its cohesion to this defensive attitude toward the threat of Marxist revolution. The aim of the National Socialist Party, Hitler repeatedly declared, "is very brief: Annihilation and extermination of the Marxist world view." This was to be accomplished by an "incomparable, brilliantly orchestrated propaganda and information organization" side by side with a movement "of the most ruthless force and most brutal resolution, prepared to oppose all terrorism on the part of the Marxists with tenfold greater terrorism." At about the same time, for similar reasons, Mussolini was founding his Fasci di combattimento. Henceforth, the new movements were to be identified by the general name of "Fascism." But the fear of revolution would not have been enough to endow the movement with that fierce energy, which for a time seemed to stem the universal trend toward democracy. After all, for many people revolution meant hope. A stronger and more elemental motivation had to be added. And in fact Marxism was feared as the precursor of a far more comprehensive assault upon all traditional ideas. It was viewed as the contemporary political aspect of a metaphysical upheaval, as a "declaration of war upon the European . . . idea of culture." Marxism itself was only the metaphor for something dreaded that escaped definition.

Anxiety was the permanent emotion of the time. It sprang from the intuition that the end of the war meant not only the end of familiar prewar Europe with its grandeur and its urge to world domination, its monarchies, and gilt-edged securities, but also the end of an era. Along with the old forms of government, the accustomed framework of life was being destroyed. The unrest, the radicalism of the politicalized masses, the disorders of revolution were interpreted as the afterpains of the war and simultaneously as harbingers of a new, strange, and chaotic age. "That is why the foundations of life quake beneath our feet."

Rarely has any age been so aware of its own transitional state. In accelerating the process, the war also created a general consciousness of it. For the first time Europe had a glimpse of what awaited it. Pessimism, so long the basic attitude of an elite minority, abruptly became the mood of the whole period.

The war had led to gigantic new forms of organization, which helped the capitalistic system attain its full development. Rationalization and the assembly line, trusts and tycoons pitilessly exposed the structural inferiority of smaller economic units.

The trend to bigness was also expressed in the extraordinary increase in cartels—from several hundred to approximately twenty-five hundred—so that in industry "only a few outsiders" remained unattached to some cartel. The number of independent businesses in the major cities had diminished by half in the thirty years before the World War. Now that war and inflation had destroyed their material base, their number dwindled more rapidly. The cruelty of the corporation, which absorbed, consumed, and dropped the individual, was felt more keenly than ever before. Fear of individual economic disaster became generalized. A considerable literature grew up around the theme that the individual's function was disappearing, that man was becoming a cog in a machine he could not understand. "In general, life seems full of dread."

This fear of a standardized, termitelike existence was expressed in the hostility to increasing urbanization, to the canyon streets and grayness of the cities, and in lamentations over the factory chimneys cropping up in quiet valleys. In the face of a ruthlessly practiced "transformation of the planet into a single factory for the exploitation of its materials and energies," belief in progress for the first time underwent a reversal. The cry arose that civilization was destroying the world, that the earth was being made into "a Chicago with a sprinkling of agriculture."

. . .

This first phase of the postwar era was characterized both by fear of revolution and anticivilizational resentments; these together, curiously intertwined and reciprocally stimulating each other, produced a syndrome of extraordinary force. Into the brew went the hate and defense complexes of a society shaken to its foundations. German society had lost its imperial glory, its civil order, its national confidence, its prosperity, and its familiar authoritites. The whole system had been turned topsy-turvy, and now many Germans blindly and bitterly wanted back what they thought had been unjustly taken from them. These general feelings of unhappiness were intensified and further radicalized by a variety of unsatisfied group interests. The class of white-collar workers, continuing to grow apace, proved especially susceptible to the grand gesture of total criticism. For the industrial revolution had just begun to affect office workers and was reducing the former "non-commissioned officers of capitalism" to the status of last victims of "modern slavery." It was all the worse for them because unlike the proletarians they had never developed a class pride of their own or imagined that the breakdown of the existing order was going to lead to their own apotheosis. Small businessmen were equally susceptible because of their fear of being crushed by corporations, department stores, and rationalized competition. Another unhappy group consisted of farmers who, slow to change and lacking capital, were fettered to backward modes of production. Another group were the academics and formerly solid bourgeois who felt themselves caught in the tremendous suction of proletarianization. Without outside support you found yourself "at once despised, declassed; to be unemployed is the same as being a communist," one victim stated in a questionnaire of the period. No statistics, no figures on rates of inflation, bankruptcies, and suicides can describe the feelings of those threatened by unemployment or poverty, or can express the anxieties of those others who still possessed some property and feared the consequences of so much accumulated discontent. Public institutions in their persistent weakness offered no bulwark against the seething collective emotions. It was all the worse because the widespread anxiety no longer, as in the time of Lagarde and Langbehn, was limited to cries of woe and impotent prophecies. The war had given arms to the fearful.

The vigilante groups and the free corps that were being organized in great numbers, partly on private initiative, partly with covert government support, chiefly to meet the threat of Communist revolution, formed centers of bewildered but determined resistance to the *status quo*. The members of these paramilitary groups were vaguely looking around for someone to lead them into a new system. At first there was another reservoir of militant energies alongside the paramilitary groups: the mass of homecoming soldiers. Many of these stayed in the barracks dragging out a pointless military life, baffled and unable to say good-bye to the warrior dreams of their recent youth. In the front-line trenches they had glimpsed the outlines of a new meaning to life; in the sluggishly resuming normality of the postwar period they tried in vain to find that meaning again. They had not fought and suffered for years for the sake of this weakened regime with its borrowed ideals which, as they saw it, could be pushed around by the most contemptible of their former enemies. And they also feared, after the exalting sense of life the war had given them, the ignobility of the commonplace bourgeois world.

It remained for Hitler to bring together these feelings and to appoint himself their spearhead. Indeed, Hitler regarded as a phenomenon seems like the synthetic product of all the anxiety, pessimism, nostalgia, and defensiveness we have discussed. For him, too, the war had been education and liberation. If there is a "Fascistic" type, it was embodied in him. More than any of his followers he expressed the underlying psychological, social, and ideological motives of the movement. He was never just its leader; he was also its exponent.

His early years had contributed their share to that experience of overwhelming anxiety which dominated his intellectual and emotional constitution. That lurking anxiety can be seen at the root of almost all his statements and reactions. It had everyday as well as cosmic dimensions. Many who knew him in his youth have described his pallid, "timorous" nature, which provided the fertile soil for his lush fantasies. His "constant fear" of contact with strangers was another aspect of that anxiety, as was his extreme distrust and his compulsion to wash frequently, which became more and more pronounced in later life. The same complex is apparent in his oft-expressed fear of venereal disease and his fear of contagion in general. He knew that "microbes are rushing at me." He was ridden by the Austrian Pan-German's fear of being overwhelmed by alien races, by fear of the "locust-like immigration of Russian and Polish Jews," by fear of "the niggerizing of the Germans," by fear of the Germans' "expulsion from Germany," and finally by fear that the Germans would be "exterminated." He had the

Völkische Boebachter print an alleged French soldier's song whose refrain was: "Germans, we will possess your daughters!" Among his phobias were American technology, the birth rate of the Slavs, big cities, "industrialization as unrestricted as it is harmful," the "economization of the nation," corporations, the "morass of metropolitan amusement culture," and modern art, which sought "to kill the soul of the people" by painting meadows blue and skies green. Wherever he looked he discovered the "signs of decay of a slowly ebbing world." Not an element of pessimistic anticivilizational criticism was missing from his imagination.

What linked Hitler with the leading Fascists of other countries was the resolve to halt this process of degeneration. What set him apart from them, however, was the manic single-mindedness with which he traced all the anxieties he had ever felt back to a single source. For at the heart of the towering structure of anxiety, black and hairy, stood the figure of the Jew: evil-smelling, smacking his lips, lusting after blonde girls, eternal contaminator of the blood, but "racially harder" than the Aryan, as Hitler uneasily declared as late as the summer of 1942. A prey to his psychosis, he saw Germany as the object of a world-wide conspiracy, pressed on all sides by Bolshevists, Freemasons, capitalists, Jesuits, all hand in glove with each other and directed in their nefarious projects by the "bloodthirsty and avaricious Jewish tyrant." *The* Jew had 75 per cent of world capital at his disposal. He dominated the stock exchanges and the Marxist parties, the Gold and Red Internationals. He was the "advocate of birth control and the idea of emigration." He undermined governments, bastardized races, glorified fratricide, fomented civil war, justified baseness, and poisoned nobility: "the wirepuller of the destinies of mankind." The whole world was in danger, Hitler cried imploringly; it had fallen "into the embrace of this octopus." He groped for images in which to make his horror tangible, saw "creeping venom," "belly-worms," and "adders devouring the nation's body." In formulating his anxiety he might equally hit on the maddest and most ludicrous phrases as on impressive or at least memorable ones. Thus he invented the "Jewification of our spiritual life," "the mammonization of our mating instinct," and "the resulting syphilization of our people." He could prophesy: "If, with the help of his Marxist creed, the Jew is victorious over the other peoples of the world, his crown will be the funeral wreath of humanity and the planet will, as it did millions of years ago, move through the ether devoid of men."

The appearance of Hitler signaled a union of those forces that in crisis conditions had great political potential. The Fascistic movements all centered on the charismatic appeal of a unique leader. The leader was to be the resolute voice of order controlling chaos. He would have looked further and thought deeper, would know the despairs but also the means of salvation. This looming giant had already been given established form in a prophetic literature that went back to German folklore. Like the mythology of many other nations unfortunate in their history, that of the Germans has its sleeping leaders dreaming away the centuries in the bowels of a mountain, but destined some day to return to rally their people and punish the guilty world. Into the twenties pessimistic literature repeatedly called up these longings, which were most effectively expressed in the famous lines of Stefan George:

> He shatters fetters, sweeps the rubble heaps
> Back into order, scourges stragglers home
> Back to eternal justice where grandeur once more is grand.
> Lord once more lord.
> Rule once more rule. He pins
> The true insigne to the race's banner.
> Through the storms and dreadful trumpet blasts
> Of reddening dawn he leads his band of liegemen
> To daylight's work of founding the New Reich.

. . .

The leader cult, viewed in terms of the "fiction of permanent warfare," was in one sense the translation of the principles of military hierarchy to political organization. The leader was the army officer lifted to superhuman heights and endowed with supernal powers. Those powers were conferred by the craving to believe and the yearning to surrender self. The tramp of marching feet on all the pavements of Europe attested to the belief in militaristic models as offering a solution to the problems of society. It was the future-minded youth in particular who were drawn to these models, having learned through war, revolution, and chaos to prize "geometrical" systems.

The same factors underlay the paramilitary aspects of the Fascistic movements, the uniforms, the rituals of saluting, reporting, standing at attention. The insigne of the movements all came down to a few basic motifs—various forms of crosses (such as the St. Olaf's cross of the Norwegian Nasjonal Samling and the red St. Andrew's cross of Portugal's National Syndicalists), also arrows, bundles of fasces, scythes. These symbols were constantly displayed on flags, badges, standards, or armbands. To some extent they were meant as defiance of the boring old bourgeois business of tailcoats and stiff collars. But primarily they seemed more in keeping with the brisk technological spirit of the age. Then, too, uniforms and military trappings could conceal social differences and bring some dash to the dullness and emotional barrenness of ordinary civilian life.

. . .

The success of Fascism in contrast to many of its rivals was in large part due to its perceiving the essence of the crisis, of which it was itself the symptom. All the other parties affirmed the process of industrialization and emancipation, whereas the Fascists, evidently sharing the universal anxiety, tried to deal with it by translating it into violent action and histrionics. They also managed to leaven boring, prosaic everyday life by romantic rituals: torchlight processions, standards, death's heads, battle cries, and shouts of *Heil,* by the "new marriage of life with danger," and the idea of "glorious death." They presented men with modern tasks disguised in the costumery of the past. They deprecated material concerns and treated "politics as an area of self-denial and sacrifice of the individual for an idea." In taking this line they were addressing themselves to deeper needs than those who promised the masses higher wages. Ahead of all their rivals, the Fascists appeared to have recognized that the Marxist or liberal conception of man as guided only by reason and material interests was a monstrous abstraction.

Thus Fascism served the craving of the period for a general upheaval more effectively than its antagonists. It alone seemed to be articulating the feeling that everything had gone wrong, that the world had been led into an impasse. That Communism made fewer converts was not due solely to its stigma of being a class party and the agency of a foreign power. Rather, Communism suffered from a vague feeling that it represented part of the wrong turn the world had taken and part of the disease it pretended it could cure. Communism seemed not the negation of bourgeois materialism but merely its obverse, not the superseding of an unjust and inadequate system, but its mirror image turned upside down.

Hitler's unshakable confidence, which often seemed sheer madness, was based on the conviction that he was the only real revolutionary, that he had broken free of the existing system by reinstating the rights of human instincts. In alliance with these interests, he believed, he was invincible, for the instincts always won out in the end "against economic motivation, against the pressure of public opinion, even against reason." No doubt the appeal to instinct brought out a good deal of human baseness. No doubt what Fascism wanted to restore was often a grotesque parody of the tradition they purported to honor, and the order they hailed was a hollow sham. But when Trotsky contemptuously dismissed the adherents of Fascistic movements as "human dust," he was only revealing the Left's characteristic ineptness in dealing with people's needs and impulses. That ineptness led to a multitude of clever errors of judgment by those who purported to understand the spirit of the age better than anyone else.

Fascism satisfied more than romantic needs. Sprung from the anxieties of the age, it was an elemental uprising in favor of authority, a revolt on behalf of order. Such paradox was its very essence. It was rebellion and subordination, a break with tradition and the sanctification of tradition, a "people's community" and strictest hierarchy, private property and social justice. But whatever the slogans it appropriated, the imperious authority of a strong state was always implied. "More than ever the peoples today have a desire for authority, guidance and order," Mussolini declared.

Mussolini spoke of the "more or less decayed corpse of the goddess Liberty." He argued that liberalism was about to "close the portals of its temple, which the peoples have deserted" because "all the political experiences of the present are antiliberal." And in fact throughout Europe, especially in the countries that had gone over to a liberal parliamentary system only after the end of the World War, there had been growing doubts of adequacy of the parliamentarism. These doubts became all the stronger the more these countries moved into the present age. There would be the feeling that the country lacked the means to meet the challenges of the transition: that the available leadership was not equal to the crisis. Witnessing the endless parliamentary disputes, the bitterness and bargaining of partisan politics, people began to long for earlier days, when rule was by decree and no one had to exercise a choice. With the exception of Czechoslovakia, the parliamentary system collapsed throughout the newly created nations of eastern and central Europe and in many of the countries of southern Europe: in Lithuania, Latvia, Estonia, Poland, Hungary, Rumania, Austria, Italy, Greece, Turkey, Spain, Portugal, and finally in Germany. By 1939 there were only nine countries with parliamentary regimes. And many of the nine, like the French Third Republic, had stabilized in a *drôle d'état*, others in a monarchy. "A fascist Europe was already a possibility."

Thus it was not the case of a single aggrieved and aggressive nation trying to impose a totalitarian pattern on Europe. The liberal age was reaching its twilight in a widespread mood of disgust and the mood manifested itself under all kinds of auspices, reactionary and progressive, ambitious and altruistic. From 1921 on, Germany had lacked a Reichstag majority that professed faith in the parliamentary system with any conviction. The ideas of liberalism had scarcely any advocates but many potential adversaries; they needed only an impetus, the stirring slogans of a leader.

THE HOLOCAUST:
1. HIMMLER SPEAKS
TO THE SS

HEINRICH HIMMLER

Heinrich Himmler (1900–1945) was one of the most powerful leaders of Nazi Germany. He was the head of the SS—the Schutzstaffel, the blackshirted elite army—which, among other responsibilities, ran the many concentration camps. Hitler gave Himmler the task of implementing the "final solution of the Jewish question": the policy of killing the Jewish population of Germany and the other countries the Nazis ruled. The horror that resulted is today often referred to by the biblical word "holocaust."

The following reading consists of an excerpt from a speech Himmler gave to SS leaders on October 4, 1943. What seemed to be Himmler's concern in this speech? How does he seem able to rationalize genocide? What kind of general support for the extermination of the Jews does this excerpt suggest existed?

I also want to make reference before you here, in complete frankness, to a really grave matter. Among ourselves, this once, it shall be uttered quite frankly; but in public we will never speak of it. Just as we did not hesitate on June 30, 1934, to do our duty as ordered, to stand up against the wall comrades who had transgressed,* and shoot them, so we have never talked about this and never will. It was the tact which I am glad to say is a matter of course to us that made us never discuss it among ourselves, never talk about it. Each of us shuddered, and yet each one knew that he would do it again if it were ordered and if it were necessary.

I am referring to the evacuation of the Jews, the annihilation of the Jewish people. This is one of those things that are easily said. "The Jewish people is going to be annihilated," says every party member. "Sure, it's in our program, elimination of the Jews, annihilation—we'll take care of it." And then they all come trudging, 80 million worthy Germans, and each one has his one decent Jew. Sure, the others are swine, but this one is an A-1 Jew. Of all those who talk this way, not one has seen it happen, not one has been through it. Most of you must know

From Heinrich Himmler's secret speech at Posen, reprinted in *A Holocaust Reader*, edited by Lucy Dawidowicz. New York: Behrman House, 1976.
* A reference to the "blood purge," in which Hitler ordered the SS to murder the leaders of the SA, a Nazi group he wished to suppress.—Ed.

what it means to see a hundred corpses lie side by side, or five hundred, or a thousand. To have stuck this out and—excepting cases of human weakness—to have kept our integrity, that is what has made us hard. In our history, this is an unwritten and never-to-be-written page of glory, for we know how difficult we would have made it for ourselves if today—amid the bombing raids, the hardships and the deprivations of war—we still had the Jews in every city as secret saboteurs, agitators, and demagogues. If the Jews were still ensconced in the body of the German nation, we probably would have reached the 1916–17 stage by now.*

The wealth they had we have taken from them. I have issued a strict order, carried out by SS-Obergruppenfuhrer Pohl, that this wealth in its entirety is to be turned over to the Reich as a matter of course. We have taken none of it for ourselves. Individuals who transgress will be punished in accordance with an order I issued at the beginning, threatening that whoever takes so much as a mark of it for himself is a dead man. A number of SS men—not very many—have transgressed, and they will die, without mercy. We had the moral right, we had the duty toward our people, to kill this people which wanted to kill us. But we do not have the right to enrich ourselves with so much as a fur, a watch, a mark, or a cigarette or anything else. Having exterminated a germ, we do not want, in the end, to be infected by the germ, and die of it. I will not stand by and let even a small rotten spot develop or take hold. Wherever it may form, we together will cauterize it. All in all, however, we can say that we have carried out this heaviest of our tasks in a spirit of love for our people. And our inward being, our soul, our character has not suffered injury from it.

---

* Here Himmler is apparently referring to the stalemate on Germany's western front in World War I.—Ed.

THE HOLOCAUST:
2. TREBLINKA

JEAN-FRANÇOIS STEINER

Treblinka, in Poland, was one of several Nazi death camps. (Auschwitz was the largest camp.) In these "death factories," the Nazis murdered

---

*millions of Jews as well as many thousands of gypsies, socialists, Soviet
prisoners, and other people. In this selection, Steiner, who lost his father
at Treblinka, reveals how "rational" and "scientific" mass murder can be.
How could this happen? Can it happen again?*

. . . Each poorly organized debarkation [of deportees from trains arriving at Treblinka] gave rise to unpleasant scenes—uncertainties and
confusion for the deportees, who did not know where they were going
and were sometimes seized with panic.

So, the first problem was to restore a minimum of hope. Lalka* had
many faults, but he did not lack a certain creative imagination. After a
few days of reflection he hit upon the idea of transforming the platform
where the convoys [trains] arrived into a false station. He had the
ground filled in to the level of the doors of the cars in order to give the
appearance of a train platform and to make it easier to get off the
trains. . . . On [a] wall Lalka had . . . doors and windows painted in gay
and pleasing colors. The windows were decorated with cheerful curtains
and framed by green blinds which were just as false as the rest. Each
door was given a special name, stencilled at eye level: "Stationmaster,"
"Toilet," "Infirmary" (a red cross was painted on this door). Lalka
carried his concern for detail so far as to have his men paint two doors
leading to the waiting rooms, first and second class. The ticket window,
which was barred with a horizontal sign reading, "Closed," was a little
masterpiece with its ledge and false perspective and its grill, painted line
for line. Next to the ticket window a large timetable announced the
departure times of trains for Warsaw, Bialystok, Wolkowysk, etc. . . .
Two doors were cut into the [wall]. The first led to the "hospital,"
bearing a wooden arrow on which "Wolkowysk" was painted. The
second led to the place where the Jews were undressed; that arrow said
"Bialystok." Lalka also had some flower beds designed, which gave the
whole area a neat and cheery look.

. . . The windows were more real than real windows; from ten yards
away you could not tell the difference. The arrows were conspicuous and
reassuring. The flowers, which were real, made the whole scene resemble a pretty station in a little provincial town. Everything was perfect. . . .

Lalka also decided that better organization could save much time in
the operations of undressing and recovery of the [deportees'] baggage.
To do this you had only to rationalize the different operations, that is, to
organize the undressing like an assembly line. But the rhythm of this
assembly line was at the mercy of the sick, the old and the wounded,
who, since they were unable to keep the pace, threatened to bog down
the operation and make it proceed even more slowly than before. . . .

* Kurt Franz, whom the prisoners called Lalka, designed the highly efficient system of
extermination at Treblinka.—Ed.

Individuals of both sexes over the age of ten, and children under ten, at a maximum rate of two children per adult, were judged fit to follow the complete circuit*, as long as they did not show serious wounds or marked disability. Victims who did not correspond to the norms were to be conducted to the "hospital" by members of the blue commando and turned over to the Ukrainians [guards] for special treatment. A bench was built all around the ditch of the "hospital" so that the victims would fall of their own weight after receiving the bullet in the back of the head. This bench was to be used only when Kurland** was swamped with work. On the platform, the door which these victims took was surmounted by the Wolkowysk arrow. In the Sibylline language of Treblinka, "Wolkowysk" meant the bullet in the back of the neck or the injection. "Bialystok" meant the gas chamber.

Beside the "Bialystok" door stood a tall Jew whose role was to shout endlessly, "Large bundles here, large bundles here!" He had been nicknamed "Groysse Pack." As soon as the victims had gone through, Groysee Pack and his men from the red commando carried the bundles at a run to the sorting square, where the sorting commandos immediately took possession of them. As soon as they had gone through the door came the order, "Women to the left, men to the right." This moment generally gave rise to painful scenes.

While the women were being led to the left-hand barracks to undress and go to the hairdresser, the men, who were lined up double file, slowly entered the production line. This production line included five stations. At each of these a group of "reds" shouted at the top of their lungs the name of the piece of clothing that it was in charge of receiving. At the first station the victim handed over his coat and hat. At the second, his jacket. (In exchange, he received a piece of string.) At the third he sat down, took off his shoes, and tied them together with the string he had just received. (Until then the shoes were not tied together in pairs, and since the yield was at least fifteen thousand pairs of shoes per day, they were all lost, since they could not be matched up again.) At the fourth station the victim left his trousers, and at the fifth his shirt and underwear.

After they had been stripped, the victims were conducted, as they came off the assembly line, to the right-hand barracks and penned in until the women had finished: ladies first. However, a small number chosen from among the most able-bodied, were singled out the door to carry the clothing to the sorting square. They did this while running

---

* The "complete" circuit was getting off the train, walking along the platform through the door to the men's or women's barracks, undressing, and being led to the gas chamber "showers."—Ed.

** Kurland was a Jew assigned to the "hospital," where he gave injections of poison to those who were too ill or crippled to make the complete circuit.—Ed.

naked between two rows of Ukrainian guards. Without stopping once they threw their bundles onto the pile, turned around, and went back for another.

Meanwhile the women had been conducted to the barracks on the left. This barracks was divided into two parts: a dressing room and a beauty salon. "Put your clothes in a pile so you will be able to find them after the shower," they were ordered in the first room. The "beauty salon" was a room furnished with six benches, each of which could seat twenty women at a time. Behind each bench twenty prisoners of the red commando, wearing white tunics and armed with scissors, waited at attention until all the women were seated. Between hair-cutting sessions they sat down on the benches and, under the direction of a *kapo* [prisoner guard] who was transformed into a conductor, they had to sing old Yiddish melodies.

Lalka, who had insisted on taking personal responsibility for every detail, had perfected the technique of what he called the "Treblinka cut." With five well-placed slashes the whole head of hair was transferred to a sack placed beside each hairdresser for this purpose. It was simple and efficient. How many dramas did this "beauty salon" see? From the very beautiful young woman who wept when her hair was cut off, because she would be ugly, to the mother who grabbed a pair of scissors from one of the "hairdressers" and literally severed a Ukrainian's arm; from the sister who recognized one of the "hairdressers" as her brother to the young girl, Ruth Dorfman, who, suddenly understanding and fighting back her tears, asked whether it was difficult to die and admitted in a small brave voice that she was a little afraid and wished it were all over.

When they had been shorn the women left the "beauty salon" double file. Outside the door, they had to squat in a particular way also specified by Lalka, in order to be intimately searched. Up to this point, doubt had been carefully maintained. Of course, a discriminating eye might have observed that . . . the smell was the smell of rotting bodies. A thousand details proved that Treblinka was not a transient camp, and some realized this, but the majority had believed in the impossible for too long to begin to doubt at the last moment. The door of the barracks, which opened directly onto the "road to heaven," represented the turning point. Up to here the prisoners had been given a minimum of hope, from here on this policy was abandoned.

This was one of Lalka's great innovations. After what point was it no longer necessary to delude the victims? This detail had been the subject of rather heated controversy among the Technicians. At the Nuremberg trials, Rudolf Höss, Commandant of Auschwitz, criticized Treblinka where, according to him, the victims knew that they were going to be killed. Höss was an advocate of the towel distributed at the door to the gas chamber. He claimed that his system not only avoided disorder, but was more humane, and he was proud of it. But Höss did not invent this "towel techique"; it was in all the manuals, and it was utilized at Treblinka until Lalka's great reform.

Lalka's studies had led to what might be called the "principle of the cutoff." His reasoning was simple: since sooner or later the victims must realize that they were going to be killed, to postpone this moment was only false humanity. The principle "the later the better" did not apply here. Lalka had been led to make an intensive study of this problem upon observing one day completely by chance, that winded victims died much more rapidly than the rest. This discovery had led him to make a clean sweep of accepted principles. Let us follow his industrialist's logic, keeping well in mind that his great preoccupation was the saving of time. A winded victim dies faster. Hence, a saving of time. The best way to wind a man is to make him run—another saving of time. Thus Lalka arrived at the conclusion that you must make the victims run. A new question had then arisen: at what point must you make the victims run and thus create panic (a further aid to breathlessness)? The question had answered itself: as soon as you have nothing more to make them do. Franz located the exact point, the point of no return: the door of the barracks.

The rest was merely a matter of working out the details. Along the "road to heaven" and in front of the gas chambers he stationed a cordon of guards armed with whips, whose function was to make the victims run, to make them rush into the gas chambers of their own accord in search of refuge. One can see that this system is more daring than the classic system, but one can also see the danger it represents. Suddenly abandoned to their despair, realizing that they no longer had anything to lose, the victims might attack the guards. Lalka was aware of this risk, but he maintained that everything depended on the pace. "It's close work," he said, "but if you maintain a very rapid pace and do not allow a single moment of hesitation, the method is absolutely without danger." There were still further elaborations later on, but from the first day, Lalka had only to pride himself on his innovation: it took no more than three quarters of an hour, by the clock, to put the victims through their last voyage, from the moment the doors of the cattle cars were unbolted to the moment the great trap doors of the gas chambers were opened to take out the bodies. Three quarters of an hour, door to door, compared to an hour and a quarter and sometimes even as much as two hours with the old system; it was a record. . . .

But let us return to the men. The timing was worked out so that by the time the last woman had emerged from the left-hand barracks, all the clothes had been transported to the sorting square. The men were immediately taken out of the right-hand barracks and driven after the women into the "road to heaven," which they reached by way of a special side path. By the time they arrived at the gas chambers the toughest, who had begun to run before the others to carry the bundles, were just as winded as the weakest. Everyone died in perfect unison for the greater satisfaction of that great Technician Kurt Franz, the Stakhanovite [model worker] of extermination.

Since a string of twenty cars arrived at the platform every half hour, the Lalka system made it possible to fully process twelve trains of twenty cars each—or four convoys, or twenty-four thousand persons—between seven o'clock in the morning and one-fifteen in the afternoon.

The rest of the day was devoted to the sorting of the clothing in Camp Number One and the disposal of the bodies in Camp Number Two.

Transported by two prisoners on litterlike affairs, the bodies, after they were removed from the gas chambers, were carefully stacked, to save room, in immense ditches in horizontal layers, which alternated with layers of sand. In this realm, too, Lalka introduced a number of improvements.

Until the great reform, the "dentists" had extracted gold teeth and bridges from the corpses by rummaging through the big piles that accumulated during the morning in front of the trap doors of the gas chambers. It was not very efficient, as Lalka realized. Thus he got the idea of stationing a line of dentists between the gas chambers and the ditches, a veritable gold filter. As they came abreast of the dentists, the carriers of the bodies, without setting down their litters, would pause long enough for the "dentists" to examine the mouths of the corpses and extract what ever needed extracting. For a trained "dentist" the operation never required more than a minute. He placed his booty in a basin which another "dentist" came to empty from time to time. After the take had been washed in the well, it was brought to a barracks where other "dentists" sorted, cleaned and classified it.

Meanwhile, the carriers of the bodies resumed their race—all moving from one place to another was done on the double—to the ditch. Here Lalka had made another improvement: previously the body carriers had gone down and stacked their bodies themselves. Lalka, that maniac for specialization, created a commando of body stackers which never left the bottom of the ditch. When they arrived, the carriers heaved their burdens with a practiced movement, the role of personal initiative being reduced to the minimum, and returned to the trap doors of the gas chambers by a lower route, as on a gymnastic platform, so as not to disturb the upward movement. When all the corpses had been removed from the gas chambers, which was generally between noon and one o'clock, the ramp commando, in charge of removal of the bodies joined the carrier commando. The burial rites lasted all afternoon and continued even into the night. Lalka had made it a rule that nobody was to go to bed until the last corpse had been stacked in its place.

13. World War II and the Cold War

AN OVERVIEW OF WORLD WAR II

CARTER FINDLEY AND JOHN ROTHNEY

This brief overview of World War II by two historians places the conflict in a genuinely global context. When did World War II begin? How did it combine separate drives for empire? What changed the balance of the war in favor of the Allies? What is the broad significance of World War II in world history?

The habit of looking at the twentieth-century world from the perspective of European dominance is hard to shake. Even now, four decades after that dominance collapsed at the end of World War II, historians often date the war from Hitler's invasion of Poland in 1939. Americans often date the war from the Japanese attack on the U.S. fleet at Pearl Harbor on December 7, 1941. By then Britain had been fighting Germany for a year alone, while German armies overran most of Europe. Britain found an ally against Hitler only when he invaded the Soviet Union on June 22, 1941, the day the war begins in Russian history books.

For many non-Europeans, however, World War II dates from well before 1939. For the Chinese, it began in 1931 against the Japanese in Manchuria. For the Ethiopians, virtually the only Africans not under European rule, it began with the Italian invasion in 1935.

The significance of these conflicting dates is that World War II merged originally separate drives for empire into one conflict. One drive began with Hitler's war with Britain and France over Poland, the last surviving creation of the Versailles system. This last of Europe's "civil wars" became a German campaign for "living space," which culminated in a Hitlerian empire stretching across Europe.

The second drive for empire began with Japan's penetration of China. Profiting from Hitler's attack on the European colonial powers, the

Carter Vaughn Findley and John A. M. Rothney: *Twentieth-Century World*, pp. 259–261. Copyright © 1986 by Houghton Mifflin Company. Used by permission.

Japanese extended their control over a large part of the East Asian mainland and the islands of the southwest Pacific, including the Dutch East Indies and the Philippines. By the end of 1941, the German and Japanese drives for empire had converged to make World War II a conflict of continents. It pitted Europe, under Hitler's rule, against the worldwide British Empire, which also had to face much of Asia, under the dominance of Japan. Had Germany not attacked the Soviet Union, and had Japan not attacked the United States, those other two continent-sized powers might not have been drawn into the struggle. Until Hitler attacked, Stalin had adhered to the Nazi-Soviet pact of August 1939. A clear majority of U.S. citizens favored neutrality in the war until the Japanese attacked them.

Russian and American participation brought World War II to a turning point by mid-to-late 1942. Until then, the so-called Axis powers (Germany, Japan, and Italy) had achieved an unbroken series of victories. German armies surged to the northern tip of Norway, to the shores of the Greek peninsula and the Black Sea, and over much of the North African desert. The Japanese swept to the eastern frontiers of India and to the arctic fringes of North America in the Aleutian Islands.

Even in this early period, however, the Axis leaders made fateful mistakes. Hitler failed to defeat Britain. He neither invaded it nor cut its lifelines across the Atlantic and through the Mediterranean. Meanwhile, he repeated Napoleon's fatal blunder of invading Russia while Britain remained unconquered. The Japanese leaders did not join in this attack on their hereditary enemy, but tried to avert U.S. interference with their empire-building by destroying the U.S. Pacific fleet. Following the attack on Pearl Harbor, it was Hitler who declared war on the United States, not the United States on Hitler.

It was these uncoordinated Axis attacks that forced together what Churchill called the Grand Alliance of Britain, the Soviet Union, and the United States. Together, these dissimilar Allies were too strong for the Axis. Consistently victorious through most of 1942, the Axis encountered nothing but defeat thereafter. Germany and subjugated Europe had been a match for Britain, despite the troops sent by the Dominions, like Canada, Australia, and New Zealand. But the Russian war destroyed Hitler's armies, and the U.S. agreement to give priority to Germany's defeat made it certain. After mid-1942, the Americans, the British, and their allies also steadily pushed the Japanese back. When the Soviet Union, after Hitler's defeat, joined Japan's enemies in 1945, Japanese prospects became hopeless, even without the awful warning of two American nuclear attacks—the first in history and the last, so far.

Throughout the war, the Axis powers failed to cooperate effectively. They also did not mobilize their home fronts as effectively as the Allies. Despite German rhetoric about uniting the peoples of Europe and Japanese claims to be leading an Asian crusade against imperialism, neither Germany nor Japan was able to mobilize the enthusiasm of a majority in the lands they overran. Instead their treatment of conquered peoples was marked by cruelty and greed, which inspired even civilians to abandon passivity for active resistance.

After World War I, people quickly concluded that most of the slogans for which they had fought were hollow. After World War II, the revelations of Japanese and Nazi brutality kept alive the sense that this second global conflict had been fought for a just cause. But if the war defeated evil regimes, this struggle of continents also destroyed the power of Europe as a whole and the European-dominated global system. Within a generation after 1945, even Britain, bankrupt and exhausted in victory, would grant independence to most of its Asian and African colonies. From this "end of empire" would soon emerge the Third World of countries reluctant to subordinate themselves to either the United States or the Soviet Union, the only great powers left after 1945.

Not only in the already threatening conflict of these two superpowers does the world of 1945 foreshadow the world of the 1980s. Even more intensively than in 1914–1918, the pressures of total war had expanded the powers of governments, transformed societies, and revolutionized the economies of the world. Moreover, with official encouragement, scientists had produced a weapon so incomparably deadly that thoughtful people wondered whether human beings still had a future. We still live with that unprecedented uncertainty of 1945. In this respect as in most, World War II marks the turning point of the twentieth-century world, though few people foresaw this transformation when Hitler's armies crossed the Polish border on September 1, 1939.

JAPAN'S WAR AIMS

TOKUTOMI IICHIRO

This selection provides a Japanese perspective on Japan's war against the United States and Great Britain and offers insight into Japanese war aims in Asia. It was written as a commentary on the Emperor's declaration of war by Tokutomi, Japan's leading nationalist writer. What did he seem to

Tokutomi Iichiro, "Commentary on the Imperial Rescript Declaring War on the United States and British Empire," reprinted in *Sources of Japanese Tradition*, vol. II, edited by William Theodore De Barry. New York: Columbia University Press, 1958.

intend as the "Light of Greater East Asia"? Who would seem to benefit, and who would lose, in the "East Asia Co-Prosperity Sphere"?

Now that we have risen up in arms, we must accomplish our aim to the last. Herein lies the core of our theory. In Nippon [Japan] resides a destiny to become the Light of Greater East Asia and to become ultimately the Light of the World. However, in order to become the Light of Greater East Asia, we must have three qualifications. The first is strength. In other words, we must expel Anglo-Saxon influence from East Asia with our strength.

To speak the truth, the various races of East Asia look upon the British and Americans as superior to the Nippon race. They look upon Britain and the United States as more powerful nations than Nippon. Therefore, we must show our real strength before all our fellow-races of East Asia. We must show them an object lesson. It is not a lesson in words. It should be a lesson in facts.

In other words, before we can expel the Anglo-Saxons and make them remove all their traces from East Asia, we must annihilate them. In this way only will the various fellow races of Greater East Asia look upon us as their leader. I believe that the lesson which we must first show to our fellow-races in Greater East Asia is this lesson of cold reality.

The second qualification is benevolence. Nippon must develop the various resources of East Asia and distribute them fairly to all the races within the East Asia Co-Prosperity Sphere to make them share in the benefits. In other words, Nippon should not monopolize the benefits, but should distribute them for the mutual prosperity of Greater East Asia.

We must show to the races of East Asia that the order, tranquillity, peace, happiness, and contentment of East Asia can be gained only by eradicating the evil precedent of the encroachment and extortion of the Anglo-Saxons in East Asia, by effecting the real aim of the co-prosperity of East Asia, and by making Nippon the leader of East Asia.

The third qualification is virtue. East Asia embraces various races. Its religions are different. Moreover, there has practically been no occasion when these have mutually united to work for a combined aim. It was the favorite policy of Anglo-Saxons to make the various races of East Asia compete and fight each other and make them mutually small and powerless. We must, therefore, console them, bring friendship among them, and make them all live in peace with a boundlessly embracing virtue.

In short, the first is the Grace of the Sacred Sword, the second, the Grace of the Sacred Mirror, and the third, the Grace of the Sacred Jewels. If we should express it in other words, we must have courage, knowledge, and benevolence. If Nippon should lack even one of the above three, it will not be able to become the Light of Asia.

FDR ASKS FOR WAR
AGAINST JAPAN

The day after Japan attacked the U.S. naval base at Pearl Harbor in Hawaii, President Franklin D. Roosevelt asked Congress to declare war on Japan. What reasons does Roosevelt give? How does he feel about the outcome of the war? What is the tone of his speech?

Yesterday, December 7, 1941—a date which will live in infamy—the United States of America was suddenly and deliberately attacked by naval and air forces of the Empire of Japan.

The United States was at peace with that nation and, at the solicitation of Japan, was still in conversation with its Government and its Emperor looking toward the maintenance of peace in the Pacific. Indeed, one hour after Japanese air squadrons had commenced bombing in Oahu, the Japanese Ambassador to the United States and his colleague delivered to the Secretary of State a formal reply to a recent American message. While this reply stated that it seemed useless to continue the existing diplomatic negotiations, it contained no threat or hint of war or armed attack.

It will be recorded that the distance of Hawaii from Japan makes it obvious that the attack was deliberately planned many days or even weeks ago. During the intervening time the Japanese Government has deliberately sought to deceive the United States by false statements and expressions of hope for continued peace.

The attack yesterday on the Hawaiian Islands has caused severe damage to American naval and military forces. Very many American lives have been lost. In addition American ships have been reported torpedoed on the high seas between San Francisco and Honolulu.

Yesterday the Japanese Government also launched an attack against Malaya. Last night Japanese forces attacked Hong Kong. Last night Japanese forces attacked Guam. Last night Japanese forces attacked the Philippine Islands. Last night the Japanese attacked Wake Island. This morning the Japanese attacked Midway Island.

Japan has, therefore, undertaken a surprise offensive extending throughout the Pacific area. The facts of yesterday speak for themselves. The people of the United States have already formed their opinions and well understand the implications to the very life and safety of our nation.

As Commander-in-Chief of the Army and Navy, I have directed that all measures be taken for our defense.

Reprinted in *Documents of American History*, seventh edition, edited by Henry Steele Commager. New York: Appleton-Century-Crofts, 1963.

Always will we remember the character of the onslaught against us.

No matter how long it may take us to overcome this premeditated invasion, the American people in their righteous might will win through to absolute victory.

I believe I interpret the will of the Congress and of the people when I assert that we will not only defend ourselves to the uttermost but will make very certain that this form of treachery shall never endanger us again.

Hostilities exist. There is no blinking at the fact that our people, our territory and our interests are in grave danger.

With confidence in our armed forces—with the unbonded determination of our people—we will gain the inevitable triumph—so help us God.

I ask that the Congress declare that since the unprovoked and dastardly attack by Japan on Sunday, December seventh, a state of war has existed between the United States and the Japanese Empire.

A VILLAGE CALLED LE CHAMBON

PHILIP HALLIE

Nazi Germany took over Austria in 1938 and Czechoslovakia in 1938 and 1939. Poland was conquered in 1939, starting World War II in Europe, and much of Western Europe in 1940. Nazi control was sometimes direct and sometimes maintained with the collaboration of nominally independent client regimes, like that headquartered in Vichy, France. Regimes like Vichy were responsible for putting a local face on Nazi domination. When the Nazis ordered the expulsion of Jews, Vichy and a chain of local, provincial, and national officialdom complied. Even ordinary citizens, out of their own anti-Semitic fantasies, fear of the authorities, or personal jealousies, complied. The sending of millions of people to their deaths was the result of a single decision by the Nazi regime, but it was also the result of many individual decisions, some as easy as looking the other way.

This is not another selection on the Nazi death camps. This is, rather,

Prelude from *Lest Innocent Blood Be Shed* by Philip P. Hallie. Copyright © 1979 by Philip P. Hallie. Reprinted by permission of Harper & Row, Publishers, Inc.

a story of hope. It is the introduction to Philip Hallie's Lest Innocent Blood Be Shed. *What happened in the little village of Chambon? What lessons does it teach us?*

There was once an art critic, I have been told, who had a sure way of identifying ancient Maltese art objects: he found himself crying before them. John Keats had a similar reaction to excellence: the thought of his beloved Fanny Brawne, or of anything he associated with her, "goes through me like a spear," he said.

Of course, these are symptoms of an awareness of excellence. They are mere reactions, not rules that we ordinary people can use to separate excellent things from dross. But any doctor will tell you that symptoms are important, and just as pain can be a symptom of disease, painful joy can be a reliable reaction to excellence.

One afternoon I was reading some documents relating to Adolf Hitler's twelve-year empire. It was not the politics of these years that was at the center of my concern; it was the cruelty perpetrated in the death camps of Central Europe. For years I had been studying cruelty, the slow crushing and grinding of a human being by other human beings. I had studied the tortures white men inflicted upon native Indians and then upon blacks in the Americas, and now I was reading mainly about the torture experiments the Nazis conducted upon the bodies of small children in those death camps.

Across all these studies, the pattern of the strong crushing the weak kept repeating itself and repeating itself, so that when I was not bitterly angry, I was bored at the repetition of the patterns of persecution. When I was not desiring to be cruel with the cruel, I was a monster—like perhaps, many others around me—who could look upon torture and death without a shudder, and who therefore looked upon life without a belief in its preciousness. My study of evil incarnate had become a prison whose bars were my bitterness toward the violent, and whose walls were my horrified indifference to slow murder. Between the bars and the walls I revolved like a madman. Reading about the damned I was damned myself, as damned as the murderers, and as damned as their victims. Somehow over the years I had dug myself into Hell, and I had forgotten redemption, had forgotten the possibility of escape.

On this particular day, I was reading in an anthology of documents from the Holocaust, and I came across a short article about a little village in the mountains of southern France. As usual, I was reading the pages with an effort at objectivity; I was trying to sort out the forms and elements of cruelty and of resistance to it in much the same way a veterinarian might sort out ill from healthy cattle. After all, I was doing this work not to torture myself but to understand the indignity and the dignity of man.

About halfway down the third page of the account of this village, I was annoyed by a strange sensation on my cheeks. The story was so simple and so factual that I had found it easy to concentrate upon *it*, not upon my own feelings. And so, still following the story, and thinking about how neatly some of it fit into the old patterns of persecution, I reached up to my cheek to wipe away a bit of dust, and I felt tears upon my fingertips. Not one or two drops; my whole cheek was wet.

"Oh," my sentinel mind told me, "you are losing your grasp on things again. Instead of learning about cruelty, you are becoming one more of its victims. You are doing it again." I was disgusted with myself for daring to intrude.

And so I closed the book and left my college office. When I came home, my operatic Italian wife and my turbulent children, as they have never failed to do, distracted me noisily. I hardly felt the spear that had gone through me. But that night when I lay on my back in bed with my eyes closed, I saw more clearly than ever the images that had made me weep. I saw the two clumsy khaki-colored buses of Vichy French police pull into the village square. I saw the police captain facing the pastor of the village and warning him that if he did not give up the names of the Jews they had been sheltering in the village, he and his fellow pastor, as well as the families who had been caring for the Jews, would be arrested. I saw the pastor refuse to give up these people who had been strangers in his village, even at the risk of his own destruction.

Then I saw the only Jew the police could find, sitting in an otherwise empty bus. I saw a thirteen-year-old boy, the son of the pastor, pass a piece of his precious chocolate through the window to the prisoner, while twenty gendarmes who were guarding the lone prisoner watched. And then I saw the villagers passing their little gifts through the window until there were gifts all around him—most of them food in those hungry days during the German occupation of France.

Lying there in bed, I began to weep again. I thought, Why run away from what is excellent simply because it goes through you like a spear? Lying there, I knew that always a certain region of my mind contained an awareness of men and women in bloody white coats breaking and rebreaking the bones of six- or seven- or eight-year-old Jewish children in order, the Nazis said, to study the processes of natural healing in young bodies. All of this I knew. But why not know joy? Why not leave root room for comfort? Why add myself to millions of victims? Why must life be for me that vision of those children lying there with their children's eyes looking up at the adults who were breaking a leg for the second time, a rib cage for the third time? Something had happened, had happened for years in that mountain village. Why should I be afraid of it?

To the dismay of my wife, I left the bed unable to say a word, dressed, crossed the dark campus on a starless night, and read again those few pages on the village of Le Chambon-sur-Lignon. And to my surprise, again the spear, again the tears, again the frantic, painful pleasure that spills into the mind when a deep, deep need is being satisfied, or when a deep wound is starting to heal.

That night, I decided to try to understand all this. I decided to understand it so that I could hold it more firmly than one can hold a tear, or an image. Since I was a student and a teacher of ethics, I would use what I had learned about man's standards of ethical excellence to help me understand the blessing—at least for me—of Le Chambon. Those involuntary tears had been an expression of moral praise, praise pressed out of my whole personality like the juice of a grape. And part of that personality had been the ideas of goodness and of evil that I had been learning and teaching for decades.

But I was not going to make Le Chambon an "example" of goodness or moral nobility; I was not going to use this story to explain some abstract idea of ethics. Ends are more valuable than means; understanding that story was my end, my goal, and I was going to use the words of philosophical ethics only as a means for achieving this goal. Or, to be more accurate, I was going to use the words of ethics to help me understand my deeply felt ethical praise for the deeds of the people of Le Chambon.

A year later, Pastor Édouard Theis was holding my arm to keep from slipping on an icy road in Le Chambon. The winter wind of the plateau, *la burle*, was blowing in its strange way: instead of pushing the snow away from us, off the plateau on which Le Chambon stands, it whirled the snow low and close around our feet. It hardly moved the tall pines on both sides of the road. It caught in its whorls the low, long-fingered evergreen bushes on the sides of the road. The bushes thrashed their green fingers around us, pointing in a thousand directions and in no direction at all. The people of the plateau used the long twigs to make their brooms in the old days, and so instead of calling the bushes by their proper name, *les genêts*, they called them *les balais* (brooms).

Night was almost at its darkest. The Protestant pastor and I were coming back from a day of interviews with some of the people of Le Chambon. Theis was miserable with influenza and still heavy with sadness, two years old, of having lost his wife, Mildred. Everything—the wind, the slippery roads, the wild fingers of the broom—everything expressed loss, pointless loss, a whirling in deepening darkness. "Oh," Pastor Theis had said during one of our interviews, "I have been *unstable* since the death of Mildred Theis." And his heavy head, his big, curved nose that descended to a point, his wide shoulders—all seemed to be collapsing. This was the man who had helped another pastor, André Trocmé, make the village of Le Chambon one of the main forces in France for saving the lives of Jewish refugees during the four years of

Nazi occupation of France. In the last months of those years, when he was on the Gestapo's black list, he had guided refugees through the mountains of eastern France, through the French police and German troops to the border of Switzerland and safety.

Though he reached for me to keep from falling on those icy mountain roads, he was helping me to keep from slipping as we walked together slowly. I had seen pictures of him in his thirties: the "rock of Le Chambon," the massive presence with a full, almost round face and big, heavy shoulders. But now Theis was seventy-five years old, and I felt under his coat (actually two thin, ragged raincoats) a thin, trembling man.

My God, I thought as we walked through *la burle*, we're losing everything. It's as if the broom were sweeping everything away, or inward and downward into darkness. At our last interview we had been talking with Madame Marion and her daughter, two of the strong women of Le Chambon during the Occupation. The precise, sixty-year-old daughter had told me her version of Theis's return to Le Chambon from a detention camp. She told me that when Theis and the other leader of Le Chambon stepped off the train, there were the villagers, waiting, with an open path through them. There was absolute silence at the railroad station. Not a word was said; there was not even a cry from a child and no shuffling of feet, she said. She told me that the two returning leaders had walked through the open path, and villagers had silently closed behind them and followed them away from the station.

Theis, when he heard this, was surprised. "I remember no silence. Perhaps if Trocmé were here, he would remember it," he said.

"Why," the younger Marion insisted in her quick, factual way, "Monsieur Theis, they were silent, and silent for a very good reason. The Gestapo was there, and so were some collaborators from Vichy. They were looking for an excuse to arrest you again. Didn't you notice?"

"Oh, perhaps I did notice," Theis murmured, "and I have forgotten. But I am not sure. I am not sure at all. And André Trocmé is dead." The story of Le Chambon was being swept out of human memory.

The Baal Shem-Tov, the founder of Hasidism, the Jewish movement that finds God in good and evil—in everything—once said, "In remembrance resides the secret of redemption." This saying appears at the top of a citation from the state of Israel, a citation that attests to the fact that André Trocmé, the spiritual leader of the village of Le Chambon, "at peril of his life, saved Jews during the epoch of extermination." This citation accompanied the Medal of Righteousness that Israel awarded to Trocmé. If the secret of redemption lies in remembering, it is lost in forgetting. After more than thirty years, the story of Le Chambon lay in less than a dozen little-known pages, most of them rather vague and inaccurate. The whole story could be found only in the memories of a few people who were now old and sick.

. . .

But it was not easy to find out what had happened in this village. From the point of view of the history of nations, something very small had happened here. The story of Le Chambon lacked the glamour, the wingspread of other wartime events. Victories and defeats of nations are written large in men's minds because the lives and fortunes of so many human beings depend upon them. World War II, between the Axis and the Allies, was a public phenomenon; military, journalistic, and governmental reports made it abundantly available to the public. It impressed itself powerfully and deeply upon the minds of mankind, both during and after the war. The metaphors that describe it have a flamboyant cast: the war itself was a "world war," with many "heroes"; there were "theaters of war," and soldiers who participated in major "campaigns" received "battle stars."

No such language applies to what happened in Le Chambon. In fact, words like "war" are inappropriate to describe it, and so are words like "theater." While the story of Le Chambon was unfolding, it was being recorded nowhere. What was happening was clandestine because the people of Le Chambon had no military power comparable to that of the Nazis occupying France, or comparable to that of the Vichy government of France, which was collaborating with the Nazi conquerors. If they had tried to confront their opponents publicly, there would have been no contest, only immediate and total defeat. Secrecy, not military power, was their weapon.

The struggle in Le Chambon began and ended in the privacy of people's homes. Decisions that were turning points in that struggle took place in kitchens, and not with male leaders as the only decision-makers, but often with women centrally involved. A kitchen is a private, intimate place; in it there are no uniforms, no buttons or badges symbolizing public duty or public support. In the kitchen of a modest home only a few people are involved. In Le Chambon only the lives of a few thousand people were changed, compared to the scores of millions of human lives directly affected by the larger events of World War II.

The "kitchen struggle" of Le Chambon resembles rather closely a certain kind of conflict that grew more and more widespread as the years of the Occupation passed. Guerrilla action, clandestine, violent resistance to the German occupants, was as much a part of the history of that Occupation as the story of that little commune. Secrecy was as vital to guerrilla warfare as it was to the resistance of the people of Le Chambon, and so was a minimum of permanent records. In both cases military weakness dictated that there be few records and much secrecy.

But the kitchen struggles differed greatly from the bush battle (the *Maquis*, the name given to the wing of the armed resistance which had no direct connections with de Gaulle's Secret Army, refers to *le maquis*, the low, prickly bushes that grow on dry, hilly land). The guerrillas were fighting for the liberation of their country. Some of them received their orders from de Gaulle's exiled French government (Free France), and others owed their allegiance to the Soviet Union; still others had no particular political allegiance, but they were all parts of military units. Especially in time of war such units are primarily concerned with achieving by violent means a victory over the enemies of those units. Their primary duty is not to save lives but to save the life of some public entity; and especially in time of war they cherish heroism—living and dying gloriously for a public cause—more than they cherish compassion. The consciences of individuals in military units tend to be in lock-step with the self-interest of the units. In fact, for the bush warriors as for the uniformed warriors, public duty took precedence over personal conscience.

But the people of Le Chambon whom Pastor André Trocmé led into a quiet struggle against Vichy and the Nazis were not fighting for the liberation of their country or their village. They felt little loyalty to governments. Their actions did not serve the self-interest of the little commune of Le Chambon-sur-Lignon in the department of Haute-Loire, southern France. On the contrary, those actions flew in the face of that self-interest: by resisting a power far greater than their own they put their village in grave danger of massacre, especially in the last two years of the Occupation, when the Germans were growing desperate. Under the guidance of a spiritual leader they were trying to act in accord with their consciences in the very middle of a bloody, hate-filled war.

And what this meant for them was nonviolence. Following their consciences meant refusing to hate or kill any human being. And in this lies their deepest difference from the other aspects of World War II. Human life was too precious to them to be taken for any reason, glorious and vast though that reason might be. Their consciences told them to save as many lives as they could, even if doing this meant endangering the lives of all the villagers; and they obeyed their consciences.

But acts of conscience are not important news, especially while a war is going on. Only actions directly related to the national self-interest receive a measure of fame then. And this is why the Partisan Sharp-shooters of the left and the Secret Army of General Charles de Gaulle were nationally though secretly revered during the Occupation, and were praised to the skies afterward. This is also why the armed resistance produced heroes like General de Gaulle himself, and the passionately beloved coordinator of the armed French Resistance, Jean Moulin.

There are no such nationally known names in the story of Le Chambon. When France was liberated, there were no triumphal marches for André Trocmé and his villagers through the streets of Paris or Marseilles. And this was as it should have been: they had not contributed directly to saving the life of the French nation. They were not so much French patriots as they were conscientious human beings.

THE ATLANTIC CHARTER AND THE YALTA DECLARATION ON LIBERATED EUROPE

The United States did not enter World War II until December 1941, after Japan attacked Pearl Harbor and Germany declared war against the United States. Even before then, however, the United States had begun helping Great Britain in the war.

In August 1941 President Roosevelt met with Prime Minister Winston Churchill to discuss their hopes for the future. The statement they produced is called the Atlantic Charter.

At the start of the war Germany and the Soviet Union had collaborated in dividing up Poland. But in June 1941 Germany invaded the Soviet Union. Thereafter the Soviet Union, the United States, and Great Britain were allies in the war. In February 1945, as it was becoming clear that the war was nearing its end, Stalin, Roosevelt, and Churchill met at Yalta in the Soviet Union to plan for the postwar world. One of their main topics was the future of the countries in Europe that were being liberated from the rule of the Nazis.

Were the goals of the Atlantic Charter and the Yalta Declaration realistic? Have they been realized? What has happened to the wartime alliance of the Soviet Union, the United States, and Great Britain?

THE ATLANTIC CHARTER

The President of the United States of America and the Prime Minister, Mr. Churchill, representing His Majesty's Government in the United Kingdom, being met together, deem it right to make known certain common principles in the national policies of their respective countries on which they base their hopes for a better future for the world.

First, their countries seek no aggrandizement, territorial or other;

Both documents are reprinted in *Documents of American History*, seventh edition, edited by Henry Steele Commager. New York: Appleton-Century-Crofts, 1963.

Second, they desire to see no territorial changes that do not accord with the freely expressed wishes of the peoples concerned;

Third, they respect the right of all peoples to choose the form of government under which they will live; and they wish to see sovereign rights and self government restored to those who have been forcibly deprived of them;

Fourth, they will endeavor, with due respect for their existing obligations, to further the enjoyment by all States, great or small, victor or vanquished, of access, on equal terms, to the trade and to the raw materials of the world which are needed for their economic prosperity;

Fifth, they desire to bring about the fullest collaboration between all nations in the economic field with the object of securing, for all, improved labor standards, economic advancement and social security;

Sixth, after the final destruction of the Nazi tyranny, they hope to see established a peace which will afford to all nations the means of dwelling in safety within their own boundaries, and which will afford assurance that all the men in all the lands may live out their lives in freedom from fear and want;

Seventh, such a peace should enable all men to traverse the high seas and oceans without hindrance;

Eighth, they believe that all of the nations of the world, for realistic as well as spiritual reasons must come to the abandonment of the use of force. Since no future peace can be maintained if land, sea or air armaments continue to be employed by nations which threaten, or may threaten, aggression outside of their frontiers, they believe, pending the establishment of a wider and permanent system of general security, that the disarmament of such nations is essential. They will likewise aid and encourage all other practicable measures which will lighten for peace-loving peoples the crushing burden of armaments.

YALTA DECLARATION ON LIBERATED EUROPE

The Premier of the Union of Soviet Socialist Republics, the Prime Minister of the United Kingdom and the President of the United States of America have consulted with each other in the common interests of the peoples of their countries and those of liberated Europe. They jointly declare their mutual agreement to concert during the temporary period of instability in liberated Europe the policies of their three Governments in assisting the peoples liberated from the domination of Nazi Germany and the peoples of the former Axis satellite states of Europe to solve by democratic means their pressing political and economic problems.

The establishment of order in Europe and the rebuilding of national economic life must be achieved by processes which will enable the liberated peoples to destroy the last vestiges of nazism and fascism and to create democratic institutions of their own choice. This is a principle of the Atlantic Charter—the right of all peoples to choose the form of government under which they will live—the restoration of sovereign rights and self-government to those peoples who have been forcibly deprived of them by the aggressor nations.

To foster the conditions in which the liberated peoples may exercise these rights, the three Governments will jointly assist the people in any European liberated state or former Axis satellite state in Europe where, in their judgment conditions require, (a) to establish conditions of internal peace; (b) to carry out emergency measures for the relief of distressed peoples; (c) to form interim governmental authorities broadly representative of all democratic elements in the population and pledged to the earliest possible establishment through free elections of Governments responsive to the will of the people; and (d) to facilitate where necessary the holding of such elections.

The three Governments will consult the other United Nations and provisional authorities or other Governments in Europe when matters of direct interest to them are under consideration.

When, in the opinion of the three Governments, conditions in any European liberated state or any former Axis satellite state in Europe make such action necessary, they will immediately consult together on the measures necessary to discharge the joint responsibilities set forth in this declaration.

By this declaration we affirm our faith in the principles of the Atlantic Charter, our pledge in the Declaration by the United Nations and our determination to build in cooperation with other peace-loving nations world order, under law, dedicated to peace, security, freedom and general well-being of all mankind.

THE COLD WAR AS HISTORY

LOUIS J. HALLE

In this reading the political scientist and former U.S. State Department planner Louis J. Halle puts the conflict between the United States and the

Abridged from *The Cold War as History* by Louis J. Halle. Copyright © 1967 by Louis J. Halle. Reprinted by permission of Harper & Row, Publishers, Inc.

Soviet Union in a broad historical perspective. What is that perspective? How is Soviet behavior a continuation of Russian policy before the communist revolution? What, according to Halle, is the main motivation behind Soviet foreign policy? How important is communism and capital- ism in the conflict between the United States and Soviet Union?

THE BEHAVIOR OF MOSCOW AS A REFLECTION OF RUSSIA'S HISTORIC EXPERIENCE

Writing in the 1830's, Alexis de Tocqueville made the following remark-able prophecy:

> There are on earth today two great people, who, from different points of departure, seem to be advancing toward the same end. They are the Russians and the Anglo-Americans.
>
> Both have grown great in obscurity; and while the attention of mankind was occupied elsewhere they have suddenly taken their places in the first rank among the nations, and the world has learned, almost at the same time, both of their birth and of their greatness.
>
> All the other peoples appear to have attained approximately their natural limits, and to have nothing left but to conserve their positions; but these two are growing: all the others have stopped or continue only by endless effort; they alone advance easily and rapidly in a career of which the limit cannot yet be seen.
>
> The American struggles against the obstacles that nature places before him; the Russian is at grips with humanity. The one combats wilderness and savagery, the other combats civilization decked in all its armament: moreover, the conquests of the American are won by the plowshare, those of the Russian by the sword.
>
> To attain his end, the first depends on the interest of the individual person, and allows the force and intelligence of individuals to act freely, without directing them. The second in some way concentrates all the power of society in one man.
>
> The one has liberty as the chief way of doing things; the other servitude.
>
> Their points of departure are different, their paths are divergent; never-theless, each seems summoned by a secret design of providence to hold in his hands, some day, the destinies of half the world.[1]

One may draw two conclusions from the fact that de Tocqueville was able to make this prediction so long ago.

One is that what is predictable must (always barring a cataclysm) be inevitable. Nothing is surely predictable except as it is bound to happen. If it may or may not happen, then one cannot predict its happening with authority; one can only guess and gamble that it will happen. But de Tocqueville was not guessing and gambling. He saw the future devel-

---

1. Translated from *De la Démocratie en Amérique*, concluding passage of the first half— i.e., of Vol. I.

opment of America and Russia as implicit in their contemporary circumstances. He saw their future in their present as one sees the leaf in the bud. Therefore we may conclude that the polarization of the world between two superpowers was not the accidental product of accidental circumstances.

Walter Lippmann once wrote that prophecy "is seeing the necessary amidst confusion and insignificance. . . ." The development that de Tocqueville prophesied so long ago belonged to the realm of the necessary.

The other conclusion that I draw from his prophecy is that the role of Communism in the polarization of the world is secondary, that it does not belong to the realm of the necessary. For de Tocqueville, when he wrote his prophecy, knew nothing of a young university student in Germany called Karl Marx, or of an unborn revolutionary called Lenin. He did not foresee the coming of Communism to Russia. He did not anticipate the substitution of a Communist regime for the czarist regime. He foresaw that what in fact came to pass would come to pass regardless of the ideological label attached to the authoritarian regime that governed Russia.

The implications of this seem to me essential to an understanding of the Cold War. The behaviour of Russia under the Communists has been Russian behaviour rather than Communist behaviour. Under the Communists Russia has continued to behave essentially as it behaved under the czars. There has been the same centralization and authoritarianism. There has been the same conspiratorial approach to international relations. There has been the same profound mistrust of the outside world. There has been the same obsession with secrecy and with espionage. There has been the same cautiousness, the same capacity for retreat. There has been the same effort to achieve security by expanding the Russian space, by constantly pushing back the menacing presence of the foreigners across the Russian borders.

What the Revolution of 1917 did was simply to reinvigorate the traditional principle of authoritarianism in Russia. It replaced a decadent and enfeebled authoritarian dynasty with a new, vigorous, and ruthlessly determined authoritarian dynasty. All this is implicit in the fact that de Tocqueville was able to predict both the polarization of the world and the ideological contest between the two superpowers without foreseeing Marxism-Leninism.

The Cold War, then, represents an historical necessity to which the Communist movement is incidental rather than essential.

By contrast with America, Russia has always been a closed society. It has been a secret society under the czars as under the Communists— and, at an earlier stage, under the princes of Muscovy as under the czars. It has been a society in which all the functions of a Government that was constitutionally all-powerful have traditionally been carried on in the dark, out of a fear that has been repeatedly justified in the awful history of the Russian people. Consequently Russia, neither Asian nor seeming quite European, speaking a language not understood outside its confines, has had about it an air of darkness and mystery that is the antithesis of the aura that surrounds the American society.

Of other societies that have been hostile and aggressive it has been evident that they were driven by ambition. Athens, Rome, Hitler's Germany, and pre-war Japan were driven by ambition. These societies were intoxicated by their dreams of power. It would be wrong to assign a like cause to the long history of Russia's expansion and hostility. And today as well, I think, we are misled by an essentially nominal situation when we say that Moscow's expansion and hostility represent an ambition to spread its so-called "Communist system" throughout the world. Such an ambition is, at best, secondary.

From the beginning in the ninth century, and even today, the prime driving force in Russia has been fear. Fear, rather than ambition, is the principal reason for the organization and expansion of the Russian society. Fear, rather than ambition in itself, has been the great driving force. The Russians as we know them today have experienced ten centuries of constant, mortal fear. This has not been a disarming experience. It has not been an experience calculated to produce a simple, open, innocent, and guileless society.

If all my ancestors for ten centuries back had died violent deaths at the hands of their neighbors it is quite likely that I would have been brought up from childhood to be suspicious and hostile toward my neighbors. It is likely that I would have been brought up to be dangerous to my neighbors, that I would have been brought up to the practice of an astute course of deception designed to outwit and to foil them. And while I might on occasion feel myself profoundly attracted to them, as one is always attracted to a powerful enemy, no smiles of friendship on their part would ever persuade me to relax my guard in their company. Like Foreign Minister Molotov visiting his wartime ally, Prime Minister Churchill, I would keep a loaded revolver by my bedside.

Throughout Russian history real circumstances have justified the fear by which the Russians have been governed. For ten centuries they have survived the greatest trials experienced by any people in the world today only because they have been so governed. They have survived those trials only because they learned at an early stage to trust no one, to be suspiciously alert, to keep their own counsel, and to substitute guile for superior strength where superior strength was lacking.

· · ·

From the days of Ivan the Great until our own time, a period of five centuries, the history of Moscow is one of steady, continuing expansion. Yet this expansion, in a way peculiar to Russia, is not an aggressive expansion. Right up to our own day it is a defensive expansion, an expansion prompted by the lack of natural defensive frontiers in a world of mortal danger on all sides. Where mountain-ramparts or impassable waters are lacking, sheer space must do in their stead. The huddled defensive community—in Kiev, in Novgorod, in Smolensk, or in Moscow—is impelled, by whatever means, to drive the encircling danger back. And the process of driving the danger back becomes, to the eye of the outsider, the process of imperial expansion.

Throughout this expansion, and until our own day, Russia continues to be embattled and besieged. It is true that Moscow threw off the Tartar yoke in 1480. In 1571, however, the Tartars of the Crimea captured and burned Moscow. According to the reports, they killed 800,000 Russians and carried away 130,000 prisoners. This was the kind of incident that would be repeated time and again throughout the long history of Russia's defensive expansion—down to Hitler's invasion and slaughter of the Russians in our own day.

After the sixteenth century, however, the threats to Russia's survival all came from the west. In 1606 Russia was invaded, and Moscow was captured, by a Polish army. For six years, then, Muscovy was largely under Polish occupation, while Moscow was either occupied or withstanding siege. In 1611 Moscow was burned down again, all except for the Kremlin and the inner town. That same year, Swedish troops captured Novgorod.

In 1613, with the liberation of Moscow from the Poles, the coronation of Michael Romanov inaugurated a new dynasty. There followed a long series of wars with Swedes, Poles, Turks. And all the time Russia was expanding steadily. To the east, it expanded at last across Siberia. To the south, it expanded along the shores of the Black Sea. To the west, under Peter the Great, it emerged on the Baltic. In 1812 it was the French who invaded Russia. The Russian earth was scorched. Again Moscow fell into the hands of the invader.

The repeated blows continued in the twentieth century as for a thousand years before. In 1917 the Russian state collapsed completely, if temporarily, under the assault of Kaiser William's army. The invaders advanced deep into Russia. Virtually all the territory gained since the days of Peter the Great was lost. And with the loss of Finland the Russian frontier was forced back to within artillery-range of the new capital, St. Petersburg, that Peter had established on the Baltic. The loss of the whole Ukraine meant the economic ruin of Russia.

However, under the hammer-blows, first of the German assault, then of assault by the expeditionary forces of the Western allies, including the United States, the Russian state was reconstituted, a new dictatorship was forged by Lenin and then Stalin, and again the innate strength of the Russian land and people was gathered up, at terrible sacrifice, to withstand the next attack.

The next attack was to come under the directing will of Adolf Hitler. Again all the best Russian earth would be scorched. Again, when the assault was over, the land would be littered with the dead bodies of Russians, of which between seven and eight million were left dead when the Nazi tide had at last receded. And again the end of it all would be a further expansion of territory under Moscow's sway, this time to embrace most of Europe to a line a hundred miles west of Berlin.

So, in the face of continual assault and defeat, Russia would emerge to fulfill de Tocqueville's prophecy, a giant power under the sway of one man [Stalin] holding in its hands the destinies of half the world.

THE REAL ISSUE OF THE COLD WAR
AND ITS MYTHIC FORMULATIONS

In ideological terms, the Cold War presented itself as a worldwide contest between liberal democracy and Communism. Each side looked forward to the eventual supremacy of its system all over the earth. The official Communist goal was the liberation of mankind from capitalist oppression. Ideologically minded Westerners interpreted this as signifying that Moscow was trying to impose its own authoritarian system on a world that it meant to rule. Americans, for their part, had traditionally looked forward to the liberation of mankind from the oppression of autocracy, and to the consequent establishment of their own liberal system throughout the world. To the ideologists in Moscow this meant that "the imperialist ruling circles" in America were trying to enslave all mankind under the yoke of Wall Street.

The ideological view of human affairs has always had an irresistible popular appeal because it conforms to the child's image of a world divided between two species, the good (we) and the wicked (they). According to this image, the essence of life is the struggle between good and evil so represented. The two contesting species take many different forms but are always essentially the same. On one occasion they may take the form of the cops and the robbers, on another that of the cowboys and the Indians, on another that of "peace-loving" and "aggressor" nations. In orthodox Marxism they take the form of proletarians and the capitalists. This is the universal fairy-tale of mankind, to which we are all brought up. Any struggle cast in terms of it must properly be total. It would be improper for the cops to negotiate a compromise settlement with the robbers, or to limit the efforts they make to overcome them by such rules of combat as would be appropriate in a boxing-match, where the moral issue is absent. Christians in the Middle Ages were limited by explicit rules of chivalry and ecclesiastical law when they fought one another, but not when they fought pagans. When they fought pagans the only proper objective was that of eliminating them, or what they represented, from the face of the earth. Similarly, to the extent that the Cold War was to be regarded as an ideological contest there could be no geographical limitation to it, and it could properly end only when one side had, at last, destroyed the other.

The ideological view, however, is in its essence mythical. The grand eschatological objectives that go with it tend to have little or no expression beyond the nominal. They are not, in any case, objectives toward which the daily operations of government are actually directed. At no time, after the first years of the Bolshevik regime, was the operative policy of Moscow directed in any immediate or meaningful sense toward the objective of a single classless and stateless society encircling the globe. This was, rather, a nominal objective that pertained to a mythological future. As such, however, it had a noble simplicity that made it more real to the man in the street than such operative objectives as that of acquiring the "glacis" of secure territory along the western frontier of the traditional Russian state.

This is not to say that the ideology, with its grand objective, did not make a difference. It made a great difference. Not only did it constantly threaten to draw the makers of policy into foolish and dangerous adventures (for example, the 1920 march on Warsaw), it gave a mythic justification to the distrust of the outside world that, in fact, had other roots; it provided its votaries with a sense of mission; it furnished a cover of respectability for political practices that, in their nakedness, would have seemed shameful; it made those who were driven by terrible necessity to the perpetration of sinister deeds feel themselves morally justified. From the first, however, the deeds themselves were directed toward more limited and practical objectives that were not essentially different from the traditional objectives of the Russian state. While the nominal ideology had an influence that one could only regard as dangerous, what was determinative for action was the complex of considerations, representing power-politics, that stemmed from the self-interest of the Russian state.

President Wilson's objective of making the world "safe for democracy" had, in a detached view, implications not altogether unrelated to those arising from the ideological objectives associated with the Russian state since 1917. The influence of that abiding objective was, on occasion, dangerous—as in the ideological interventions that the United States undertook in Latin America immediately after World War II, as in its commitment to the maintenance of liberal democracy in China. In the long run, however, what was generally determinative for the operating policy of the United States, as for that of Soviet Russia, was its own vital interests in a world of power-politics.

In practice neither the United States nor the Soviet Union was bent on establishing its rule over the earth. Each, however, could be represented, with a certain show of plausibility, as seeking to do so. The Cold War would tend to be intractable and unlimitable to the extent that each side allowed itself to be entranced by the nominal and ideological questions at issue, subordinating the real, strategic questions.

14. Dependence and Independence in Asia

LETTER OF AN INDIAN JUDGE

ARVIND NEHRA

The burdens of colonialism increased for all after World War I, but perhaps no class experienced greater emotional tension than the rising native colonial elite, educated in the West to collaborate in the rule of the colonies. Caught in the middle layers of the colonial bureaucracy where they were without final authority but within easy reach of their discontented and sometimes revolutionary compatriots, they were unwelcome among the Europeans and distrusted at home.

This letter from one such colonial official, an Indian judge sent to Burma by the British, gives us a sense of some of those tensions. The fact that he corresponded with an "English Gentlewoman" was unusual enough. The author's candor is even more striking. This letter was written several years after he first met the English lady who "took pity" and talked to him at a Government House party in Calcutta. In what ways does the writer identify with the English? In what ways does he identify with Indians or Burmese? Is his role as official for the English ultimately good or bad for the Burmese?

Christmas is not legitimately any feast of mine save that it is the feast of children, and being myself a Father my heart must be soft towards all children. For this reason it is rapidly becoming a feast of mine. I can now rely upon a letter from you at that season, with your news. I find it difficult to believe that this large boy in the snapshot is indeed David. Time falls away so fast one does not realize that it is going.

I remain in Rangoon, but shall shortly be promoted. I am now a full-fledged Judge of the High Court. My next move will no doubt be India and I shall be glad to get back there, for the news we get is far from good. What is to come of all this agitation for Home Rule, I cannot make out.

Here in Burma there is also a certain unrest, but it is not very much as yet. The sun shines, there is a Religious Festival to keep, someone makes a large tiger and plays music inside him, and the Burman forgets. Indeed at heart he is no Politician, and has no aspirations beyond a full stomach. In my opinion at the bottom of all Political aspirations it boils down to that. It is only when a people becomes poverty-stricken that it grows discontented and seeks to better its ways with quack medicines.

I have now four children. Arvind, my firstborn, is a strong boy of seven. Your David must now be nine. There are two other sons and a daughter. Mala has indeed done her duty and becomes now very stout. It is a pity but it cannot be helped. At twenty-seven she is quite the old lady. Our women fade quickly, and they do not care. To grow old and stout with child-bearing, it is an honourable thing, and one that nobody fears. As yet there are no beauty parlours in our midst, save those dark arts our old women impart to the Brides.

Rangoon is very changed. The streets are now thronged with motor cars, and there are still two more Clubs building. Everybody appears to be immensely rich, and indeed we draw here princely pay. It is pleasant, but always in my secret heart I wonder, is it wise? Because at the back of it all, there sits always the small man in the jungle, the little man with two or three rice fields, and he it is who is taxed to pay all this money and only as long as he is contented and satisfied can there be any quiet in the land. Already travelling in the Districts, I have heard murmurs.

There has come amongst us also, since the War, a new kind of official. He is not the type of man the East got years ago, but a new kind of whom I would say that he was born tired. And he has come out East, like Mr. Nigel Hill, not from any sense of vocation such as fired the young men in the days when Mr. Kipling wrote his poems, but because he must live, and wishes as soon as possible to draw a pension. And always he hates the damn country.

At first I treated it lightly thinking it was a pose like the young man at Cambridge who said "I never do any work," and then was always swotting behind closed doors when he pretended to sleep. Of late I come to the conclusion this is not so. For many things are troublesome here now, and nothing is done. Only we continue to do exactly what was laid down yesterday. Nothing new is allowed under the sun, even when the old is obviously worn threadbare, and bad. From time to time I have spoken to you about taxes. I shall now quote you an instance. There is in the Districts much real poverty because of the fall in the price of rice. Rice, which the cultivator now sells at from sixty to seventy rupees one hundred baskets, he at one time got over one hundred rupees for. But the tax remains the same as when he got one hundred rupees. We are rapidly approaching a state of things when the profit upon the rice is nothing, and still he has the tax to pay.

Perhaps you will ask why the tax cannot fall automatically with the price of the rice? Because, Lady Sahib, the cost of Government administration does not fall, it grows every year heavier. It is a bad thing for a country when the small man in the jungle murmurs and grows discontented.

Meanwhile, Government salaries continue large, much larger than the same men could ever hope to get had they remained in England. I myself receive a salary that is ridiculously high. It is pleasant and I enjoy it, but in my heart alone I doubt if it is wise. And all around us, red brick buildings are springing up, the realization of this or that high-flown scheme, often not too well thought out.

I who admire and love England so much, often feel to-day that she is like one who has taken bad advice and is for a moment deserting her better judgments, for profligate ways. Certainly the Western Administration of to-day is too expensive, and too complicated for the Eastern nations, and that is at the root of all the troubles realized and brewing. When it is written of any country, "The people cried out under the burden of the taxes" then that chapter is to be a sad one.

One sees a repercussion of all this in the Courts where there are many crimes from poverty, and much violence in the District, resisting tax collections, but so far it is on a small scale, little. The sun shines and the Burman forgets.

Do I offend you, Lady Sahib, in writing to you like this? I hope not. In my present position there is not a soul to whom I can speak out and frankly, for whatever my private convictions may be, officially I must uphold the system entirely and without reservation. No one realizes more than I the necessity for absolute loyalty on the part of Government Servants in these days, and how any move that is made must be made by the body as a whole, not here one and there one.

To-night I shall dine with a brother Judge in his beautiful house out beside the Lakes. From time to time I am now asked to dine in the British Community but always I see in the eyes of my Hostess that old terror lest I shall not behave properly at table. We shall have eight courses to eat, and many expensive drinks, and all the talk will be of how hard up everyone is and what difficult times these are. There will be only elderly English ladies from the Hospital and Schools present, for the difficulties of these mixed dinner parties is an acute one, and no one appreciates it now more than myself.

For this, Lady Sahib, is the problem stripped of all its frills and varnish. I am an Indian, and have growing sons, and if my sons mix with your daughters, perhaps they will fall in love with one another. The colour problem is the sex problem, the problem of the outcast and half-breed. However much we may like one another, we do not wish our children to inter-marry. All our inhibitions and our precautions and our fortifications against each other's communities are because of this one great and not-alluded-to fact. To the pure bred, the half-breed must always be a disaster. Could one ever overcome that instinctive feeling? Would it be desirable if one did?

In America I am told they are evolving a superman from all the nations under the sun. I would prefer to see him for myself, before passing any opinion on this result of the melting pot.

As I grow older, I think there is no colour problem, but this one of sex, just as there are no National Problems, only problems of Finance. A country has vested interests in another country, and like Pharaoh of old, when they struggle for freedom, she will not let them go. There is no new plot under the sun, Lady Sahib. Only the same old story told over and over again, with perhaps some new scenery here and there for politeness' sake.

But Nations, like people, dislike hard facts. They prefer to put a small and elegant petticoat on the naked truth. And so vested interests are called moral obligations because we feel better about it that way. So we break people's heads, lest they should break each other's.

GANDHI

JAWAHARLAL NEHRU

Mahatma Gandhi and Jawaharlal Nehru were the two most important leaders of India's national independence movement. Although they worked together and Nehru was Gandhi's choice as the first Indian prime minister, they expressed in their personalities and ideas two very different Indias. How would you describe these two Indias? Whose India did the judge, Arvind Nehra, prefer? Was it Gandhi's or Nehru's vision of the future that was realized? Who do you think was a better guide for India?

I imagine that Gandhiji is not so vague about the objective as he sometimes appears to be. He is passionately desirous of going in a certain direction, but this is wholly at variance with modern ideas and conditions, and he has so far been unable to fit the two, or to chalk out all the intermediate steps leading to his goal. Hence the appearance of vagueness and avoidance of clarity. But his general inclination has been clear enough for a quarter of a century, ever since he started formulating his philosophy in South Africa. I do not know if those early writings still represent his views. I doubt if they do so in their entirety, but they do help us to understand the background of his thought.

"India's salvation consists," he wrote in 1909, "in unlearning what she

From *Toward Freedom: The Autobiography of Jawaharlal Nehru*. New York: John Day Company, 1941.

has learned during the last fifty years. The railways, telegraphs, hospitals, lawyers, doctors, and suchlike have all to go; and the so-called upper classes have to learn consciously, religiously, and deliberately the simple peasant life, knowing it to be a life giving true happiness." And again: "Every time I get into a railway car or use a motor bus I know that I am doing violence to my sense of what is right"; "to attempt to reform the world by means of highly artificial and speedy locomotion is to attempt the impossible."

All this seems to me utterly wrong and harmful doctrine, and impossible of achievement. Behind it lies Gandhiji's love and praise of poverty and suffering and the ascetic life. For him progress and civilization consist not in the multiplication of wants, of higher standards of living, "but in the deliberate and voluntary restriction of wants, which promotes real happiness and contentment, and increases the capacity for service." If these premises are once accepted, it becomes easy to follow the rest of Gandhiji's thought and to have a better understanding of his activities. But most of us do not accept those premises, and yet we complain later on when we find that his activities are not to our liking.

Personally I dislike the praise of poverty and suffering. I do not think they are at all desirable, and they ought to be abolished. Nor do I appreciate the ascetic life as a social ideal, though it may suit individuals. I understand and appreciate simplicity, equality, self-control; but not the mortification of the flesh. Just as an athlete requires to train his body, I believe that the mind and habits have also to be trained and brought under control. It would be absurd to expect that a person who is given to too much self-indulgence can endure much suffering or show unusual self-control or behave like a hero when the crisis comes. To be in good moral condition requires at least as much training as to be in good physical condition. But that certainly does not mean asceticism or self-mortification.

Nor do I appreciate in the least the idealization of the "simple peasant life." I have almost a horror of it, and instead of submitting to it myself I want to drag out even the peasantry from it, not to urbanization, but to the spread of urban cultural facilities to rural areas. Far from this life's giving me true happiness, it would be almost as bad as imprisonment for me. What is there in "The Man with the Hoe" to idealize over? Crushed and exploited for innumerable generations, he is only little removed from the animals who keep him company.

> Who made him dead to rapture and despair,
> A thing that grieves not and that never hopes,
> Stolid and stunned, a brother to the ox?

This desire to get away from the mind of man to primitive conditions where mind does not count, seems to me quite incomprehensible. The very thing that is the glory and triumph of man is decried and discouraged, and a physical environment which will oppress the mind and prevent its growth is considered desirable. Present-day civilization is full of evils, but it is also full of good; and it has the capacity in it to rid itself of those evils. To destroy it root and branch is to remove that capacity from it and revert to a dull, sunless, and miserable existence. But even if that were desirable it is an impossible undertaking. We cannot stop the river of change or cut ourselves adrift from it, and psychologically we who have eaten of the apple of Eden cannot forget that taste and go back to primitiveness.

It is difficult to argue this, for the two standpoints are utterly different. Gandhiji is always thinking in terms of personal salvation and of sin, while most of us have society's welfare uppermost in our minds. I find it difficult to grasp the idea of sin, and perhaps it is because of this that I cannot appreciate Gandhiji's general outlook.

CHINA:
1. THE NEW AWAKENING

HAROLD ISAACS

This brief selection from Harold Isaacs' The Tragedy of the Chinese Revolution, *a recent history, recalls the impact of Ch'en Tu-hsiu's* New Youth *magazine in 1915. Spirits that had risen with Sun Yat-sen's revolution in 1911, only to become depressed by its apparent failure, rose again with Ch'en's call to a new generation.*

How did Ch'en's appeal reverse traditional Confucian values? Why do you think it had such an enormous appeal?

China's economic spurt during the First World War opened all the sluices of change. Along a thousand channels new ideas, new thoughts, new aspirations found their way into the country and crashed against the dead weight of the past like mighty waves against a grounded hulk. Among the intellectuals the mood of despair and discouragement engendered by the failure of the 1911 Revolution gave way to the

From *The Tragedy of the Chinese Revolution*, second revised edition, by Harold R. Isaacs. Reprinted with the permission of the publishers, Stanford University Press. © 1951, 1961 by the Board of Trustees of the Leland Stanford Junior University.

beginnings of a vigorous cultural renaissance which rapidly drew a whole new generation into its orbit. New leaders, new forces came to the fore. Out of the thinned ranks of the revolutionary intellectuals of 1911 emerged the figure of Ch'en Tu-hsiu, scion of an Anhwei Mandarin family, who began posing the tasks of revolt more boldly, more clearly, more courageously than anyone who had preceded him. To his side rallied the men who with him were going to make over the life of a whole generation and who in later years would enter and lead opposing armies on the battlefields of social conflict.

The task of the new generation, proclaimed Ch'en Tu-hsiu, was "to fight Confucianism, the old tradition of virtue and rituals, the old ethics and the old politics . . . the old learning and the old literature." In their place he would put the fresh materials of modern democratic thought and natural science.

> We must break down the old prejudices, the old way of believing in things as they are, before we can begin to hope for social progress [wrote Ch'en in 1915 in his magazine, *New Youth*]. We must discard our old ways. We must merge the ideas of the great thinkers of history, old and new, with our own experience, build up new ideas in politics, morality, and economic life. We must build the spirit of the new age to fit it to new environmental conditions and a new society. Our ideal society is honest, progressive, positive, free, equalitarian, creative, beautiful, good, peaceful, cooperative, toilsome, but happy for the many. We look for the world that is false, conservative, negative, restricted, inequitable, hidebound, ugly, evil, war-torn, cruel, indolent, miserable for the many and felicitous for the few, to crumble until it disappears from sight. . . .
>
> I hope those of you who are young will be self-conscious and that you will struggle. By self-consciousness I mean that you are to be conscious of the power and responsibility of your youth and that you are to respect it. Why do I think you should struggle? Because it is necessary for you to use all the intelligence you have to get rid of those who are decaying, who have lost their youth. Regard them as enemies and beasts; do not be influenced by them, do not associate with them.
>
> Oh, young men of China! Will you be able to understand me? Five out of every ten whom I see are young in age, but old in spirit. . . . When this happens to a body, the body is dying. When it happens to a society, the society is perishing. Such a sickness cannot be cured by sighing in words; it can only be cured by those who are young, and in addition to being young, are courageous. . . . We must have youth if we are to survive, we must have youth if we are to get rid of corruption. Here lies the hope for our society.

This memorable call was really the opening manifesto of the era of the second Chinese Revolution. Ch'en Tu-hsiu was a professor at the time at Peking National University, where new ideas and new impulses were stirring and where a new spirit was germinating. Ch'en's magazine was eagerly snatched up by students in every school and college in the country. When it was published, wrote one student, "it came to us like a clap of thunder which awakened us in the midst of a restless dream. . . ."

CHINA:
2. DREAMS OF YOUTH

LU HSUN

Lu Hsun (1881–1936) was one of China's greatest modern writers. He attended the Naval Academy at Nanking and then went to study medicine in Japan, but, as he relates here, he became increasingly distressed by China's "weak and backward" state. Literature seemed to him a more valuable pursuit. Impressed with the New Youth *magazine, he wrote his first story,* A Madman's Diary, *for* New Youth *in 1918 and then never stopped writing. While he supported the aims of the communist revolution and was hailed by Mao Tse-tung (Mao Zedong), he never became a party member.*

What made Lu Hsun turn to literature? How could literature seem more important than the Navy or medicine? What is the meaning of Lu Hsun's story of an "iron house without windows"?

When I was young I, too, had many dreams. Most of them came to be forgotten, but I see nothing in this to regret. For although recalling the past may make you happy, it may sometimes also make you lonely, and there is no point in clinging in spirit to lonely bygone days. However, my trouble is that I cannot forget completely, and these stories have resulted from what I have been unable to erase from my memory.

For more than four years I used to go, almost daily, to a pawnbroker's and to a medicine shop. I cannot remember how old I was then; but the counter in the medicine shop was the same height as I, and that in the pawnbroker's twice my height. I used to hand clothes and trinkets up to the counter twice my height, take the money proffered with contempt, then go to the counter the same height as I to buy medicine for my father who had long been ill. On my return home I had other things to keep me busy, for since the physician who made out the prescriptions was very well-known, he used unusual drugs: aloe root dug up in winter,

From *A Call to Arms* by Lu Hsun. Peking: 1922.

sugar-cane that had been three years exposed to frost, twin crickets, and *ardisia* . . . all of which were difficult to procure. But my father's illness went from bad to worse until he died.

I believe those who sink from prosperity to poverty will probably come, in the process, to understand what the world is really like. I wanted to go to the K—— school in N——[1] perhaps because I was in search of a change of scene and faces. There was nothing for my mother to do but to raise eight dollars for my travelling expenses, and say I might do as I pleased. That she cried was only natural, for at that time the proper thing was to study the classics and take the official examinations. Anyone who studied "foreign subjects" was looked down upon as a fellow good for nothing, who, out of desperation, was forced to sell his soul to foreign devils. Besides, she was sorry to part with me. But in spite of that, I went to N—— and entered the K—— school; and it was there that I heard for the first time the names of such subjects as natural science, arithmetic, geography, history, drawing and physical training. They had no physiology course, but we saw woodblock editions of such works as *A New Course on the Human Body* and *Essays on Chemistry and Hygiene*. Recalling the talk and prescriptions of physicians I had known and comparing them with what I now knew, I came to the conclusion those physicians must be either unwitting or deliberate charlatans; and I began to sympathize with the invalids and families who suffered at their hands. From translated histories I also learned that the Japanese Reformation had originated, to a great extent, with the introduction of Western medical science to Japan.

These inklings took me to a provincial medical college in Japan. I dreamed a beautiful dream that on my return to China I would cure patients like my father, who had been wrongly treated, while if war broke out I would serve as an army doctor, at the same time strengthening my countrymen's faith in reformation.

I do not know what advanced methods are now used to teach microbiology, but at that time lantern slides were used to show the microbes; and if the lecture ended early, the instructor might show slides of natural scenery or news to fill up the time. This was during the Russo-Japanese War, so there were many war films, and I had to join in the clapping and cheering in the lecture hall along with the other students. It was a long time since I had seen any compatriots, but one day I saw a film showing some Chinese, one of whom was bound, while many others stood around him. They were all strong fellows but appeared completely apathetic. According to the commentary, the one with his hands bound was a spy working for the Russians, who was to

1. The Kiangnan Naval Academy in Nanking.

have his head cut off by the Japanese military as a warning to others, while the Chinese beside him had come to enjoy the spectacle.

Before the term was over I had left for Tokyo, because after this film I felt that medical science was not so important after all. The people of a weak and backward country, however strong and healthy they may be, can only serve to be made examples of, or to witness such futile spectacles; and it doesn't really matter how many of them die of illness. The most important thing, therefore, was to change their spirit, and since at that time I felt that literature was the best means to this end, I determined to promote a literary movement. There were many Chinese students in Tokyo studying law, political science, physics and chemistry, even police work and engineering, but not one studying literature or art. However, even in this uncongenial atmosphere I was fortunate enough to find some kindred spirits. We gathered the few others we needed, and after discussion our first step, of course, was to publish a magazine, the title of which denoted that this was a new birth. As we were then rather classically inclined, we called it *Xin Sheng* (*New Life*).

When the time for publication drew near, some of our contributors dropped out, and then our funds were withdrawn, until finally there were only three of us left, and we were penniless. Since we had started our magazine at an unlucky hour, there was naturally no one to whom we could complain when we failed; but later even we three were destined to part, and our discussions of a dream future had to cease. So ended this abortive *New Life*.

Only later did I feel the futility of it all; at that time I did not really understand anything. Later I felt if a man's proposals met with approval, it should encourage him; if they met with opposition, it should make him fight back; but the real tragedy for him was to lift up his voice among the living and meet with no response, neither approval nor opposition, just as if he were left helpless in a boundless desert. So I began to feel lonely.

And this feeling of loneliness grew day by day, coiling about my soul like a huge poisonous snake. Yet in spite of my unaccountable sadness, I felt no indignation; for this experience had made me reflect and see that I was definitely not the heroic type who could rally multitudes at his call.

However, my loneliness had to be dispelled, for it was causing me agony. So I used various means to dull my senses, both by conforming to the spirit of the time and turning to the past. Later I experienced or witnessed even greater loneliness and sadness, which I do not like to recall, preferring that it should perish with me. Still my attempt to deaden my senses was not unsuccessful—I had lost the enthusiasm and fervour of my youth.

In S——[2] Hostel there were three rooms where it was said a woman

2. Shaohsing.

had lived who hanged herself on the locust tree in the courtyard. Although the tree had grown so tall that its branches could no longer be reached, the rooms remained deserted. For some years I stayed here, copying ancient inscriptions. I had few visitors, there were no political problems or issues in those inscriptions, and my only desire was that my life should slip quietly away like this. On summer nights, when there were too many mosquitoes, I would sit under the locust tree, waving my fan and looking at the specks of sky through the thick leaves, while the caterpillars which came out in the evening would fall, icy-cold, on to my neck.

The only visitor to come for an occasional talk was my old friend Chin Hsin-yi. He would put his big portfolio down on the broken table, take off his long gown, and sit facing me, looking as if his heart was still beating fast after braving the dogs.

"What is the use of copying these?" he demanded inquisitively one night, after looking through the inscriptions I had copied.

"No use at all."

"Then why copy them?"

"For no particular reason."

"I think you might write something. . . ."

I understood. They were editing the magazine *New Youth*, but hitherto there seemed to have been no reaction, favourable or otherwise, and I guessed they must be feeling lonely. However I said:

"Imagine an iron house without windows, absolutely indestructible, with many people fast asleep inside who will soon die of suffocation. But you know since they will die in their sleep, they will not feel the pain of death. Now if you cry aloud to wake a few of the lighter sleepers, making those unfortunate few suffer the agony of irrevocable death, do you think you are doing them a good turn?"

"But if a few awake, you can't say there is no hope of destroying the iron house."

True, in spite of my own conviction, I could not blot out hope, for hope lies in the future. I could not use my own evidence to refute his assertion that it might exist. So I agreed to write, and the result was my first story, *A Madman's Diary*. From that time onwards, I could not stop writing. . . .

CHINA:
3. THE IMPORTANCE OF
THE PEASANT PROBLEM

MAO TSE-TUNG

Chinese intellectuals like Ch'en and Lu Hsun played an important role in revolutionizing the young, especially young, middle-class students. In many ways they helped shape the thought of a new generation. One of the members of this new generation was Mao Tse-tung (Mao Zedong) (1893–1976), who began his political activity as a student in 1915. He participated in the May 4th Movement of 1919, a student protest against the decision of the Paris Peace Conference to turn German colonies over to Japan rather than China. He participated in the organization of the Chinese Communist Party in 1921, and he directed the attention of Chinese Marxists to the importance of the peasants. While Soviet Marxism had depended on the revolutionary role of the working classes, Mao showed that a Chinese revolution depended on the peasantry. In this selection from his Report on an Investigation of the Peasant Movement in Hunan *(1927), he explains why.*

What reasons does Mao give for supporting the peasants? What signs does he show of their increasing power? Who thought the peasant revolts were "terrible?" Why did Mao disagree? Why, according to Mao, did some people think the peasants were "going too far"? Was Mao right about the peasants?

During my recent visit to Hunan I made a first-hand investigation of conditions in the five counties of Hsiangtan, Hsianghsiang, Hengshan, Liling and Changsha. In the thirty-two days from January 4 to February 5, I called together fact-finding conferences in villages and county towns, which were attended by experienced peasants and by comrades working in the peasant movement, and I listened attentively to their reports and collected a great deal of material. Many of the hows and whys of the peasant movement were the exact opposite of what the gentry in Hankow and Changsha are saying. I saw and heard of many strange things of which I had hitherto been unaware. I believe the same is true of many other places, too. All talk directed against the peasant movement must be speedily set right. All the wrong measures taken by

From *Report on an Investigation of the Peasant Movement in Hunan* by Mao Tse-tung. Peking: Foreign Language Press, 1967.

the revolutionary authorities concerning the peasant movement must be speedily changed. Only thus can the future of the revolution be benefited. For the present upsurge of the peasant movement is a colossal event. In a very short time, in China's central, southern and northern provinces, several hundred million peasants will rise like a mighty storm, like a hurricane, a force so swift and violent that no power, however great, will be able to hold it back. They will smash all the trammels that bind them and rush forward along the road to liberation. They will sweep all the imperialists, warlords, corrupt officials, local tyrants and evil gentry into their graves. Every revolutionary party and every revolutionary comrade will be put to the test, to be accepted or rejected as they decide. There are three alternatives. To march at their head and lead them? To trail behind them, gesticulating and criticizing? Or to stand in their way and oppose them? Every Chinese is free to choose, but events will force you to make the choice quickly.

GET ORGANIZED!

The development of the peasant movement in Hunan may be divided roughly into two periods with respect to the counties in the province's central and southern parts where the movement has already made much headway. The first, from January to September of last year, was one of organization. In this period, January to June was a time of underground activity, and July to September, when the revolutionary army was driving out Chao Heng-ti,* one of open activity. During this period, the membership of the peasant associations did not exceed 300,000–400,000, the masses directly under their leadership numbered little more than a million, there was as yet hardly any struggle in the rural areas, and consequently there was very little criticism of the associations in other circles. Since its members served as guides, scouts and carriers of the Northern Expeditionary Army, even some of the officers had a good word to say for the peasant associations. The second period, from last October to January of this year, was one of revolutionary action. The membership of the associations jumped to two million and the masses directly under their leadership increased to ten million. Since the peasants generally enter only one name for the whole family on joining a peasant association, a membership of two million means a mass following of about ten million. Almost half the peasants in Hunan are now organized. In counties like Hsiangtan, Hsianghsiang, Liuyang, Changsha, Liling, Ninghsiang, Pingkiang, Hsiangyin, Hengshan, Hengyang, Leiyang, Chenhsien and Anhua, nearly all the peasants have

---

* Chao Heng-ti, the ruler of Hunan, was defeated by the Northern Expeditionary Army in 1926.—Ed.

combined in the peasant associations or have come under their leadership. It was on the strength of their extensive organization that the peasants went into action and within four months brought about a great revolution in the countryside, a revolution without parallel in history.

DOWN WITH THE LOCAL TYRANTS AND EVIL GENTRY! ALL POWER TO THE PEASANT ASSOCIATIONS!

The main targets of attack by the peasants are the local tyrants, the evil gentry and the lawless landlords, but in passing they also hit out against patriarchal ideas and institutions, against the corrupt officials in the cities and against bad practices and customs in the rural areas. In force and momentum the attack is tempestuous; those who bow before it survive and those who resist perish. As a result, the privileges which the feudal landlords enjoyed for thousands of years are being shattered to pieces. Every bit of the dignity and prestige built up by the landlords is being swept into the dust. With the collapse of the power of the landlords, the peasant associations have now become the sole organs of authority and the popular slogan "All power to the peasant associations" has become a reality. Even trifles such as a quarrel between husband and wife are brought to the peasant association. Nothing can be settled unless someone from the peasant association is present. The association actually dictates all rural affairs, and, quite literally, "whatever it says, goes." Those who are outside the associations can only speak well of them and cannot say anything against them. The local tyrants, evil gentry and lawless landlords have been deprived of all right to speak, and none of them dares even mutter dissent. In the face of the peasant associations' power and pressure, the top local tyrants and evil gentry have fled to Shanghai, those of the second rank to Hankow, those of the third to Changsha and those of the fourth to the county towns, while the fifth rank and the still lesser fry surrender to the peasant associations in the villages.

"Here's ten yuan. Please let me join the peasant association," one of the smaller of the evil gentry will say.

"Ugh! Who wants your filthy money?" the peasants reply.

Many middle and small landlords and rich peasants and even some middle peasants, who were all formerly opposed to the peasant associations, are now vainly seeking admission. Visiting various places, I often came across such people who pleaded with me, "Mr. Committeeman from the provincial capital, please be my sponsor!"

In the Ching Dynasty, the household census compiled by the local authorities consisted of a regular register and "the other" register, the former for honest people and the latter for burglars, bandits and similar undesirables. In some places the peasants now use this method to scare those who formerly opposed the associations. They say, "Put their names down in the other register!"

Afraid of being entered in the other register, such people try various devices to gain admission into the peasant associations, on which their minds are so set that they do not feel safe until their names are entered. But more often than not they are turned down flat, and so they are always on tenterhooks; with the doors of the association barred to them, they are like tramps without a home or, in rural parlance, "mere trash." In short, what was looked down upon four months ago as a "gang of peasants" has now become a most honourable institution. Those who formerly prostrated themselves before the power of the gentry now bow before the power of the peasants. No matter what their identity, all admit that the world since last October is a different one.

"IT'S TERRIBLE!" OR "IT'S FINE!"

The peasants' revolt disturbed the gentry's sweet dreams. When the news from the countryside reached the cities, it caused immediate uproar among the gentry. Soon after my arrival in Changsha, I met all sorts of people and picked up a good deal of gossip. From the middle social strata upwards to the Kuomintang* right-wingers, there was not a single person who did not sum up the whole business in the phrase, "It's terrible!" Under the impact of the views of the "It's terrible!" school then flooding the city, even quite revolutionary-minded people became down-hearted as they pictured the events in the countryside in their mind's eye; and they were unable to deny the word "terrible." Even quite progressive people said, "Though terrible, it is inevitable in a revolution." In short, nobody could altogether deny the word "terrible." But, as already mentioned, the fact is that the great peasant masses have risen to fulfil their historic mission and that the forces of rural democracy have risen to overthrow the forces of rural feudalism. The patriarchal-feudal class of local tyrants, evil gentry and lawless landlords has formed the basis of autocratic government for thousands of years and is the corner-stone of imperialism, warlordism and corrupt officialdom. To overthrow these feudal forces is the real objective of the national revolution. In a few months the peasants have accomplished what Dr. Sun Yat-sen wanted, but failed, to accomplish in the forty years he devoted to the national revolution. This is a marvellous feat never before achieved, not just in forty, but in thousands of years. It's fine. It is not "terrible" at all. It is anything but "terrible." "It's terrible!" is obviously a theory for combating the rise of the peasants in the interests of the

---

* The Nationalist Party founded in 1912 and led by Sun Yat-sen.—Ed.

landlords; it is obviously a theory of the landlord class for preserving the old order of feudalism and obstructing the establishment of the new order of democracy, it is obviously a counter-revolutionary theory. No revolutionary comrade should echo this nonsense. If your revolutionary viewpoint is firmly established and if you have been to the villages and looked around, you will undoubtedly feel thrilled as never before. Countless thousands of the enslaved—the peasants—are striking down the enemies who battened on their flesh. What the peasants are doing is absolutely right; what they are doing is fine! "It's fine!" is the theory of the peasants and of all other revolutionaries. Every revolutionary comrade should know that the national revolution requires a great change in the countryside. The Revolution of 1911 did not bring about this change, hence its failure. This change is now taking place, and it is an important factor for the completion of the revolution. . . .

CHINA:
4. THE CHINESE PEOPLE HAS STOOD UP

MAO TSE-TUNG

The Chinese revolution was both communist and nationalist. It sought the liberation not only of the peasantry from the landlords but also of the Chinese people from foreign oppression. In this speech, given on the eve of the founding of the Chinese People's Republic on September 21, 1949, Mao expressed the nationalist side of the revolution.

How is the emphasis of this speech different from the previous documents? Are the goals of communism and nationalism in opposition or merely different in emphasis?

. . . Our conference is one of great nationwide popular unity.

Such great nationwide popular unity has been achieved because we have vanquished the Kuomintang reactionary government, which is aided by American imperialism. In the course of little more than three years, the heroic Chinese People's Liberation Army, an army such as the

Reprinted in Mao Tse-tung, *Selected Works*, IV. San Francisco: China Books, 1965.

world has seldom seen, crushed the offensive of the several million troops of the American-supported Kuomintang reactionary government, thereby enabling us to swing over to the counter-offensive and the offensive. . . .

We have a common feeling that our work will be recorded in the history of mankind, and that it will clearly demonstrate that the Chinese, who comprise one quarter of humanity, have begun to stand up. The Chinese have always been a great, courageous, and industrious people. It was only in modern times that they have fallen behind, and this was due solely to the oppression and exploitation of foreign imperialism and the domestic reactionary government.

For more than a century, our predecessors never paused in their indomitable struggles against the foreign and domestic oppressors. These struggles include the Revolution of 1911, led by Sun Yat-sen, the great pioneer of China's revolution. Our predecessors instructed us to carry their work to completion. We are doing this now. We have united ourselves and defeated both our foreign and domestic oppressors by means of the people's liberation war and the people's great revolution, and we proclaim the establishment of the People's Republic of China.

Henceforth, our nation will enter the large family of peace-loving and freedom-loving nations of the world. It will work bravely and industriously to create its own civilization and happiness, and will, at the same time, promote world peace and freedom. Our nation will never again be an insulted nation. We have stood up. Our revolution has gained the sympathy and acclamation of the broad masses throughout the world. We have friends the world over.

Our revolutionary work is not yet concluded. . . . The imperialists and the domestic reactionaries will certainly not take their defeat lying down. . . . Daily, hourly, they will try to restore their rule in China. . . . We must not relax our vigilance. . . .

The people's democratic dictatorship and unity with international friends will enable us to obtain rapid success in our construction work. . . . Our population of 475 million and our national territory of 9,597 million square kilometres are factors in our favour. It is true that there are difficulties ahead of us, a great many of them. But we firmly believe that all the difficulties will be surmounted by the heroic struggle of all the people of our country. The Chinese people has had ample experience in overcoming difficulties. If we and our predecessors could come through the long period of extreme difficulties and defeat the powerful domestic and foreign reactionaries, why can we not build up a prosperous and flourishing country after our victory? . . .

An upsurge in cultural construction will inevitably follow in the wake of the upsurge of economic construction. The era in which the Chinese were regarded as uncivilized is now over. We will emerge in the world as a nation with a high culture.

Our national defence will be consolidated and no imperialist will be allowed to invade our territory again. . . .

Let the domestic and foreign reactionaries tremble before us. Let them say that we are no good at this and no good at that. Through the Chinese people's indomitable endeavours, we will steadily reach our goal.

THE VIETNAMESE DECLARATION OF INDEPENDENCE (SEPTEMBER 2, 1945)

HO CHI MINH

One of the many results of World War II was the stirring of independence movements in the European colonies. Many of these colonies had been conquered by Japan during the war and entertained hopes of independence after the defeat of Japan. Vietnam was one example. In any case, the Vietminh, the communist-Vietnamese nationalist movement, had fought the Japanese throughout the war. They did not expect the victorious Allies to turn the colony back to France. No one then would have imagined that independence would have to wait a nine-year war with the French followed by twenty years of war with the United States.

What seems to be Ho Chi Minh's attitude toward the United States and France in 1945? Notice the striking similarity of the form of the declaration to the American Declaration of Independence. Why do you suppose he did that?

"All men are created equal. They are endowed by their Creator with certain inalienable rights; among these are Life, Liberty, and the pursuit of Happiness."

This immortal statement was made in the Declaration of Independence of the United States of America in 1776. In a broader sense, this means: All the peoples on the earth are equal from birth, all the peoples have a right to live, to be happy and free.

From *Selected Works*, III, by Ho Chi Minh. Hanoi: Foreign Languages Publishing House, 1960–1962.

The Declaration of the French Revolution made in 1791 on the Rights of Man and the Citizen also states: "All men are born free and with equal rights, and must always remain free and have equal rights."

Those are undeniable truths.

Nevertheless, for more than eighty years, the French imperialists, abusing the standard of Liberty, Equality, and Fraternity, have violated our Fatherland and oppressed our fellow-citizens. They have acted contrary to the ideals of humanity and justice.

In the field of politics, they have deprived our people of every democratic liberty.

They have enforced inhuman laws; they have set up three distinct political regimes in the North, the Center and the South of Vietnam in order to wreck our national unity and prevent our people from being united.

They have built more prisons than schools. They have mercilessly slain our patriots; they have drowned our uprisings in rivers of blood.

They have fettered public opinion; they have practised obscurantism against our people.

To weaken our race they have forced us to use opium and alcohol.

In the field of economics, they have fleeced us to the backbone, impoverished our people, and devastated our land.

They have robbed us of our rice fields, our mines, our forests, and our raw materials. They have monopolized the issuing of bank-notes and the export trade.

They have invented numerous unjustifiable taxes and reduced our people, especially our peasantry, to a state of extreme poverty.

They have hampered the prospering of our national bourgeoisie; they have mercilessly exploited our workers.

In the autumn of 1940, when the Japanese Fascists violated Indochina's territory to establish new bases in their fight against the Allies, the French imperialists went down on their bended knees and handed over our country to them.

Thus, from that date, our people were subjected to the double yoke of the French and the Japanese. Their sufferings and miseries increased. The result was that from the end of last year to the beginning of this year, from Quang Tri province to the North of Vietnam, more than two million of our fellow-citizens died from starvation. On March 9, the French troops were disarmed by the Japanese. The French colonialists either fled or surrendered showing that not only were they incapable of "protecting" us, but that, in the span of five years, they had twice sold our country to the Japanese.

On several occasions before March 9, the Vietminh League urged the French to ally themselves with it against the Japanese. Instead of agreeing to this proposal, the French colonialists so intensified their terrorist activities against the Vietminh members that before fleeing they massacred a great number of our political prisoners detained at Yen Bay and Caobang.

Notwithstanding all this, our fellow-citizens have always manifested toward the French a tolerant and humane attitude. Even after the Japanese putsch of March 1945, the Vietminh League helped many Frenchmen to cross the frontier, rescued some of them from Japanese jails, and protected French lives and property.

From the autumn of 1940, our country had in fact ceased to be a French colony and had become a Japanese possession.

After the Japanese had surrendered to the Allies, our whole people rose to regain our national sovereignty and to found the Democratic Republic of Vietnam.

The truth is that we have wrested our independence from the Japanese and not from the French.

The French have fled, the Japanese have capitulated, Emperor Bao Dai has abdicated. Our people have broken the chains which for nearly a century have fettered them and have won independence for the Fatherland. Our people at the same time have overthrown the monarchic regime that has reigned supreme for dozens of centuries. In its place has been established the present Democratic Republic.

For these reasons, we, members of the Provisional Government, representing the whole Vietnamese people, declare that from now on we break off all relations of a colonial character with France; we repeal all the international obligation that France has so far subscribed to on behalf of Vietnam and we abolish all the special rights the French have unlawfully acquired in our Fatherland.

The whole Vietnamese people, animated by a common purpose, are determined to fight to the bitter end against any attempt by the French colonialists to reconquer their country.

We are convinced that the Allied nations which at Tehran and San Francisco have acknowledged the principles of self-determination and equality of nations, will not refuse to acknowledge the independence of Vietnam.

A people who have courageously opposed French domination for more than eight years, a people who have fought side by side with the Allies against the Fascists during these last years, such a people must be free and independent.

For these reasons, we, members of the Provisional Government of the Democratic Republic of Vietnam, solemnly declare to the world that Vietnam has the right to be a free and independent country—and in fact is so already. The entire Vietnamese people are determined to mobilize all their physical and mental strength, to sacrifice their lives and property in order to safeguard their independence and liberty.

15. Dependence and Independence in Africa and The Middle East

CHILDHOOD IN THE NIGERIAN VILLAGE OF AKÉ

WOLE SOYINKA

Western influence was not only political. It was also cultural and technological. In fact, the spread of Western technology paved the way for other aspects of "westernization." In an African village, the appearance of Western electricity, news, and politics was all of a piece. Here are the memories of one African childhood, that of the Nigerian playwright Wole Soyinka in British West Africa. Soyinka won the Nobel Prize for literature in 1986.

As you read the story, notice how many things have been newly introduced into young Soyinka's world. How are these Western ways and inventions understood, absorbed, and integrated? Do you see any signs of earlier westernization, perhaps even before Soyinka was born? In what ways was African society strengthened by colonialism? In what ways was it weakened? In what ways did African society remain independent of it?

Workmen came into the house. They knocked lines of thin nails with narrow clasps into walls. The lines turned with corners and doorways and joined up with outside wires which were strung across poles. The presence of these workmen reminded me of another invasion. At the end of those earlier activities we no longer needed the oil-lamps, kerosene lanterns and candles, at least not within the house. We pressed down a switch and the room was flooded with light. Essay's [the author's father] instructions were strict—only he, or Wild Christian [the author's mother] could give the order for the pressing of those switches. I recalled that it took a while to connect the phenomenon of the glowing bulb with the switch, so thoroughly did Essay keep up the deception. He pretended it was magic, he easily directed our gaze at the glass bulb while he muttered his magic spell. Then he solemnly intoned:

"Let there be light."

Afterwards he blew in the direction of the bulb and the light went out.

But finally, we caught him out. It was not too difficult to notice that he always stood at the same spot, that that spot was conveniently near a small white-and-black object which had sprouted on the wall after the workmen had gone. Still, the stricture continued. The magic light was expensive and must be wisely used.

Now the workmen were threading the walls again, we wondered what the new magic would produce. This time there was no bulb, no extra switches on the wall. Instead, a large wooden box was brought into the house and installed at the very top of the tallboy, displacing the old gramophone which now had to be content with one of the lower shelves on the same furniture. The face of the box appeared to be made of thick plaited silk.

But the functions continued to be the same. True, there was no need to put on a black disc, no need to crank a handle or change a needle, it only required that the knob be turned for sounds to come on. Unlike the gramophone however, the box could not be made to speak or sing at any time of the day. It began its monologue early in the morning, first playing "God Save the King." The box went silent some time in the afternoon, resumed late afternoon, then, around ten or eleven in the evening, sang "God Save the King" once more and went to sleep.

Because the box spoke incessantly and appeared to have no interest in a response, it soon earned the name *As' oromagb' esi.*[1] An additional line was added to a jingle which had been formed at the time of the arrival of electricity. Belatedly, that jingle had also done honour to Lagos where the sacred monopoly of the umbrella by royalty had first been broken;

Elektiriki ina oba
Umbrella el'eko
As' oromagb' esi, iro oyinbo.[2]

At certain set hours, the box delivered THE NEWS. The News soon became an object of worship to Essay and a number of his friends. When the hour approached, something happened to this club. It did not matter what they were doing, they rushed to our house to hear the Oracle. It was enough to watch Essay's face to know that the skin would be peeled off the back of any child who spoke when he was listening to

1. One who speaks without expecting a reply.
2. Electricity, government light Umbrella, for the Lagos elite Rediffusion, white man's lies.

The News. When his friends were present, the parlour with its normal gloom resembled a shrine, rapt faces listened intently, hardly breathing. When The Voice fell silent all faces turned instinctively to the priest himself. Essay reflected for a moment, made a brief or long comment and a babble of excited voices followed.

The gramophone fell into disuse. The voice of Denge, Ayinde Bakare, Ambrose Campbell; a voice which was so deep that I believed it could only have been produced by a special trick of His Master's Voice, but which father assured me belonged to a black man called Paul Robeson*—they all were relegated to the cocoon of dust which gathered in the gramophone section. Christmas carols, the songs of Marian Anderson**; oddities, such as a record in which a man did nothing but laugh throughout, and the one concession to a massed choir of European voices—the Hallelujah Chorus—all were permanently interned in the same cupboard. Now voices sang, unasked, from the new box. Once that old friend the Hallelujah Chorus burst through the webbed face of the box and we had to concede that it sounded richer and fuller than the old gramophone had ever succeeded in rendering it. Most curious of all the fare provided by the radio however were the wranglings of a family group which were relayed every morning, to the amusement of a crowd, whole laughter shook the box. We tried to imagine where this took place. Did this family go into the streets to carry on their interminable bickering or did the idle crowd simply hang around their home, peeping through the windows and cheering them on? We tried to imagine any of the Aké families we knew exposing themselves this way—the idea was unthinkable. It was some time, and only by listening intently before I began to wonder if this daily affair was that dissimilar from the short plays which we sometimes acted in school on prize-giving day. And I began also to respond to the outlandish idiom of their humour.

Hitler monopolized the box. He had his own special programme and somehow, far off as this war of his whim appeared to be, we were drawn more and more into the expanding arena of menace. Hitler came nearer home every day. Before long the greeting Win-The-War replaced some of the boisterous exchanges which took place between Essay and his friends. The local barbers invented a new style which joined the repertory of Bentigo, Girls-Follow-Me, Oju-Aba, Missionary Cut and others. The women also added Wi-de-woh to their hair-plaits, and those of them who presided over the local foodstalls used it as a standard response to complaints of a shortage in the quantity they served. Essay and his correspondents vied with one another to see how many times the same envelope could be used between them. Windows were blacked

---

*The American actor and bass singer.—Ed.
**The American contralto, the first black person to be named permanent member of the Metropolitan Opera Company.—Ed.

over, leaving just tiny spots to peep through, perhaps in order to obtain an early warning when Hitler came marching up the path. Household heads were dragged to court and fined for showing a naked light to the night. To reinforce the charged atmosphere of expectations, the first aeroplane flew over Abeokuta; it had a heavy drone which spoke of Armageddon and sent Christians fleeing into churches to pray and stay the wrath of God. Others simply locked their doors and windows and waited for the end of the world. Only those who had heard about these things, and flocks of children watched in fascination, ran about the fields and the streets, following the flying miracle as far as they could, shouting greetings, waving to it long after it had gone and returning home to await its next advent.

INDEPENDENCE IN TROPICAL AFRICA

L. S. STAVRIANOS

The period since most African nations achieved independence has not been marked by great successes, as this selection demonstrates. What, according to this historian, are the causes for such a poor showing? Did political independence include economic independence? What were some of the limitations placed on the autonomy of African states? The author compares the independence of the Ivory Coast and Kenya with that of Zaire. What does this comparison suggest about Africa's future? What should be done?

Just as the first postwar decade witnessed the liberation of Asia, so the second witnessed the liberation of Africa. Nationalist movements had gotten under way during the interwar years, but in retrospect they were "archaic and prehistoric." They consisted of "followers grouped around an influential protector." These "followers" comprised a small professional elite with no ties to the great rural mass. Their influence was limited to a few towns such as Dakar, Accra, Lagos and Khartoum-Omdurman. They were interested primarily in improving their position

Excerpts from pp. 665–672, 674–677, and 679 (under the title "Independence in Tropical Africa") from *Global Rift* by L. S. Stavrianos. Copyright © 1981 by L. S. Stavrianos. By permission of William Morrow & Company.

within the colonial framework; hence their demand for Africanization of the bureaucracy, the judiciary and the elected local legislatures. It seemed quite natural and justified that a senior British colonial official should state at a 1939 conference that "at any rate in Africa we can be sure that we have unlimited time in which to work."

Such comfortable conviction was shattered by the Second World War. Many Africans served overseas, no less than 120,000 in Burma alone. During their campaigning in Burma, and while stationed in their bases in India and Ceylon, the Africans noted that the British received higher pay and more privileges, even when they were of the same rank. The Africans also were affected by contact with Asian activists who were more advanced in their political theories and organization. The Indian Congress Party had a direct influence on Kwame Nkrumah and his Convention People's Party (CPP), which was based on the Gandhian principle of absolute nonviolence. CPP members out of prison sported P.G. (Prison Graduate) caps, which were the Gandhi caps with the letters P.G. affixed. Nkrumah also borrowed from Gandhi the concept of a mass-based party for winning political concessions, and became known as the "Gandhi of Ghana." The influence of Asia increased tremendously with the winning of independence by several Asian colonies. Africans naturally asked why they too should not be rid of the bonds of colonialism.

Most important was the great wartime economic expansion because of the urgent demand for African raw materials. British West African producers more than doubled the value of their exports between 1938 and 1946. Likewise the value of Congo exports increased fourteen times between 1939 and 1953, while government revenues rose four times. The general economic upsurge led to a boom in the building of schools, construction of roads and the improvement of housing, sanitation and medical services. These innovations, together with the impact of the returning veterans, combined to shake up and awaken tropical Africa. Native cash farmers were making more money than ever before. African workmen were moving up the ladder to semiskilled and even into a few skilled industrial jobs. More Africans were getting positions as government clerks, court interpreters, head messengers and agricultural demonstrators. City populations soared to an unprecedented degree, so that between 1931 and 1960 these typical African cities increased as follows (in thousands): Dakar, 54 to 383; Abidjan, 10.2 to 180; Accra, 60.7 to 325.9; Leopoldville, 30.2 to 389.5; and Nairobi, 29.8 to 250.8.

The resulting social disruption engendered a new breed of political leaders, impatient and aggressive, like Kwame Nkrumah, Nnamdi Azikiwe, Jomo Kenyatta, Sekou Touré, Leopold Senghor and Félix Houphouet-Boigny. Unlike the Casley-Hayfords and Blaise Diagnes of the interwar years, the new leaders organized mass parties involving the lower middle class and the peasants. These parties were better organized and more disciplined than the earlier associations, and their members made good use of the improved roads to penetrate into remote villages in private cars, party vans and even bicycles. The new nationalist leaders also operated internationally, meeting at the Fifth Pan-African Congress in London in 1945 to challenge the colonial powers to honor the Atlantic Charter applied only to victims of Axis aggression, while the French declared at Brazzaville in 1944 that the introduction, "even in a far-off future, of self-government in the colonies is out of the question."

This intransigence appeared natural at the time, but it was soon reversed in the face of the nationalist triumphs in Indochina and Algeria. The significance of these stunning events of the colonial world as a whole was noted by Frantz Fanon:

> A colonized people is not alone. In spite of all that colonialism can do, its frontiers remain open to new ideas and echoes from the world outside. . . . The great victory of the Vietnamese people at Dien Bien Phu is no longer strictly speaking, a Vietnamese victory. Since July, 1954, the question which the colonial peoples have asked themselves has been, "What must be done to bring about another Dien Bien Phu? How can we manage it?" Not a single colonized individual could ever again doubt how best to use the forces at their disposal, how to organize them, and when to bring them into action. This encompassing violence does not work upon the colonized people only; it modifies the attitude of the colonialists who become aware of manifold Dien Bien Phus. This is why a veritable panic takes hold of the colonialist governments in turn. Their purpose is to capture the vanguard, to turn the movement of liberation toward the right, and to disarm the people: quick, quick, let's decolonize. Decolonize the Congo before it turns into another Algeria. Vote the constitutional framework for all Africa, create the French Communauté, renovate that same Communauté, but for God's sake, let's decolonize quick. . . .

Decolonization did take place quickly. The British took the lead in the Gold Coast, where Nkrumah's Convention People's Party won an overwhelming majority in the 1951 election. Nkrumah was in prison on Election Day, but the British governor, sensing the trends of events, released him and gave him and his colleagues top administrative posts. After this apprenticeship in self-government, the Gold Coast became in 1957 the independent state of Ghana. With the colonial dam broken at one point, it was impossible to hold back the flood. Nigeria, the most populous country in Africa with its 25 million people, became independent in 1960, and was followed by the other British West African colonies, Sierra Leone and Gambia, in 1961 and 1963, respectively.

The Paris governments were as conciliatory south of the Sahara as they were stubborn to the north. In 1956 France enacted a "framework law" that granted representative institutions to its twelve West African territories and to the island of Madagascar. Two years later the new De

Gaulle regime, brought into power by the crisis in Algeria, decided to avoid a similar ordeal in tropical Africa. The sub-Saharan colonies were given the option of voting either for full independence or for autonomy as separate republics in the French "Community" that was to replace the empire. At first this strategy appeared to be successful; in the ensuing referendum, all the territories except Guinea, which was under the influence of the trade union leader, Sekou Touré, voted for autonomy. The arrangement, however, proved transitory. In 1959, Senegal and the French Sudan asked for full independence within the French Community as the Federation of Mali. When this was granted, four other territories—the Ivory Coast, Niger, Dahomey and Upper Volta—went a step farther and secured independence outside the French Community. By the end of 1960, all the former colonies of both French West Africa and French Equatorial Africa had won their independence, and all but one had become members of the United Nations.

Because of the paternalism of Brussels and the intervention of the superpowers, the Belgian Congo underwent prolonged fighting before winning independence, as will be noted below. Likewise in East Africa, the presence of a white settler community necessitated the Mau Mau rebellion to force the British Colonial Office to accept the independent state of Kenya in 1963. The neighboring states of Uganda and Tanganyika (later, with Zanzibar, Tanzania) made the transition to statehood without turmoil. The net result was the emergence of thirty-two independent African countries during the decade after Ghana's debut in 1957. The few colonies that remained in the continent stood out painfully as obsolete hangovers from the past.

The onrush of decolonization did not signify that independent status was granted gratuitously or indiscriminately. At least three factors determined the time and place for conferring independent statehood. One was the economic and military power of the mother country. Britain and France had sufficient strength and confidence to be willing to concede independence with reasonable expectation that they would be able to defend their interests in their ex-colonies against encroachment by other Great Powers. In most cases their calculation proved correct, and they continued to dominate the economies of the new African states and to provide many of the technicians, administrators and educators. By contrast the Portuguese, lacking the economic and military resources of the British and French, refused to surrender political control over their colonies, as they justifiably feared European, American and Japanese interlopers. Thus it was Portugal's weakness that forced her to resist decolonization and to continue fighting against African liberation movements long after Britain and France had bowed out. This paradox was explicitly recognized by the Portuguese Overseas Minister, Adriano Moreira: "We know that only political power is a defense against the economic and financial invasion of our territories by

. . . former colonial powers." Not only did Portuguese officials recognize this power consideration but so did their colonial subjects. In Guinea-Bissau, Amilcar Cabral, the leading African theorist and practitioner of revolution, observed in 1965:

> Portuguese colonialism in our time is characterized fundamentally by a very simple fact: Portuguese colonialism, or if you prefer, the Portuguese economic infrastructure, cannot afford the luxury of neocolonialism. In view of this, we can understand the whole attitude, the whole stubbornness of Portuguese colonialism toward our people. If Portugal had an advanced economic development, if Portugal could be classed as a developed country, we certainly would not be at war with Portugal.

The second factor determining the time and place of decolonization was the role of the superpowers—the United States and the Soviet Union. Neither one had appreciable influence in Africa before World War II, but the weakening of the colonial powers during the war gave Russia and America an opportunity that both promptly exploited. Russia was the weaker of the two, because of its inferior economic and military resources and because it lacked the contacts within Africa and with the colonial powers that the United States enjoyed. But the Soviet Union was able partly to make up for this weakness by supporting African governments and liberation movements more freely than the United States, which had to take into account the interests of its Western allies and of its corporations. Thus the Soviet Union at various times and with varying results gave overt or covert aid and/or arms to Nasser's Egypt, Nkrumah's Ghana, Touré's Guinea, Barre's Somalia, Selassie's Ethiopia and the revolutionary movements in the Portuguese colonies. America's postwar role in Africa vacillated between determination to buttress the status quo against Soviet intrusion, and desire to break into the lucrative economic preserves of Britain, France, Belgium and Portugal. The mineral-rich Belgian Congo affords the classic example of superpower intervention in African affairs—first in 1959–61 and then again in 1978. A more recent example is that of the Central African Empire, where Jean Bokassa was installed in office in 1965 by the French, and then unceremoniously ousted by them in 1979 when his unpredictable barbarities became embarrassing.

The third and probably most important factor determining the course of decolonization was the political complexion of the organizations and leaders agitating for independence. In postwar Africa as throughout the Third World in all centuries, independent status was conceded selectively, depending on the prospective degree of social change. If the expectation was for merely political change, independence was usually conceded rather than resorting to extreme repressive measures. But if there was any likelihood of social restructing that threatened metropolitan and local vested interests, then all possible measures were used to keep the social revolutionaries out of power. In such cases the usual outcome was the gradual co-option of the revolutionary leaders who, lured by the prospect of wealth and office, changed their political coloration and became the supporters (and beneficiaries) of the status quo.

A typical example of such co-option is the case of Félix Houphouet-Boigny of the Ivory Coast. During and immediately after World War II he militantly opposed French rule and the local French planters. In 1946 he publicly praised "the precious help given to the Overseas Territories by the Communists in their struggle against the common enemy, imperialist and colonialist reaction. . . ." By 1950 Houphouet-Boigny had completely reversed his position. He severed his ties with the Communists, cooperated closely with Paris and opposed independence when it became an option in 1958. After the course of events brought independence to the Ivory Coast along with the other French sub-Saharan colonies, Houphouet-Boigny became President, and to the present day preserves as close economic and cultural ties with France as in colonial times.

Very different was the experience of Kwame Nkrumah of Gold Coast Colony. After being released from prison in 1951, he declared flatly: "I am a friend of Britain. . . . I want for the Gold Coast Dominion status within the British Commonwealth. I am no Communist and never have been. . . ." This statement encouraged the British to grant independence to the Gold Coast and to accept Nkrumah as its President. But when economic setbacks caused Nkrumah to switch to socialist economic policies, Western attitudes and policies toward him changed completely. According to an ex-CIA agent, John Stockwell, Washington was involved in the 1966 army coup that deposed Nkrumah: "The Accra (CIA) station was encouraged by headquarters to maintain contacts with dissidents of the Ghanian army. . . . So close was the station's involvement that it was able to coordinate the recovery of some classified Soviet military equipment . . . as the coup took place . . . inside CIA headquarters the Accra station was given full, if unofficial credit for the eventual coup."

The above factors behind Africa's decolonization were responsible for three types of postliberation regimes: nationalist, social revolutionary and white settler. Considering the nationalist regimes, they varied considerably in their institutions and policies. For the sake of convenience they may be divided into two types: the conservative neocolonial and the reformist state capitalist.

A basic feature of the neocolonial society was its emphasis on production for foreign markets as the prerequisite for getting started on the road to economic growth. This led to the encouragement of cash crops at the expense of traditional food production. Cash crops were stimulated by the allotment of the best arable lands, by supporting road and railway systems, by government-sponsored irrigation schemes and by a wide range of scientific inputs, including fertilizers, pesticides and high-yield seeds. In addition to emphasizing cash-crop production, the conservative regimes strove to attract foreign capital by creating a hospitable investment climate through such measures as tax holidays, protective tariffs and free repatriation of profits.

This economic strategy underlay the first African national economic plans, usually prepared by Western experts. As the decade of the sixties unfolded, it became clear that the multiplier effects expected from cash-crop exports and from foreign investments were not materializing. Prices for raw-material exports declined, while the cost of manufactured imports rose. Food production for domestic markets lagged, causing increasing food costs for urban dwellers, as well as large-scale food imports, which upset the trade balance. Displaced peasants streamed into cities, where jobs were lacking because the foreign-financed industrialization was capital-intensive and geared to producing only luxury or semiluxury items for a limited middle-class market. The tragedy of uprooted African peasants crowded into urban shanty towns was heightened by the fact that peasant farmers, given a modicum of opportunity, can better the large plantations not only in terms of output per unit of land, but more important, in terms of cost per unit produced. In Kenya, for example, peasant families who took over the farms of former European settlers made impressive gains, in some cases nearly doubling the level of output.

Under these circumstances the typical African conservative regime ended up with a dual economy, comprising an encapsulated export-producing enclave surrounded by a traditional, underdeveloped agrarian sector. The enclave is sustained by a cheap labor supply from the underdeveloped sector and by an array of government-provided incentives. The multinational corporations, which control imports and exports as well as plantations and mines, realize high returns on their investments because of their domination of world markets through their global marketing structures. The result is the siphoning of surplus value out of African countries to such a degree that U.S. corporations between 1965 and 1975 extracted a net total of $2,998 billion out of Africa, or 25 percent more than they invested there.

The classic example of a neocolonial state is the Congo, now known as Zaïre. When Belgium granted the colony independence in June 1960, Patrice Lumumba emerged as the only Congolese leader with any pretense of more than a regional following. His unwillingness to accept manipulation made him unacceptable to Brussels and, more important, to Washington. Just as the nationalistic Mossadeq was eliminated in Iran on suspicion of being a Soviet stooge, so the nationalistic Lumumba was condemned in telegraphic instructions from CIA Director Allen Dulles (Aug. 26, 1960): "IN HIGH QUARTERS HERE IT IS THE CLEARCUT

CONCLUSION THAT IF LUMUMBA CONTINUES TO HOLD HIGH OFFICE, THE INEVITABLE RESULT WILL AT LEAST BE CHAOS AND AT WORSE PAVE THE WAY TO COMMUNIST TAKEOVER OF THE CONGO. . . . HIS REMOVAL WILL BE AN URGENT AND PRIME OBJECTIVE. . . . THIS SHOULD BE A HIGH PRIORITY OF OUR COVERT ACTION. . . ."

Without going into the long and sordid record (set forth in the 1975 U.S. Senate report on *Alleged Assassination Plots Involving Foreign Leaders*), Dulles' orders were in fact carried out. Lumumba was murdered on January 21, 1961, and according to Stockwell, a CIA agent drove about in Lubumbashi (then Elizabethville) "with Lumumba's body in the trunk of his car, trying to decide what to do with it." Lumumba was then succeeded by his CIA-supported chief of staff, Joseph Mobutu.

American investments in Zaïre thereupon increased sharply, totalling by 1977 $1 billion in mining, construction and oil, as well as $500 million in U.S. bank loans. According to information by a State Department official in 1976, "the United States viewed the position of Zaïre within Africa as roughly similar to that of Brazil in South America"—that is, mineral-rich, strategically located and pro-Western. The official added: "There was a thrust within the State Department to bolster Zaïre in the hope it could extend its hegemony throughout the continent."

The difficulty with this American strategy was that, as usual, it was based solely on geopolitical considerations and ignored the condition and aspirations of the people actually involved. In this case, the Mobutu regime was notoriously inefficient and corrupt, with a quarter to a third of the national GNP being siphoned off by the ruling clique. The resulting mass suffering and disaffection became evident when on May 13, 1978, a force of twenty-five hundred to thirty-five hundred guerrillas of the National Front for the Liberation of the Congo attacked the copper mining town of Kolwezi. With the aid of urban and rural sympathizers they captured the city and its mines in two days. Since this was the post-Vietnam era, the Carter administration limited overt support to Mobutu to $17.5 million of "nonlethal" military aid. But covertly the administration encouraged and financed other countries— Western and Third World—to intervene with armed force. U.S. Air Force planes transported Belgian soldiers from Brussels to Zaïre, while French planes airlifted French Legionnaires and Moroccan troops. French and Belgian military advisers directed all intelligence and logistical operations, while West Germany and China provided food and medicines.

Mobutu continues to revel in his eleven palaces and to cruise on Zaïre River accompanied by four of France's master chefs; his subjects continue to subsist on manioc, with one third suffering from deficiencies in both protein and caloric intake; and the vital cobalt and copper, not to mention debt-repayment installments, continue to flow to Western countries. Economist Albert Ndele, governor of the Central Bank of

Zaïre from 1961 to 1970, warns the West of the fragility of their creation: "There is unbelievable poverty and misery in my country. A recent report says there is 70 percent infant mortality in Kinshasa. Even the medicines given by charity are sold to the people—by Mobutu's family. The road system is a shambles. The sanitary situation is as bad. The same is true of education. If you think that Mobutu is the man for the West, you had better think again." Also noteworthy is the observation of a European-educated Zaïrian doctor: "The West likes to say this conduct is very African, very compatible with our tradition of chieftains. That, of course, is nonsense. Mobutu is not in the least a product of our African heritage. He is nothing more than a product of Western capitalism."

President Julius Nyerere, in a lecture to the foreign envoys in his capital, also has expressed his views on current Western activities in Zaïre:

> We must reject the principle that external powers have the right to maintain in power African governments that are universally recognized to be corrupt, or incompetent, or a bunch of murderers, when their peoples try to make a change. Africa cannot have its present governments frozen into position for all time by neocolonialism, or because there are cold-war or ideological conflicts between the big powers. The peoples of an individual African country have as much right to change their corrupt government in the last half of the 20th century as, in the past, the British, French and Russian peoples had to overthrow their own rotten regimes. Are African peoples to be denied that same right?

Africa affords examples of more successful neocolonial states than Zaïre, outstanding being Kenya and the Ivory Coast. In the latter country, Houphouet-Boigny has staunchly espoused the economic institutions and policies inherited from colonial times. "I have nothing to do with this false policy of nationalization. Our policy is to attract foreign capital, not nationalize business. We want our foreign friends to make a profit, and if they do, pay us a reasonable part." This economic strategy has yielded an average annual per capita income of $300, an 8 percent annual growth of GNP and a favorable trade balance from the export of coffee, cocoa, timber, bananas, pineapples and other agricultural products.

But this represents economic growth rather than balanced national economic development. It is economic growth that has led to French control of 40 percent of total investment capital in the country, with another 25 percent shared by Britain, the United States and Japan. The remaining 35 percent is owned by 40,000 French citizens resident in the country, several hundred Lebanese and 3 percent of the Ivorians. Thus the impressive economic statistics have involved little "trickling down" of the benefits of growth. The infant mortality rate is 138 per 1,000 births (as against 28 in Cuba), life expectancy is 35 years and the illiteracy rate is 60 percent. Natural resources are being abused as recklessly as the human. According to forestry experts, Ivory Coast forest stock "has sustained a level of destruction that cannot last for more than three or four more years." The Ivory Coast often is referred to as "the only African country that works." But it should be asked: For what purpose does it work, and for whose benefit?

The above pattern prevails also in Kenya, where President Jomo Kenyatta, like Houphouet-Boigny, adopted strongly pro-Western business-oriented policies. The first billboard outside the Nairobi airport reads: "General Motors Kenya Limited—With Full Confidence in the Economic Future of Kenya." The confidence is warranted, for Kenya offers a well-developed infrastructure network, a stable investment climate and the right of foreign corporations to remit all their profits. Nairobi, like Abidjan of the Ivory Coast, is a modern capital city of banks, business buildings, luxury hotels, well-stocked restaurants and fashionable night-clubs. But only a few blocks away from these symbols of affluence begin the sprawling ghettos, with hungry people living in shacks without running water. Crime, especially robbery, is booming in Nairobi, as is prostitution. Nor are conditions better in the countryside, where over 80 percent of the country's 13 million people live. A 1977 United Nations survey, undertaken with the cooperation of the Kenyan government, disclosed that 72 percent of household heads never attended school, one third of the children suffer from malnutrition, less than 2 percent of the households have electricity and half the women trudge at least three times each day between their villages and the springs, with large, heavy urns on their backs. An American who worked in Kenya in the 1960s and 1970s has analyzed why both the animal and human populations of that country are starving. His account is noteworthy, as it graphically describes the food-crop-to-cash-crop trend that is devastating Third World countries in Asia and Latin America as well as in Africa:

Pity the poor beasts: The last of the world's great herds are dying. East Africa's primitive savannah country is shrinking as the land comes under the farmers' ploughs. Thus are the herds vanishing, pushed from their natural grounds. Within the forseeable future, the glory of the primeval migrations across Africa's plains will be gone forever. . . .

A ride through Kenya's rich farm country quickly reveals that much of Africa's best agricultural land is not used to feed people. Nor is it used for the starving wildlife. Instead, this wonderful soil supports export crops. Thousands of acres grow coffee trees—for coffee to be consumed in Germany, England and America. Drive north of Nairobi and you find an endless vista of pineapples—fruit to be loaded onto jetliners and shipped fresh to Europe. Head westward into the Rift Valley and you find ranches and farms used for cattle raising and for growing wheat. While these last two efforts produce food which is consumed within Kenya, the consumers are not farmers vying with the wildebeest for a precious resource but the people who live in the burgeoning cities. The irony is that these new city dwellers only a few years back were farmers capable of feeding themselves. . . .

The real problem in Kenya is that land is used for cash crops instead of for foodstuffs. Kenya has enough productive farmland to feed all of its people without destroying the habitat of the wild animals. There is no necessity for choosing between the life of a human and that of a gazelle. If a more balanced economic and agricultural system can be created, both humans and beasts will survive on the African plains.

On the other hand, Kenya boasts one of the largest black middle classes in Africa. Although the national economy is dominated by Europeans, and to a lesser extent by Arabs and Indians, nevertheless the black elite is prosperous. It profits from its share of the economy, and especially from its control of the state apparatus, which is a lucrative source of sub-rosa income. Bribes are essential to acquire anything, whether it be a driver's license, a construction contract or a peddler's permit. Some have protested against this well-oiled system, but with little success. Josia Kariuki, a popular member of parliament, attacked the blatant social inequity, dismissing the existing Kenya as a country of ten millionaires and ten million beggars. In March 1975 he was shot in the streets of Nairobi. A parliamentary investigation implicated police officials and top Kenyatta aides.

Despite these anomalies, the fact remains that the growing black middle class in countries such as Kenya and the Ivory Coast provides a measure of stability that is lacking in a society such as that of Zaïre, where only a handful have access to the trough. If enough blacks derive benefit from the status quo, then the vast dispossessed majority cherish the hope of upward mobility and refrain from militant mass action. This is why former Secretary of State Kissinger and State Department specialists proposed a "Kenya model" for an independent black-ruled Rhodesia, before this option evaporated with Robert Mugabe's electoral victory.

The experiences of the neocolonial states suggest that domestic institutions and international economic relationships inherited from the colonial era cannot overcome the underdevelopment that has persisted since independence. These institutions and relationships were designed to satisfy foreign rather than local interests, and have continued to do so to the present day.

Translated into terms of human lives, the post-World War II experience of most African states has been an unmitigated disaster. In 1976 Africa, with 7.5 percent of the world's population, subsisted with only 1.2 percent of the world's GNP [Gross National Product]. Per-capita GNP is $277 for Africa, $315 for Asia and $1,050 for Latin America. Africa's illiteracy rate is 74 percent, as against 47 percent in Asia and 24 percent in Latin America. Life expectancy for Africans is less than 40 years, 1 of every 4 has insufficient food, 1 of every 2 cannot find a job,

7 percent of Africa's population takes 40 percent of the income and the resulting inequities in life-styles are eroding the traditional communal spirit of African society. "There is increasing evidence," concludes one observer, "that injustices meted out by blacks to their racial brethren may in some instances make white rule look rather benevolent." This judgment is corroborated by the testimony of the dispossessed blacks. "Sometimes the black bosses are worse than the whites," states a black servant in Nairobi. "They hate us poor very much."

Such economic and social disruption inevitably has political repercussions. The job market has failed to keep pace with the burgeoning supply of diploma holders, creating the serious problem of the "unemployed school leaver." This in turn has led to a resurgence of tribalism, as the unemployed graduates organize on ethnic lines to compete in a situation of increasing scarcity. National leaders perforce use ethnic groups as the basis of their support, leading to unstable conditions and political fragmentation. Since the indigenous middle class generally lacks an independent economic base, political office has become the principal means for personal gain. By extending control over the economy, the new rulers are able to manipulate the national surplus. "African socialism" has become a smoke screen for corruption and self-aggrandizement. The resulting mass disaffection invites intervention of the military, which by 1980 ruled twenty African countries. These circumstances explain the startling warning by Edden Kdjo, secretary-general of the Organization of African Unity (OAU), at its meeting in Lagos in April 1980:

> Africa is passing through such terrible times that the question is now survival. The future remains unclear. We are being cheerful to say that should things continue as they are, only eight or nine African countries out of the 50 OAU members could still survive a few years from now.

THE SOUTH AFRICAN "FREEDOM CHARTER"

South Africa has always been dominated by a small white minority, consisting of British and Dutch "Afrikaner." Blacks, people of mixed race,

Reprinted in *Nelson Mandela—The Struggle Is My Life: His Speeches and Writings Brought Together with Historical Documents and Accounts of Mandela in Prison by Fellow Prisoners.* New York: Pathfinder Press, 1986.

and Indians have always suffered discrimination. With the political ascendancy of the Nationalist Party in 1948, however, segregation (apartheid) became more pronounced and institutionalized. Black workers were, and still are, subjected to harsh discipline, life in company barracks without their families, and arrest at the whim of the security police. "Pass laws" required blacks to carry identity cards or "passes," which were necessary to travel into towns where only whites could live or from one bleak black enclave to another.

In 1955, the African National Congress (ANC), the principal opposition force, called a "Congress of the People" to represent all South Africans for the first time in the nation's history. Three thousand delegates came, two thousand of whom were black; the other thousand were about equally divided among mixed, or "colored," Indians, and whites. Thus it was a South Africa in miniature that adopted this "Freedom Charter" at that Congress.

What does the Freedom Charter tell you about the actual conditions of life for blacks in South Africa? What seem to be the easiest demands to achieve? What would be the most difficult? Are any of these demands unreasonable? Does the realization of all of these demands require a political revolution in South Africa?

PREAMBLE

We, the people of South Africa, declare for all our country and the world to know:

That South Africa belongs to all who live in it, black and white, and that no government can justly claim authority unless it is based on the will of the people;

That our people have been robbed of their birthright to land, liberty and peace by a form of government founded on injustice and inequality;

That our country will never be prosperous or free until all our people live in brotherhood, enjoying equal rights and opportunities;

That only a democratic state, based on the will of all of the people, can secure to all their birthright without distinction of colour, race, sex or belief;

And therefore, we, the people of South Africa, black and white, together—equals, countrymen and brothers—adopt this FREEDOM CHARTER. And we pledge ourselves to strive together, sparing nothing of our strength and courage, until the democratic changes here set out have been won.

THE PEOPLE SHALL GOVERN!

Every man and woman shall have the right to vote for and stand as a candidate for all bodies which make laws.

All the people shall be entitled to take part in the administration of the country.

The rights of the people shall be the same regardless of race, colour or sex.

All bodies of minority rule, advisory boards, councils and authorities shall be replaced by democratic organs of self-government.

ALL NATIONAL GROUPS SHALL HAVE EQUAL RIGHTS!

There shall be equal status in the bodies of state, in the courts, and in the schools for all national groups and races;

All people shall have equal rights to use their own languages and to develop their own folk culture and customs;

All national groups shall be protected by law against insults to their race and national pride;

The preaching and practice of national, race or colour discrimination and contempt shall be a punishable crime;

All apartheid laws and practices shall be set aside.

THE PEOPLE SHALL SHARE IN THE COUNTRY'S WEALTH!

The national wealth of our country, the heritage of all South Africans, shall be restored to the people;

The mineral wealth beneath the soil, the banks and monopoly industry shall be transferred to the ownership of the people as a whole;

All other industries and trade shall be controlled to assist the well-being of the people;

All people shall have equal rights to trade where they choose, to manufacture and to enter all trades, crafts and professions.

THE LAND SHALL BE SHARED AMONG THOSE WHO WORK IT!

Restriction of land ownership on a racial basis shall be ended, and all the land re-divided amongst those who work it, to banish famine and land hunger;

The state shall help the peasants with implements, seed, tractors and dams to save the soil and assist the tillers;

Freedom of movement shall be guaranteed to all who work on the land;

All shall have the right to occupy land wherever they choose;

People shall not be robbed of their cattle, and forced labour and farm prisons shall be abolished.

ALL SHALL BE EQUAL BEFORE THE LAW!

No one shall be imprisoned, deported or restricted without a fair trial;

No one shall be condemned by the order of any Government official;

The courts shall be representative of all the people;

Imprisonment shall be only for serious crimes against the people, and shall aim at re-education, not vengeance;

The police force and army shall be open to all on an equal basis and shall be the helpers and protectors of the people;

All laws which discriminate on grounds of race, colour or belief shall be repealed.

ALL SHALL ENJOY EQUAL HUMAN RIGHTS!

The law shall guarantee to all their right to speak, to organise, to meet together, to publish, to preach, to worship and to educate their children;

The privacy of the house from police raids shall be protected by law;

All shall be free to travel without restriction from countryside to town, from province to province, and from South Africa abroad;

Pass laws, permits and all other laws restricting these freedoms shall be abolished.

THERE SHALL BE WORK AND SECURITY!

All who work shall be free to form trade unions, to elect their officers and to make wage agreements with their employers;

The state shall recognise the right and duty of all to work; and to draw full unemployment benefits;

Men and women of all races shall receive equal pay for equal work;

There shall be a forty-hour working week, a national minimum wage, paid annual leave, and sick leave for all workers, and maternity leave on full pay for all working mothers;

Miners, domestic workers, farm workers and civil servants shall have the same rights as all others who work;

Child labour, compound labour, the tot system[1] and contract labour shall be abolished.

THE DOORS OF LEARNING AND OF CULTURE SHALL BE OPENED!

The government shall discover, develop and encourage national talent for the enhancement of our cultural life;

All the cultural treasures of mankind shall be open to all, by free exchange of books, ideas and contact with other lands;

The aim of education shall be to teach the youth to love their people and their culture, to honour human brotherhood, liberty and peace;

Education shall be free, compulsory, universal and equal for all children;

Higher education and technical training shall be opened to all by means of state allowances and scholarships awarded on the basis of merit;

Adult illiteracy shall be ended by a mass state education plan;

Teachers shall have all the rights of other citizens;

The colour bar in cultural life, in sport and in education shall be abolished.

THERE SHALL BE HOUSES, SECURITY AND COMFORT!

All people shall have the right to live where they choose, to be decently housed, and to bring up their families in comfort and security;

Unused housing space to be made available to the people;

Rent and prices shall be lowered, food plentiful and no one shall go hungry;

A preventive health scheme shall be run by the state;

Free medical care and hospitalisation shall be provided for all, with special care for mothers and young children;

Slums shall be demolished, and new suburbs built where all have transport, roads, lighting, playing fields, crèches and social centres;

The aged, the orphans, the disabled and the sick shall be cared for by the state;

Rest, leisure and recreation shall be the right of all;

Fenced locations and ghettos shall be abolished, and laws which break up families shall be repealed.

1. The system used on the wine farms of the Western Cape, where labourers are paid or part-paid in kind, by being supplied at various times of the day, as well as the end of the week, with "tots" of cheap strong wine. This and the other labour abuses mentioned still exist in the 1980s.

THERE SHALL BE PEACE AND FRIENDSHIP!

South Africa shall be a fully independent state, which respects the rights and sovereignty of all nations;

South Africa shall strive to maintain world peace and the settlement of all international disputes by negotiations—not war;

Peace and friendship amongst all our people shall be secured by upholding the equal rights, opportunities and status of all;

The people of the protectorates—Basutoland, Bechuanaland and Swaziland[2]—shall be free to decide for themselves their own future;

The right of all the peoples of Africa to independence and self-government shall be recognised, and shall be the basis of close co-operation.

Let all who love their people and their country now say, as we say here:

"THESE FREEDOMS WE WILL FIGHT FOR, SIDE BY SIDE, THROUGHOUT OUR LIVES, UNTIL WE HAVE WON OUR LIBERTY."

2. Now the independent states of Lesotho, Botswana and Swaziland.

THE PALESTINE PROBLEM: 1. THE ARAB CASE

After the defeat of the Ottoman Empire in World War I, the League of Nations gave Great Britain a mandate to administer the region known as Palestine. British rule was beset by, on one hand, pressure from the Zionist movement to establish a Jewish homeland in Palestine and, on the other, pressure from Palestinian Arabs and neighboring Arab states to resist the Zionist demands. In the meantime, Zionist-inspired Jewish immigration to Palestine—mainly from Europe—continued and then increased with the rise of anti-Semitism after Hitler's coming to power in Germany in 1933. As World War II ended, the situation in Palestine worsened: both Zionist and Arab pressures intensified, with both sides resorting sometimes to violence. The horrendous experience of the

"The Arab Case for Palestine: Evidence Submitted by the Arab Office, Jerusalem, to the Anglo-American Commission of Inquiry, March 1946," as reprinted in *The Israel-Arab Reader*, second edition, edited by Walter Laqueur. New York: Bantam, 1970.

*Jewish people in Europe under Hitler's murderous rule naturally added to
the difficulty of resolving the problem.*

*In November 1945 the United States and Great Britain established a
commission to investigate the issue. This reading contains a portion of
the Arab presentation to the commission. Why did Arabs oppose a Jewish
state? What claims to Palestine did they make? Would they have accepted
a nonreligious state that included Jews and Arabs? Was any compromise
possible at this point? Why did the Arabs oppose the partition of
Palestine?*

1. The whole Arab people is unalterably opposed to the attempt to
impose Jewish immigration and settlement upon it, and ultimately to
establish a Jewish State in Palestine. Its opposition is based primarily
upon right. The Arabs of Palestine are descendants of the indigenous
inhabitants of the country, who have been in occupation of it since the
beginning of history; they cannot agree that it is right to subject an
indigenous population against its will to alien immigrants, whose claim is
based upon a historical connection which ceased effectively many
centuries ago. Moreover they form the majority of the population; as
such they cannot submit to a policy of immigration which if pursued for
long will turn them from a majority into a minority in an alien state; and
they claim the democratic right of a majority to make its own decisions
in matters of urgent national concern.

. . .

2. . . .The entry of incessant waves of immigrants prevents normal
economic and social development and causes constant dislocation of the
country's life; in so far as it reacts upon prices and values and makes the
whole economy dependent upon the constant inflow of capital from
abroad it may even in certain circumstances lead to economic disaster. It
is bound moreover to arouse continuous political unrest and prevent the
establishment of that political stability on which the prosperity and
health of the country depend. This unrest is likely to increase in
frequency and violence as the Jews come nearer to being the majority
and the Arabs a minority.

Even if economic and social equilibrium is re-established, it will be to
the detriment of the Arabs. The superior capital resources at the
disposal of the Jews, their greater experience of modern economic
technique and the existence of a deliberate policy of expansion and
domination have already gone far toward giving them the economic
mastery of Palestine. The biggest concessionary companies are in their
hands; they possess a large proportion of the total cultivable land, and
an even larger one of the land in the highest category of fertility; and the
land they possess is mostly inalienable to non-Jews. The continuance of

land-purchase and immigration, taken together with the refusal of Jews to employ Arabs on their lands or in their enterprises and the great increase in the Arab population, will create a situation in which the Arab population is pushed to the margin of cultivation and a landless proletariat, rural and urban, comes into existence. This evil can be palliated but not cured by attempts at increasing the absorptive capacity or the industrial production of Palestine; the possibility of such improvements is limited, they would take a long time to carry out, and would scarcely do more than keep pace with the rapid growth of the Arab population; moreover in present circumstances they would be used primarily for the benefit of the Jews and thus might increase the disparity between the two communities.

Nor is the evil economic only. Zionism is essentially a political movement, aiming at the creation of a state: immigration, land-purchase and economic expansion are only aspects of a general political strategy. If Zionism succeeds in its aim, the Arabs will become a minority in their own country; a minority which can hope for no more than a minor share in the government, for the state is to be a Jewish state, and which will find itself not only deprived of that international status which the other Arab countries possess but cut off from living contact with the Arab world of which it is an integral part.

• • •

8. In the Arab view, any solution of the problem created by Zionist aspirations must satisfy certain conditions:

(i) It must recognize the right of the indigenous inhabitants of Palestine to continue in occupation of the country and to preserve its traditional character.

(ii) It must recognize that questions like immigration which affect the whole nature and destiny of the country, should be decided in accordance with democratic principles by the will of the population.

(iii) It must accept the principle that the only way by which the will of the population can be expressed is through the establishment of responsible representative Government. (The Arabs find something inconsistent in the attitude of Zionists who demand the establishment of a free democratic commonwealth in Palestine and then hasten to add that this should not take place until the Jews are in a majority.)

(iv) This representative Government should be based upon the principle of absolute equality of all citizens irrespective of race and religion.

(v) The form of Government should be such as to make possible the development of a spirit of loyalty and cohesion among all elements of the community, which will override all sectional attachments. In other words it should be a Government which the whole community could regard as their own, which should be rooted in their consent and have a moral claim upon their obedience.

(vi) The settlement should recognize the fact that by geography and history Palestine is inescapably part of the Arab world; that the only alternative to its being part of the Arab world and accepting the implications of its position is complete isolation, which would be disastrous from every point of view; and that whether they like it or not the Jews in Palestine are dependent upon the goodwill of the Arabs.

(vii) The settlement should be such as to make possible a satisfactory definition within the framework of U.N.O. of the relations between Palestine and the Western Powers who possess interests in the country.

(viii) The settlement should take into account that Zionism is essentially a political movement aiming at the creation of a Jewish state and should therefore avoid making any concession which might encourage Zionists in the hope that this aim can be achieved in any circumstances.

. . .

The idea of partition and the establishment of a Jewish state in a part of Palestine is inadmissible for the same reasons of principle as the idea of establishing a Jewish state in the whole country. If it is unjust to the Arabs to impose a Jewish state on the whole of Palestine, it is equally unjust to impose it in any part of the country. Moreover, as the Woodhead Commission showed, there are grave practical difficulties in the way of partition; commerce would be strangled, communications dislocated and the public finances upset. It would also be impossible to devise frontiers which did not leave a large Arab minority in the Jewish state. This minority would not willingly accept its subjection to the Zionists, and it would not allow itself to be transferred to the Arab state. Moreover, partition would not satisfy the Zionists. It cannot be too often repeated that Zionism is a political movement aiming at the domination at least of the whole of Palestine; to give it a foothold in part of Palestine would be to encourage it to press for more and to provide it with a base for its activities. Because of this, because of the pressure of population and in order to escape from its isolation it would inevitably be thrown into enmity with the surrounding Arab states and this enmity would disturb the stability of the whole Middle East.

THE PALESTINE PROBLEM:
2. ISRAEL'S PROCLAMATION
OF INDEPENDENCE

The Anglo-American commission failed to resolve the problem. In 1947 Britain informed the United Nations, which had replaced the League of Nations, that it could not continue indefinitely to administer Palestine. The United Nations then called for the partition of Palestine into Jewish and Arab states. On May 14, 1948, the Jews of Palestine proclaimed the independent State of Israel. The next day—when British authority officially ended—armies from the Arab nations invaded Israel. But the Arabs were defeated. At the end of the war, Israel controlled 77 percent of the former Palestine rather than the 57 percent the United Nations had allotted to a Jewish state. In the course of the war, 900,000 of the 1,300,000 Arabs who had been living in the Israeli part of Palestine became refugees.

What reasons does the document below give for the establishment of Israel? What provision does the new state seem ready to make for Palestinian Arabs? Do these differ from the rights of Jews?

The Land of Israel was the birthplace of the Jewish people. Here their spiritual, religious and national identity was formed. Here they achieved independence and created a culture of national and universal significance. Here they wrote and gave the Bible to the world.

Exiled from the Land of Israel the Jewish people remained faithful to it in all the countries of their dispersion, never ceasing to pray and hope for their return and the restoration of their national freedom.

Impelled by this historic association, Jews strove throughout the centuries to go back to the land of their fathers and regain their statehood. In recent decades they returned in their masses. They reclaimed the wilderness, revived their language, built cities and villages, and established a vigorous and ever-growing community, with its own economic and cultural life. They sought peace, yet were prepared to defend themselves. They brought the blessings of progress to all inhabitants of the country and looked forward to sovereign independence.

In the year 1897 the First Zionist Congress, inspired by Theodor Herzl's vision of the Jewish State, proclaimed the right of the Jewish people to national revival in their own country.

This right was acknowledged by the Balfour Declaration of November

"State of Israel Proclamation of Independence," as reprinted in *The Israel-Arab Reader*, second edition, edited by Walter Laqueur. New York: Bantam, 1970.

2, 1917, and re-affirmed by the Mandate of the League of Nations, which gave explicit international recognition to the historic connection to the Jewish people with Palestine and their right to reconstitute their National Home.

The recent holocaust, which engulfed millions of Jews in Europe, proved anew the need to solve the problem of the homelessness and lack of independence of the Jewish people by means of the re-establishment of the Jewish State, which would open the gates to all Jews and endow the Jewish people with equality of status among the family of nations.

The survivors of the disastrous slaughter in Europe, and also Jews from other lands, have not desisted from their efforts to reach Eretz-Yisrael, in face of difficulties, obstacles and perils; and have not ceased to urge their right to a life of dignity, freedom and honest toil in their ancestral land.

In the second World War the Jewish people in Palestine made their full contribution to the struggle of the freedom-loving nations against the Nazi evil. The sacrifices of their soldiers and their war effort gained them the right to rank with the nations which founded the United Nations.

On November 29, 1947, the General Assembly of the United Nations adopted a Resolution requiring the establishment of a Jewish State in Palestine. The General Assembly called upon the inhabitants of the country to take all the necessary steps on their part to put the plan into effect. This recognition by the United Nations of the right of the Jewish people to establish their independent State is unassailable.

It is the natural right of the Jewish people to lead, as do all other nations, an independent existence in its sovereign State.

Accordingly we, the members of the National Council, representing the Jewish people in Palestine and the World Zionist Movement, are met together in solemn assembly today, the day of termination of the British Mandate for Palestine; and by virtue of the natural and historic right of the Jewish people and of the Resolution of the General Assembly of the United Nations.

We hereby proclaim the establishment of the Jewish State in Palestine, to be called Medinath Yisrael (The State of Israel).

•   •   •

The State of Israel will be open to the immigration of Jews from all countries of their dispersion; will promote the development of the country for the benefit of all its inhabitants; will be based on the principles of liberty, justice and peace as conceived by the Prophets of Israel; will uphold the full social and political equality of all its citizens, without distinction of religion, race, or sex; will guarantee freedom of religion, conscience, education and culture; will safeguard the Holy Places of all religions; and will loyally uphold the principles of the United Nations Charter.

The State of Israel will be ready to co-operate with the organs and representatives of the United Nations in the implementation of the Resolution of the Assembly of November 29, 1947, and will take steps to bring about the Economic Union over the whole of Palestine.

We appeal to the United Nations to assist the Jewish people in the building of its State and to admit Israel into the family of nations.

In the midst of wanton aggression [by Arab states], we yet call upon the Arab inhabitants of the State of Israel to preserve the ways of peace and play their part in the development of the State, on the basis of full and equal citizenship and due representation in all its bodies and institutions—provisional and permanent.

We extend our hand in peace and neighbourliness to all the neighbouring states and their peoples, and invite them to co-operate with the independent Jewish nation for the common good of all. The State of Israel is prepared to make its contribution to the progress of the Middle East as a whole.

Our call goes out to the Jewish people all over the world to rally to our side in the task of immigration and development, and to stand by us in the great struggle for the fulfilment of the dream of generations for the redemption of Israel.

WOMEN AND THE ISLAMIC REVOLUTION IN IRAN

RUHOLLAH KHOMEINI

Ruhollah Khomeini (b. 1902) was the leader of the Iranian Revolution. A revered religious teacher, or ayatollah, he had opposed Shah Mohammed Reza Pahlavi since 1962. Khomeini was in exile near Paris when the revolutionary crisis in Iran came to a climax. He returned to Iran in triumph on January 31, 1979, fifteen days after the Shah fled the country.

Reprinted in *Islam and Revolution: Writings and Declarations* by Imam Khomeini, translated and annotated by Hamid Algar. London: KPI Ltd., 1985.

Instead of governing from the capital city of Tehran, Khomeini later retired to his home in the religious center of Qum, where he supervised affairs from behind the scenes.

The following speech, given in Qum in March 1979, is addressed to the women of Iran. For what does Ayatollah Khomeini praise Iranian women? Why does he say that Islam has improved the status of women? From what he says, do you think that the Islamic Revolution has improved the condition of women in Iran?

Greetings without limit to the women of Iran! Peace be upon you, respected sisters. The mercy of God be upon you, lionhearted women, whose noble efforts have delivered Islam from the fetters of enslavement to foreigners. Beloved and courageous sisters, you fought shoulder-to-shoulder with the men and ensured the victory of Islam. I thank you, women of Iran and women of Qum. May God and the Imam of the Age be pleased with you. Carrying your infants in your arms, you came into the streets and supported Islam with your ardent demonstrations. I have heard what happened in Qum and other cities; I have heard what happened on Chahar Mardan Street in Qum. I take pride in all the courageous deeds accomplished by the women of Iran, in Qum and other cities, for you have been in the vanguard of our triumph and have encouraged the men. We are all indebted to your courage, lionhearted women.

Islam has particular regard for women. Islam appeared in the Arabian Peninsula at a time when women had lost their dignity, and it raised them up and gave them back their pride. Islam made women equal with men; in fact, it shows a concern for women that it does not show for men. In our revolutionary movement, women have likewise earned more credit than men, for it was the women who not only displayed courage themselves, but also had reared men of courage. Like the Noble Qur'an [Koran] itself, women have the function of rearing and training true men. If nations were deprived of courageous women to rear true men, they would decline and collapse.

The laws of Islam are for the benefit of both man and woman, and woman must have a say in the fundamental destiny of the country. Just as you have participated in our revolutionary movement, indeed played a basic role in it, now you must also participate in its triumph, and must not fail to rise up again whenever it is necessary. The country belongs to you and, God willing, you will rebuild it.

In the earliest age of Islam, the women participated in wars together with the men, and we see that then as now the women fought shoulder-to-shoulder with the men, or even in front of them. They might lose their infants and children, but they would still resist the enemy.

We want our women to attain the high rank of true humanity. Women must have a share in determining their destiny. The repressive regime of the Shah wanted to transform our warrior women into pleasure-seekers, but God determined otherwise. They wanted to treat woman as a mere object, a possession, but Islam grants woman a say in all affairs just as it grants man a say. All the people of Iran, men and women alike, must repair the ruins that the previous regime has bequeathed to us; the hands of men alone will not suffice to accomplish the task. Men and women must collaborate in this respect.

There is one particular question to which attention should be paid. When women wish to marry, there are certain prerogatives they can stipulate for themselves that are contrary neither to the *shari'a* [holy law] nor to their own self-respect. For example, a woman can stipulate that if her future husband turns out to be of corrupt moral character or if he mistreats her, she would possess the right to execute a divorce. This is a right that Islam has granted to women. If Islam has imposed certain restrictions on both women and men, it is for the benefit of both. Similarly, just as Islam has granted man the right to divorce, it has also granted it to woman, on condition that the parties stipulate at the time of the marriage that if the husband behaves in a certain manner, the wife will have the right to execute a divorce. Once the man has accepted such a stipulation, he can never repudiate it. Apart from making it possible to include such a stipulation in the marriage contract, Islam forbids the husband to mistreat his wife; if he habitually mistreats her, he is to be punished and the *mujtahid* [legal authority] will grant the wife a divorce.

May God Almighty adorn all of you with dignity, health, happiness, and perfect faith and character.

Peace be upon you, beloved and respected ladies.

16. Dependence and Independence in the Americas

REVOLUTION AND THE INTELLECTUAL IN LATIN AMERICA

ALAN RIDING

The role of the writer, artist, or intellectual in Latin America is different from what it is in the United States. Intellectuals are more respected and popular than in the United States, and they are more actively concerned with political issues. Many, in fact, serve as political advisers. These are some of the conclusions of this essay. Why does this seem to be the case? What in Latin American history accounts for this difference? Has this ever been the case in the United States, or elsewhere? Under what circumstances? What other social classes play important political roles in Latin America and the United States?

While Latin American intellectuals vary from communists to supporters of the United States, the majority of them appear to be socialists. Why is this? Why are there so few supporters of a strong U.S. role in the hemisphere?

On his way from Mexico City to Stockholm to receive the 1982 Nobel Prize in Literature, and again on the way back, Gabriel García Márquez stopped over in Cuba to see his close friend and political mentor, Fidel Castro. The Colombian novelist is a frequent traveler to Havana, but these two visits took on special significance: He was emphasizing his political identification with Cuba at the moment of his greatest literary glory.

In contrast, Octavio Paz, the Mexican poet and essayist, has not visited Havana since the 1959 Cuban revolution. He once sympathized with the announced objectives of the new regime, but became disenchanted when, in his words, the revolution was "confiscated" by Marxists. He now considers the Cuban people no more fortunate than they were before the overthrow of the rightist dictatorship of Fulgencio Batista.

García Márquez and Paz live seven miles apart in Mexico City and are great admirers of each other's writing, but they are no longer close friends. Politics, their common obsession, has divided them. They have become symbols of the two opposing views in the rising political debate among Latin America's intellectuals.

At the heart of the polemic is the search for new political models for a continent viewed by the intellectuals as desperately in need of change. Latin America's writers, artists and academics look about them and see country after country locked into political systems that eliminate freedom in the name of fighting Communism—or, conversely, in the name of combating United States "imperialism." They see economic structures that condemn millions to perpetual poverty—except where leftist revolutions have brought programs of social betterment at the cost of political liberty. Positions are often expressed through sympathy for—or doubts about—Castro's Cuba, Sandinist Nicaragua and the guerrilla movements in El Salvador and Guatemala. But more complex dilemmas are also involved, confronting politics and morality, testing loyalty and honesty and raising troubling questions about justice and freedom.

What gives the debate its importance is that intellectuals exercise enormous political influence in Latin America. It is they who provide respectability to governments in power and legitimacy to revolts and revolutionary movements, they who articulate the ideas and contribute the images through which Latin Americans relate to power, they who satisfy the decidedly Latin need for a romantic and idealistic raison d'être.

Literary fame, then, has given political clout not only to García Márquez and Paz but to other writers—Jorge Luis Borges, Julio Cortázar, Carlos Fuentes and Mario Vargas Llosa among them—whose works constitute the contemporary Latin American literary boom. And their activism is emulated by hundreds of less-known intellectuals who consider themselves the political conscience of society.

Most of these intellectuals feel drawn to the left. Few are card-carrying Communists, but most of them accept García Márquez's view of the United States as the main obstacle to political and social change in Latin America. In line with this conviction, they vociferate their criticism of Washington and its right-wing allies in the hemisphere and swallow their reservations about the Cuban and Nicaraguan revolutions.

Ranged against them in the debate is a minority of intellectuals who equate dictatorships of the left and the right. For them, Cuba's Castro is as bad as Chile's Gen. Augusto Pinochet Ugarte. Yet one seldom hears them defending United States policy, and their general viewpoint seems to be one of a socialist ideal far removed from the reality of the region.

The lines that divide the two camps are often blurred, and as much energy is dedicated to arguing various socialist options as to debating the merits of Marxism and capitalism.

"Why is it like this?" Mario Vargas Llosa, the Peruvian novelist, asked in a recent essay. "Why is it that instead of being basically creators and artists, writers in Peru and other Latin American countries must above all be politicians, agitators, reformers, social publicists and moralists?"

The question may be even more puzzling to people in the United States, where the political influence of writers and other intellectuals is exercised far more subtly and indirectly, and politics mainly has to do with specific issues rather than ideologies. Successive administrations in Washington have ignored the swirling debate in Latin America, or viewed it with deep suspicion, denying García Márquez and many other authors permanent visas for unrestricted entry into the United States.

There is a certain irony in this, for García Márquez, though fiercely critical of Washington's hemispheric policies, is a strong champion of United States culture. Having lived in Paris in the mid-1950's, he feels that European thought has become a prisoner of abstractions, that "the era of Sartre and Camus has long been over," and that "Americans are the literary giants of the 20th century." Acknowledging William Faulkner as his literary mentor, he holds that "there is no way one can relate to contemporary cultural life without going to the United States." All the greater, then, his frustration over the State Department's restrictive rules.

The problem, however, is not limited to American visa regulations. By holding aloof from this hidden dimension of the region's politics, the United States is passing up an opportunity to present its case to Latin America's principal opinion molders—a failure in the exercise of influence that could have large political consequences. These Latin writers are wrestling with issues—endemic poverty, human rights, chronic militarism and the conflict between left and right—that are of universal concern. Intellectuals may not be the principal actors in the Latin drama, but they define the issues. Before causes win out, it is their ideas that triumph. Nothing less than the continent's long-range political evolution may be at stake.

The Latin intellectual's position grows out of the society in which he lives. In a region characterized by weak social institutions, inadequate public education and little democratic tradition, intellectuals automatically belong to a prestigious elite. And because Latin American politics invariably revolves around personalities, men of talent are looked to for wisdom and leadership.

Taken together, the intellectuals of Latin America form a kind of unofficial parliament in which the major political events of the day are discussed, integrated into the regional agenda, or allowed to fade from the public consciousness. The Falkland Islands war of 1982 is a case in point. At the time, the intellectual community was sharply divided between those who refused to support a repressive Argentine military regime, despite their acceptance of Argentine claims to sovereignty over the islands, and those who thought that British "aggression" from across the seas required hemispheric solidarity. Yet the Falkland war never engaged the intellectuals deeply, and, less than a year later, it has left little trace in the public mind.

This kind of political eminence rarely brings wealth—few Latin writers can survive on their royalties and only García Márquez, whose books have been translated into many languages, can be called rich. But it does make writers into powerful political symbols, particularly if they have been recognized abroad, and few of today's top Latin American authors show many qualms about making full use of this power. The Mexican writer Juan Rulfo, who seems almost bashful about the renown that his novel, "Pedro Páramo," brought him, is one of a small handful of writers who prefer to keep out of the limelight. The others usually separate their activism from their creativity and use journalism as their principal political vehicle. And they clearly feel a strong need to speak out and to be heard. It is as if they see themselves mirrored in the power structure and become hypnotized by their image.

García Márquez, at 54, remains the most active of the continent's writer-politicians, frequently to be seen in the company of world leaders from Managua to New Delhi. A stocky man with wiry hair and a mischievous smile, he clearly relishes his fame. Yet, brought up in the steamy political parlors of Colombia's Caribbean coast, he prefers, in his words, the intrigue of "secret diplomacy," as if politics were the art of whispering.

Prior to the 1979 Nicaraguan revolution, for example, he served as a secret intermediary between the Sandinists and several governments of the region. Around the same time, he privately negotiated the release of numerous political prisoners in Cuba. More recently, he has been "conspiring," as he puts it, to promote peace talks between El Salvador's warring factions.

But he has never been attracted by political office. In the late 1970's, he turned down an invitation from a coalition of leftist parties to run for the presidency of Colombia. Late last year, he declined an ambassadorship offered him by Colombia's new President, Belisario Betancur. Instead, he is planning to invest his Nobel Prize money in founding a newspaper in Bogotá. "I am an emergency politician," he explains. "If I were not a Latin American, I would not be in politics. But how can the intellectual enjoy the luxury of debating the destiny of the soul when the problems are of physical survival, health, education, ignorance and so on?"

Octavio Paz, in contrast, rarely leaves his apartment on the Paseo de la Reforma, Mexico City's principal avenue. He is a gentle man, but is no less consumed by politics than García Márquez. For more than 20 years, he served as a Mexican diplomat, resigning as Ambassador to India in 1968 to protest the Mexican Army's bloody suppression of an anti-Government student movement. Now, at the age of 68, with a lifetime of political activity behind him, he prefers to sit in his book-lined study, surrounded by Asian art, and to dedicate himself to writing poetry and political and philosophical essays.

He edits the literary and political monthly Vuelta, and until recently he delivered political commentaries on Mexico's main television channel. But he sees his principal role as one of simply thinking. "Very few Latin American intellectuals of the left or the right have done much thinking," he says. "Very few. It's a serious reflection. They spout commonplaces. I don't reproach García Márquez for using his skill as a writer to defend his ideas. I reproach him because his ideas are poor. There is an enormous difference between what I do and what García Márquez does. I try to think and he repeats slogans."

As a general rule, the writers join their political activity with prolific literary output—and, at times, their books, too, have broad political impact. For example, García Márquez and the late novelists Miguel Angel Asturias and Alejo Carpentier all wrote about the phenomenon of the old-fashioned Latin American dictator—*el caudillo*—and turned him into a figure of ridicule. Many writers are so prominent as public figures—García Márquez and Paz are good examples—that they have a political following among people who have not read their books.

While they come from different countries, the writers' audience is continental, not only because they project a strong sense of a common Latin American identity but because the issues they raise are familiar throughout the region. Almost without exception, they write widely syndicated columns and give frequent interviews—more often about politics than about literature—that are read across Latin America. They frequently gather at conferences that issue sweeping declarations on world issues. And while their political opinions may be challenged, their moral authority is rarely questioned.

The phenomenon, of course, is not new to Latin America. It goes back at least as far as the symbiotic relationship between intellectuals and politics in Athens, Rome and the Renaissance courts. The leaders of the American, French and Russian revolutions were intellectuals, as were most of the political figures who brought independence in the 1960's to the European colonies in Africa and Asia. And, as recently as last month [February, 1983], President Francois Mitterrand of France considered it worthwhile to invite some 300 writers, artists, moviemakers, economists and philosophers from around the world to Paris for a conference splendidly entitled "Creation and Development."

Thus, the Latin American intellectual owes his role not only to the fact that so relatively few others in his society are well educated: He is also heir to a general European tradition. What distinguishes him even from the European intellectual, however, is the special tradition of dogma that he inherited from Catholic Spain and that still weighs down political thought in the hemisphere.

For three centuries after the Spanish Conquest, most Latin intellectuals came from the ranks of the clergy and observed the limitations on free thought dictated by the Spanish Inquisition. Such minimal dissent as existed could only come from within the church. Priests, for example, were the first to protest the enslavement of the Indians in colonial Mexico. Yet whatever the intellectual debate at the time, it revolved around the prevailing Catholic dogma. Priests organized Mexico's independence movement against Spain, but their troops followed the standard of the Virgin of Guadalupe. Even the Liberal Reforms that swept across Latin America in the 19th century became almost dogmatic in their anticlericalism.

This doctrinaire past facilitated the transition to Marxism following the 1917 Bolshevik revolution in Moscow. In Latin America, Marxism became the new creed and intellectuals its new priests, while the state was assigned the church's old role of organizing society. "We are the sons of rigid ecclesiastic societies," says the Mexican novelist Carlos Fuentes. "This is the burden of Latin America—to go from one church to another, from Catholicism to Marxism, with all its dogma and ritual. This way we feel protected."

Years later, in the 1960's, many Latin American Catholic priests were themselves to be drawn by Marxism in their search for answers to the continent's social ills, and the two dogmas were fused in a new category of Christian Marxists. Among most intellectuals, however, the debate remained dominated by Marxism. And today, as in the past, the political crises that regularly convulse the world of Latin America's intellectuals are essentially crises of faith, in which loyalty to the Marxist ideal is tested by the shortcomings of the Socialist reality. And, ironically, throughout this century, each generation of writers and artists has gone through its own traumatic experience, wanting to believe anew, yet finding difficulty in marrying principles with practice.

Octavio Paz was an unknown young writer when he went to Paris in the late 1930's. Like many intellectuals from the New World, he was drawn by the crusade against Fascism symbolized by the Spanish Civil War. In Paris, he came in contact with leading European intellectuals who, almost to a man, seemed entranced by the Soviet experience. "I was very influenced by Marxism," he recalls. "I was never a member of the Communist Party, but I was very close to them—first to the Stalinists and then to the Trotskyists. I also explored anarchist thought."

But like many other leftist writers, Paz was soon disillusioned by Moscow's behavior—first the expulsion of Leon Trotsky from the Soviet Union (and his subsequent murder in Mexico), then the Moscow purge trials of the 1930's, and, finally, the German-Soviet nonaggression pact of 1939. The impact of these events was felt in Communist parties throughout Latin America, provoking purges of anti-Stalinist factions that rebelled against the pro-Moscow leadership.

For Paz's generation, it was a watershed. A handful of prominent figures—including the great Mexican muralists Diego Rivera and David Alfaro Siqueiros and the late Chilean poet and Nobel laureate Pablo Neruda—remained faithful to "*el partido*," but the region's Communist parties shrank and stagnated into irrelevance. For most intellectuals, the road to the socialist Utopia no longer passed through Moscow.

But the search continued, and the warm welcome that Latin America's intelligentsia gave to the 1959 Cuban revolution reflected the anxiety of the quest. At one level, Castro's victory offered the hope that other Latin American dictators could be toppled by ragtag bands of idealistic youths. But it also seemed to deal with the "problem" of Moscow by exuding a revolutionary spirit that was the antithesis of the Soviet Union's repressive and bureaucratic form of Communism, and it confronted what most intellectuals considered to be Latin America's main problem—the need to break free of the political and economic domination of the United States. Cuba thus gave birth to a new truly Latin American dogma—*La Revolución*—that conveniently focused on Havana rather than Moscow and was dedicated largely to excoriating the "evils" of United States "imperialism."

Many writers and artists for the first time found a cause close to home with which they could identify. The Argentine novelist Julio Cortázar—a huge man who is now 68, and looks 20 years younger—had settled in Paris in the early 1950's to dedicate himself to "esthetic concerns" far removed from politics. Yet, to him, the Cuban revolution came as a kind of revelation. "I made my first trip to Havana in 1961," he recalls, "and when I saw the panorama, with all its problems, its difficulties, its contradictions, it was in some ways like being born again." Since then, politics has been an important part of his life, and he has become a fervent defender of Castro's Cuba—and, more recently, of the Nicaraguan revolution.

The Rev. Ernesto Cardenal, a poet and priest who now serves as Nicaragua's Minister of Culture, underwent a similar experience. Feeling a need to redefine his faith in more political terms, he at first found the answer in a "theology of liberation," which committed the clergy to work with the poor. But for Father Cardenal—with his long white hair and beard, his jeans and his perpetual beret, he looks more like a poet than a priest—it was his visit to Cuba in 1970 that made the crucial difference.

"It was like a second conversion," he says. "Before then, I saw myself as a revolutionary, but I had confused ideas. I was trying to find a third way, which was the Revolution of the Gospel, but then I saw that Cuba was the Gospel put into practice. And only when I converted to Marxism could I write religious poetry."

In the early years of the Cuban revolution, with Havana under constant pressure from the United States, Latin intellectuals were almost unanimous in their sympathy for the Castro regime. And even as they saw domestic freedoms evaporating in Cuba, they argued that these were "temporary" restrictions forced on the regime by "imperialism." By way of compensation, they pointed to Cuba's considerable achievements in improving the lot of the rural poor and in bringing health and education to the population.

But as Castro's repressions bit ever deeper into the cultural sphere, the mood gradually changed. An event in 1971 brought matters to a head. A Cuban poet, Heberto Padilla, was jailed for his stubbornly outspoken dissidence and was forced to make a humiliating "confession" in order to obtain his freedom. Many leading Cuban writers, including Carlos Franqui and Guillermo Cabrera Infante, had quietly opted for exile even before then, but the Padilla affair became such a scandal that most Latin intellectuals were forced to protest.

Just as the Moscow trials destroyed the leftist consensus four decades earlier, so the Padilla case shattered the concept of revolutionary infallibility for the new generation of Latin American writers and artists and raised difficult political and moral dilemmas. For Octavio Paz, by then already distanced from Cuba, the Padilla case was a morally repugnant symptom of totalitarian dictatorship. Vargas Llosa was one of those who broke with Havana over the episode. Others, such as García Márquez and Cortázar, were dismayed by the affair but saw it as a "mistake" attributable to political sectarianism, which they pledged to combat "from the inside."

"One thing that is very reproachable is that we intellectuals only define ourselves when we are affected personally," García Márquez said recently. "It was only when there were problems with intellectuals in Cuba that intellectuals began to break with Cuba, and I think this is politically immature."

The "mistake" of alienating an important group of Latin intellectuals was a surprising one for a man of Castro's evident astuteness, and he set about to undo the damage after appointing a new Minister of Culture, Armando Hart. The Casa de las Américas, Cuba's principal publishing house in the cultural field, was a particularly useful instrument, giving many young leftist writers throughout the region their first opportunity to see their work in print and organizing large conferences of intellectuals, invitations to which were seen by many as synonymous with literary recognition. By 1980, several Latin writers who had broken with Cuba over the Padilla affair had revisited the island.

But it was the extreme right in the region that contributed most to restoring the intellectuals' allegiance to Cuba. In the early 1970's, thousands of writers and academics in such countries as Brazil, Chile, Uruguay, Argentina and Bolivia were persecuted by military dictatorships and forced to flee. In exile, they received political support from Havana. And while many were not Marxists and had personal reservations about Cuba, they had no interest in criticizing their most faithful friend. Their public passions were therefore reserved exclusively for their home Governments and for the United States, which frequently supported these regimes.

Even today, the Reagan Administration's continuing hostility toward Cuba serves to insure intellectual loyalty to Havana. Carlos Fuentes, who was born into a family of Mexican diplomats and has spent more of his life abroad than in Mexico, now lives in Princeton, N.J. and has not visited Cuba since 1962 because of his political differences with Castro. Yet he, too, deplores the thrust of Washington's policy, declaring: "The day the United States stops attacking Cuba, it will no longer be possible for Cuba to mobilize intellectual opinion in the region. All Latin Americans have felt they must keep silent so as not to help imperialism."

The same sense of protectiveness pervades the intellectuals' view of Nicaragua. Solidarity with the Sandinist revolution has grown in direct proportion to the rise of hostility toward the Managua regime on the part of the United States. Cortázar, García Márquez, Fuentes—even Vargas Llosa, who distinguishes between Cuba and Nicaragua—have all visited Managua at the invitation of the Sandinist leadership, and have all been sufficiently impressed by what they saw to denounce the Reagan Administration's efforts to undermine the new Government. (Their reaction has been shared, incidentally, by such European visitors as Günter Grass and Graham Greene.)

"What can we say about a country that comes out of 45 years of dictatorship?" said Fuentes after a visit to Managua last January. "It has avoided a blood bath. It has avoided a Maximum Leader. My attitude is to let these countries resolve their own problems. I'd like to ask Reagan: 'What right have you to meddle in things you don't understand?'"

When United States military units joined Honduran troops for war games close to Honduras's border with Nicaragua last month, the Sandinist Government, charging that the maneuvers were a form of hostile pressure, mobilized its own forces. But its most effective weapon, perhaps, was a delegation of intellectuals from other Latin American countries, including Cortázar and the Salvadoran poet Claribel Alegría, and even from the United States, who participated in a "peace vigil" near the Honduran border. Reports were flown to the scene, and the word went out to the hemisphere: While the United States engaged in saber rattling, Nicaragua defended itself with a moral shield.

The readiness of the region's intellectuals to identify with Nicaragua has yet another explanation—the country's strong tradition of following the political lead of its writers. From the time of Rubén Darío, the modernist poet who made Nicaragua famous even before the world had heard of the Somoza dictatorship, Nicaragua has been a land of poets. Many, such as José Coronel Urtecho, Ernesto Cardenal and Pablo Antonio Cuadra, are famous throughout Latin America. Others served more modestly as family or village poets, enjoying as much prestige as the local doctor, teacher or priest.

It was natural, then, for the Sandinists to mobilize this talent—the protest music of Carlos Mejía Godoy as well as the poetry of rebel leaders and ordinary guerrillas—against the Somoza regime. And today, many top Sandinist officials are also writers. One of the revolutionary *comandantes*, Omar Cabezas, won an award from the Casa de las Américas for his memoirs as an insurgent. The head of the ruling junta, Daniel Ortega Saavedra, is a respected poet, while another junta member, Sergio Ramirez Mercado, is a well-known novelist. Since the revolution, some 50 poetry workshops have sprung up in the army, police and the trade unions, and even in peasant organizations.

Visiting writers are, therefore, welcomed by officials who are also fellow intellectuals. They are not unaware, of course, of the press censorship and other restrictions on political freedom that are part of the Sandinist revolution. Almost invariably, however, they blame these curbs on the harassment of Nicaragua emanating from the United States, and they point to the burst of artistic creativity since the revolution as evidence that cultural freedom survives.

.   .   .

There is one final irony—that this very political instability, this process of decomposition and renovation, has contributed to the richness of the region's literature. Latin America's social models may, so far, have failed, but its writers have made the failures memorable. In the end, Latin America's perceptions of itself will probably be shaped more lastingly by such books as García Márquez's "One Hundred Years of Solitude" and Paz's "The Labyrinth of Solitude" than by any political pronouncement by either author.

A THEOLOGY OF LIBERATION

GUSTAVO GUTIERREZ

There are many groups in Latin America that are stronger than the intellectuals. The landowning class, of course, and the military have been most powerful. The peasants, even without power, are still the majority of the population. Urban classes—workers and owners—are becoming increasingly influential. But all of this we could say about any developing society in Asia or Africa. What makes Latin America unique is the addition of another class, another force for change or conservatism: the clergy.

Since the first clergy arrived with the conquistadors they have been an important political force in the Americas. They have spoken out on every issue, sometimes on the side of the oppressed, often on the side of the powerful.

In recent years, more of the clergy have sided with the poor and powerless than ever before. "Liberation theology" is one example of that development. In this essay, one of the early advocates of "a theology of liberation" examines two ways of understanding Latin American poverty. In the 1950s, he says, there was the "development" model, but that did not work. Now a "theory of dependence" makes more sense, he suggests. What does he mean by these two explanations of poverty? Which do you find more convincing? What does any of this have to do with religion or theology anyway?

THE OPTION BEFORE THE LATIN AMERICAN CHURCH

We have seen that one of the most fruitful functions of theology—and one in which we are particularly interested in this work—is critical reflection, the fruit of a confrontation between the Word accepted in faith and historical praxis.

Historical developments can help us to discover unsuspected facets of revelation as well as to understand the nature of the Church in greater depth, express it better, and adjust it more successfully to our times. For this reason the commitment of Christians in history constitutes a true *locus theologicus*.

In this connection it is useful to recall, at least in broad outline, the new awareness of the reality of the continent which Latin Americans have acquired as well as the way in which they understand their own liberation. We will also look at the options which important sectors of the Church are making here in the only predominantly Christian continent among those inhabited by oppressed peoples. The Latin American Church indeed faces peculiar and acute problems related to the process of liberation.

THE PROCESS OF LIBERATION IN LATIN AMERICA

Dependence and *liberation* are correlative terms. An analysis of the situation of dependence leads one to attempt to escape from it. But at the same time participation in the process of liberation allows one to acquire a more concrete living awareness of this situation of domination, to perceive its intensity, and to want to understand better its mechanisms. This participation likewise highlights the profound aspirations which play a part in the struggle for a more just society.

An Awareness of the Latin American Reality

After a long period of real ignorance of its own reality (except for a brief period of optimism induced by vested interests) Latin America is now progressing from a partial and anecdotal understanding of its situation to a more complete and structural one.

The most important change in the understanding of the Latin American reality lies, first, in going beyond a simple, tearful description with an attendant accumulation of data and statistics, and, second, in having no false hopes regarding the possibility of advancing smoothly and by preestablished steps towards a more developed society. The new approach consists in paying special attention to the root causes of the situation and considering them from a historical perspective. This is the point of view which Latin Americans are beginning to adopt in the face of the challenge of an ever more difficult and contradictory situation.

The Decade of Developmentalism

Latin America in the '50s was characterized by great optimism regarding the possibility of achieving self-sustained economic development. To do this it was necessary to end the stage of *foreign-oriented growth* (exportation of primary products and importation of manufactured products), which made the Latin American countries dependent exclusively upon foreign trade. The more developed countries in the area had already begun to do this. There would then begin an *inward development*. By means of the substitution of imports, expansion of the internal market, and full industrialization, this would lead to an independent society.

Fernando Henrique Cardoso and Enzo Faletto wrote that "it could not be denied that at the beginning of the decade of the '50s some of the necessary preconditions were present for this new stage in the Latin American economy, at least in countries such as Argentina, Mexico, Chile, Colombia and Brazil. This approach was based on a favorable set of historical circumstances and was theoretically formulated in serious economic studies. In the political sphere, it was adopted by the populist movements which at different times and with varying influence arose in Latin America.

The developmentalist policies current at that time were supported by international organizations. From their point of view underdeveloped countries thus were considered backward, having reached a lower level than the developed countries. They were obligated, therefore, to repeat more or less faithfully the historical experience of the developed countries in their journey towards modern society. For those located in the heart of the Empire, this modern society was characterized by high mass consumption.

Developmentalist policies did not yield the expected results. One of their proponents acknowledged that "after more than half of the decade of the '60s has passed, the *gap* between the two worlds is growing bigger, rather than slowly decreasing as was expected. . . . While from 1960 to 1970 the developed nations will have increased their wealth by 50 percent, the developing countries, two-thirds of the world's population, will continue to struggle in poverty and frustration." The developmentalist approach has proven to be unsound and incapable of interpreting the economic, social, and political evolution of the Latin American continent.

. . .

The Theory of Dependence

For some time now, another point of view has been gaining ground in Latin America. It has become ever clearer that underdevelopment is the end result of a process. Therefore, it must be studied from a historical perspective, that is, in relationship to the development and expansion of the great capitalist countries. The underdevelopment of the poor countries, as an overall social fact, appears in its true light: as the historical by-product of the development of other countries. The dynamics of the capitalist economy lead to the establishment of a center and a periphery, simultaneously generating progress and growing wealth for the few and social imbalances, political tensions, and poverty for the many.

. . .

The imbalance between developed and underdeveloped countries—caused by the relationships of dependence—becomes more acute if the cultural point of view is taken into consideration. The poor, dominated nations keep falling behind; the gap continues to grow. The underdeveloped countries, in relative terms, are always farther away from the cultural level of the center countries; for some it is difficult ever to recover the lost ground. Should things continue as they are, we will soon be able to speak of two human groups, two kinds of people: "Not only sociologists, economists, and political theorists, but also psychologists and biologists have pointed with alarm to the fact that the incessant widening of the distance between the developed and the underdeveloped countries is producing a marked separation of two human groups; this implies the appearance, in a short time, of a true anthropological differentiation. . . . At each level of progress and each stage of development, the industrialized countries advance and accumulate strength which allows them to reach new collective goals of a number and degree much higher than those attainable by the underdeveloped countries."

The Liberation Movement

To characterize Latin America as a dominated and oppressed continent naturally leads one to speak of liberation and above all to participate in the process. Indeed, *liberation* is a term which expresses a new posture of Latin Americans.

The failure of reformist efforts has strengthened this attitude. Among more alert groups today, what we have called a new awareness of Latin American reality is making headway. They believe that there can be authentic development for Latin America only if there is liberation from the domination exercised by the great capitalist countries, and especially by the most powerful, the United States of America. This liberation also implies a confrontation with these groups' natural allies, their compatriots who control the national power structure. It is becoming more evident that the Latin American peoples will not emerge from their present status except by means of a profound transformation, a *social revolution*, which will radically and qualitatively change the conditions in which they now live. The oppressed sectors within each country are becoming aware—slowly, it is true—of their class interests and of the painful road which must be followed to accomplish the breakup of the status quo. Even more slowly they are becoming aware of all that the building of a new society implies.

• • •

There is also present in this process of liberation, explicitly or implicitly, a further ramification which it is well to keep in mind. The liberation of our continent means more than overcoming economic, social, and political dependence. It means, in a deeper sense, to see the becoming of mankind as a process of the emancipation of man in history. It is to see man in search of a qualitatively different society in which he will be free from all servitude, in which he will be the artisan of his own destiny. It is to seek the building up of *a new man*. Ernesto Che Guevara wrote, "We revolutionaries often lack the knowledge and the intellectual audacity to face the task of the development of a new human being by methods different from the conventional ones, and the conventional methods suffer from the influence of the society that created them."

This vision is what in the last instance sustains the liberation efforts of Latin Americans. But in order for this liberation to be authentic and complete, it has to be undertaken by the oppressed people themselves and so must stem from the values proper to these people. Only in this context can a true cultural revolution come about.

THE SCALPELS OF AREQUIPA

RICHARD SELZER

The relationship between the United States and Latin America is a confusing and contradictory one. It is certainly not all exploitation, all "dependency." This reading tells of how a group of U.S. plastic surgeons travelled on their own to perform important operations in Peru without thought of gain, except that which comes from thankful smiles and almost miraculous work.

But the ironies of this peculiar aid mission are not lost on the author either. How is it that the North Americans have developed cosmetic surgery to such a degree, while Latin Americans lack the most basic medical care? What about the "other reasons" the doctors have come: the experience, the practice, the exotic, playing god; is that not a new form of Yankee imperialism? Then there is an accident. North Americans, even at their best, bring pain as well as healing. What does this account tell you about the relationship between the United States and Latin America? What, ideally, should that relationship be?

Interplast. It is one of those ugly names for which Americans with an entrepreneurial need to describe themselves have a penchant. It stands for International Plastic Surgery, Incorporated. The organization—which sends out expeditions of surgeons, anesthesiologists, nurses, and technicians to perform reconstructive plastic surgery in so-called undeveloped countries—was founded in 1969 by Donald Laub, who twenty-five years ago was one of my interns when I was chief resident in surgery at Yale. In his other life Don practices in Palo Alto, California. Among other things, he has performed what is perhaps the largest number of sex-change operations in the world—over four hundred of them—but now he and I are sitting on a hotel porch in Arequipa, Peru, sipping coca tea.

"Why did you start Interplast?" I ask him, and he tells me that in the beginning it was to get patients for his residents to operate on. As the great majority of cases in the States are private, there is insufficient clinical material for the training of plastic surgeons. A simple solution was to practice abroad. But almost at once, in the face of the need, the overwhelming numbers, and the severity of the various deformities, the priorities were reversed and the needs of the visited rather than the visitors came first.

The length of this expedition will be two weeks. We are a team of twenty.

I am an interloper here. A turkey among peacocks. Just so is a mere generalist among a pride of plastic surgeons. Still, I have been engrafted upon this expedition. My colleagues will be Peruvian doctors and nurses. I shall remove the gallbladders of the Indians here, reset their intestines, ligate and strip their varicose veins—the same work I do every day in New Haven. But I have also come to observe, which is to behold and perceive.

Our trip from North to South America is hardly Xenophon's march from Babylon to the Bosporus; still, it is in the heroic mold. Twenty people, all unused to and resisting regimentation, each with that certain "sweet arrogance" that belongs to men and women trained to a fare-thee-well in their life's work—it is not easy. In Miami, a surgeon wanders away and is nearly lost; in Lima, a nurse stops listening and misses a vital connection. Yet in the end we have been coaxed and prodded on and off the succession of planes, buses, and cars that have carried us to Peru. Seventy crates and cartons of equipment have been ushered through customs. Interplast uses none of the precious resources of the host country. We have brought our own: sterile gauze, hemostats, scalpels—all.

We are assembled in the lobby of the Hotel Crillón, in Lima. The next morning we fly to Arequipa, in the southern highlands. We shall work there in the government provincial hospital named Honorio Delgado. In the evening an exuberance possesses us. It is a kind of glee at the prospect of shared labor and adventure. Friendships which had been initiated in airports along the way are cemented. Absent is the wariness of new acquaintances inching toward intimacy. There is no taking of measure, no hesitation. The team is being forged. A MASH mentality prevails. Veterans of previous expeditions regale novices with tales of surgical derring-do. The initiates sigh and fidget. Later I fall asleep dreaming of Peru. Of condors and gold. Of llamas and emerald mountains. Of cruel Pizarro and his conquistadores.

The flight from Lima to the mountain city of Arequipa takes little more than one hour, but I think the direction must be straight up. Abruptly, Peru vanishes and we are engulfed in fog. Peaks and crags dodge our wings and miss, but barely. The plane flutters, banks, rolls all but over, and we are on the ground. It is less a descent and landing than a careful insertion into Arequipa. Half of us are to be housed in Peruvian homes, the rest are wedged, three to a tiny room, at Turistas, a pink-and-green hotel made of volcanic rock. We do not stop to unpack but rush to the hospital to begin our work. The great clinic, we are told, is already in session. CONSULTARIO CIRUGIA PLASTICA DE INTERPLAST, reads the sign on the wall. Black crayon on yellow paper. Within minutes we are fully engaged in the examination and selection of patients for the days of surgery ahead.

The hospital of Honorio Delgado is slowly, imperceptibly settling into a state of splendid ruination. One day it will be the twentieth century's medical Machu Picchu. Every floor bears great gouges where tile and stone have crumbled. Every ceiling is a constellation of cracks. Should something break, it will stay broken. There is no such thing as restoration or replacement. Honorio Delgado has run out of catgut, scrub suits, dressings. Rubber gloves are mended and reused the next day and the day after that. Each scrap of gauze is retrieved from a bucket, washed and folded, and made ready to blot another patient's blood. The scalpels of Arequipa enjoy longevity. If these knives could speak, they would spin tales of the dozens of incisions each of them has made. At Yale or Stanford, a knife has a lifetime of a single operation. Each procedure here is dictated by the cost of the material needed to do it. The staff is paid, but poorly. Carlos Galdo, the chief of men's surgery and the equal, at least, of most of the surgeons I have known, earns $300 a month. Before an emergency appendectomy, the patient must buy suture material, gauze, and knife blade to be used upon him. If there is no money, as is usual, the residents themselves must buy the material, paying for the right to heal their patients. But Interplast, ah Interplast, has come to Peru, its cartons bursting with throwaway knives, suture material of every caliber and variety (catgut, nylon, Vicryl, silk), tanks of anesthetic gas, intravenous fluids, and an array of clever instruments (dermatomes, staples, retractors, endotracheal tubes). We are both proud of and embarrassed by our plenty. Under the awed gazes of our hosts we squirm. Always, we are the rich gringos.

Clinic is held in two tiny examining rooms in which at no time are there fewer than a dozen people. Four examinations are being conducted simultaneously. In one corner Iris Figueroa, a beautiful fourteen-year-old girl, glows among our white coats. Her mother holds up the girl's right hand for us to see. It has but one finger, the index, which protrudes like a talon. The rest are absent save for a cluster of soft nubbins bunched at the knuckles.

Leo is our hand surgeon. "What is your name?" he asks her.

"Iris," she says and lowers her gaze.

"Wiggle your thumb," says Leo.

His English is translated into Spanish by a nurse. But what can he mean? There is no thumb. He means only to see if she moves the bone at the base of what should have been her thumb, the one hidden in the featureless pad of tissue in which all five metacarpals exist uselessly. Iris tries to wiggle it; she tries very hard to do what the doctor has asked her to, even shakes her head at the effort. There is no movement to be seen. Still, palpating, Leo feels *something* at work within that pad of flesh.

"We can separate this ray out," he says, thinking out loud, "make a web space, deepen it all the way to the wrist. Then she will be able to pinch." The girl's mother lifts Iris's other hand and we see that this one too is blank, blind, dumb. And fingerless. For a moment we are still. Then:

"Is she right- or left-handed?" The interpreter is busy.

"Right," she says at last. And we smile as though we have just received the best news. And we have. All this while, the girl has been eating our faces with her eyes.

"Put her on the schedule," says Leo. "I'll do her tomorrow."

"There's no more room on the schedule tomorrow," says Fran Taylor. She has charge of making out the operations list. "In fact, you're all booked up for the whole two weeks." Leo says nothing, only looks down at the small unfinished hand, paw really, that he is holding. "It's just the way it is," says Fran. "We can't do them all."

"You tell her, then," says Leo. There is a short volley of Spanish. Something pale and vague flits from the face of the girl. I think it must be hope. Her head drops down and away. She is trying not to show what is churning inside. But courage has its limits, in Peru as everywhere else, and there are tears. With her single finger she reaches up to wipe them away.

"No room?" Leo asks again. He cannot seem to understand.

"No room," says Fran.

"Give her a high-priority slip for next year. We'll be back next year," he says to Iris. "I'll fix it then." Fran writes out a slip of paper, marks it "priority," and hands it to the mother of the girl.

However, a surgical schedule is not graven in stone. Just when you think you've got it made out once and for all, along come fever, cough, infection—all the mischances of the body—to cause one operation to be canceled at the last minute and another to be put in its place. Lest a precious slot on the list be wasted, substitutes must wait at the ready. There is an understudy kind of chanciness about it. The Indians know this, and they do not leave us until they are certain there is no hope.

Paper is shuffled, the door is let open a bit, and a woman leads a seven-year-old boy into the room. He climbs up on the table that Iris has just left. Where his lip should be, a nude rubbery insect from which a single tooth projects.

"What's your name?" asks Don.

"Miguel." Don laughs as though the name itself were funny.

"Say 'el gato,' Miguel," he says "Say 'Coca-Cola.' " The boy looks at his mother. She nods.

"El gato," says Miguel. "Coca-Cola." But it is only an approximation. The vowels leak out of his nose; the consonants are blunted, furry.

"Unilateral cleft lip and cleft palate," says Don. "We ought to get it fixed now. Later, there will be less chance for speech improvement. He's at the right age."

"Now," says Fran, "you know there's no space for it. Why do you make me say it again and again?" She tells the mother it cannot be done, tells her to bring him back next year. She gives her a slip of paper. They rise to leave.

"Good-bye, Miguelito," says Don. "*Adiós, amigo.*" It is the boy's turn to smile.

Just at noon the sun comes out for the first time. In its rays the hospital of Honorio Delgado blanches. Through the tiny window of the examining room we see the huge snowy cone of Misti, one of the three volcanoes that ring the city of Arequipa. It is dead, they say. Burnt out. But I don't know about that. There is just the whiff of temper in that bit of cloud the peak has snagged. What mountain could hold its peace in the face of so much heartbreak? Once, I arrived in Paris some hours later than I had planned, only to find that the hotel had given away my room reservation. "*Complet,*" announced the desk clerk, dismissing me with her back. Very Parisian, I was to learn, after dragging luggage the heft of boulders into a dozen other lobbies in search of shelter, to be met each time with another "*complet.*" It is a small thing to sit up all night in a foreign city waiting for the dawn. I know that. "No room" in Peru is worse than "*complet*" in Paris. Still, as I watch the disappointed children leave the clinic, I think of that cold and tired night.

I step out into the waiting room, from which the throng spills to the out-of-doors, where there is a topiary garden—shrubs in the shape of a llama, a condor, an ocelot, an angel, each one carved precisely as if by a surgeon of Interplast. From this garden I spy on the patients. How beautiful they are. Tiny. Even the tallest of them is shorter than the least of us. Every shade of brown and gold is represented in their skin. Their hair is full and black. All their sexuality seems to reside in their hair. Again and again the children are scooped up and pressed into their mothers. The children eye each other's deformities with solemnity. The mothers, too, cast quick glances. It is said that the Incas were all exterminated during the Spanish conquest, that their race is extinct. But I don't believe it. The genes of the Incas are here in this courtyard full of *serranos*. Now and then I see a perfect pre-Columbian face, and then I am sure.

Here, in this legendary waiting room, one would think deformity the natural state of mankind. No child but with his cleft lip, burn scar, webbed hand. The marred and the scarred far outnumber the others. The children are quiet, reserved. There is no restlessness in them. Only, they wait. The longing in their faces is all for a clever scalpel, a tiny row of meticulously placed sutures that will redeem their lives. See how the examining-room door opens again. Something billows forth from the crowd. Yet no one moves. It is only their breath that has surged. The lucky name is called out: "Fabian Platera Choquehuanca." A woman carries a fully swathed infant into the examining room. The rest inhale, exhale, and settle into waiting. Many have come on foot from great distances, from villages high in the Andes. Still, they are not disgruntled. Nor are there predatory lawyers circling at the periphery. There is only the eternal eloquence of the wound. All at once, from the examining room, another "no room," followed by a hush in which I think to hear the volcano rumbling. I go back to duty. The door bangs open and a young boy of eight runs in and hugs Fran. They cling to each other, laughing. There is a barrage of Spanish. Fran explains:

"He had a double cleft lip. We fixed it last year. He and his mother have come all the way from Puno to show us. Look. You can't even tell." She turns to the boy.

"You are handsome," she says. He laughs and races out of the room.

Another day. Another ten cleft lips and palates. We are pushing to get them all done, all that we have promised, before we leave.

A short lesson in embryology: Mesenchyme is that all-purpose undifferentiated tissue of which we are largely composed early in fetal life. Mesenchyme is not stationary, but flows, folding upon itself, rising into ridges, incorporating within itself little sacs and hollows. Within the first trimester of pregnancy it happens, sometimes—far oftener in Peru than in the United States, it seems—that the mesenchyme destined to form the upper jaw, the lip, and the palate fails to fuse in the midline of the face, or even to migrate to the midline of the face. And so there is a cleft where there should have been an uninterrupted smooth and attractive joining. Such an intrauterine mishap runs in families. Should a mother or a sibling have a cleft lip, then the odds turn grimmer for the unborn. Inbreeding, it is said, plays a part, the grouping and concentration of negative influences. And malnutrition. And multiparity in which an eleventh or twelfth child is born to a woman in her forties or later. For the Indians of Peru such risks are high. They live in such a state of genetic vulnerability. Interplast has come here to repair and reconstruct, to correct the inborn errors to which society and culture have made these people susceptible. So we tell ourselves and others. So we believe. But that is not the only reason we have come. Honesty insists that we have each of us come for our own entirely other reasons. The surgical residents have come for the experience of operating on great numbers of these deformities. Within two weeks they will have performed more of these operations than most surgeons will do in a lifetime. For some, it is the opportunity for virtue that we are seeking. Such opportunities are not without the element of self-aggrandizement. For still others it is the exhilaration of the exotic that beckons, or the lovely sense of camaraderie that is to be found in working together for a purpose we think high. Last, there is the need for human beings to challenge themselves. In surgery it is best done by tackling the most difficult of clinical situations and prevailing. Next to the control of the birthrate, the correction of malnutrition, genetic counseling, and the teaching of simple hygiene, all our surgery is nothing. Still, that we have come to do it is enough for us.

In the operating room the ancient pedagogy of surgery goes on, but here as in Babel. The doctors and nurses of Arequipa speak no English; we, no Spanish. Still, hand guides hand within a sleeping patient. Voices murmur.

"*Paciencia, paciencia. Lento, por favor.*" And after a difficult technique newly mastered, "*Felicitaciones, amigo.*"

As usual, the surgeons are confident, the anesthesiologists nervous. It is the role of the anesthesiologist to rein the surgeon in, restrain, lest in his enthusiasm the surgeon endanger life. These associates are the conscience of the operating room. They, the statesmen. We, the warriors.

¡*Miracolo*! It is Iris Figueroa who is the patient on the operating table. A last-minute cancellation. An infant with too low a blood count, crackles in his lungs. An anesthesiologist has said no. The infant's misfortune is Iris's good luck. Now we are in the middle of the surgery. The skin flaps have been cut. A full-thickness skin graft has been taken from the girl's groin. There is still much to do.

Anesthetist: "How much longer will you be at it?"

Surgeon: "Another hour and a half or so. Why?"

Anesthetist: "The trouble is . . . we are almost out of oxygen. The tank is on empty."

Surgeon: "No."

Anesthetist: "Yes."

Surgeon, angrily: "How could you let that happen?" Then, flatly: "We'll have to find a good place to stop."

Anesthetist: "That would be *right now*. I'm going to have to wake her up."

Surgeon: "Can you wait one minute?"

Anesthetist: "No."

Just then, the door to the operating room opens and a huge headless tank is rolled, wobbled, carried even, into the room. Two tiny Peruvian nurses are supplying the brawn. They are dwarfed by the giant tank. They use their breasts and their breath to propel it forward. A monkey wrench is found, and the tubing is switched from the dead tank to this new one. A knob is turned. All eyes are on the gauge. No one knows how much, if any, oxygen the tank holds. The needle pops to the halfway mark. It is enough. The surgeon and the anesthetist breath heavily, as though it were they who had run out of air.

Surgeon: "Now can we get on with it?"

Anesthetist: "Trouble is, now there's no oxygen in the recovery room. This is their tank. The only one."

Surgeon: "Suture!"

· · ·

Sunday. Carlos Galdo has arranged an outing for us to a restored eighteenth-century grain mill. After weeks of surgery, clinics, and rounds, we are eager for leisure. We are a caravan of four cars each holding five *Interplasticos*. There is much hilarity. At El Molino there will be a feast: octopus marinated in lime juice, slices of charcoal-broiled beef heart, pisco, and beer. And dancing, without which a party is not a party in Peru. Peruvians cannot imagine a party where people sit around and converse. What fun is that? they ask. Not much, we admit. The mill is about twenty miles from Arequipa, in the country. I am in the backseat of the last car. Near the halfway mark we cross a narrow bridge that spans a deep gorge at the bottom of which is a swiftly running river. Having crossed, we immediately find that the road ascends sharply, then curves out of sight. The leading cars have already disappeared from view. It is in mid-ascent of that incline that fate casts upon Interplast its most ironic smile. The car stalls. Before the hand brake can be applied, we have rolled backward a few feet and struck a small car filled with people. It is an ancient blue Volkswagen. The driver of that Volkswagen leaps from the car, neglecting, in his ardor for battle, to close the door. Now he and our driver are fully engaged in a passionate discussion which promises to be interminable. I get out of the car to assess the damage. None to our car, I see; only a dent in the front bumper of the other. Never mind, I say. I'll give him money. Let's get going. Just then, thinking to disengage us from the Volkswagen, our driver releases the hand brake prior to starting the motor. It is a lapse. We roll back a bit. The hand brake is reapplied. But not before we have once again nudged the Volkswagen. This time, it begins to roll backward down the hill toward the bridge. I chase after it, thinking, I suppose, to reach in and pull up the hand brake. But I cannot catch the car. Faster and faster it rolls. Through the windshield I see the faces of the passengers. Indians, I see. Their eyes are wide with terror. Their mouths are open for shrieking. Just before the bridge, the little blue car takes a small, sickening turn to the left, achieves the rim of the chasm, tips up at the front, and plunges backward into the ravine. All this I watch from a few feet away. And hear the crash far below. For a moment I pause at the edge, then leap. The sides of the gorge are not quite straight. There are stunted shrubs to grab, rocks to brace a foot against. It is an utterly graceless scramble downward, at least half of which is made on skidding buttocks, heels. A series of bounces, really, until that final plummet into the river. A mouthful of raw sewage.

I am twenty feet from the rock ledge where the car has come to rest on its side. From the wreck, whimpering. They are alive! I see three old men. They are covered with blood. The river beneath the ledge is red with it. I try to pull one of the men through a window, but he is wedged. Now I am joined by Bill and Michael. They are both young and strong. I am merely reckless. We shout to each other above the noise of the river. Our voices echo against the walls of the chasm. The air is stagnant, palpable. Michael climbs on top of the car and tries to open the door. It will not open. He pounds it with his fist, a rock. At last it gives, and we pass the three old men from one of us to the next. They are Franciscan monks. They wear long brown habits and rosaries. Somehow, this makes it worse. From the bridge, people throw ponchos in which the injured will be carried up to the road. Other men have come down to help. One of the monks has sustained an avulsion of his forehead and scalp. Blood from the great wound films his face. He is blinded by it. I wipe the wound with my hand, find the artery that is spurting at the base of the gouge, pinch it between thumbnail and fingernail. The bleeding slows, virtually stops. We lay him on a poncho and begin to climb. He is immensely heavy and I must use one hand to pinch the artery. The other is more tired than it has ever been in my life. No mountaineer ever looked more longingly at the summit of Everest than I at the bridge high above. At last we reach the top, and I unpinch my fingers from the blood vessel. The bleeding has stopped. It does not resume. The three wounded men are placed in the back of a trunk and taken to Honorio Delgado. The next day we will visit them on rounds. Rows of cotton sutures will crisscross their smiles. From swollen purple mouths they will cast blessings upon us. There will be no single word of reproach. All the same, we will be filled with guilt. We who came to repair and have ended by damaging. Conquistadores!

At last, Carlos and the others have come back to find us. He insists that we go on to El Molino. Shattered, and so malleable, we do. There we find kindly massage, tumblers of pisco. In two hours we are dry. And tipsy. And dancing. Later, on the way back to Arequipa, we stop at the bridge and go to stand again at the edge of the precipice. A rank air hisses up from the depths. Like ones who have emerged from the mouth of hell, we are returned to a state of childhood horror. You are making too much of it, we say to one another. And know that we are making far too little. We pick up stones and toss them over the side. The one I throw takes hours to strike the bottom. It has a muffled sound like the impact of flesh. A noise like that could kill you. I would not go down there again for Saint Francis himself.

A last visit to Honorio Delgado. What a far cry it is from my sleek and gleaming hospital in New Haven—all glass and prestressed concrete. And yet, so like. A hospital is only a building until you hear the slate hooves of dreams galloping upon its roof. You listen then and know that here is no mere pile of stone and precisely cut timber but an inner space full of pain and relief. Such a place invites mankind to heroism. For us, Honorio Delgado has become an instrument with which to confront life, a rock that stands firm against the incessant lapping of fate. Even at *la peña*, at the mill, at the bottom of the ravine, this hospital clung to us like a she-wolf. We could smell her maternal odors penetrating to our hearts. Tomorrow we leave Peru carrying with us the pathetic belief that the way to heal the world is to take it in for repairs. One on one. One at a time.

17. The Fate of Humanity

THE COST OF THE ARMS RACE

JOHN KENNETH GALBRAITH

In this selection, John Kenneth Galbraith, the economist and former presidential adviser, discusses some of the causes and implications of the arms race between the United States and the Soviet Union. What, according to Galbraith, are the technological and bureaucratic causes of the arms race? How, according to him, does this arms race affect our security and our economy?

There are, of course, many forces perpetuating the arms race; nothing is gained by simplification. One is the technological competition. Each power develops the weapons of ever-greater destructive capacity and precision that render obsolete those of the other. Each, foreseeing such obsolescence, strives to develop those that will, in turn, render those of the other side ineffective and then obsolete. A large and learned community of experts with their own language and values—scientists, engineers, and politicians—nurtures and guides this process.

The technological dynamic is sustained by the economic, bureaucratic, and scientific interest of these specialists—the interest of which President Dwight D. Eisenhower spoke in his best-remembered speech, when he warned on leaving office against "this acquisition of unwarranted influence, whether sought or unsought, by the military-industrial complex." This interest, the bureaucratic interest in particular, cannot be identified specifically with one side or the other. And in both the United States and the Soviet Union it is strongly reinforced by an appeal to fear—fear of what the other side is doing, fear of being thought soft on a potential enemy. In a passage from his memoirs that deserved wider attention than it received, Nikita Khrushchev tells of a conversation at Camp David with President Eisenhower:

> "Tell me, Mr. Khrushchev, [the President asked,] how do you decide the question of funds for military expenses?" Then, before I had a chance to say anything, he said, "Perhaps first I should tell you how it is with us. . . .

"It's like this. My military leaders come to me and say, 'Mr. President, we need such and such a sum for such and such a program. . . . If we don't get the funds we need, we'll fall behind the Soviet Union.' So I give in. That's how they wring money out of me. They keep grabbing for more, and I keep giving it to them. Now tell me, how is it with you?"

Here is Khrushchev's reply:

"It's just the same. Some people from our military department come and say, 'Comrade Khrushchev, look at this! The Americans are developing such and such a system. We could develop the same system, but it would cost such and such.' I tell them there's no money; it's all been allotted already. So they say, 'If we don't get the money we need and if there's a war, then the enemy will have superiority over us.' So we discuss it some more, and I end up by giving them the money they ask for."[1]

The final and influential force sustaining the weapons competition is the commonly held belief that it safeguards an economic, political, and social system—a way of life. On the American side we are defending free enterprise and free institutions; these are under attack from socialism and Communism; weaponry, whatever the cost and risk, is the means by which we protect them. The Soviet Union, looking out on a predominantly capitalist world, has a reciprocal response. In such manner those committed to a larger social faith—to belief in freedom and free enterprise or socialism and Communism—are swept into support of the weapons race.

If we are to counter the forces that perpetuate it, we must recognize, above all, that the weapons competition does not, in fact, defend social and economic systems, neither that of the United States nor that of the Soviet Union. It is presently putting both systems gravely at risk, the risk of returning them to a society that far antedates both capitalism and socialism and for which even the words are irrelevant. As always, the historical process. Capitalism and socialism are the highly sophisticated products of this process, and nuclear conflict will have an equally shattering effect on both. Transportation, communications, the food supply, the monetary economy itself will succumb. So also the political institutions of the free world, as well as the even more complex structure required by socialism. Remaining at most on either side will be a medieval economy, unfortunate survivors grubbing hopelessly in the contaminated soil. There will be no freedom, no democracy; these were unknown in the medieval existence not because they had yet to be invented but because in a poverty-ridden context they are irrelevant. None should doubt it; the ashes of capitalism will be indistinguishable by

1. *Khrushchev Remembers* (Boston: Little, Brown, 1970), pp. 519–520. The authenticity of this document, once subject to some challenge, is now generally accepted. There should, of course, be the usual warning about conversations remembered long after the fact.

even the most perceptive surviving ideologue from the ashes of Communism.

However, one thing will, indeed, have been accomplished: the differences between the rich countries and the poor will at long last have been eliminated. It is worth reflecting that, by reasonable calculation, the life and well-being of the average citizen of the United States or Russia is even now as much at risk as that of the poorest villager in India. But not even the villager is secure from the dangers of nuclear conflict. The fallout, the ozone effects, the contamination from a full-scale confrontation or from that limited war that some strategic theorists, in a striking immunity to sanity, think possible will, like the rain, come upon the just and the unjust—the innocent and the responsible—alike.

The technological dynamic in the United States and the Soviet Union must be arrested; the supporting bureaucratic and economic interest must be overcome. Likewise the fear of addressing the problem. By far the most direct and understandable way of doing this is through a bilateral freeze on the development, production, and deployment of further nuclear weapons as the prelude to negotiation on their reduction—and, one hopes, their eventual elimination. The freeze is not impractical, illusory, or visionary; it is a highly sensible, highly practical design for removing the issue from the nearly exclusive control of the nuclear theologians, as they have been called. These are the people for whom the technical and military intricacies involved in the development and deployment of weapons and the policy on arms control negotiation have become an intellectual preserve from which the public, including those urging effective nonsymbolic arms control, are righteously excluded on grounds of ignorance or naiveté. It is a delegation of power, the most fatal in our time, that can no longer be tolerated.

·   ·   ·

Arms expenditure, we are coming also to realize, is deeply adverse to good economic performance in the older industrial countries and notably in the United States and the Soviet Union. In her useful and authoritative *World Military and Social Expenditures, 1981*, Ruth Leger Sivard concludes:

> Among ten developed countries for which historical data are available [for the years 1960–1979], the slowest growth in investment and manufacturing productivity has occurred in two countries (UK and US) where military expenditures are the highest in relation to GNP. The best investment and productivity record is in Japan, where the military-to-GNP ratio has been very low and productivity has grown at an amazing 8 percent per year. [Germany with relatively low defense expenditures had also a favorable rate of growth in productivity.]

The poorest record may well be in the Soviet Union, where the proportion of GNP devoted to military programs is higher than in the NATO countries, perhaps twice as high.

She assigns the reasons for the link between costly military effort and productivity:

An arms race . . . drains investment and research resources[,] . . . limits the potential for growth and innovation. On the civilian side, this means an economy less prepared to compete in world markets, less able to provide its citizens with improved conditions of living.[2]

Through the decade of the 1970s the United States used from 5 to 8 percent of Gross National Product for military purposes, while the Germans used between 3 and 4 percent—in most years relatively about half as much. The Japanese in this same period devoted less than 1 percent of their Gross National Product annually to military use. In 1977, to take a fairly typical year, American military spending was $441 per capita; that of Germany, $252 per capita; that of Japan, a mere $47 per capita. It was from the capital so saved and invested that a substantial share of the civilian capital investment came which brought these latter countries to the industrial eminence that now challenges so successfully that of the United States. Again the figures are striking. Through the decade of the seventies American investment in fixed nonmilitary and nonresidential investment ranged from 16.9 percent of Gross National Product to 19.0 percent. That of Germany ranged upward from 20.6 to 26.7 percent. The Japanese range in these years was from 31.0 percent to a towering 36.6 percent. The investment in improvement of civilian plant was broadly the reciprocal of what went for weapons.[3]

2. Ruth Leger Sivard, *World Military and Social Expenditures, 1981* (Lessburg, Virginia: World Priorities, 1981), p. 19.
3. Figures are from *The Statistical Abstract of the United States* and *International Economic Indicators*, December 1980.

THE NUCLEAR WINTER

CARL SAGAN

The world's arsenal of nuclear weapons has grown enormously since the first atomic bombs were exploded in 1945. Here the astronomer Carl Sagan suggests that the effects of nuclear war would be far greater than is usually imagined. What, according to Sagan, would be the effects of such a war? What can we do to prevent it?

Into the eternal darkness, into fire, into ice.
                          —*Dante, The Inferno*

Except for fools and madmen, everyone knows that nuclear war would be an unprecedented human catastrophe. A more or less typical strategic warhead has a yield of 2 megatons, the explosive equivalent of 2 million tons of TNT. But 2 million tons of TNT is about the same as all the bombs exploded in World War II—a single bomb with the explosive power of the entire Second World War but compressed into a few seconds of time and an area 30 or 40 miles across. . . .

In a 2-megaton explosion over a fairly large city, buildings would be vaporized, people reduced to atoms and shadows, outlying structures blown down like matchsticks and raging fires ignited. And if the bomb were exploded on the ground, an enormous crater, like those that can be seen through a telescope on the surface of the Moon, would be all that remained where midtown once had been. There are now more than 50,000 nuclear weapons, more than 13,000 megatons of yield, deployed in the arsenals of the United States and the Soviet Union—enough to obliterate a million Hiroshimas.

But there are fewer than 3000 cities on the Earth with populations of 100,000 or more. You cannot find anything like a million Hiroshimas to obliterate. Prime military and industrial targets that are far from cities are comparatively rare. Thus, there are vastly more nuclear weapons than are needed for any plausible deterrence of a potential adversary.

Nobody knows, of course, how many megatons would be exploded in a real nuclear war. There are some who think that a nuclear war can be "contained," bottled up before it runs away to involve many of the world's arsenals. But a number of detailed analyses, war games run by the U.S. Department of Defense and official Soviet pronouncements, all indicate that this containment may be too much to hope for. Once the bombs begin exploding, communications failures, disorganization, fear, the necessity of making in minutes decisions affecting the fates of millions and the immense psychological burden of knowing that your own loved ones may already have been destroyed are likely to result in a nuclear paroxysm. Many investigations, including a number of studies for the U.S. government, envision the explosion of 5000 to 10,000 megatons—the detonation of tens of thousands of nuclear weapons that now sit quietly, inconspicuously, in missile silos, submarines and long-range bombers, faithful servants awaiting orders.

The World Health Organization, in a recent detailed study chaired by Sune L. Bergstrom (the 1981 Nobel laureate in physiology and medicine), concludes that 1.1 billion people would be killed outright in such a nuclear war, mainly in the United States, the Soviet Union, Europe, China and Japan. An additional 1.1 billion people would suffer serious injuries and radiation sickness, for which medical help would be unavailable. It thus seems possible that more than 2 billion people—almost half of all the humans on Earth—would be destroyed in the immediate aftermath of a global thermonuclear war. This would represent by far the greatest disaster in the history of the human species and, with no other adverse effects, would probably be enough to reduce at least the Northern Hemisphere to a state of prolonged agony and barbarism. Unfortunately, the real situation would be much worse.

In technical studies of the consequences of nuclear weapons explosions, there has been a dangerous tendency to underestimate the results. This is partly due to a tradition of conservatism which generally works well in science but which is of more dubious applicability when the lives of billions of people are at stake. In the Bravo test of March 1, 1954, a 15-megaton thermonuclear bomb was exploded on Bikini Atoll. It had about double the yield expected, and there was an unanticipated last-minute shift in the wind direction. As a result, deadly radioactive fallout came down on Rongelap in the Marshall Islands, more than 200 kilometers away. Almost all of the children on Rongelap subsequently developed thyroid nodules and lesions, and other longterm medical problems, due to the radioactive fallout.

Likewise, in 1973, it was discovered that high-yield airbursts will chemically burn the nitrogen in the upper air, converting it into oxides of nitrogen; these, in turn, combine with and destroy the protective ozone in the Earth's stratosphere. The surface of the Earth is shielded from deadly solar ultraviolet radiation by a layer of ozone so tenuous that, were it brought down to sea level, it would be only 3 millimeters thick. Partial destruction of this ozone layer can have serious consequences for the biology of the entire planet.

These discoveries, and others like them, were made by chance. They were largely unexpected. And now another consequence—by far the most dire—has been uncovered, again more or less by accident.

The U.S. Mariner 9 spacecraft, the first vehicle to orbit another planet, arrived at Mars in late 1971. The planet was enveloped in a global dust storm. As the fine particles slowly fell out, we were able to measure temperature changes in the atmosphere and on the surface. Soon it became clear what had happened:

The dust, lofted by high winds off the desert into the upper Martian atmosphere, had absorbed the incoming sunlight and prevented much of it from reaching the ground. Heated by the sunlight, the dust warmed the adjacent air. But the surface, enveloped in partial darkness, became much chillier than usual. Months later, after the dust fell out of the atmosphere, the upper air cooled and the surface warmed, both returning to their normal conditions. We were able to calculate accurately, from how much dust there was in the atmosphere, how cool the Martian surface ought to have been.

Afterwards, I and my colleagues, James B. Pollack and Brian Toon of NASA's Ames Research Center, were eager to apply these insights to the Earth. In a volcanic explosion, dust aerosols are lofted into the high atmosphere. We calculated by how much the Earth's global temperature should decline after a major volcanic explosion and found that our results (generally a fraction of a degree) were in good accord with actual measurements. Joining forces with Richard Turco, who has studied the effects of nuclear weapons for many years, we then began to turn our attention to the climate effects of nuclear war. [The scientific paper, "Global Atmospheric Consequences of Nuclear War," is written by R. P. Turco, O. B. Toon, T. P. Ackerman, J. B. Pollack and Carl Sagan. From the last names of the authors, this work is generally referred to as "TTAPS."]

We knew that nuclear explosions, particularly groundbursts, would lift an enormous quantity of fine soil particles into the atmosphere (more than 100,000 tons of fine dust for every megaton exploded in a surface burst). Our work was further spurred by Paul Crutzen of the Max Planck Institute for Chemistry in Mainz, West Germany, and by John Birks of the University of Colorado, who pointed out that huge quantities of smoke would be generated in the burning of cities and forests following a nuclear war.

Groundbursts—at hardened missile silos, for example—generate fine dust. Airbursts—over cities and unhardened military installations—make fires and therefore smoke. The amount of dust and soot generated depends on the conduct of the war, the yields of the weapons employed and the ratio of groundbursts to airbursts. So we ran computer models for several dozen different nuclear war scenarios. Our baseline case, as in many other studies, was a 5000-megaton war with only a modest fraction of the yield (20 percent) expended on urban or industrial targets. Our job, for each case, was to follow the dust and smoke generated, see how much sunlight was absorbed and by how much the temperatures changed, figure out how the particles spread in longitude and latitude, and calculate how long before it all fell out of the air back onto the surface. Since the radioactivity would be attached to these same fine particles, our calculations also revealed the extent and timing of the subsequent radioactive fallout.

Some of what I am about to describe is horrifying. I know, because it horrifies me. There is a tendency—psychiatrists call it "denial"—to put it out of our minds, not to think about it. But if we are to deal intelligently, wisely, with the nuclear arms race, then we must steel ourselves to contemplate the horrors of nuclear war.

The results of our calculations astonished us. In the baseline case, the amount of sunlight at the ground was reduced to a few percent of normal—much darker, in daylight, than in a heavy overcast and too dark for plants to make a living from photosynthesis. At least in the Northern Hemisphere, where the great preponderance of strategic targets lies, an unbroken and deadly gloom would persist for weeks.

Even more unexpected were the temperatures calculated. In the baseline case, land temperatures, except for narrow strips of coastline, dropped to minus 25° Celsius (minus 13° Fahrenheit) and stayed below freezing for months—even for a summer war. (Because the atmospheric structure becomes much more stable as the upper atmosphere is heated and the lower air is cooled, we may have severely *under*estimated how long the cold and dark would last.) The oceans, a significant heat reservoir, would not freeze, however, and a major ice age would probably not be triggered. But because the temperatures would drop so catastrophically, virtually all crops and farm animals, at least in the Northern Hemisphere, would be destroyed, as would most varieties of uncultivated or undomesticated food supplies. Most of the human survivors would starve.

In addition, the amount of radioactive fallout is much more than expected. Many previous calculations simply ignored the intermediate time-scale fallout. That is, calculations were made for the prompt fallout—the plumes of a radioactive debris blown downwind from each target—and for the long-term fallout, the fine radioactive particles lofted into the stratosphere that would descend about a year later, after most of the radioactivity had decayed. However, the radioactivity carried into the upper atmosphere (but not as high as the stratosphere) seems to have been largely forgotten. We found for the baseline case that roughly 30 percent of the land at northern midlatitudes could receive a radio-active dose greater than 250 rads, and that about 50 percent of northern midlatitudes could receive a dose greater than 100 rads. A 100-rad dose is the equivalent of about 1000 medical X-rays. A 400-rad dose will, more likely than not, kill you.

The cold, the dark and the intense radioactivity, together lasting for months, represent a severe assault on our civilization and our species. Civil and sanitary services would be wiped out. Medical facilities, drugs, the most rudimentary means for relieving the vast human suffering, would be unavailable. Any but the most elaborate shelters would be useless, quite apart from the question of what good it might be to emerge a few months later. Synthetics burned in the destruction of the cities would produce a wide variety of toxic gases, including carbon monoxide, cyanides, dioxins and furans. After the dust and soot settled out, the solar ultraviolet flux would be much larger than its present value. Immunity to disease would decline. Epidemics and pandemics would be rampant, especially after the billion or so unburied bodies began to thaw. Moreover, the combined influence of these severe and simultaneous stresses on life are likely to produce even more adverse consequences—biologists call them synergisms—that we are not yet wise enough to foresee.

So far, we have talked only of the Northern Hemisphere. But it now seems—unlike the case of a single nuclear weapons test—that in a real nuclear war, the heating of the vast quantities of atmospheric dust and soot in northern midlatitudes will transport these fine particles toward and across the Equator. We see just this happening in Martian dust storms. The Southern Hemisphere would experience effects that, while less severe than in the Northern Hemisphere, are nevertheless extremely ominous. The illusion with which some people in the Northern Hemisphere reassure themselves—catching an Air New Zealand flight in a time of serious international crisis, or the like—is now much less tenable, even on the narrow issue of personal survival for those with the price of a ticket.

But what if nuclear wars *can* be contained, and much less than 5000 megatons is detonated? Perhaps the greatest surprise in our work was that even small nuclear wars can have devastating climatic effects. We considered a war in which a mere 100 megatons were exploded, less than one percent of the world arsenals, and only in low-yield airbursts over cities. This scenario, we found, would ignite thousands of fires, and the smoke from these fires alone would be enough to generate an epoch of cold and dark almost as severe as in the 5000-megaton case. The threshold for what Richard Turco has called the Nuclear Winter is very low.

Could we have overlooked some important effect? The carrying of dust and soot from the Northern to the Southern Hemisphere (as well as more local atmospheric circulation) will certainly thin the clouds out over the Northern Hemisphere. But, in many cases, this thinning would be insufficient to render the climatic consequences tolerable—and every time it got better in the Northern hemisphere, it would get worse in the Southern.

Our results have been carefully scrutinized by more than 100 scientists in the United States, Europe and the Soviet Union. There are still arguments on points of detail. But the overall conclusion seems to be agreed upon: There are severe and previously unanticipated global consequences of nuclear war—subfreezing temperatures in a twilit radioactive gloom lasting for months or longer.

Scientists initially underestimated the effects of fallout, were amazed that nuclear explosions in space disabled distant satellites, had no idea that the fireballs from high-yield thermonuclear explosions could deplete the ozone layer and missed altogether the possible climatic effects of nuclear dust and smoke. What else have we overlooked?

Nuclear war is a problem that can be treated only theoretically. It is not amenable to experimentation. Conceivably, we have left something important out of our analysis, and the effects are more modest than we calculate. On the other hand, it is also possible—and, from previous experience, even likely—that there are further adverse effects that no one has yet been wise enough to recognize. With billions of lives at stake, where does conservatism lie—in assuming that the results will be better than we calculate, or worse?

Many biologists, considering the nuclear winter that these calculations describe, believe they carry somber implications for life on Earth. Many species of plants and animals would become extinct. Vast numbers of surviving humans would starve to death. The delicate ecological relations that bind together organisms on Earth in a fabric of mutual dependency would be torn, perhaps irreparably. There is little question that our global civilization would be destroyed. The human population would be reduced to prehistoric levels, or less. Life for any survivors would be extremely hard. And there seems to be a real possibility of the extinction of the human species.

It is now almost 40 years since the invention of nuclear weapons. We have not yet experienced a global thermonuclear war—although on more than one occasion we have come tremulously close. I do not think our luck can hold forever. Men and machines are fallible, as recent events remind us. Fools and madmen do exist, and sometimes rise to power. Concentrating always on the near future, we have ignored the long-term consequences of our actions. We have placed our civilization and our species in jeopardy.

Fortunately, it is not yet too late. We can safeguard the planetary civilization and the human family if we so choose. There is no more important or more urgent issue.

THE EARTH IN DEFICIT

THOMAS BERRY

Economic deficits are nothing compared to a deficit in nature, according to this contemporary author, a Christian theologian. But often the causes are the same. What does the author mean by a deficit in nature? What are the causes of a natural deficit? What has to be done to return to a balanced natural world?

The reality of our present economy is such that we must have certain forebodings not simply as regards the well-being of the human community but even of the planet itself in its most basic life systems. Economic dysfunction is generally expressed in terms of deficit expenditure. Income does not balance outflow. In the natural world there exists an amazing richness of life expression in the ever-renewing cycle of the seasons. There is a minimum of entropy. The inflow of energy and the outflow are such that the process is sustainable over an indefinite period of time—so long as the human process is integral with these processes of nature, so long is the human economy sustainable into the future. The difficulty comes when the industrial mode of our economy disrupts the natural processes, when human technologies are destructive of earth technologies. In such a situation the productivity of the natural world and its life systems is diminished. When nature goes into deficit, then we go into deficit. When this occurs to a limited extent on a regional basis it can often enough be remedied. The difficulty is when the entire planetary system is affected. The earth system is most threatened when the human economy goes out of balance and frantic efforts toward a remedy lead to a reckless plundering of the land, spending our capital as our interest diminishes.

If we look at the specific data available on the United States economy we find that we now have a GNP [Gross National Product] of close to 4 trillion dollars. We also have a national debt of over 2 trillion dollars, an annual budgetary deficit of some 200 billion, an infrastructure disintegration requiring repairs of 750 billion, an annual trade deficit of over 100 billion, third world financial loans unlikely to be repaid of 350 billion, an annual military expenditure of 300 billion. All of these can be considered as financial deficits.

But seldom does anyone speak of the earth deficit, the deficit involved in the closing down of the basic life system of the planet through abuse

From Thomas Berry, "Wonderworld as Wasteland: The Earth in Deficit," in *Cross Currents*, Winter 1985–1986. Reprinted with permission of Convergence, Inc.

of the air, the soil, the water and the vegetation. Yet the earth deficit is the real deficit, the ultimate deficit, the deficit so absolute in some of its major consequences as to be beyond adjustment from any source in heaven or earth. Since the earth system is the ultimate guarantor of all deficits, a failure here is a failure of last resort. Neither economic viability nor improvement in life conditions for the poor can be realized in such circumstances. They can only worsen, especially when we consider rising population levels throughout the developing world.

This deficit in its extreme expression is not only a resource deficit but the death of a living process, not simply the death of *a* living process but of *the* living process—a living process which exists, so far as we know, only on the planet earth. This is what makes our problems definitively different from those of any other generation of whatever ethnic, cultural, political or religious tradition or of any other historical period. For the first time we are determining the destinies of the earth in a comprehensive and irreversible manner. The immediate danger is not *possible* nuclear war but *actual* industrial plundering.

Economics on this scale is not simply economics of the human community; it is economics of the earth community in its comprehensive dimensions. Nor is this a question of profit or loss in terms of personal or community well-being in a functioning earth system. Economics has invaded the earth system itself. Our industrial economy is closing down the planet in the most basic modes of its functioning. The air, the water, the soil are already in a degraded condition. Forests are dying on every continent. The seas are endangered. Aquatic life forms in lakes and streams and in the seas are contaminated. The rain is acid.

So the litany could go on. In this country we are losing over four billion tons of topsoil each year. The great aquifers of the Plains region are diminished beyond their capacity for refilling. Our industrial agriculture is no longer participation in the productive cycle of the natural world; it is the extinction of the very conditions on which these productive cycles depend.

While it is unlikely that we could ever extinguish life in an absolute manner, we are eliminating species at a rate never before known in historic time and in a manner never known in biological time. Destruction of the tropical rain forests of the planet will involve destroying the habitat of perhaps half the living species of earth. Although its strictly economic implications have still not been worked out, it should be clear that an exhausted planet is an exhausted economy.

Until recently both textbook economics and corporation practise have ignored or given minimal attention to the implications of the data. Such deficits were simply external or unreal costs of doing business, costs that were not entered into the bookkeeping records until social protest brought about environmental impact statements, limits on pollution of the environment, clean-up of waste sites, and liability for personal damage resulting from toxic disruption of the basic life systems. Even the existence of such cleanup needs should be telling us something: that the industrial system itself in its present form is a failing system. Yet we can be sure that whatever fictions exist in Wall Street bookkeeping the earth is a faithful scribe, a faultless calculator, a superb bookkeeper; we will be held responsible for every bit of our economic folly.

Only now do we begin to consider that there is an economics of the human as a species as well as an economics of the earth as a functional community, and that the primary objective of economic science, the engineering profession, technological invention, industrial processing, financial investment, and corporation management, must be the integration of human well-being within the context of the well-being of the natural world. This is the primary purpose of economics. Only within the ever-renewing processes of the natural world is there any future for the human community. Not to recognize this is to make economics a deadly affair.

The exploitation itself was and still is experienced not as deterioration of the planet or as a new mode of exhaustion of the planet but as an extension of the emergent creative process leading to a kind of wonderworld existence. This is "progress," a belief so entrancing for the modern world that no doubt of its validity is permitted. Even though this belief has long ago been severely critiqued and its limitations indicated, it remains the functional basis of our economy. The GNP must increase each year. Everything must be done on a larger scale, with little awareness of the catastrophe involved built into the exponential rate of increase. However rational modern economics might be, the dynamics of economics is obviously noneconomic but visionary, a commitment supported by myth and a sense of having the magic powers of science to overcome any difficulty encountered when human processes reach their limits.

This visionary approach can be seen in the new surge of the industrial economy, the rising level of stock market quotations, the shifting of currency values, the formation of the great conglomerates, the giant corporation mergers, the new mystique of the entrepreneur. . . .

Thus the mythic drive to control our world continues, even though so much is known about the earth, its limited resources, the interdependence of life systems, the delicate balance of its ecosystems, the consequences of disturbing the atmospheric conditions, of contaminating the air, the soil, the waterways and the seas, the limited quantity of fossil fuels in the earth, the inherent danger of chemicals discharged into natural surroundings. Although much of this has been known for generations, neither the study nor the commercial-industrial practise of economics has shown any capacity to break free from the mythic commitment to progress, or any awareness that we are in reality creating wasteworld rather than wonderworld. This mythic commitment to continuing economic growth is such that none of our major newspapers or newsweeklies considers having a regular ecological section, equivalent to sports or business or arts or entertainment, although the ecological issues are more important than any of these, more important than the daily national and international political news. The real history that is being made is inter-species and human-earth history, not inter-nation history. Our real threat is from the retaliatory powers of the abused earth, not from other nations.

THE UNIVERSAL DECLARATION OF HUMAN RIGHTS

The Universal Declaration of Human Rights was adopted by the United Nations General Assembly on December 10, 1948. The vote was unanimous, although the Soviet Bloc, South Africa, and Saudi Arabia abstained. The Declaration continues the Western tradition of political liberty incorporated in the U.S. Bill of Rights (the first ten amendments to the U.S. Constitution) and the French Declaration of the Rights of Man and Citizen.

To what extent does the Universal Declaration go beyond the ideas of those documents? Since 1948 some newly independent countries have included the Declaration in their national constitutions. Should the United States do that? To what extent is the Declaration followed today? Can you give examples of compliance or of violations? What gives the Declaration its authority? How might international compliance be increased?

ARTICLE 1

All human beings are born free and equal in dignity and rights. They are endowed with reason and conscience and should act towards one another in a spirit of brotherhood.

ARTICLE 2

Everyone is entitled to all the rights and freedoms set forth in this Declaration, without distinction of any kind, such as race, colour, sex,

From *The Universal Declaration of Human Rights*. New York: The United Nations, 1963.

language, religion, political or other opinion, national or social origin, property, birth or other status.

Furthermore, no distinction shall be made on the basis of the political, jurisdictional or international status of the country or territory to which a person belongs, whether it be independent, trust, non-self-governing or under any other limitation of sovereignty.

ARTICLE 3

Everyone has the right to life, liberty and the security of person.

ARTICLE 4

No one shall be held in slavery or servitude; slavery and the slave trade shall be prohibited in all their forms.

ARTICLE 5

No one shall be subjected to torture or to cruel, inhuman or degrading treatment or punishment.

ARTICLE 6

Everyone has the right to recognition everywhere as a person before the law.

ARTICLE 7

All are equal before the law and are entitled without any discrimination to equal protection of the law. All are entitled to equal protection against any discrimination in violation of this Declaration and against any incitement to such discrimination.

ARTICLE 8

Everyone has the right to an effective remedy by the competent national tribunals for acts violating the fundamental rights granted him by the constitution or by law.

ARTICLE 9

No one shall be subjected to arbitrary arrest, detention or exile.

ARTICLE 10

Everyone is entitled in full equality to a fair and public hearing by an independent and impartial tribunal, in the determination of his rights and obligations and of any criminal charge against him.

ARTICLE 11

1. Everyone charged with a penal offence has the right to be presumed innocent until proven guilty according to law in a public trial at which he has had all the guarantees necessary for his defence.

2. No one shall be held guilty for any penal offence on account of any act or omission which did not constitute a penal offence, under national or international law, at the time when it was committed. Nor shall a heavier penalty be imposed than the one that was applicable at the time the penal offence was committed.

ARTICLE 12

No one shall be subjected to arbitrary interference with his privacy, family, home or correspondence, nor to attacks upon his honour and reputation. Everyone has the right to the protection of the law against such interference or attacks.

ARTICLE 13

1. Everyone has the right to freedom of movement and residence within the borders of each State.

2. Everyone has the right to leave any country, including his own, and to return to his country.

ARTICLE 14

1. Everyone has the right to seek and to enjoy in other countries asylum from persecution.

2. This right may not be invoked in the case of prosecutions genuinely arising from non-political crimes or from acts contrary to the purposes and principles of the United Nations.

ARTICLE 15

1. Everyone has the right to a nationality.

2. No one shall be arbitrarily deprived of his nationality nor denied the right to change his nationality.

ARTICLE 16

1. Men and women of full age, without any limitation due to race, nationality or religion, have the right to marry and to found a family. They are entitled to equal rights as to marriage, during marriage and at its dissolution.

2. Marriage shall be entered into only with the free and full consent of the intending spouses.

3. The family is the natural and fundamental group unit of society and is entitled to protection by society and the State.

ARTICLE 17

1. Everyone has the right to own property alone as well as in association with others.

2. No one shall be arbitrarily deprived of his property.

ARTICLE 18

Everyone has the right to freedom of thought, conscience and religion; this right includes freedom to change his religion or belief, and freedom, either alone or in community with others and in public or private, to manifest his religion or belief in teaching, practice, worship and observance.

ARTICLE 19

Everyone has the right to freedom of opinion and expression; this right includes freedom to hold opinions without interference and to seek, receive and impart information and ideas through any media and regardless of frontiers.

ARTICLE 20

1. Everyone has the right to freedom of peaceful assembly and association.

2. No one may be compelled to belong to an association.

ARTICLE 21

1. Everyone has the right to take part in the government of his country, directly or through freely chosen representatives.

2. Everyone has the right of equal access to public services in his country.

3. The will of the people shall be the basis of the authority of government; this will shall be expressed in periodic and genuine elections which shall be by universal and equal suffrage and shall be held by secret vote or by equivalent free voting procedures.

ARTICLE 22

Everyone, as a member of society, has the right to social security and is entitled to realization through national effort and international co-operation and in accordance with the organization and resources of each State, of the economic, social and cultural rights indispensable for his dignity and the free development of his personality.

ARTICLE 23

1. Everyone has the right to work, to free choice of employment, to just and favourable conditions of work and to protection against unemployment.

2. Everyone, without any discrimination, has the right to equal pay for equal work.

3. Everyone who works has the right to just and favourable remuneration ensuring for himself and his family an existence worthy of human dignity, and supplemented, if necessary, by other means of social protection.

4. Everyone has the right to form and to join trade unions for the protection of his interests.

ARTICLE 24

Everyone has the right to rest and leisure, including reasonable limitation of working hours and periodic holidays with pay.

ARTICLE 25

1. Everyone has the right to a standard of living adequate for the health and well-being of himself and his family, including food, clothing, housing and medical care and necessary social services, and the right to security in the event of unemployment, sickness, disability, widowhood, old age or other lack of livelihood in circumstances beyond his control.

2. Motherhood and childhood are entitled to special care and assistance. All children, whether born in or out of wedlock, shall enjoy the same social protection.

ARTICLE 26

1. Everyone has the right to education. Education shall be free, at least in the elementary and fundamental stages. Elementary education shall be compulsory. Technical and professional education shall be made generally available and higher education shall be equally accessible to all on the basis of merit.

2. Education shall be directed to the full development of the human personality and to the strengthening of respect for human rights and fundamental freedoms. It shall promote understanding, tolerance and friendship among all nations, racial or religious groups, and shall further the activities of the United Nations for the maintenance of peace.

3. Parents have a prior right to choose the kind of education that shall be given to their children.

ARTICLE 27

1. Everyone has the right freely to participate in the cultural life of the community, to enjoy the arts and to share in scientific advancement and its benefits.

2. Everyone has the right to the protection of the moral and material interests resulting from any scientific, literary or artistic production of which he is the author.

ARTICLE 28

Everyone is entitled to a social and international order in which the rights and freedoms set forth in this Declaration can be fully realized.

ARTICLE 29

1. Everyone has duties to the community in which alone the free and full development of his personality is possible.

2. In the exercise of his rights and freedoms, everyone shall be subject only to such limitations as are determined by law solely for the purpose of securing due recognition and respect for the rights and freedoms of

others and of meeting the just requirements of morality, public order and the general welfare in a democratic society.

3. These rights and freedoms may in no case be exercised contrary to the purposes and principles of the United Nations.

ARTICLE 30

Nothing in this Declaration may be interpreted as implying for any State, group or person any right to engage in any activity or to perform any act aimed at the destruction of any of the rights and freedoms set forth herein.